Business Mathematics for Colleges

Tenth Edition

James E. Deitz, Ed.D.
Heald Colleges of California

James L. Southam, Ph.D.
San Francisco State University

COLLEGE DIVISION South-Western Publishing Co.

Cincinnati Ohio

REGIONAL TECHNICAL COLLEGE GALWAY
0 5 JUL 1995
CASTLEBAR CAMPUS LIBRARY

047897

MB76JB

ISBN: 0-538-81187-0

Library of Congress Catalog Card Number: 91-62099

    3 4 5 6 7 8 9 H 9 8 7 6 5 4
Printed in the United States of America

Sponsoring Editor: James M. Keefe
Developmental Editor: Sara E. Bates
Production Editors: Nancy J. Ahr
                     Leslie Kauffman
Associate Editors: Suzanne Dorsey
                     Jackie Myrick
                     Robert D. Sandman
Interior and Cover Designer: Craig LaGesse Ramsdell
Photo Editor: Diana Robbins Carter
Cover Illustrator/Photographer: Frank Miller
Marketing Manager: Tania Hindersman

To the Student

In modern business, everyone needs knowledge of and skill in business mathematics. The Tenth Edition of BUSINESS MATHEMATICS FOR COLLEGES will assist you in developing your knowledge and skill by presenting the necessary fundamental principles and applying these principles in a series of practical business problems.

The following suggestions will aid you in using this book:

1. For each section, read the text, and study the steps and the examples carefully before beginning an assignment.

2. Read carefully the instructions for each group of assignment problems before attempting to solve them. Master the technique for solving word problems as presented on pages 33-34.

3. Do your own work. You learn by doing the calculations yourself. Ask your instructor for help if you have any difficulty in understanding what you are to do or how to do it.

4. Before working each problem try to approximate your answer. The text presents methods for doing this.

5. Try to use shortcuts in your calculations. You will find shortcuts presented in several chapters.

6. Improve your writing of figures through regular practice so that you will not make errors as a result of mistaking one number for another.

7. Align figures in columns to avoid errors in addition and subtraction.

8. Practice problems have been provided in all chapters. These problems do not require the use of a calculator. Master the fundamental processes before you depend on a calculator. Be able to work employment test problems without any mechanical device, since many potential employers may not allow its use.

9. Space is allowed on the assignment sheets for you to calculate most problems. *Show each step* in your solution so that if you make an error, your instructor can help you locate the cause of your difficulty.

10. If you need additional practice, ask your instructor about the microcomputer study guide.

11. Write your name and the date at the top of the first page of each assignment before you submit it to the instructor.

12. Record your score or grade for each assignment on the Progress Record at the end of your book.

Many students have used the earlier editions of this text in preparing themselves for business. The authors hope that this new edition will provide even greater assistance to the thousands of students who will become the business people of the future.

James E. Deitz
James L. Southam

Contents

Part One
Fundamentals of Mathematics in Business

Chapter 1
Fundamental Processes

OBJECTIVES
After completing this chapter, you should be able to:

• Add, subtract, multiply, and divide with greater ease
• Estimate multiplication and division solutions

Numbers are used in practically every aspect of business—to represent prices, to measure weights and quantities, to check the time worked by employees, and to indicate profit and general value.

It is important that students who plan to enter business gain competence in handling numbers. The purpose of this chapter is to review the fundamental mathematical processes and to provide practice in the use of certain short-cuts using numbers.

ADDITION

About half of the calculations used in business involve addition. The more skilled you become in recognizing the sum of any two digits, the more rapidly and accurately you will be able to add.

Number Combinations

Certain aids can help you in adding more accurately and rapidly. One of the most helpful of these is combining any two numbers that total 10. The combinations that total 10 are illustrated below. Practice the combinations until you can identify them instantly.

1	2	3	4	5
9	8	7	6	5

In the reverse order:

9	8	7	6	5
1	2	3	4	5

When these combinations are found in any column of numbers, they should be added as 10.

In example a., you might add the numbers in the right-hand column by saying, as you count down the column, "9 plus 4 is 13, plus 6 is 19, plus 3 is 22, plus 7 is 29, plus 8 is 37" (or simply "13, 19, 22, 29, 37"). By using the combinations of 10, however, you can simply add down the column by saying "9 plus 10 is 19, plus 10 is 29, plus 8 is 37" (or "9, 19, 29, 37").

The number 3, which is to be carried over to the top of the next column, is written in a small figure above the number 7 in the center column. The combinations of 10 are used in adding the center column by simply saying "10, 20, 30."

In adding the left-hand column, you can simply say "8, 18, 28, 32."

It also is helpful to instantly recognize combinations of three numbers that total 10. These basic combinations are:

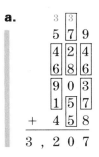

1	1	1	1	2	2	2	3
1	2	3	4	2	3	4	3
8	7	6	5	6	5	4	4

These numbers in each combination may appear in a different sequence. For example, the numbers 2, 3, and 5 may appear in any one of six arrangements:

2	3	2	3	5	5
3	2	5	5	2	3
5	5	3	2	3	2

When these numbers totaling 10 are in sequence in a column, they should be combined and added as 10. In example b., you might add the numbers in the right-hand column by saying, as you add down the column, "10, 18, 28, 38, 41." The number 4, which is carried over, is written as a small figure above the 5 in the first column. The combinations of 10's are used in adding the left-hand column by saying "9, 19, 29, 39, 47."

Addition of Repeated Digits
When adding a column in which most of the digits are the same, it is often quicker to count the number of repeated digits, and then multiply the digit by that number. (See "Steps for Multiplying Two Numbers" later in this chapter.) In example c., the ones column totals 33 (10 + 10 + 13). The tens column shows five 4's equaling 20: 5 × 4 = 20. The carry over of 3 and the 5 are then added to the 20 for a total of 28 in the tens column. The total in the problem is 283.

Checking Addition
It is always desirable to check the accuracy of your addition. This is done by adding the columns again in the opposite direction—that is, if you added down, add up for the check.

Horizontal Addition
It is often necessary in business papers and records to add numbers horizontally, or across the line, to save the time of recopying the numbers vertically. Several horizontal additions may be checked by adding the columns vertically and by then adding these totals horizontally. This is called *cross-checking*. The sums obtained by adding the totals horizontally and vertically should be the same.

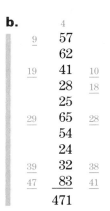

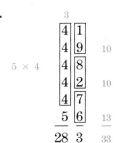

d.

282 +	346 +	723 +	409 +	716 =	2,476
113 +	806 +	629 +	916 +	620 =	3,084
240 +	318 +	718 +	312 +	309 =	1,897
716 +	501 +	423 +	716 +	114 =	2,470
872 +	417 +	909 +	704 +	472 =	3,374
2,223 +	2,388 +	3,402 +	3,057 +	2,231 =	13,301 (same total)

COMPLETE ASSIGNMENT 1-1

SUBTRACTION

Subtraction is the process of finding the difference between two numbers. When the *subtrahend* (number being subtracted) is taken from the *minuend* (number from which subtraction is being made), the result is the *difference*, as shown. When the subtrahend is less than the minuend, the result is a positive difference. When the subtrahend is greater than the minuend, the result is a negative difference. In business, a negative difference may be called a *credit balance*. A credit balance is frequently shown in parentheses.

e.

Positive Differences			*Negative Difference (Credit Balances)*	
$32.22	18.88	Minuend	12.00	$32.22
− 22.22	− 3.63	Subtrahend	− 13.50	− 42.22
$10.00	15.25	Difference	(1.50)	($10.00)

Checking Subtraction

Subtraction is checked with addition since subtraction is the opposite of addition. If 209 is subtracted from 317, the difference is 108. This can be checked by adding 108 to 209. The sum is 317. The same procedure can be used to check subtraction with a negative difference (credit balance).

f.

Subtract	*Check*	*Subtract*	*Check*
317	108	$21.10	($ 3.40)
− 209	+ 209	− 24.50	+ 24.50
108	317	($ 3.40)	$21.10

Horizontal Subtraction

Certain business forms and records are constructed so that it is necessary to subtract numbers horizontally unless time is taken to copy the numbers vertically. A number of horizontal subtractions are checked by adding the columns vertically and then subtracting these totals horizontally. This answer should equal the total of the differences in the column at the right.

g.

Minuend		*Subtrahend*		*Difference*
$ 367.65	−	$ 194.50	=	$173.15
829.30	−	516.28	=	313.02
601.40	−	479.12	=	122.28
296.74	−	82.65	=	214.09
$2,095.09	−	$1,272.55	=	$822.54 (same total)

COMPLETE ASSIGNMENT 1-2

MULTIPLICATION

Multiplication, stated simply, is "repeated addition." When two numbers (called *factors*) are multiplied, one number is repeated as many times as there are units in the other. The factor that is multiplied is called the *multiplicand*. The factor that indicates how many times to multiply is the *multiplier*. The result is the *product*. Note that in multiplication it does not matter which number is called the multiplier. Thus, $3 \times 5 = 5 \times 3$; $87 \times 100 = 100 \times 87$, etc. Also note that when multiplying numbers, the digit order will be from right to left.

Steps for Multiplying Two Numbers

1. a. Make the smaller factor the multiplier.
   b. Write the smaller factor under the larger one so that their right-hand digits are in the same column.
2. a. Multiply the multiplicand by the right-hand digit of the multiplier.
   b. Write the product directly below the line.
   c. Be sure the product's right-hand digit is lined up with the right-hand digit of the multiplier.
3. a. Multiply the multiplicand by the *second* digit of the multiplier.
   b. Write the product below and one place to the left of the Step 2 product. (Thus, this product's right-hand digit goes directly under the *second* digit of the multiplier.)
4. a. Multiply the multiplicand by the *third* digit of the multiplier.
   b. Write the product below and one place to the left of the Step 3 product. (Thus, this product's right-hand digit goes directly under the *third* digit of the multiplier.)
5. Continue following the pattern of Steps 3 and 4 as needed, each time choosing the multiplier digit that is just to the left of the one used in the prior step (for example, the fourth digit, the fifth digit, etc.) until all digits in the multiplier have been used.
6. Add the three products to get the final answer.

h.

			In other words:
	456	(multiplicand)	$7 \times 456 = 3{,}192$
Step 1	$\times\ 237$	(multiplier)	$30 \times 456 = 13{,}680$
Step 2	3 192		$200 \times 456 = 91{,}200$
Step 3	13 68		$237 \times 456 = 108{,}072$
Step 4	91 2		
Step 6	108,072	(product)	

Checking Multiplication

The best method to check multiplication is to divide the product by the multiplier to obtain the multiplicand. Example i. shows the relationship between multiplication and division. (For the division process, see the next section.)

i.

multiplicand	22	$\longleftrightarrow$	22
multiplier	$\times\ 6$	$\longleftrightarrow$	$6\overline{)132}$
product	132	$\longleftarrow$	

Multiplying Numbers Ending in 0

To multiply a number by 10, simply add a zero onto the end of the number. To multiply a number by 100, add two zeros onto the end: $10 \times 46 = 460$; $7{,}689 \times 100 = 768{,}900$.

1. Use as the multiplier the factor with the smaller number of digits after ignoring all zeros on the right-hand side of the number.
2. Ignore the right-hand zeros and multiply the remaining numbers.
3. Add to the right-hand side of the product the total number of zeros ignored in Step 2.

j. Step 1 370×200: 200

ignored

37	(1 zero)
$\times$ 2	(2 zeros)

Step 2 74 (3 zeros)

Step 3 74 & 000 = 74,000

Step 1 $1,200 \times 160,800$: 1,200

ignored

1608	(2 zeros)
$\times$ 12	(2 zeros)
3216	
1608	

Step 2 19296 (4 zeros)

Step 3 19296 & 0000 = 192,960,000

---

k.

42,674
$\times$ 401
42 674
17 069 6
17,112,274
(2 places)

Multiplying When the Multiplier Contains 0

Often the 0 is found in the center of the multiplier rather than at the end. To multiply 42,674 by 401 in example k., first multiply the multiplicand by 1, and write down the product. Then multiply by 4 (which is really 400), and write the results two places, instead of one, to the left. In other words, one extra place is left for each 0 in the multiplier. (Refer to the example displayed in the margin.)

Whenever more than one zero is found within the multiplier, the multiplication process is similar. To multiply 33,222 by 2,004 as in example l., first multiply 33,222 by 4. Then, multiply 33,222 by 2, writing the answer three places to the left. Remember, space must be left for the two zeros (1 + 2 extra places = 3 places).

l.

33,222
$\times$ 2,004
132 888
66 444
66,576,888
(3 places)

Rule: Zero times any number is zero, and any number times zero is zero. Thus, $4 \times 0 = 0$, and $0 \times 567 = 0$.

Multiplying the Product of Two Factors

Sometimes in business you will need to multiply two factors, then multiply the product of those factors by a third factor. As shown in example m., you first multiply the first two factors and then multiply that product by the third factor.

m.

$21 \times 30 \times 12 = 7,560$

21	630
$\times$ 30	$\times$ 12
630	1,260
	6 30
	7,560

Multiplying by 25

A shortcut for multiplying by 25 is to multiply by 100 (add two zeros), and divide by 4. (For the division process, see the next section.)

n. 321 $\times$ 25 828 $\times$ 25 6,640 $\times$ 25

32,100 $\div$ 4 = 8,025 82,800 $\div$ 4 = 20,700 664,000 $\div$ 4 = 166,000

Multiplying by 50

A shortcut for multiplying by 50 is to multiply by 100 (add two zeros), and divide by 2. (For the division process, see the next section.)

o. 732 × 50　　　　　　　1,245 × 50　　　　　　　$28.20 × 50
　　73,200 ÷ 2 = 36,600　124,500 ÷ 2 = 62,250　$2,820.00 ÷ 2 = $1,410.00

Estimating

Mentally estimating an approximate answer is a good method for checking whether or not your product is a reasonable answer.

Steps to Estimate a Multiplication Answer

1. Round the *multiplicand* and *multiplier* to the nearest *10* for 2-digit numbers, the nearest *100* for 3-digit numbers, the nearest *1,000* for 4-digit numbers, etc.
2. Drop the zeros to the right of the non-zero numbers.
3. Mentally multiply the non-zero numbers to determine the base product.
4. Add back *all* zeros dropped in Step 2.

p.

Problem	Round To	Drop Zeros	Base Product	Add Back Zeros (Approximate Answer)	Real Answer
68 × 21	70 × 20	7 × 2	14	1,400	1,428
473 × 1,957	500 × 2,000	5 × 2	10	1,000,000 −	925,661
7,869 × 43,242	8,000 × 40,000	8 × 4	32	320,000,000	340,271,298
147,203 × 13	100,000 × 10	1 × 1	1	1,000,000 +	1,913,639
9 × 511,739	9 × 500,000	9 × 5	45	4,500,000	4,605,651
882 × 39 × 134	900 × 40 × 100	9 × 4 × 1	36	3,600,000	4,609.332

− Since both the multiplicand and multiplier were rounded to *larger* numbers, the real answer will be *lower* than the approximate answer.

+ Since both the multiplicand and multiplier were rounded to *smaller* numbers, the real answer will be *higher* than the approximate answer.

COMPLETE ASSIGNMENT 1-3

DIVISION

Division is the process of finding how many times one number (the *divisor*) is contained in another (the *dividend*). The result is called the *quotient*. If anything remains after division is completed, it is called the *remainder*. In example q., 47 ÷ 2 = 23 (with 1 left over), 47 is the dividend, 2 the divisor, 1 the remainder, and the answer of 23 with a remainder of (1) is the quotient.

q.

```
                    23(1)   quotient
        divisor   2)47      dividend
                    4
                    ‾
                    7
                    6
                    ‾
                    1       remainder
```

1. a. Write the divisor.
    b. Draw the division bracket ($\overline{)\qquad}$).
    c. Write in the dividend.
2. Take as the first partial dividend the least number of digits at the left of the dividend that will contain the divisor.
3. a. Write the number of times the divisor will go into the partial dividend selected in Step 2.
    b. Multiply the divisor by this answer, write the product under the partial dividend, and subtract.
    c. To the internal remainder thus obtained, bring down the next digit of the dividend for the second partial dividend.
4. Divide as before, and continue until all the digits of the dividend have been used.

r.
```
          Step 3a
            174
    164)28,675   Step 2
        16 4
        12 27    Step 3b
        11 48    Step 3c
           795
           656   Step 4
           139
        (remainder)
```

s.
```
       20,108
   34)683,672
      68
       3 6
       3 4
        272
        272
          0
```

As illustrated in example s., when the partial dividend is smaller than the divisor, a zero must be placed in the quotient above that digit. This process is continued until the partial dividend is at least as large as the divisor. Then the long division steps are continued.

Checking Division

To check division, simply multiply the quotient by the divisor, and add any remainder to the product. The result will equal the original dividend. (Refer to examples r. and s.)

```
        174                20,108
     ×  164              ×     34
        696               80 432
     10 44               603 24
     17 4                683,672
     28,536
     + 139   (remainder)
     28,675
```

NOTE: Division is the opposite of multiplication.

t.

Multiplication	Division
$4 \times 6 = 24$	$24 \div 4 = 6$
$36 \times 52 = 1{,}872$	$1{,}872 \div 36 = 52$

Dividing by 10

To divide by 10, drop the digit at the extreme right of the dividend; the dropped digit will be the remainder.

u. $790 \div 10 = 79$ (0 remainder) $3{,}562 \div 10 = 356$ (2 remainder)

Dividing by 100

To divide by 100, drop the two right-hand digits of the dividend, and use them as the remainder.

v. $81{,}400 \div 100 = 814$ (0 remainder) $257{,}948 \div 100 = 2{,}579$ (48 remainder)

Dividing When Divisor and Dividend End with Zeros

When a divisor and dividend both end with zeros, an easy shortcut is to delete the ending zeros common to both, and then divide.

w.

Problem with both divisor and dividend ending with zeros	Zeros common to divisor and dividend have been dropped	Answer	
$8{,}400 \div 200$	$84 \div 2$	42	
$46{,}000 \div 2{,}300$	$460 \div 23$	20	
$42{,}000 \div 100$	$420 \div 1$	420	
$20{,}000{,}000 \div 4{,}000$	$20{,}000 \div 4$	5,000	
$2{,}760 \div 270$	$276 \div 27$	10	(6 remainder or R6)
$3{,}200 \div 1{,}000$	$32 \div 10$	3	(2 remainder or R2)

Estimating

Before doing long division problems, it is best to estimate mentally an approximate whole-number answer. Later, when working with decimals, fractions, and electronic calculators, the process of mentally estimating whole-number answers helps to avoid major and embarrassing errors.

Steps to Estimate a Long Division Whole-Number Answer

1. Round the *divisor* and *dividend* to the nearest *10* for 2-digit numbers, the nearest *100* for 3-digit numbers, the nearest *1,000* for 4-digit numbers, etc.
2. Drop the number of zeros common to both.
3. Mentally divide the remaining divisor into the remaining dividend. (NOTE: for decimal information shown in the Real Answer column, see Chapters 7 and 8.)

x.

Problem	Round To	Drop Zeros	Approximate Answer	Real Answer
77 ÷ 39	80 ÷ 40	8 ÷ 4	2	1.97
196 ÷ 63	200 ÷ 60	20 ÷ 6	3+	3.11
2,891 ÷ 114	3,000 ÷ 100	30 ÷ 1	30	25.36
592 ÷ 29	600 ÷ 30	60 ÷ 3	20	20.41
18,476 ÷ 384	20,000 ÷ 400	200 ÷ 4	50	48.11
917 ÷ 186	900 ÷ 200	9 ÷ 2	4+	4.93
21,716,412 ÷ 40,796	20,000,000 ÷ 40,000	2,000 ÷ 4	500	532.32
99,624 ÷ 476	100,000 ÷ 500	1,000 ÷ 5	200	209.29
29,200 ÷ 316	30,000 ÷ 300	300 ÷ 3	100	92.41

+ Since 20 ÷ 6 and 9 ÷ 2 would result in a remainder, it is reasonable to assume the real answer will be *larger*.

COMPLETE ASSIGNMENT 1-4

Chapter terms for review

credit balance
cross-checking
difference
dividend
divisor
factors
minuend

multiplicand
multiplier
product
quotient
remainder
subtrahend

Assignment 1-1: Addition Review

A **(10 points)** — Add the following. Where possible, use combinations of tens (1 point for each correct answer).

1.	**2.**	**3.**	**4.**	**5.**	**6.**	**7.**	**8.**	**9.**	**10.**
14	41	19	34	97	50	72	82	38	94
56	29	51	33	44	54	99	43	39	71
25	17	14	43	33	54	99	47	22	56
85	13	96	33	36	52	21	15	71	29
53	36	81	37	76	47	89	93	45	55
52	44	28	36	32	59	47	58	47	84
35	15	11	34	72	54	63	34	25	31
32	55	43	32	34	55	40	22	13	98
48	62	51	38	76	55	62	46	29	76
32	66	76	32	27	35	68	73	79	62

Score for A (10)

B **(20 points)** — Add the following (1 point for each correct answer).

11.	**12.**	**13.**	**14.**	**15.**	**16.**	**17.**	**18.**
209	782	127	920	347	852	251	883
486	280	145	751	399	428	271	114
225	438	665	359	354	112	244	312
219	473	818	822	334	238	234	588
684	655	682	807	192	959	589	736

19.	**20.**	**21.**	**22.**	**23.**	**24.**	**25.**	**26.**
275	479	652	322	203	650	651	444
342	413	386	108	776	162	616	397
615	180	366	128	417	297	496	855
898	418	344	722	304	946	659	811
505	415	359	922	687	321	628	313

27.	**28.**	**29.**	**30.**
549	682	862	356
587	314	411	294
870	262	422	987
543	734	295	263
531	444	973	128

Score for B (20)

C **(10 points)** — Add the following (1 point for each correct answer).

31.	**32.**	**33.**	**34.**	**35.**
$ 78.25	$ 16.71	$ 34.42	$ 27.61	$128.02
49.41	243.80	127.81	71.96	43.92
38.12	72.73	84.25	389.91	104.64

36. $ 20.65	**37.** $ 799.99	**38.** $100.16	**39.** $106.14	**40.** $ 34.76
83.27	695.95	12.85	211.26	40.52
87.18	346.99	14.35	38.93	24.72

Score for C (10)

D (10 points) — Add the following (1 point for each correct answer).

41. $ 248.28	**42.** $ 201.22	**43.** $ 234.81	**44.** $ 238.69	**45.** $ 506.30
820.14	513.14	371.60	982.30	221.42
306.80	280.54	271.37	376.48	348.86
521.98	2,647.55	408.55	728.90	237.64

46. $ 703.91	**47.** $ 126.92	**48.** $ 442.71	**49.** $ 525.13	**50.** $ 872.66
422.38	32.15	71.93	44.78	769.56
721.05	873.19	416.90	208.17	907.14
446.21	872.52	236.19	6,481.29	270.80

Score for D (10)

E (50 points) — Add the columns vertically and horizontally. Get a master total (1 point for each vertical and horizontal total; 2 points for the master total).

51.

42	37	20	49	36	84	_____
16	92	14	30	29	33	_____
55	60	72	90	14	83	_____
14	20	70	66	29	47	_____
72	56	55	19	10	32	_____
33	20	43	29	51	15	_____
35	70	36	74	11	36	_____

52.

$ 27.42	$ 12.88	$ 26.17	$ 13.13	_____
16.38	71.32	33.14	66.66	_____
17.55	43.15	26.77	33.33	_____
71.14	16.26	20.12	18.88	_____

53.

26	24	31	49	52	48	_____
32	28	55	35	27	43	_____
33	17	44	36	25	15	_____
34	16	23	77	16	14	_____
19	21	44	16	88	22	_____
22	18	37	13	16	24	_____
17	63	19	41	25	35	_____

54.

$ 71.12	$ 26.08	$ 17.17	$ 28.83	_____
12.55	95.05	20.01	37.99	_____
16.48	39.02	18.55	50.05	_____
77.09	16.41	20.44	20.66	_____

Score for E (50)

Part One   Fundamentals of Mathematics in Business

Assignment 1-2: Subtraction Review

A (10 points) — Subtract the following ($\frac{1}{2}$ point for each correct answer).

1. 77 − 16	**2.** 50 − 23	**3.** 72 − 25	**4.** 63 − 29	**5.** 53 − 48	**6.** 38 − 49	**7.** 92 − 16	**8.** 83 − 65

9. 60 − 10	**10.** 39 − 36	**11.** 40 − 31	**12.** 13 − 26	**13.** 73 − 14	**14.** 37 − 22	**15.** 68 − 39	**16.** 99 − 27

17. 57 − 43	**18.** 91 − 69	**19.** 62 − 29	**20.** 82 − 36

Score for A (10)

B (10 points) — Subtract the following. Then check your subtraction by adding the subtrahend and the difference and comparing your total to the minuend ($\frac{1}{2}$ point for each correct answer.)

21. 584 − 173	**22.** 963 − 874	**23.** 92 − 491	**24.** 714 − 30	**25.** 927 − 333

26. 7,116 − 2,007	**27.** $14.08 − 73.16	**28.** 10,381 − 6,300	**29.** 331,000 − 198,700	**30.** $1,016.14 − 300.21

Score for B (10)

C (10 points) — Subtract the following (1 point for each correct answer).

31. $97.17 − 23.19	**32.** $15.67 − 0.88	**33.** $71.69 − 10.87	**34.** $43.21 − 47.18	**35.** $65.27 − 34.56

36. $90.61 − 20.50	**37.** $71.65 − 65.43	**38.** $37.09 − 23.27	**39.** $34.27 − 23.46	**40.** $62.18 − 11.97

Score for C (10)

D (15 points) — Subtract the following ($1\frac{1}{2}$ points for each correct answer).

41. $8,042.88 − 3,400.07	**42.** $964.38 − 201.83	**43.** $9,011.09 − 795.08	**44.** $7,430.29 − 2,597.73	**45.** $3,385.03 − 233.42

46.	$1,029.27	47.	$235,168.82	48.	$87,218.14	49.	$51,222.93	50.	$53,541.76
	− 89.27		− 88,591.24		− 14,001.22		− 87,131.91		− 23,986.48

E **(15 points)** — Sometimes it is necessary to make a double subtraction. The following problems are of this type (3 points for each correct final answer).

51.	$7,672.18	52.	$ 11,739.93	53.	$734.12	54.	$745.89	55.	$1,837,042.03
	− 564.27		− 3,142.18		− 672.18		− 250.15		− 6,218.18
	− 124.13		− 1,694.25		− 13.14		− 624.13		− 39,917.16

F **(20 points)** — In some cases, more than two subtractions in a series are necessary. Each of the problems below involves a series of three consecutive subtractions (4 points for each correct final answer).

56.	$3,000.00	57.	$61,218.70	58.	$19,257.28	59.	$87,620.32	60.	$350,496.83
	− 98.07		− 935.46		− 10,392.14		− 7,614.18		− 384.17
	− 221.10		− 44,752.38		− 3,343.86		− 48,612.56		− 254,957.84
	− 3,162.14		− 5,083.17		− 4,708.15		− 31,072.14		− 70,885.26

G **(20 points)** — Subtract across each row; then add each of the three columns (1 point for each correct answer).

61.	3,540 − 3,543 = _____	62.	$ 42.35 − $ 20.35 = _____
	5,625 − 2,982 = _____		86.12 − 50.18 = _____
	9,207 − 4,264 = _____		46.92 − 46.12 = _____
	3,000 − 2,971 = _____		75.28 − .49 = _____
	6,388 − 5,295 = _____		70.80 − 30.80 = _____
	2,019 − 1,978 = _____		85.67 − 26.49 = _____
	5,261 − 2,168 = _____		45.67 − 19.14 = _____

Assignment 1-3: Multiplication Review

A (20 points) — Multiply ($\frac{1}{2}$ point for each correct answer).

1. $2 \times 12 =$ ____	**2.** $8 \times 15 =$ ____	**3.** $13 \times 40 =$ ____	**4.** $12 \times 36 =$ _____
5. $9 \times 10 =$ ____	**6.** $5 \times 15 =$ ____	**7.** $15 \times 16 =$ ____	**8.** $70 \times 6 =$ _____
9. $8 \times 9 =$ ____	**10.** $6 \times 12 =$ ____	**11.** $12 \times 12 =$ ____	**12.** $50 \times 8 =$ _____
13. $6 \times 8 =$ ____	**14.** $8 \times 12 =$ ____	**15.** $4 \times 20 =$ ____	**16.** $55 \times 80 =$ _____
17. $6 \times 6 =$ ____	**18.** $7 \times 22 =$ ____	**19.** $8 \times 11 =$ ____	**20.** $11 \times 800 =$ _____
21. $2 \times 14 =$ ____	**22.** $9 \times 22 =$ ____	**23.** $8 \times 17 =$ ____	**24.** $31 \times 50 =$ _____
25. $9 \times 8 =$ ____	**26.** $9 \times 20 =$ ____	**27.** $5 \times 16 =$ ____	**28.** $15 \times 5 =$ _____
29. $4 \times 7 =$ ____	**30.** $11 \times 20 =$ ____	**31.** $10 \times 12 =$ ____	**32.** $50 \times 50 =$ _____
33. $8 \times 6 =$ ____	**34.** $11 \times 11 =$ ____	**35.** $11 \times 14 =$ ____	**36.** $99 \times 9 =$ _____
37. $12 \times 5 =$ ____	**38.** $12 \times 11 =$ ____	**39.** $12 \times 15 =$ ____	**40.** $16 \times 7 =$ _____

Score for A (20)

B (15 points) — Find the products (1 point for each correct answer).

41. $\begin{array}{r} 1,728 \\ \times\ 42 \end{array}$	**42.** $\begin{array}{r} 3,026 \\ \times\ 372 \end{array}$	**43.** $\begin{array}{r} 38,246 \\ \times\ 8,297 \end{array}$	**44.** $\begin{array}{r} 5,017 \\ \times\ 201 \end{array}$	**45.** $\begin{array}{r} 3,600 \\ \times\ 300 \end{array}$
46. $\begin{array}{r} 7,179 \\ \times\ 71 \end{array}$	**47.** $\begin{array}{r} 8,222 \\ \times\ 509 \end{array}$	**48.** $\begin{array}{r} 67,406 \\ \times\ 3,006 \end{array}$	**49.** $\begin{array}{r} 1,236 \\ \times\ 444 \end{array}$	**50.** $\begin{array}{r} 27,000 \\ \times\ 420 \end{array}$
51. $\begin{array}{r} 8,125 \\ \times\ 79 \end{array}$	**52.** $\begin{array}{r} 4,017 \\ \times\ 375 \end{array}$	**53.** $\begin{array}{r} 36,084 \\ \times\ 1,312 \end{array}$	**54.** $\begin{array}{r} 10,216 \\ \times\ 9,000 \end{array}$	**55.** $\begin{array}{r} 19,800 \\ \times\ 8,900 \end{array}$

Score for B (15)

C (5 points) — Multiply by using shortcuts (1 point for each correct answer).

56. $\begin{array}{r} 3,684 \\ \times\ 50 \end{array}$	**57.** $\begin{array}{r} 4,999 \\ \times\ 50 \end{array}$	**58.** $\begin{array}{r} 5,642 \\ \times\ 25 \end{array}$	**59.** $\begin{array}{r} 3,212 \\ \times\ 50 \end{array}$	**60.** $\begin{array}{r} 1,376 \\ \times\ 25 \end{array}$

Score for C (5)

D (20 points) — Multiply the three factors (4 points for each final product).

61. $17 \times 22 \times 31 =$ _____

62. $47 \times 16 \times 70 =$ _____

63. $33 \times 33 \times 33 =$ _____

64. $217 \times 106 \times 202 =$ _____

65. $\$915 \times 40 \times 20 =$ _____

Score for D (20)

E (10 points) — Complete the 5 multiplication problems, then add the 5 products (1 point for each correct answer; 5 points for total).

66. 12 × $12.00 = _____

67. 27 × 8.16 = _____

68. 104 × 3.52 = _____

69. 6 × 92.92 = _____

70. 55 × 32.50 = _____

71.   Total = _____

Score for E (10)

F (30 points) — Estimate an answer for each of the following problems. Show your rounding, dropping of zeros with base product, and final estimate (2 points for each correct answer).

Problem	Rounding	Dropped Zeros & Base Product	Estimated Answer
72. 1,095 × 427	_____	_____	_____
73. 78,221 × 6,099	_____	_____	_____
74. 34,007 × 80	_____	_____	_____
75. 56 × 1,528	_____	_____	_____
76. 18 × 2,855 × 93	_____	_____	_____

Score for F (30)

Assignment 1-4: Division Review

A **(10 points)** — Divide the following problems mentally. Write only your answers ($\frac{1}{2}$ point for each correct quotient).

1. $72 \div 6 =$ _____	**2.** $90 \div 6 =$ _____	**3.** $96 \div 8 =$ _____
4. $110 \div 5 =$ _____	**5.** $126 \div 3 =$ _____	**6.** $154 \div 7 =$ _____
7. $88 \div 22 =$ _____	**8.** $144 \div 12 =$ _____	**9.** $169 \div 13 =$ _____
10. $135 \div 9 =$ _____	**11.** $990 \div 33 =$ _____	**12.** $187 \div 11 =$ _____
13. $156 \div 12 =$ _____	**14.** $900 \div 15 =$ _____	**15.** $336 \div 12 =$ _____
16. $84 \div 12 =$ _____	**17.** $104 \div 2 =$ _____	**18.** $300 \div 20 =$ _____
19. $119 \div 7 =$ _____	**20.** $225 \div 15 =$ _____	

Score for A (10)

B **(30 points)** — Estimate an answer for each of the following division problems. Show your rounding, dropping of zeros, and final estimate (2 points for each correct answer).

Problem	Rounding	Dropped Zeros	Estimated Answer
21. $4,909 \div 487 =$	_____	_____	_____
22. $888 \div 47 =$	_____	_____	_____
23. $19,762 \div 1,111 =$	_____	_____	_____
24. $366 \div 17 =$	_____	_____	_____
25. $988,888 \div 1,999 =$	_____	_____	_____

Score for B (30)

C **(10 points)** — Divide by shortcut methods. Express remainders in parentheses (1 point for each correct answer).

26. $3,450 \div 10 =$ _____	**27.** $12,800 \div 100 =$ _____
28. $58,700 \div 100 =$ _____	**29.** $2,200 \div 50 =$ _____
30. $7,800 \div 20 =$ _____	**31.** $6,450 \div 320 =$ _____
32. $9,005 \div 100 =$ _____	**33.** $387 \div 10 =$ _____
34. $38,500 \div 1,000 =$ _____	**35.** $3,250,000 \div 10,000 =$ _____

Score for C (10)

D **(50 points)** — Divide. Show remainder in parentheses after the whole number in the quotient (2 points for each correct answer).

36. $21\overline{)478}$	**37.** $13\overline{)2,795}$	**38.** $23\overline{)14,076}$	**39.** $7\overline{)4,919}$

40.

$$36\overline{)6,436}$$

41.

$$23\overline{)478}$$

42.

$$271\overline{)50,001}$$

43.

$$33\overline{)97,382}$$

44.

$$926\overline{)926,007}$$

45.

$$77\overline{)12,770}$$

46.

$$506\overline{)10,238}$$

47.

$$9\overline{)818,173}$$

48.

$$700\overline{)362,497}$$

49.

$$111\overline{)34,173}$$

50.

$$88\overline{)97,817}$$

51.

$$13\overline{)\$67,209}$$

52.

$$6\overline{)\$13.20}$$

53.

$$54\overline{)78,540}$$

54.

$$51\overline{)100}$$

55.

$$26\overline{)111,013}$$

56.

$$66\overline{)73,428}$$

57.

$$1,014\overline{)20,016}$$

58.

$$66\overline{)17,209}$$

59.

$$65\overline{)372,000}$$

60.

$$29\overline{)58,004,316}$$

Part One   Fundamentals of Mathematics in Business

Chapter 2
Electronic Calculators

OBJECTIVES
After completing this chapter, you should be able to:

• Understand the features of a basic electronic calculator
• Use a calculator for business computations

Students who study business mathematics and accounting today use calculators. These modern miracles of calculation reduce computation time in long and complex problems, especially for multiplication and division.

Small, reasonably priced, hand-held calculators are adequate for working problems in this book and solving problems common to business. Pocket-size calculators can be purchased for under $10. For this amount, you can purchase a calculator that will perform regular addition, subtraction, multiplication, and division; it will probably have an eight-digit display, floating decimal point, percentage key, memory register, and the ability to work problems using repeat addition-subtraction and constant multipliers and divisors.

Desk-top calculators also have become very popular. Many models can be purchased for under $50. These calculators feature a tape so that calculations can be printed and verified. Their keys are large enough that an experienced person can use the touch method of entering numbers without looking at the keys.

FEATURES IMPORTANT FOR BUSINESS

Most calculators used for business are quite simple to use and very similar in operation. There are basic features to look for in a calculator that is purchased for business. The following features are recommended:

1. *Eight- to twelve-digit capacity.* For business, eight or more digits are preferable.
2. *Floating decimal point.* This feature places the decimal point automatically, carrying out calculations from two decimal places to the maximum capacity of the calculator's display.

3. *Power source.* Most hand-held calculators use solar power or silver-oxide batteries that allow up to 2,000 hours of normal operation. These are recommended highly. For other calculators that use nine-volt, size AA, or size AAA batteries, spare batteries should *always* be kept available in case of battery failure.

4. *Percent key (%).* This key eliminates the need to convert a percentage to a decimal before multiplying or dividing. For most calculators, this key reduces the number of steps required in percentage calculations by commanding the calculator to give a net percentage answer.

5. *Memory register.* This feature enables the user to store an amount and then add to it, subtract from it, recall it for review, multiply it, or divide it again and again until the register is cleared.

6. *Repeat addition-subtraction.* This feature provides that a number, once entered, can be automatically repeated in addition and subtraction by depressing the equals key.

7. *Constant multipliers and divisors.* This feature provides that a number, once entered, can be automatically repeated as a multiplier or divisor by entering the new dividend or multiplicand and depressing the equals key. The constant is usually the last number entered in division problems (divisor) and is usually the first number entered in multiplication problems (multiplier).

THE DECIMAL POINT

Many calculations have a decimal point. A decimal point is a period (.) used to separate a whole number on the left of the decimal from a less than whole number on the right of the decimal.

a. $37.42 — the decimal separates the whole dollars (37) from the less than whole dollar (42 cents).

Decimals, which are not limited to representing dollars and cents, are a regular part of business calculations. Often decimal amounts are limited to a certain number of figures shown on the right side of a decimal. Many electronic calculators show up to 8 figures on the right side of the decimal point. Frequently, these should be reduced, or "rounded", to just two figures.

To round a number containing three or more figures on the right side of the decimal to two decimal places, start at the decimal and count to the right. If the third figure is 4 or less, leave the second figure as it is. If the third is 5 or greater, increase the second figure by one.

b. 37.414 rounded to two decimal places is 37.41
37.415 rounded to two decimal places is 37.42
82.333333 rounded to four decimal places is 82.3333
82.666666 rounded to four decimal places is 82.6667

Examples of decimals and rounding for use in this chapter are limited to their simplest form. Decimals, along with special rounding techniques, will be fully explained in Chapters 7 and 8.

DISPLAY UNITS

Most hand-held calculators use *LED* (*Light Emitting Diodes*) or *LC* (*Liquid Crystal*) display units. LED numbers usually appear in red or green light. LC numbers usually appear in soft white light. Both display modes are good for business purposes. In addition to displaying numbers and decimal points, most of today's calculators also show when the display number is negative by a minus sign (−), when a number is in the memory register by a dot or an M, and when the entry or results exceed the capacity of the display by some type of overflow indicator.

BASIC KEYS AND THEIR CAPABILITIES

The first booklet to read for instructions about a calculator is the one provided by the manufacturer. You should always read and do the sample problems in the manufacturer's instruction booklet. The following descriptions are compiled from a number of these booklets. They cover the basic key functions common to most hand-held calculators.

On Off On-Off	....	Controls power. NOTE: The Off key usually clears the calculator, including the memory.
C Clear Key	....	Clears the calculator except for the memory register.
AC All Clear Key	....	Clears the calculator, including the memory register.
0 - 9 Numeral Keys	....	Used to enter numbers.
CE Clear Entry	....	Used to clear numbers keyed incorrectly but not yet entered. Does not clear total or memory.
. Decimal Point Key	....	Puts a decimal point into a number.
+ Addition Key	....	Adds.
− Subtraction Key	....	Subtracts.
× Multiplication Key	....	Multiplies.
÷ Division Key	....	Divides.
= Equals Key	....	Orders the *sum*, the *difference*, the *product*, or the *quotient*.
+/- Change Sign Key	....	Converts a positive number to a negative number and vice versa.
% Percent Key	....	Orders computed answer to move decimal two places to the left.
√ Square Root Key	....	Computes the square root of the number in the display. Used primarily in scientific calculations; seldom used in business.

For Memory Calculators:

M+ Memory Plus Key	....	Adds the number in the display to the memory. NOTE: Used to add the results of regular register multiplication (the product) and division (the quotient) to the memory register.

M– Memory Minus Key . . . . Subtracts the number in the display from the memory.

MR Memory Recall Key . . . . Displays the contents of the memory register. NOTE: Does not clear the memory.

MC Memory Clear Key . . . . Displays the contents of the memory register and clears the memory register.

BASIC OPERATIONS

The following calculator operations are commonly used in business mathematics. Although you have undoubtedly read and practice similar problems using your own calculator's instruction booklet, you should work through the following illustrations. The steps shown can be used with most hand-held and small desk-top calculators. However, because of the number of different manufacturers, your calculator might not use the exact steps shown here. Note the differences and work the problems until you get the answers given. Consult your own instruction booklet when differences arise.

Addition: 200 + 300 + 400 = 900

Enter	C	200		+		300		+		400		=
Display	0	200	200		300		500		400		900

Subtraction: 45.6 − 12.3 = 33.3

Enter	C	45.6		−		12.3		=
Display	0	45.6	45.6		12.3		33.3

Addition-Subtraction Chain: 3.91 + 14.21 − 1.03 + 2.16 − 10 = 9.25

Enter	C	3.91		+		14.21		−		1.03		+		2.16		−		10		=
Display	0	3.91	3.91		14.21	18.12		1.03	17.09		2.16	19.25		10	9.25

Multiplication: 300 × 5 = 1,500

Enter	C	300		×		5		=
Display	0	300	300		5		1,500

Multiplication by % Key (automatically moves decimal 2 places to the left): 300 × 5%(0.05) = 15

Enter	C	300		×		5		%
Display	0	300	300		5		15

Multiplication, Subtraction, and % Key chain: 670 × 3 − 1,800 × 20% = 42

Enter	C	670		×		3		−		1,800		×		20		%
Display	0	670	670		3	2,010		1,800	210		20	42

Multiplication Chain: 1.23 × 45.6 × 789 = 44,253.432

Enter	C	1.23		×		45.6		×		789		=
Display	0	1.23	1.23		45.6	56.088		789	44,253.432

Division: 400 ÷ 8 = 50

Enter	C	400	÷	8	=
Display	0	400	400	8	50

Division by % Key (automatically moves decimal 2 places to the left):
400 ÷ 8%(0.08) = 5,000

Enter	C	400	÷	8	%
Display	0	400	400	8	5,000

Division Chain: 400 ÷ 50 ÷ 3 = 2.6666666

Enter	C	400	÷	50	÷	3	=
Display	0	400	400	50	8	3	2.6666666

Division-Multiplication Chain: 123 ÷ 456 × 789 = 212.8223683

Enter	C	123	÷	456	×	789	=
Display	0	123	123	456	0.2697368	789	212.8223683

Constant Multiplication: 250 × 4 = 1,000; 250 × 5 = 1,250; 250 × 6 = 1,500
Machine with constant program (in older-model calculators, the constant key might be the second number entered rather than the first):

Enter	C	250	×	4	=	5	=	6	=
Display	0	250	250	4	1,000	5	1,250	6	1,500

Machine without constant program, but with memory register:

Enter	C	MC	250	M+	×	4	=	MR	×	5	=	MR	×
Display	0	0	250	250	250	4	1,000	250	250	5	1,250	250	250

	6	=
	6	1,500

Constant Division: 208 ÷ 26 = 8; 312 ÷ 26 = 12; 624 ÷ 26 = 24
Machine with constant program:

Enter	C	208	÷	26	=	312	=	624	=
Display	0	208	208	26	8	312	12	624	24

Machine without constant program, but with memory register:

Enter	C	MC	26	M+	208	÷	MR	=	312	÷	MR	=	624	÷
Display	0	0	26	26	208	208	26	8	312	312	26	12	624	624

	MR	=
	26	24

Memory Problem-Hold and Recall Intermediate Answers: (3 × 5) + (6 × 11) + (13 × 20) = 341

Enter	C	MC	3	×	5	M+	6	×	11	M+	13	×	20	M+	MR
Display	0	0	3	3	5	15	6	6	11	66	13	13	20	260	341

BUSINESS APPLICATIONS

c. Find the closing checkbook balance: Opening balance = $387.50; checks = $17.20, $13.82, $17.60, and $29.40; deposit = $298.40. (Answer: Balance = $607.88)

Enter	C	387.50	−	17.20	−	13.82	−	17.60	−
Display	0	387.50	387.50	17.20	370.30	13.82	356.48	17.60	338.88

	29.40	+	298.40	=
	29.40	309.48	298.40	607.88

d. Find the average miles per gallon for an automobile driven 370 miles and using 20 gallons of gas. (Answer: Average miles per gallon = 18.5)

Enter	C	370	÷	20	=
Display	0	370	370	20	18.5

e. Total the invoice for 9 items @ $11.00, 7 items @ $14.00, and 3 items @ $15.00, plus 6% sales tax. (Answer: Total invoice = $256.52)

Enter	C	MC	9	×	11	=	M+	7	×	14	=	M+	3	×	15
Display	0	0	9	9	11	99	99	7	7	14	98	98	3	3	15

	=	M+	MR	×	0.06	=	+	MR
	45	45	242	242	0.06	14.52	14.52	242

or, with % key:

Enter	MR	×	6	%	+	=
Display	242	242	6	14.52	14.52	256.52

or

Enter	C	MC	9	×	11	M+	7	×	14	M+	3	×	15	M+	MR	×
Display	0	0	9	9	11	99	7	7	14	98	3	3	15	45	242	242

	0.06	M+	MR
	0.06	14.52	256.52

Chapter terms for review

constant divisors
constant multipliers
eight-digit capacity
floating decimal point
LC (Liquid Crystal)
LED (Light Emitting Diodes)

memory register
percent key
power source
repeat addition-subtraction
twelve-digit capacity

Assignment 2-1: Basic Operations

A (50 points)— Use a calculator to solve the following problems. Calculate in the order presented (left to right). Round answers to four decimal places using only the fifth decimal place in the rounding process. Show negative numbers in parentheses ($\frac{1}{2}$ point for each correct answer).

Add:

1. $37 + 28 + 56 =$ _____
2. $3.12 + 0.014 + 17 + 4.3 + 1.6 =$ _____
3. $211 + 0.056 + 0.001 + 173 =$ _____
4. $3.62 + 0.01 + 6.03 + 19.999 =$ _____
5. $201,623 + 11 + 0.1 + 308 =$ _____
6. $13 + 2,000 + 14.14 + 9 =$ _____
7. $1,150 + 1.155 + 11.5 =$ _____
8. $106 + 1,114.3 + 50.2 + 14 =$ _____
9. $0.0016 + 0.3 + 1.6 + 0.004 =$ _____
10. $17 + 13 + 0.42 + 0.008 =$ _____

Subtract:

11. $2,000 - 1,099 =$ _____
12. $4.123 - 2.123 =$ _____
13. $5,001 - 4,777 =$ _____
14. $0.107 - 0.12 =$ _____
15. $11,117 - 0.03 =$ _____
16. $24.006 - 19.603 =$ _____
17. $29 - 30.16 =$ _____
18. $29 - 20.16 =$ _____
19. $14 - 0.14 =$ _____
20. $2.3 - 4.013 =$ _____

Add-subtract:

21. $13 - 24 + 16.01 =$ _____
22. $57 + 12 - 14.113 + 6.11 - 0.116 =$ _____
23. $3,000 + 3,000 + 3,000 - 16 - 0.016 =$ _____
24. $472 + 13 + 0.96 + 33 - 874 =$ _____
25. $0.004 - 17 - 0.32 - 0.16 + 33 =$ _____
26. $10 + 0.21 + 19 - 0.731 =$ _____
27. $800 - 2,116 + 23 + 14 =$ _____
28. $16 - 18 + 0.115 + 0.113 + 0.9919 =$ _____
29. $28,107 - 107 - 800 - 1,200 - 713 - 87 =$ _____
30. $29 - 28.001 + 17.69 - 0.03 =$ _____

Multiply:

31. $36 \times 14 =$ _____
32. $72 \times 2.3 =$ _____
33. $36 \times 3.6 =$ _____
34. $28,936.8 \times 36 =$ _____
35. $11 \times 1.1 \times 111 \times 0.11 =$ _____
36. $27.602 \times 0.0013 =$ _____
37. $8,732 \times 12 \times 0.06 \times 12 =$ _____
38. $0.03 \times 0.16 =$ _____
39. $239 \times 23 \times 9 \times 0.002 =$ _____
40. $12 \times 30 \times 9.1 \times 0.106 =$ _____

Divide:

41. $33 \div 19 =$ _____

42. $0.33 \div 0.19 =$ _____

43. $39 \div 36 =$ _____

44. $0.39 \div 0.36 =$ _____

45. $44 \div 61 =$ _____

46. $44 \div 0.61 =$ _____

47. $200 \div 0.4 =$ _____

48. $382 \div 383 =$ _____

49. $1.4 \div 379 =$ _____

50. $379 \div 1.4 =$ _____

51. $40 \div 40 \div 40 \div 40 =$ _____

52. $80 \div 80 \div 80 \div 80 =$ _____

53. $3.7 \div 0.0000617 =$ _____

54. $617 \div 3.7 =$ _____

55. $0.007 \div 0.16328 =$ _____

56. $28 \div 14 \div 2 =$ _____

57. $679 \div 703 =$ _____

58. $0.04 \div 36 \div 0.02 =$ _____

59. $29 \div 0.02314 =$ _____

60. $17 \div 34 =$ _____

61. $1.3 \div 7.2 =$ _____

62. $89 \div 0.89 =$ _____

63. $39 \div 0.39 =$ _____

64. $714 \div 1,016 =$ _____

65. $0.36 \div 0.036 =$ _____

66. $3,116,215 \div 5 =$ _____

67. $7,316 \div 12 =$ _____

68. $417 \div 0.06 \div 6 =$ _____

69. $1.4 \div 1,401 =$ _____

70. $3,709 \div 4,132 =$ _____

71. $28 \div 0.0034602 =$ _____

72. $4,038 \div 4,037 =$ _____

73. $36 \div 321 =$ _____

74. $14 \div 15 \div 16 \div 17 =$ _____

75. $679 \div 700 =$ _____

76. $2,001 \div 3,001 =$ _____

77. $679 \div 504 =$ _____

78. $378 \div 0.03 =$ _____

79. $9.03 \div 9.04 =$ _____

80. $22 \div 2 \div 11 =$ _____

Chain calculations:

81. $36 \div 6 \times 1.2 + 4 - 2.2 =$ _____

82. $2.162 - 13 \times 0.16 + 66 =$ _____

83. $0.005 \div 3.6 \times 1.2 + 1.3 - 6 =$ _____

84. $2,216,000 + 1,114,230 \times 2.03 =$ _____

85. $0.005 \div 360 \times 0.12 + 13 - 0.6 =$ _____

86. $17 \div 17 \div 17 \times 34 =$ _____

87. $38,716,140 \times 2 \div 99,968 =$ _____

88. $0.138 \times 14 - 23 \times 6 =$ _____

89. $14,707 \div 14,000 \times 6 =$ _____

90. $0.016 \times 0.016 =$ _____

91. $0.05 \div 0.12 \times 110 + 0.11 - 3.3 =$ _____

92. $38 - 14 \times 26 \div 0.13 \times 18 =$ _____

93. $0.005 \div 0.03 \times 0.12 + 13.1 - 60 =$ _____

94. $0.005 \times 0.03 \times 0.12 - 1.31 \times 60 =$ _____

95. $6 \times 0.13 \div 8 + 28 - 17 =$ _____

96. $108 - 216 \times 3 \div 0.14 + 300 =$ _____

97. $42 \div 346 \times 0.01 - 36 + 28 =$ _____

98. $283 \div 3 + 16 + 16 + 16 + 16 =$ _____

99. $17 \times 4 \div 12 + 2.016 - 11 =$ _____

100. $28 \div 28,000 \times 3 =$ _____

Score for A (50)

B (50 points)—Round dollars and cents problems to two decimal places and all others to four decimal places using only the fifth decimal place in the rounding process ($\frac{1}{2}$ point for each correct answer).

Divide-multiply:

101. 94 ÷ 99 = _____   **102.** 94 × 99 = _____

103. 19 ÷ 4 = _____   **104.** 2.16 × 3.08 = _____

105. 17.412 × 36.001 = _____   **106.** 2.36 × 0.016 = _____

107. 14,016 ÷ 239.01 = _____   **108.** 14,016 ÷ 239 = _____

109. 19 ÷ 14 = _____   **110.** 0.012 × 11 = _____

111. 23 ÷ 14.1 = _____   **112.** 23 × 14.3 = _____

113. 29 ÷ 31 = _____   **114.** 0.60 ÷ 66 = _____

115. 293 × 12 = _____   **116.** 0.29 × 300 = _____

117. 0.068 × 12 = _____   **118.** 17,328 ÷ 1,700 = _____

119. 217 × 0.012 = _____   **120.** 289 ÷ 9,132 = _____

121. 0.72 ÷ 0.76 = _____   **122.** 17 × 0.0013 = _____

123. 2,807 × 0.3 = _____   **124.** 38 × 0.26 = _____

125. 23 ÷ 9.01 = _____   **126.** 1,101 ÷ 101,101 = _____

127. 22 ÷ 0.0003 = _____   **128.** 1.17 ÷ 2 = _____

129. 23 × 168 = _____   **130.** 4,110 ÷ 3,000 = _____

131. 27 ÷ 32 = _____   **132.** 381 × 0.17 = _____

133. 34,618,221 ÷ 28,126,308 = _____   **134.** 0.01 ÷ 0.002 = _____

135. 23,046 ÷ 12 = _____   **136.** 1,289,764 × 0.3 = _____

137. 1.138 ÷ 12 = _____   **138.** 0.714 × 628 = _____

139. 11 ÷ 12 = _____   **140.** 1 ÷ 9 = _____

Combined calculations:

141. $13.09 × 6.1 = _____   **142.** 0.01 + 0.003 = _____

143. $38.26 × 204 = _____   **144.** 3,184,220 ÷ 6 = _____

145. 13.06 − 14.19 = _____   **146.** $28.17 × 144 = _____

147. 0.07 ÷ 0.14 = _____   **148.** 27 × $10.13 = _____

149. 29.8 ÷ 30 = _____   **150.** 17 − 0.99 = _____

151. 17 ÷ 23.01 = _____   **152.** $17.01 ÷ 3 = _____

153. 0.017 − 28.1 = _____   **154.** 109 × 0.6 = _____

155. 36 + 42 = _____   **156.** 3,184,200 × 0.12 = _____

157. 78,361,028 ÷ 99,817,209 = _____   **158.** 27.1 ÷ 9 = _____

159. 17.016 × 1.9 = _____   **160.** $14.12 + $111.06 = _____

161. $141.07 ÷ 4 = _____   **162.** 16,164 ÷ 16 = _____

163. 17.381 ÷ 26.08 = _____   **164.** $7.17 × 28 = _____

165. 28.31 × 16.02 = _____   **166.** $1,174 − $0.76 = _____

167. 22.16 × 9 = _____   **168.** 14 ÷ 13.8 = _____

169. $428.17 + $36.11 = _____   **170.** 294 × 3.16 = _____

171. $28.06 × 14 = _____   **172.** 0.281 ÷ 0.0301 = _____

173. 0.281 × 3.01 = _____   **174.** 2,714 × 4 = _____

175. 214 + 0.007 = _____   **176.** $0.17 + $3 = _____

177. 36,148 × 21.2 = _____   **178.** 32 × 32.1 = _____

179. 32 ÷ 32.1 = _____   **180.** $3.01 − $7.12 = _____

Chain calculations:

181. $17 \div 1.13 \times 6 + 2 = $ _____

182. $17 \times 1.13 \div 6 - 2 = $ _____

183. $17.3 \div 17 \times 234 = $ _____

184. $3,000,000 \times 0.04 + 6 = $ _____

185. $0.016 \div 3.81624 \times 14 = $ _____

186. $318 - 18 \div 2 \times 3 - 450 = $ _____

187. $987.44 \times 99.906 \times 0.0987 = $ _____

188. $7 \times 7 \times 7 \times 77 = $ _____

189. $108.1 \times 3.07 \div 6 = $ _____

190. $\$25.00 \times 13 - \$15.00 \div 4 = $ _____

191. $117 \times 0.16 \div 3 + 14 = $ _____

192. $0.113 \div 0.2 \times 14 = $ _____

193. $209.6 \times 14 \div 37 = $ _____

194. $3 + 3 + 7 \times 6.7 = $ _____

195. $2.916 \div 29.08 \times 99 = $ _____

196. $29 + 13 - 21.4 \div 12 = $ _____

197. $920.8 \div 743.261 \div 0.083 = $ _____

198. $920 \times 26 \times 0.002 = $ _____

199. $201.3 \div 87.016 \times 2 = $ _____

200. $101 \div 2 + 2 \times 16 = $ _____

Score for B (50)

Assignment 2-2: Business Applications

A **(40 points)—Solve the following problems using a calculator (4 points for each correct answer).**

1. Find the closing balance: opening balance—$311.16; deposits—$28.50, $326.40, $36.11; checks— $1.17, $187.50, $72.40, $23.14, $20.13, $11.23, $97.30, $29.16. _____

2. Determine the total of the sales minus the refunds: Monday sales—$73.19, $29.60, $100.17, $5.63; refunds—$40.76, $56.40; Tuesday sales—$38.00, $19.76, $46.25, $38.68; refund—$7.61. _____

3. 144 items at $27.14 each plus 144 items at $13.12 each. _____

4. 28 items at $14.03 each plus $23.57 sales tax. _____

5. Total the expenses: 209 kilometers @ 20¢ per kilometer; meals—$3.45, $4.50, $17.20; lodging— $45.50. _____

6. Total the income: food sales—$362.40; clothing sales—$763.80; office supply sales—$17.40; book sales—$56.40; refund—$13.08. _____

7. You drive an automobile 517.6 miles and get 21.7 miles per gallon of gas. If gas costs $1.23 per gallon, how much was the total gas bill? _____

8. If four salespeople sold a total of $9,384.26 in merchandise, what was the average per salesperson? _____

9. Monday sales—$387.00; Tuesday sales—$517.17; Wednesday sales—$409.13; Thursday sales— $767.00; and Friday sales—$299.70. How much is the average daily sales? _____

10. Baseball cards sold at $0.65 each. Tom bought 13. Sally bought 32. Harry bought 7. Beth bought 22. The seller started with 100 cards in stock. What was the price of his remaining stock after these purchases? _____

_____
Score for A (40)

B **(60 points)—Solve the following problems using a calculator.**

11. Multiply each of the following sales amounts by 0.06 to show the amount of sales tax. Round to two decimal places. Total the sales and the amount of tax using the memory feature on your calculator (1 point for each correct tax and sales amount; 2 points for each correct total amount—Total, 24 points).

Sales Amount Before Tax	Tax (0.06)	Sales Amount With Tax
$ 512.16	_____	_____
412.30	_____	_____
42.00	_____	_____
217.80	_____	_____
96.26	_____	_____
16.12	_____	_____
908.70	_____	_____
221.24	_____	_____
777.70	_____	_____
_____	_____	_____

12. Six cars were tested for gas-mileage performance by being driven as far as they would go on 9 gallons of gas. Total miles driven are given below. Determine the miles per gallon for each car. Round answers to four decimal places (1 point for each correct answer—Total, 6 points).

Car	Total Miles Driven	Gallons Used	Miles per Gallon
A	412	9	_____
B	396	9	_____
C	307	9	_____
D	303	9	_____
E	236	9	_____
F	149	9	_____

13. Determine each separate amount, and find the subtotal of the invoice items below. Add 6% sales tax (0.06), and determine the total invoice using the memory feature on your calculator (2 points for each correct answer—Total, 20 points).

Quantity	Item	Price per Unit	Amount
4	Jackets	$ 26.20	_____
2	Belts	9.47	_____
6	Shoes—Oxford Sets	49.99	_____
9	Shirts—Sport	24.99	_____
26	Socks—Varied	3.46	_____
12	Suits—Mixed	119.00	_____
17	Ties	15.50	_____
		Subtotal	_____
		Sales Tax	_____
		Total Invoice	_____

14. For each sale made, a Smith Company salesperson receives a commission of 8.8% (.088) times the sales amount. Determine the total May commission paid each of the five salespeople and the average commission per working day (total May commission divided by the number of working days). Round each answer to the nearest cent (1 point for each correct answer—Total, 10 points).

Salesperson	May Sales	Commission Rate	Total May Commission	Working Days	Commission per Day
A	$30,124	8.8%	_____	21	_____
B	27,106	8.8	_____	21	_____
C	31,013	8.8	_____	21	_____
D	36,003	8.8	_____	21	_____
E	42,168	8.8	_____	21	_____

Score for B (60)

Part One   Fundamentals of Mathematics in Business

Chapter 3
Enhancing Number Skills

OBJECTIVES
After completing this chapter, you should be able to:

* Apply greater skill to using fundamental processes
* Use skill in applying fundamental processes to business calculations

NUMBER DRILLS

Practicing number drills will improve speed and accuracy in using the four fundamental processes. Number drills will improve your ability to think quickly. Rapid and accurate number calculations need to be made frequently in business.

In the following illustration you should be able to obtain the ten answers without using pencil, paper, or an electronic calculator. ***Each step is done left to right in the number sequence in which it appears***.

a. $7 + 3 + 8 + 4 = 22$
$27 - 2 - 5 + 8 + 2 = 30$
$60 \div 2 \div 3 \div 5 = 2$
$3 + 4 + 2 + 10 = 19$
$3 \times 4 \times 2 \times 10 = 240$
$28 \div 4 \times 5 \times 2 - 7 \div 9 = 7$
$26 \div 2 + 2 \times 2 \times 2 \div 6 + 10 = 20$
$180 \times 2 \div 6 - 20 \div 8 \times 5 = 25$
$100 \times 5 - 20 - 400 - 30 + 6 = 56$
$4,000 \div 2 + 100 \div 7 - 299 = 1$

NUMBER SENTENCES

Sometimes numbers are used in sentence form: three plus five equals eight ($3 + 5 = 8$). Another example of a *number sentence* is twenty-five minus seven divided by three equals six ($25 - 7 \div 3 = 6$).

Number sentences in which both sides of the equal sign contain calculations are called *number sentence equations*, or *equations*. For example, five plus five equals the same as twelve minus two (5 + 5 = 12 − 2); seven minus four times two equals the same as thirty divided by five (7 − 4 × 2 = 30 ÷ 5).

Basic equations are used frequently in calculating business applications, especially when comparisons between various business elements are being made. For an equation to be true, the numbers on the left of the equal sign must calculate to the same answer as the numbers on the right of the equal sign.

Rule: Moving a number to the opposite side of an equation changes its sign. In addition and subtraction problems, the sign will change from plus to minus or from minus to plus (+ to − or − to +). In multiplication and division problems, the sign will change from multiply to divide or from divide to multiply (× to ÷ or ÷ to ×). Note the example shown below.

b. 6 + 4 + 5 = 17 − 2
Change the 5 and the 2: 6 + 4 + 2 = 17 − 5
Check: 6 + 4 + 2 = 12 equals 17 − 5 = 12

3 × 8 = 48 ÷ 2
Change the 8 and the 2: 3 × 2 = 48 ÷ 8
Check: 3 × 2 = 6 equals 48 ÷ 8 = 6

A number equation may be incomplete but provide enough information to be completed. Note the examples shown below.

c. 6 + 2 = ? + 4   (? = 4)
15 − 3 = 2 + ?   (? = 10)
7 + 3 + 6 = 4 + 4 + ?   (? = 8)
20 ÷ 5 = 2 × ?   (? = 2)

Number sentence equations in business frequently compare items. Note the examples shown below.

d. 4 items at $0.50 each = 10 items at ? each (? = $0.20)
6 tickets at $3 each = 5 tickets at ? each (? = $3.60)

NUMBER RELATIONSHIPS IN A SERIES

Relationships in a series of numbers may be found by comparing the first three or four terms in the series. For example, examining the series 320, 160, 80, 40 indicates that each term is found by dividing the preceding number by 2. The next two numbers in the series would be 20 and 10.

The series 7, 14, 21 indicates the addition of 7 to each number. The next two numbers in this series would be 28 and 35.

The series 5, 15, 35, 75, 155 shows that each number results from multiplying the preceding number by 2 and then adding 5. These relationships are used frequently in employment tests. Recognizing numerical and series relationships can also be important in analyzing, communicating, and computing with numbers.

USING FUNDAMENTAL PROCESSES TO SOLVE WORD PROBLEMS

Some students have little difficulty with calculations that are expressed in numbers only. In the following illustration they would quickly answer 350.

e. $15 + 15 + 10 \times 10 - 50 = 350$

However, they might not answer $350 as quickly when the business problem in the next illustration is given, even though it uses only the elements in the number equation above.

f. A company orders carpeting for three offices containing 15 square yards, 15 square yards, and 10 square yards. A carpet dealer sells the carpet for $10 a square yard and gives a $50 discount when the sale is for three or more offices. How much would the company pay to have the three offices carpeted?

15 sq. yd. + 15 sq. yd. + 10 sq. yd. = 40 sq. yd.
40 sq. yd. × $10 = $400 gross price
$400 − $50 discount = $350 net price

Business problems using calculations simply require addition, subtraction, multiplication, and division. The following steps are taken to solve the word problem illustrated above.

Steps for Solving Word Problems

1. Read the entire problem carefully, and note what answer is asked for.
2. Note which items need to be added, which subtracted, which multiplied, and which divided.
3. Complete the calculation in the most logical and easiest sequence.

Step 1 The answer asked for in example f. is "how much" would the company pay?

Step 2 The items to be calculated in the problem are as follows:
To be added—15 sq. yd., 15 sq. yd., and 10 sq. yd.
To be subtracted—One $50 discount.
To be multiplied—The total sq. yd. times $10 per sq. yd.
To be divided—No division required.

Step 3 A sequence that is logical and easy is to:
Add sq. yd. in the 3 offices: 15 + 15 + 10 = 40.
Multiply the $10 per sq. yd. by total sq. yd.: 40 × $10 = $400.
Subtract the $50 discount: $400 − $50 = $350.

Some word problems will involve all four fundamental processes: addition, subtraction, multiplication, and division. Refer to the problem below.

g. Mary owns half of a small bakery. Last week she baked 6 cakes on Monday, 9 on Tuesday, 11 on Wednesday, 8 on Thursday, and 6 on Friday. She sold all cakes for $9 each. It cost Mary $5 to make each cake; the rest was her profit on each cake. Mary split her profit evenly with her partner. How much did her partner receive from last week's cakes?

Step 1   The answer asked for is "how much money did Mary's partner receive?"

Step 2   The items to be calculated in the problem are as follows:
To be added—6 cakes, 9 cakes, 11 cakes, 8 cakes, and 6 cakes.
To be subtracted—Cost of $5 per cake from the $9 received for the cake.
To be multiplied—Total cakes baked by the profit of $4 per cake.
To be divided—Total profit by 2 (split evenly between 2 partners).

Step 3   A sequence that is logical and easy is to:
Add the cakes baked: 6 + 9 + 11 + 8 + 6 = 40.
Subtract cost from sales price: $9 − $5 = $4 profit per cake.
Multiply the $4 profit per cake by cakes sold: 40 × $4 = $160.
Divide total profit by 2: $160 ÷ 2 = $80 received by partner.

MAKING QUICK CALCULATIONS BY "ROUNDING" NUMBERS

Quick calculations often are beneficial when working in business situations. *Rounding* odd and difficult-to-calculate amounts to even whole numbers that are easier to calculate is a technique that often is used in business. By rounding you will be able to get quick and accurate answers without having to write out the calculations.

h. How much would 5 items at $2.99 each cost?

To easily figure 5 items at $2.99, think "$2.99 is $0.01 less than $3.00." Then think "5 times $3 equals $15." Finally, think "$15 less $0.05 (5 × $0.01) is $14.95," the correct answer.

i. The total cost of 3 items is $119.85. How much does one of these items cost?

To easily figure $119.85 divided by 3, think "$119.85 is $0.15 less than $120." Then think "$120 divided by 3 = $40" and "$40 less $0.05 ($0.15 ÷ 3) is $39.95," the correct answer.

j. At 19 miles per gallon, how many miles would a car go on 16 gallons of gas?

To easily figure the total miles, think "19 is just 1 mile less than 20." Then think "16 times 20 = 320" and "320 minus 16 (16 × 1) is 304," the correct answer.

COMPLETE ASSIGNMENT 3-2

Chapter terms for review

equation

number sentence

number sentence equation

rounding

Assignment 3-1: Development of Fundamental Processes

A (20 points) — Do each step in the order in which it occurs. These problems may be used as dictated drills (1 point for each correct answer).

1. $14 + 5 + 3 + 4 =$ _____
2. $6 \times 6 - 4 \div 8 \times 2 =$ _____
3. $17 - 3 - 2 - 5 =$ _____
4. $14 \div 2 \times 5 \times 2 + 5 =$ _____
5. $80 \div 4 \div 2 \div 5 =$ _____
6. $9 \times 2 + 2 \times 6 - 20 \div 4 =$ _____
7. $3 \times 2 \times 5 \times 3 =$ _____
8. $4 - 3 \times 5 \times 5 \times 5 - 3 =$ _____
9. $25 \div 5 \times 3 + 1 + 11 + 2 - 6 =$ _____
10. $12 + 12 + 12 + 14 \div 5 \times 3 + 3 =$ _____
11. $100 \times 5 - 50 \div 9 + 5 \div 11 \times 3 =$ _____
12. $36 \div 3 \div 4 + 10 + 5 - 3 \times 3 =$ _____
13. $15 \div 3 \times 2 + 8 - 3 + 12 \div 3 =$ _____
14. $10 \times 8 + 20 \times 3 \div 6 \div 5 + 4 =$ _____
15. $9 \div 3 \times 7 + 4 + 5 \times 4 - 6 =$ _____
16. $680 \div 2 \div 2 + 10 \div 6 \times 2 + 6 =$ _____
17. $32 \times 2 \div 8 \times 100 + 200 \div 4 + 1 =$ _____
18. $12 + 10 + 3 + 26 + 29 \div 4 \times 3 =$ _____
19. $1{,}000 \times 4 \times 2 - 5{,}000 \div 6 =$ _____
20. $3 + 4 + 5 + 6 + 7 \div 5 \times 800 =$ _____

Score for A (20)

B (20 points)—Do each step in the order in which it occurs. Do these problems without using scratch paper or an electronic calculator (2 points for each correct answer).

21. 12 items at $3 each plus $2 tax = _____
22. 15 watches at $30 each less a $50 discount = _____
23. 3 lamps at $22 each plus 7 bulbs at $2 each = _____
24. 100 belts at $4 each less discounts of $60 and $30 = _____
25. 3 dozen scissors at $11.20 per dozen plus a $4 shipping charge = _____
26. 8 pounds of pears at $3 per pound plus 50¢ per pound for packaging = _____
27. $38 sale price plus $3 tax less a $12 discount plus a $3 delivery charge = _____
28. 6 bath towels at $8 each and 4 hand towels at $3 each plus $2.50 tax = _____
29. 4 dozen brushes at $25 per dozen plus $5 tax plus $7 shipping charge = _____
30. 2 shirts at $20 each, 4 ties at $5 each, and 7 pair of socks at $2 each = _____

Score for B (20)

C (20 points) — Complete the following number sentences by supplying the missing items (1 point for each correct answer).

31. $21 + 3 =$ _____ $+ 8$

32. $4 \times 20 =$ _____ $+ 4$

33. $13 +$ _____ $= 7 + 26$

34. _____ $\div 2 = 9 - 1$

35. _____ $+ 4 = 4 + 12$

36. $64 \div 32 = 900 \div$ _____

37. $400 = 17 - 2 +$ _____

38. $15 - 9 - 2 = 25 -$ _____

39. $22 - 9 =$ _____ $- 6$

40. _____ $+ 6 = 43 - 12$

41. $36 -$ _____ $= 17 + 8$

42. $(7 \times 8) - 6 =$ _____

43. $9 + 17 - 3 = 4 \times$ _____ $- 5$

44. $15 \times 2 \times 2 =$ _____

45. $160 \div 4 + 2 = 7 \times 7 -$ _____

46. $13 \times$ _____ $= 77 - 12$

47. $13 - 11 \times$ _____ $= 8 \times 8 + 16$

48. _____ $\times 9 = 81 - 9$

49. _____ $\times 3 \times 3 = 9 \div 3 \times 9$

50. $4 \times$ _____ $= 10 \times 6$

Score for C (20)

D (40 points) — In each of the following problems, a definite relationship exists among the numbers in the series. Extend the series by following the correct process (8 points for each problem; 2 points for each correct line).

51. Extend the series below through addition.

  a. 4, 8, 12, 16, _____

  b. 1, 4, 5, 8, _____

  c. 2, 4, 7, 11, 13, _____

  d. 5, 10, 20, 35, 55, _____

52. Extend the series below through subtraction.

  a. 50, 45, 40, 35, _____

  b. 50, 45, 43, 38, _____

  c. 100, 90, 81, 73, _____

  d. 610, 600, 580, 550, _____

53. Extend the series below through multiplication.

  a. 4, 8, 16, 32, _____

  b. 5, 25, 125, _____

  c. 2, 4, 20, 40, _____

  d. 2, 4, 12, 48, _____

54. Extend the series below through division.

  a. 15,625, 3,125, 625, 125, _____

  b. 729, 243, 81, 27, _____

  c. 10,000, 2,000, 1,000, 200, _____

  d. 10,000, 5,000, 1,000, 500, _____

55. Extend the series below through combinations of the four processes above.

  a. 72, 75, 69, 72, _____

  b. 200, 100, 300, 150, _____

  c. 6, 9, 18, 21, 42, _____

  d. 240, 120, 600, 300, 1,500, _____

Score for D (40)

Assignment 3-2: Word Problems

A (50 points) — Solve the following word problems (5 points for each correct answer).

1. A store regularly sold 2 cans of soup for 64¢. It advertised a special sale of 6 cans for $1.56. A customer bought 12 cans at the sale. How much did the customer save over the regular price?
_____

2. A sales representative's car gets 18 miles to a gallon of gas. It is driven 120 miles each day for 30 days. Gas costs an average of $1.27 per gallon. What was the sales representative's total 30-day cost for gas? _____

3. A store clerk sold a ruler for 67¢, three pencils for 29¢ each, notebook paper for 99¢, and an eraser for 35¢ to a customer and was given $10.00 in payment. How much change did the clerk give the customer from the $10.00? (All prices include tax.) _____

4. A college student worked at a local store for $5.00 per hour as his class schedule permitted. The student worked 3 hours each Monday, Tuesday, Wednesday, and Thursday. He also worked 2 hours each Friday and 8 hours each Saturday. How many weeks did the student work to earn $770 for a new bicycle? _____

5. A box, a crate, and a trunk weighed a total of 370 pounds. The crate weighed 160 pounds. The trunk weighed 4 pounds more than the box. What did the box weigh? _____

6. Four sales representatives rented a car and agreed to divide the cost of gas equally among themselves. Gas cost $1.45 per gallon. They used 32 gallons of gas on the trip. How much did each representative pay for gas? _____

7. A hotel has 12 floors. Each floor has 20 single-person rooms and 40 two-person rooms. What is the total guest capacity of the hotel? _____

8. A department store offers its customers socks for $1.50 for each pair or $16.50 for one dozen (12) pair. If two customers buy 1 dozen together and each pays half the cost, how much would each customer save by paying the quantity price? _____

9. Car A traveled to a destination 450 miles away at 50 miles per hour. Car B traveled to a destination 550 miles away at 55 miles per hour. How much longer did car B travel than car A? _____

10. Supply Clerk A ordered 5 staplers for $27.50 total and 2 large boxes of staples for $1.75 each. Supply Clerk B ordered a box of computer disks for $8.50 and a box of computer paper for $39.95. How much more did Clerk B spend than Clerk A? (All prices include tax.) _____

Score for A (50)

Part One Fundamentals of Mathematics in Business

B (40 points) — Solve each of the problems without writing any calculations on paper and without using a calculator or a computer (2 points for each correct answer).

11. 5 items at $1.99 = _____   **12.** 2 items at $7.98 = _____

13. 4 items at $19.98 = _____   **14.** 2 items at $49.96 = _____

15. 15 items at $0.99 = _____   **16.** 10 items at $9.99 = _____

17. 6 items at $3.95 = _____   **18.** 5 items at $1.02 = _____

19. 19 items at $40 = _____   **20.** 3 items at $19.99 = _____

21. 20 items at $40.05 = _____   **22.** 30 items at $1.99 = _____

23. 20 items at $39.98 = _____   **24.** 2 items at $5.99 = _____

25. 48 items at $5 = _____   **26.** 5 items at $1.97 = _____

27. 7 items at $7.97 = _____   **28.** 2 items at $99.98 = _____

29. 30 items at $2.98 = _____   **30.** 99 items at $1.90 = _____

Score for B (40)

C (10 points) — In each of the equations below, rewrite the equation by moving the last number on each side of the equal sign to the other side and making appropriate sign changes so that the equation is still true (1 point for each correct equation).
(Example: Given 13 + 7 + 2 = 10 + 12; Answer 13 + 7 − 12 = 10 − 2)

31. $6 + 4 + 5 = 17 - 2$

_____

32. $6 \times 2 \div 3 = 8 \div 4 \times 2$

_____

33. $9 - 3 - 3 = 2 + 1$

_____

34. $8 \div 2 \times 4 = 24 \div 3 \times 2$

_____

35. $20 + 1 - 7 = 16 - 2$

_____

36. $3 \times 3 \times 3 = 18 \div 2 \times 3$

_____

37. $12 + 3 - 5 = 7 + 3$

_____

38. $7 \times 4 \div 2 = 28 \times 2 \div 4$

_____

39. $64 - 32 - 16 = 8 + 8$

_____

40. $63 \div 7 \times 2 = 3 \times 2 \times 3$

_____

Score for C (10)

Chapter 4
Weights, Measurements, and Numerical Averages

OBJECTIVES
After completing this chapter, you should be able to:

* **Calculate using standard U.S. weights and measurements**
* **Calculate numerical averages for business**

USING FUNDAMENTAL PROCESSES IN WEIGHT AND MEASUREMENT PROBLEMS IN BUSINESS

Many aspects of business require an understanding of weights and measurements in order to solve practical problems. Engineers, contractors, buyers, suppliers, shippers, to name a few, all must be able to calculate volume, distance, quantity, etc. Closely related, an understanding of numerical averages frequently is helpful in decision making.

FIGURE 4-1   Commonly Used Business Measurements

Standard U.S. Weights and Measurements	
Distance	*Liquid*
12 inches (in.) = 1 foot (ft.)	8 ounces (oz.) = 1 cup (c.)
3 feet (ft.) = 1 yard (yd.)	2 cups (c.) = 1 pint (pt.)
5,280 feet (ft.) = 1 mile (mi.)	2 pints (pt.) = 1 quart (qt.)
1,760 yards (yd.) = 1 mile (mi.)	4 quarts (qt.) = 1 gallon (gal.)
Weights	*Volume*
16 ounces (oz.) = 1 pound (lb.)	1,728 cubic inches (cu. in.) = 1 cubic foot (cu. ft.)
2,000 pounds (lb.) = 1 ton (t.)	27 cubic feet (cu. ft.) = 1 cubic yard (cu. yd.)

Area
144 square inches (sq. in.) = 1 square foot (sq. ft.)
9 square feet (sq. ft.) = 1 square yard (sq. yd.)
43,560 square feet (sq. ft.) = 1 acre (a.)
640 acres (a.) = 1 square mile (sq. mi.)

Rule: When adding and subtracting weights and measurements, convert smaller units into larger units whenever possible, e.g., ounces into pounds, quarts into gallons, feet into yards. When subtracting weights and measurements, "borrow" quantities needed from the next higher unit.

a.

	7 yd.	2 ft.	11 in.
+	2 yd.	1 ft.	6 in.
	9 yd.	3 ft.	17 in.
		(+ 1)←(− 12)	
	9 yd.	4 ft.	5 in.
(+ 1)←(− 3)			
	10 yd.	1 ft.	5 in.

b.

	2 gal.	3 qt.	1 pt.
	3 gal.	2 qt.	1 pt.
	4 gal.		1 pt.
	9 gal.	5 qt.	3 pt.
	(+ 1)←(− 2)		
	9 gal.	6 qt.	1 pt.
(+ 1)←(− 4)			
	10 gal.	2 qt.	1 pt.

c.

	41 sq. yd.	8 sq. ft.
	11 sq. yd.	7 sq. ft.
	52 sq. yd.	15 sq. ft.
(+ 1)←(− 9)		
	53 sq. yd.	6 sq. ft.

d.

	4 (1 + 3)	
	12 (13 − 1)	1 (2 − 1)	17 (5 + 12)

	13 yd.	2 ft.	5 in.
−	3 yd.	2 ft.	9 in.
	9 yd.	2 ft.	8 in.

e.

	5 (6 − 1)	6 (2 + 4)	
	6 gal.	2 qt.	1 pt.
−	2 gal.	3 qt.	
	3 gal.	3 qt.	1 pt.

f.

	27 (28 − 1)	12 (3 + 9)
	28 sq. yd.	3 sq. ft.
−	15 sq. yd.	8 sq. ft.
	12 sq. yd.	4 sq. ft.

Business Perspective

Business operations constantly use measurement calculations to compute miles per gallon of gasoline, square yards of carpeting per area to be carpeted, ounces of perfume per bottle, price of food per pound, etc.

g. What is the total sales price of a group of spices selling at $9.60 per pound if sales are:

Sale A = 2 lb., 4 oz.
Sale B = 2 lb., 10 oz.
Sale C = 1 lb., 2 oz.

Add: 2 lb. 4 oz.   Convert: 5 lb., 16 oz. = 6 lb.
2 lb. 10 oz.   Multiply: 6 lb. × $9.60 = $57.60 total sales
1 lb. 2 oz.
5 lb. 16 oz.

h. Land sells for $2 per square foot. How much will 3 acres cost?

1 a. = 43,560 sq. ft.
Multiply: 43,560 sq. ft. per a. × 3 a. = 130,680 sq. ft.
Multiply: 130,680 sq. ft. × $2 per sq. ft. = $261,360

i. If a liquid spray sells for $6.40 per gallon:

1. How much will 1 quart cost?

Divide: $6.40 per gal. ÷ 4 qt. per gal. = $1.60 per qt. cost

2. How much will 1 pint cost?

Divide: $1.60 per qt. ÷ 2 pt. per qt. = $0.80 per pt. cost

3. How much will 3 gallons, 3 quarts, and 1 pint cost?

Multiply and add: 3 gal. × $6.40 = $19.20
3 qt. × 1.60 = 4.80
1 pt. × 0.80 = 0.80
Total cost $24.80

Rule: To find the total square feet of an area, multiply its length times its width.

j. How many square feet would be in a conference room that is 31 feet long and 18 feet wide?

31 ft. length × 18 ft. width = 558 sq. ft. of area

Rule: To find the number of square yards in a total amount of square feet, divide the total square feet by 9 (number of square feet in each square yard).

k. How many square yards are there in 558 square feet?

558 sq. ft. ÷ 9 = 62 sq. yd.

l. How much will it cost to carpet a room that measures 15 feet by 21 feet if the installed carpet costs $22 per square yard?

Multiply: 21 ft. length × 15 ft. width = 315 sq. ft. in area
Divide: 315 sq. ft. ÷ 9 = 35 sq. yd. in area
Multiply: 35 sq. yd. × $22 per sq. yd. = $770 cost for installed carpet

Rule: To find a total cubic measurement, multiply length times width times height.

m. How many cubic inches are there in one cubic foot?

12 in. long × 12 in. wide × 12 in. high = 1,728 cu. in. in one cu. ft. (See Figure 4-1)

n. How many cubic feet are there in one cubic yard?

3 ft. long × 3 ft. wide × 3 ft. high = 27 cu. ft. in one cu. yd. (See Figure 4-1)

o. How many cubic yards are there in a room measuring 21 feet long by 18 feet wide by 9 feet high?

21 ft. × 18 ft. × 9 ft. = 3,402 cu. ft.
3,402 cu. ft. ÷ 27 cu. ft. per cu. yd. = 126 cu. yd.

COMPLETE ASSIGNMENT 4-1

NUMERICAL AVERAGES

Numerical averages are used frequently in business, government, and other human activities such as sports. An *average* of several numbers is obtained by adding the numbers and dividing the total by the number of items added. (An average of this kind is also known as the *mean*.)

p. What is the average of the four numbers 112, 209, 312, and 147?

Add: 112 + 209 + 312 + 147 = 780
Divide: 780 ÷ 4 = 195 average

Using Averages In Estimating

You can use averages and estimates to figure an approximate value. For example, you can use averages to estimate the number of words on a page. On a page that has 20 lines of various lengths, you would first choose three or four lines that are typical in size for the page. Next, you would count the exact number of words in those selected lines, and figure an average number of words per line which, when multiplied by 20, gives an estimate of the number of words on the page.

q. Assume the selected three lines on a 20-line page contain the following number of words: line #1—14 words; line #2—18 words; and line #3—13 words. What is the approximate number of words on the page?

Add: 14 + 18 + 13 = 45 total words
Divide: 45 ÷ 3 = 15 average words per line
Multiply: 20 × 15 = 300 approximate number of words on page

Business Perspective

Frequently, businesses want to know the "average" sales, profits, or expenses over a given period of time. This average is found by dividing the total sales, profits, or expenses by the number of days, months, or years used in arriving at the total.

r. Last year ABC Business had monthly sales as follows: January—$38,146; February—$23,100; March—$31,617; April—$30,700; May—$46,118; June—$27,300; July—$40,300; August—$31,200; September—$28,113; October—$12,090; November—$15,268; December—$30,720. What were ABC's average monthly sales last year?

Add: $38,146 + 23,100 + 31,617 + 30,700 + 46,118 + 27,300 + 40,300 + 31,200 + 28,113 + 12,090 + 15,268 + 30,720 = $354,672
Divide: $354,672 ÷ 12 = $29,556 average monthly sales

COMPLETE ASSIGNMENT 4-2

Chapter terms for review

average
mean

Assignment 4-1: Weights and Measurements

A **(50 points) — Solve the following word problems (5 points for each correct answer).**

1. A room is 30 feet long and 24 feet wide. How much will it cost to cover the floor with carpet costing $12 a square yard (9 square feet) if 4 extra square yards are purchased for matching?

   _____

2. A company packs its fish in cans. Each can contains 12 ounces of fish. Each can weighs one ounce. Two dozen cans are packed in a carton. The carton weighs 8 ounces. A customer orders 5 cartons. If 16 ounces equal 1 pound, how many pounds does the shipment weigh?

   _____

3. A state is building a freeway. It needs a 1,936-foot length of property owned by a citizen. The width of the area needed is 90 feet. If an acre is 43,560 square feet, how much would he receive for the land at the rate of $972 per acre?

   _____

4. Carpet costs $31 per square yard. Carpet padding costs $6 per square yard. Carpet installation charges are $3 per square yard. How much will it cost to cover two areas with carpet and pad if area A measured 20 feet by 30 feet and area B measured 30 feet by 40 feet?

   _____

5. Which room would be cheaper to carpet? Room A measures 15 feet by 15 feet and is being carpeted with carpet that costs $22 per square yard installed. Room B measures 12 feet by 21 feet and is being carpeted with carpet that costs $20 per square yard installed?

   _____

6. In an effort to improve his general health, the president of Farrell Machine Company has begun exercising regularly. On one Sunday he walks at an average pace of three miles an hour. He starts his walk at 3:30 and returns at 6:00. During that time he stops to talk to a friend for 12 minutes. Later, he stops to jump rope for 15 minutes and spends 3 minutes giving directions to a stranger. How far does he walk?

_____

7. In developing a machine model for a client, an engineer uses 9 inches of black wire, 6 inches of green wire, 21 inches of white wire, and 12 inches of yellow wire. How many feet of wire does she use?

_____

8. A life guard buys rope to tie up boats at the Community Sailing Center. He needs 12 feet for boat A, 14 feet for boat B, 17 feet for boat C, and 14 feet for boat D. How many yards of rope does he need?

_____

9. The captain of a commercial cruise ship walks around the deck (which equals 1,056 feet) 15 times each day for 8 days. How many miles does she walk during that time if there are 5,280 feet in a mile?

_____

10. A florist shop owner waters the plants in his green house once a week. He puts three pints of water on each of the 16 plants in row A and two quarts of water on each of the 14 plants in row B. How many gallons of water does he use?

_____

B (50 points) — Solve the following problems.

11. Fill in the blank spaces in the following table by converting the given units into the other two units (3 points for each correct unit; 30 points total).

Table of Cubic Measure

Cubic Inches	Cubic Feet	Cubic Yards
466,560	_____	_____
_____	_____	12
233,280	_____	_____
_____	54	_____
_____	_____	

12. A swimming pool 60 feet long and 18 feet wide is filled to an average depth of 6 feet. How many *cubic yards* of water does the pool contain? (4 points)

_____

13. A grain storage structure is 24 feet long, 18 feet wide, and 30 feet high. What is the total capacity of the storage structure in cubic yards? (4 points)

_____

14. A toy manufacturer packages tiny cars in boxes 4 inches long, 3 inches wide, and 2 inches high.
   a. How many cubic inches of storage space will 72 boxes require? (3 points)

_____

   b. How many cubic feet of storage space would be required to store 288 of the tiny toy car boxes? (3 points)

_____

15. Soil containing toxic materials has to be removed from an old gas station site. The contaminated soil is in an area 90 feet by 120 feet and it has to be removed to a depth of 6 feet. Charges to remove and transport the soil are $40 per cubic yard.

a. How many cubic yards of soil are removed? (3 points)

_____

b. How much does the removal and transport cost? (3 points)

_____

_____
Score for B (50)

Assignment 4-2: Numerical Averages and Weights and Measurements

A (20 points) — Using the table below, solve the following problems (2 points for each correct answer.)

1. Calculate the totals for each department in the table below (2 points for each correct total).

Summary of Departmental Sales

Week	Medicine	Magazines	Snack Bar	Cosmetics
1	$ 365.21	$ 186.18	$ 200.46	$ 140.64
2	336.17	178.96	227.65	158.52
3	353.12	202.45	198.68	177.14
4	321.40	192.41	209.98	188.70
5	395.39	201.44	211.54	201.74
6	295.87	195.65	224.10	193.36
7	281.95	174.26	313.81	188.80
8	301.13	223.29	325.22	269.42
Total				

2. What is the total for all four departments?

_____

3. What are the average weekly sales for Medicine?

_____

4. What are the average weekly sales for Magazines?

_____

5. What are the average weekly sales for Snack Bar?

_____

6. What are the average weekly sales for Cosmetics?

_____

7. What are the average weekly sales for all four departments?

_____

Score for A (20)

B (28 points) — Figure estimates as requested from the data supplied (4 points for each correct answer).

8. A book has 250 pages. A count of words on 5 pages selected randomly give page totals of 300, 290, 304, 291, and 315. What is the approximate number of words in this book?

_____

9. A city is conducting a weekly traffic count of the number of cars that goes through its main intersection each week. The second week in March shows 976 cars, the second week in May shows 1,016 cars, and the second week in August shows 999 cars. Approximately how many cars would travel through this intersection in one year?

_____

10. An apple grove owner has 1,200 apple trees. All trees are the same age and produce about the same number of apples. Apple production for 10 trees is counted; it shows apples per tree of 207, 202, 217, 199, 196, 183, 211, 210, 180, and 195. Approximately how many apples could be expected to be produced on the 1,200 trees?

_____

11. Dunn's Department Store sales over one week are: Monday—$290, Tuesday—$400, Wednesday—$314, Thursday—$360, Friday—$412, Saturday—$450, and Sunday—$294. What would be a reasonable estimate of Dunn's sales over a period of 30 days?

_____

12. A shoe factory produces shoes 50 weeks out of each year. For the first four weeks in May its production is: week 1—976 pairs, week 2—974 pairs, week 3—972 pairs, and week 4—978 pairs. Approximately how many pairs of shoes would this factory be expected to produce in its year of production?

_____

13. The costs of electricity for a factory for 6 months are as follows: January—$562, February—$603, March—$516, April—$479, May—$393, and June—$363. What is the average monthly cost during this 6-month period?

———————————

14. Welfare costs in a certain city were as follows over a period of 5 years: $183,711; $285,651; $307,319; $329,769; and $424,975. What was the average yearly expenditure during this period?

———————————

Score for B (28)

C (52 points) — If necessary use the Standard U.S. Weights and Measurements table in Figure 4-1. Try to memorize the table components by completion of this assignment. In final answers, whenever possible, convert smaller units into larger units, such as pints into quarts and ounces into pounds (4 points for each correct answer).

15.   3 lb. 15 oz.
       + 303 lb. 12 oz.

16.   4 t. 1,600 lb.
       − 1 t.   800 lb.

17.   5 t. 1,100 lb.
       − 4 t. 1,600 lb.

18.   9 yd. 2 ft.
       − 3 yd. 2 ft. 11 in.

19.   7 yd. 2 ft.   6 in.
       12 yd. 2 ft. 11 in.
       + 3 yd. 2 ft.   9 in.

20.   2 yd. 1 ft.   4 in.
       6 yd.   10 in.
       +   2 ft.   5 in.

21. Undeveloped land on the outskirts of Napa, California is offered for sale at $1.50 per square foot. How much will 1 acre cost?

———————————

22. If 8 acres of land sells for $696,960, what is its cost per square foot?

———————————

23. Cheese sells for $7 per pound. What is the cost of three pieces that weigh respectively: 1 pound, 3 ounces; 1 pound, 7 ounces; and 2 pounds, 6 ounces?

———————————

24. Liquid soap sells for $2 per ounce. How much will one gallon cost?

———————————

25. Three rooms measure respectively 18 feet by 21 feet, 12 feet by 15 feet, and 9 feet by 9 feet. What is the total number of square feet in these three rooms?

———————————

26. If installed carpet costs $30 per square yard, how much would it cost to carpet the 3 rooms in Problem 25?

———————————

27. If a cargo of grain weighs 88,000 pounds, what would be its value when grain is selling for $420 per ton?

———————————

———————————
Score for C (52)

Part Two
Fractions and Decimals

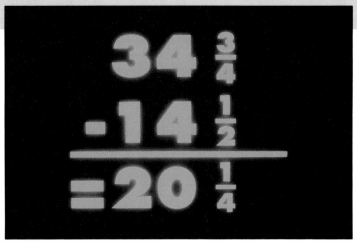

Chapter 5
Fractions: Addition and Subtraction

OBJECTIVES
After completing this chapter, you should be able to:

- Change improper fractions to mixed numbers and mixed numbers to improper fractions
- Reduce fractions to lower terms or raise them to higher terms
- Add and subtract fractions

FRACTIONS

A *fraction* expresses one or more equal parts of a whole unit, such as $\frac{3}{5}$ (three-fifths of a unit) or $\frac{1}{3}$ (one-third of a unit).

In a fraction, the number below the line shows the number of equal parts into which the unit is divided. It is called the *denominator*. The *numerator*, the number above the line, shows how many equal parts are expressed.

$\frac{2}{3}$ $\frac{\text{numerator}}{\text{denominator}}$ $\frac{\text{number of equal parts}}{\text{total parts}}$

A *proper fraction* is smaller than one whole unit. In all proper fractions, the numerator is smaller than the denominator.

$\frac{3}{5}$ $\frac{1}{3}$ $\frac{24}{75}$ $\frac{\text{numerator is smaller}}{\text{denominator is greater}}$

An *improper fraction* is one or more whole units. The numerator of an improper fraction is greater than or equal to the denominator.

$\frac{14}{5}$ $\frac{17}{6}$ $\frac{25}{25}$ $\frac{\text{numerator is greater (or equal)}}{\text{denominator is smaller (or equal)}}$

A *mixed number* represents more than one whole unit by combining a whole number and a proper fraction. Examples are $2\frac{4}{5}$, $2\frac{5}{6}$, and $6\frac{1}{4}$.

1. Divide the numerator by the denominator.
2. Put the quotient in the whole-number position.
3. Put the remainder in the fraction part numerator position.
4. Put the original denominator in the fraction part denominator position.

a. Change $\frac{13}{4}$ to a mixed number (See Point A in Figure 5-1.)

Step 1   Steps 2 and 3

$$\frac{13}{4} = 4\overline{)\begin{array}{c} 3 \text{ R}1 \\ 13 \end{array}} \quad \text{thus,} \quad \frac{13}{4} = 3\frac{1}{4}$$
$$\underline{12}$$
$$1$$

Step 4

1. Multiply the denominator of the fraction by the whole number.
2. Add the numerator of the fraction to the product of Step 1. The sum becomes the numerator of the improper fraction.
3. The denominator of the fraction of the mixed number becomes the denominator of the improper fraction.

b. Change $5\frac{1}{2}$ to an improper fraction (See Point B in Figure 5-1.)

Step 1   Step 2

$$2 \times 5 = 10 \quad \text{thus,} \quad 5\frac{1}{2} = \frac{10 + 1}{2} = \frac{11}{2}$$

Step 3

Fractions Reduced to Lower Terms

Simpler fractions are easier to use. Look carefully at Point C on the tape measure in Figure 5-1. It measures $\frac{8}{16}$ inch, $\frac{4}{8}$ inch, and $\frac{2}{4}$ inch. But almost everyone would say that the distance is "$\frac{1}{2}$ inch." The other fractions are also correct, but seem more complicated. The fraction $\frac{4}{8}$ is in lower terms than $\frac{8}{16}$; $\frac{1}{2}$ is in lower terms than both $\frac{4}{8}$ and $\frac{8}{16}$. In each fraction except $\frac{1}{2}$ the numerator and the denominator can be evenly divided by the same number, the *common divisor*, to arrive at a reduced fraction. For example, in $\frac{4}{8}$ both 4 and 8 can be evenly divided by 2 to reduce the fraction to $\frac{2}{4}$ or by 4 to reduce the fraction to $\frac{1}{2}$. The $\frac{1}{2}$ cannot be reduced by any common divisor. Thus, $\frac{1}{2}$ is in *lowest terms*.

FIGURE 5-1   Measuring tape with 8ths on top edge and 16ths on bottom edge

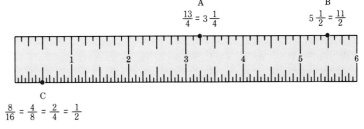

Rule: If a fraction's numerator and denominator have no common divisor greater than 1, the fraction is in lowest terms.

1. Divide both the numerator and the denominator by a common divisor greater than 1 to arrive at a reduced fraction.
2. If necessary, repeat Step 1 until the fraction is in lowest terms.

c. Reduce $\frac{30}{45}$ to lowest terms

$$\underset{\text{Step 1}}{\frac{30}{45} = \frac{30 \div 5}{45 \div 5} = \frac{6}{9}} \longrightarrow \overset{\text{Repeat}}{\underset{\text{Step 1}}{\frac{6}{9} = \frac{6 \div 3}{9 \div 3} = \frac{2}{3}}} \quad \text{or,} \quad \underset{\text{Step 1}}{\frac{30}{45} = \frac{30 \div 15}{45 \div 15} = \frac{2}{3}}$$

Notice that you shorten your work by observing that 15 is a common divisor of both 30 and 45.

Fractions Raised to Higher Terms

A fraction is raised to *higher terms* by multiplying both numerator and denominator by the **same** number. ***The new denominator must be an even multiple of the old denominator.***

Steps to Raise a Fraction to Higher Terms

1. Divide the new denominator by the old denominator. The quotient is the *common multiplier*.
2. Multiply the old numerator by the multiplier.
3. Multiply the old denominator by the multiplier.

d. Raise $\frac{3}{4}$ to twenty-fourths   Raise $\frac{2}{5}$ to sixtieths

$$\underset{\text{Step 1}}{\frac{3}{4} = \frac{?}{24}} \quad 24 \div 4 = 6 \quad \text{so} \qquad\qquad \underset{\text{Step 1}}{\frac{2}{5} = \frac{?}{60}} \quad 60 \div 5 = 12 \quad \text{so}$$

$$\underset{\text{Steps 2 \& 3}}{\frac{3}{4} = \frac{3 \times 6}{4 \times 6} = \frac{18}{24}} \qquad\qquad \underset{\text{Steps 2 \& 3}}{\frac{2}{5} = \frac{2 \times 12}{5 \times 12} = \frac{24}{60}}$$

COMPLETE ASSIGNMENT 5-1

ADDITION AND SUBTRACTION OF FRACTIONS

The steps below explain how to add and subtract fractions. ***Before adding or subtracting, all of the fractions must have the same denominator, a common denominator.*** The product of the denominators is always a common denominator, but there may be a smaller one.

Steps to Add and Subtract Fractions

1. If the denominators of the fractions are not already the same, change the fractions to have the same denominator. It will be the denominator of the answer.
2. Find the numerator of the answer. If the problem is
   a. Addition—then add the numerators of the fractions.
   b. Subtraction—then subtract one numerator from the other.
3. Reduce the answer, or write it as a mixed number in lowest terms.

e.
$$\underset{\text{Step 2}}{} \quad \underset{\text{Step 3}}{}$$
$$\frac{7}{8} + \frac{5}{8} = \frac{12}{8} = 1\frac{4}{8} = 1\frac{1}{2}$$

f.
$$\frac{3}{4} + \frac{2}{5} = \underset{\text{Step 1}}{\frac{3 \times 5}{4 \times 5} + \frac{2 \times 4}{5 \times 4}} = \underset{\text{Step 2}}{\frac{15}{20} + \frac{8}{20}} = \underset{\text{Step 3}}{\frac{23}{20}} = 1\frac{3}{20}$$

g.
$$\frac{3}{8} + \frac{5}{6} + \frac{1}{4} = \underset{\text{Step 1}}{\frac{3 \times 6}{8 \times 6} + \frac{5 \times 8}{6 \times 8} + \frac{1 \times 12}{4 \times 12}} = \underset{\text{Step 2}}{\frac{18}{48} + \frac{12}{48}} = \underset{\text{Step 3}}{\frac{70}{48}} = 1\frac{22}{48} = 1\frac{11}{24}$$

h.
$$\frac{7}{10} + \frac{2}{15} = \underset{\text{Step 1}}{\frac{7 \times 15}{10 \times 15} + \frac{2 \times 10}{15 \times 10}} = \underset{\text{Step 2}}{\frac{105}{150} + \frac{20}{150}} = \underset{\text{Step 3}}{\frac{125}{150}} = \frac{5}{6}$$

NOTE: Examples g. and h. could have been solved more easily by using smaller common denominators. In example g., 24 is also a common denominator. In example h., 30, 60, 90, and 120 are all common denominators that are smaller than 150. The solutions are correct as shown, but the intermediate numbers would be smaller. There will be less reducing if you were able to identify a smaller common denominator. Compare the solutions above with those listed below:

g. $\frac{3}{8} + \frac{5}{6} + \frac{1}{4} = \frac{3 \times 3}{8 \times 3} + \frac{5 \times 4}{6 \times 4} + \frac{1 \times 6}{4 \times 6} = \frac{9}{24} + \frac{20}{24} + \frac{6}{24} = \frac{35}{24} = 1\frac{11}{24}$

h. $\frac{7}{10} + \frac{2}{15} = \frac{7 \times 3}{10 \times 3} + \frac{2 \times 2}{15 \times 2} = \frac{21}{30} + \frac{4}{30} = \frac{25}{30} = \frac{5}{6}$

i.
$$\underset{\text{Step 2}}{} \quad \underset{\text{Step 3}}{}$$
$$\frac{7}{8} - \frac{5}{8} = \frac{2}{8} = \frac{1}{4}$$

j.
$$\frac{3}{4} - \frac{1}{5} = \underset{\text{Step 1}}{\frac{3 \times 5}{4 \times 5} - \frac{1 \times 4}{5 \times 4}} = \underset{\text{Step 2}}{\frac{15}{20} - \frac{4}{20}} = \frac{11}{20}$$

k.
$$\frac{7}{10} - \frac{2}{15} = \underset{\text{Step 1}}{\frac{7 \times 3}{10 \times 3} - \frac{2 \times 2}{15 \times 2}} = \underset{\text{Step 2}}{\frac{21}{30} - \frac{4}{30}} = \frac{17}{30}$$

Adding Mixed Numbers

A slightly different procedure is used when adding mixed numbers than when adding pure fractions. To learn how to add mixed numbers, refer to the steps below.

Steps to Add Mixed Numbers

1. If necessary, rewrite the mixed numbers so the fraction parts have common denominators.
2. Add the whole-number parts; add the fraction parts.
3. If the sum of the fraction parts is improper (example m.) change that improper fraction to a mixed number. Otherwise, skip Step 3.
4. Combine the two sums to form the mixed number answer.
5. If necessary, reduce to lowest terms the fraction part of the mixed number answer.

l.   Step 1

$$1\frac{1}{12} = 1\frac{1}{12}$$

$$+\ 4\frac{3}{4} = +\ 4\frac{9}{12}$$

Steps 2, 4, & 5 $5\frac{10}{12} = 5\frac{5}{6}$

m.   Step 1

$$3\frac{3}{8} = 3 \quad \frac{9}{24}$$

$$7\frac{5}{6} = 7 \quad \frac{20}{24}$$

$$+\ \frac{1}{4} = +\quad \frac{6}{24}$$

Step 2 $\quad 10 \quad \frac{35}{24}$

Steps 3 & 4 $\quad 10 + 1\frac{11}{24} = 11\frac{11}{24}$

Subtracting Mixed Numbers

Subtracting mixed numbers is similar to adding mixed numbers. When the fraction part in the *subtrahend* (the number being subtracted) is larger than the fraction part in the *minuend* (the number from which the subtraction is being made), a new step is needed.

Steps to Subtract Mixed Numbers

1. If necessary, rewrite the mixed numbers so the fraction parts have common denominators.
2. If the fraction part in the subtrahend is larger than the fraction part in the minuend (example o.) "borrow 1" from the whole-number part of the minuend. Otherwise, skip Step 2.
3. Subtract the whole-number parts; subtract the fraction parts.
4. Combine the two differences to form the mixed number answer.
5. If necessary, reduce to lowest terms the fraction part of the mixed number answer.

n.   Step 1   **o.**   Step 1   Step 2

$$5\frac{3}{4} = 5\frac{9}{12}$$

$$-\ 2\frac{1}{3} = -\ 2\frac{4}{12}$$

Steps 3 & 4 $3\frac{5}{12}$

$$4\frac{2}{9} = 4\frac{4}{18} = 3\frac{18}{18} + \frac{4}{18} = 3\frac{22}{18}$$

$$-\ 1\frac{5}{6} = -\ 1\frac{15}{18} = -\ 1\frac{15}{18} = -\ 1\frac{15}{18}$$

Steps 3 & 4 $2\frac{7}{18}$

COMPLETE ASSIGNMENT 5-2

Chapter terms for review

common denominator
common divisor
common multiplier
denominator
fraction
higher terms
improper fraction

lowest terms
minuend
mixed number
numerator
proper fraction
subtrahend

Assignment 5-1: Fractions and Mixed Numbers

A (20 points) — Change the improper fractions to whole numbers or to mixed numbers. Reduce fractions to lowest terms (1 point for each correct answer).

1. $\frac{4}{3}$ = _____   **2.** $\frac{13}{5}$ = _____   **3.** $\frac{3}{3}$ = _____   **4.** $\frac{32}{12}$ = _____

5. $\frac{7}{5}$ = _____   **6.** $\frac{18}{4}$ = _____   **7.** $\frac{20}{6}$ = _____   **8.** $\frac{15}{10}$ = _____

9. $\frac{5}{2}$ = _____   **10.** $\frac{11}{8}$ = _____   **11.** $\frac{27}{16}$ = _____   **12.** $\frac{50}{8}$ = _____

13. $\frac{8}{4}$ = _____   **14.** $\frac{12}{5}$ = _____   **15.** $\frac{16}{15}$ = _____   **16.** $\frac{16}{3}$ = _____

17. $\frac{9}{6}$ = _____   **18.** $\frac{25}{6}$ = _____   **19.** $\frac{60}{10}$ = _____   **20.** $\frac{47}{4}$ = _____

Score for A (20)

B (20 points) — Change the mixed numbers to improper fractions (1 point for each correct answer). Example: $4\frac{3}{8} = \frac{35}{8}$ **(Detail: 8 × 4 = 32; 32 + 3 = 35; $\frac{35}{8}$)**

21. $1\frac{2}{5}$ = _____   **22.** $4\frac{2}{3}$ = _____   **23.** $3\frac{7}{10}$ = _____   **24.** $5\frac{11}{16}$ = _____

25. $3\frac{5}{6}$ = _____   **26.** $2\frac{8}{15}$ = _____   **27.** $12\frac{1}{2}$ = _____   **28.** $3\frac{5}{8}$ = _____

29. $5\frac{3}{4}$ = _____   **30.** $3\frac{5}{12}$ = _____   **31.** $7\frac{3}{5}$ = _____   **32.** $20\frac{2}{3}$ = _____

33. $6\frac{2}{3}$ = _____   **34.** $4\frac{3}{16}$ = _____   **35.** $6\frac{8}{9}$ = _____   **36.** $32\frac{1}{4}$ = _____

37. $9\frac{1}{2}$ = _____   **38.** $8\frac{7}{8}$ = _____   **39.** $3\frac{8}{15}$ = _____   **40.** $7\frac{11}{16}$ = _____

Score for B (20)

C (40 points) — Reduce to *lowest* terms (2 points for each correct answer).

41. $\frac{2}{4}$ = _____   **42.** $\frac{2}{6}$ = _____   **43.** $\frac{4}{10}$ = _____   **44.** $\frac{4}{6}$ = _____   **45.** $\frac{4}{8}$ = _____

46. $\frac{6}{8}$ = _____   **47.** $\frac{6}{9}$ = _____   **48.** $\frac{2}{16}$ = _____   **49.** $\frac{3}{9}$ = _____   **50.** $\frac{10}{15}$ = _____

51. $\frac{9}{24}$ = _____   **52.** $\frac{6}{10}$ = _____   **53.** $\frac{3}{12}$ = _____   **54.** $\frac{9}{12}$ = _____   **55.** $\frac{4}{16}$ = _____

56. $\frac{14}{16}$ = _____   **57.** $\frac{8}{10}$ = _____   **58.** $\frac{9}{16}$ = _____   **59.** $\frac{8}{12}$ = _____   **60.** $\frac{12}{15}$ = _____

Score for C (40)

D (20 points) — Raise to *higher* terms (1 point for each correct answer).

61. $\frac{2}{3} =$ _____   62. $\frac{1}{2} =$ _____   63. $\frac{3}{4} =$ _____   64. $\frac{3}{4} =$ _____   65. $\frac{2}{5} =$ _____

66. $\frac{1}{3} =$ _____   67. $\frac{1}{2} =$ _____   68. $\frac{1}{6} =$ _____   69. $\frac{5}{6} =$ _____   70. $\frac{5}{6} =$ _____

71. $\frac{3}{8} =$ _____   72. $\frac{5}{8} =$ _____   73. $\frac{3}{5} =$ _____   74. $\frac{1}{4} =$ _____   75. $\frac{4}{5} =$ _____

76. $\frac{5}{8} =$ _____   77. $\frac{7}{9} =$ _____   78. $\frac{2}{3} =$ _____   79. $\frac{3}{10} =$ _____   80. $\frac{5}{12} =$ _____

Score for D (20)

Part Two   Fractions and Decimals

Assignment 5-2: Addition and Subtraction of Fractions and Mixed Numbers

A (45 points) — Add the following fractions and mixed numbers. Write answers as mixed numbers with fractions in lowest terms (3 points for each correct answer).

1. $\dfrac{3}{8} =$

    $+ \dfrac{2}{8} =$

2. $\dfrac{3}{4} =$

    $+ \dfrac{2}{3} =$

3. $1\dfrac{3}{5} =$

    $+ 4\dfrac{5}{6} =$

4. $\dfrac{5}{12} =$

    $+ \dfrac{11}{12} =$

5. $\dfrac{2}{5} =$

    $+ \dfrac{1}{3} =$

6. $2\dfrac{1}{3} =$

    $+ 5\dfrac{7}{9} =$

7. $\dfrac{3}{8} =$

    $+ \dfrac{5}{8} =$

8. $\dfrac{1}{2} =$

    $+ \dfrac{1}{6} =$

9. $3\dfrac{3}{8} =$

    $+ 4\dfrac{5}{6} =$

10. $\dfrac{3}{4} =$

    $\dfrac{2}{3} =$

    $+ \dfrac{1}{4} =$

11. $\dfrac{1}{2} =$

    $\dfrac{3}{5} =$

    $+ \dfrac{2}{3} =$

12. $\dfrac{4}{5} =$

    $5\dfrac{1}{6} =$

    $+ 2\dfrac{7}{10} =$

13. $\dfrac{1}{3} =$

    $\dfrac{1}{2} =$

    $+ \dfrac{5}{6} =$

14. $1\dfrac{2}{3} =$

    $4\dfrac{3}{4} =$

    $+ 2\dfrac{3}{5} =$

15. $2\dfrac{7}{15} =$

    $1\dfrac{2}{5} =$

    $+ 3\dfrac{3}{10} =$

_____

Score for A (45)

B (10 points) — The following involve fractions in only halves, quarters, eighths, or sixteenths. These types of fractions are very important in some industries. For example, eighths are used in the stock market, and sixteenths are used in building trades (2 points for each correct answer).

16. $\dfrac{1}{8} + \dfrac{3}{4} + \dfrac{3}{8} + \dfrac{1}{2} + \dfrac{5}{8} =$ _____

17. $25\dfrac{3}{8} + 12\dfrac{1}{4} + 16\dfrac{5}{8} + 14\dfrac{1}{2} =$ _____

18. $\dfrac{7}{8} + \dfrac{5}{16} + \dfrac{3}{4} + \dfrac{5}{8} + \dfrac{1}{2} =$ _____

19. $110\dfrac{7}{8} + 215\dfrac{3}{4} + 88\dfrac{1}{2} =$ _____

20. $2\dfrac{3}{16} + 5\dfrac{1}{4} + 3\dfrac{7}{8} =$ _____

C (36 points) — Subtract the following fractions and mixed numbers. Write the answer as a proper fraction or mixed number in lowest terms (3 points for each correct answer).

21. $\dfrac{7}{8} =$
$- \dfrac{3}{8} =$

22. $7\dfrac{11}{16} =$
$- 2\dfrac{5}{16} =$

23. $8\dfrac{1}{3} =$
$- 2\dfrac{5}{6} =$

24. $\dfrac{7}{12} =$
$- \dfrac{1}{3} =$

25. $4\dfrac{5}{8} =$
$- 1\dfrac{1}{4} =$

26. $3\dfrac{5}{12} =$
$- 1\dfrac{3}{4} =$

27. $\dfrac{3}{4} =$
$- \dfrac{5}{16} =$

28. $5\dfrac{2}{3} =$
$- 2\dfrac{2}{5} =$

29. $5\dfrac{1}{6} =$
$- 2\dfrac{3}{4} =$

30. $\dfrac{3}{5} =$
$- \dfrac{1}{3} =$

31. $4\dfrac{5}{6} =$
$- 2\dfrac{5}{8} =$

32. $16\dfrac{3}{16} =$
$- 5\dfrac{7}{8} =$

33. $\dfrac{3}{4} =$
$- \dfrac{2}{3} =$

34. $6\dfrac{2}{9} =$
$- 3\dfrac{5}{9} =$

35. $91\dfrac{3}{10} =$
$- 2\dfrac{8}{15} =$

Part Two   Fractions and Decimals

52- week High Low	Stock	Div	Yld.	PE	Sales 100s	High	Low	Last	Chg.

NYSE

MONDAY COMPOSITE TRADING FOR THE 1,500 MOST ACTIVE NEW YORK STOCK EXCHANGE ISSUES. STOCKS IN BOLDFACE ROSE OR FELL 3% OR MORE

					290	23⅜	23¼	23¼	— ⅛
					512	17⅜	17	17¼	+ ¼
					x307	7⅜	7⅛	7¼	...
					x138	8⅞	8⅝	8¾	...
					2814	28⅝	26	28⅝	+ 2⅝
					1715	2¾	2⅝	2⅝	...
					2992	21⅛	20¼	20½	— ⅛
					1258	5⅛	4⅜	4¾	— ⅜
					220	17¾	16¼	16⅝	— ⅝
					1097	25⅜	24⅞	25	+ ⅛
23¾ 15	FFB pfB	2.15		9.1	... 294	u23⅞	23⅝	23¾	...
33 14¼	FtFnMg	.10b	.3	11	2015	30¾	29⅛	30½	+ 1⅜
·45½ 15⅜	Flntste	3.00		9.7 5	2365	31	29⅝	30⅞	+ 1½
1⅞ ¼	FInstA		...	...	368	9/16	½	½	— 1/16
32 20	Ftln pfB	3.57e		11.6	122	20¾	20¼	20¾	+ ¼

Chapter 6
Fractions: Multiplication and Division

OBJECTIVES

After completing this chapter, you should be able to:

- **Multiply two or more fractions**
- **Divide a fraction by another fraction**
- **Use aliquot parts to simplify calculations**

MULTIPLICATION WITH FRACTIONS

Multiplication of fractions is the easiest operation involving fractions. In multiplication, you do not need common denominators. Refer to the steps below for multiplying fractions.

Steps to Multiply Fractions

1. Multiply the numerators to get the numerator of the product.
2. Multiply the denominators to get the denominator of the product.
3. Reduce the product to lowest terms.

---

a.

$$\frac{2}{3} \times \frac{4}{5} = \frac{2 \times 4}{3 \times 5} = \frac{8}{15}$$
(Steps 1 & 2)

b.

$$\frac{2}{3} \times \frac{5}{6} = \frac{2 \times 5}{3 \times 6} = \frac{10}{18} = \frac{5}{9}$$
(Steps 1 & 2) (Step 3)

c.

$$\frac{2}{3} \times \frac{4}{5} \times \frac{5}{6} = \frac{2 \times 4 \times 5}{3 \times 5 \times 6} = \frac{40}{90} = \frac{4}{9}$$
(Steps 1 & 2) (Step 3)

Cancellation

To *cancel* common factors is an expression that means to "divide out" a factor that occurs in both the numerator and denominator. You cancel common factors before multiplying the numerators and denominators. If you do all of the *cancellation* possible, then the final answer will be in lowest terms. In example b. above, it is possible to cancel a 2; in example c., it is possible to cancel a 2 and a 5 (see page 64).

b. $\dfrac{2}{3} \times \dfrac{5}{6} = \dfrac{2}{3} \times \dfrac{\overset{1}{\cancel{5}}}{\cancel{6}} = \dfrac{1 \times 5}{3 \times 3} = \dfrac{5}{9}$ **c.** $\dfrac{2}{3} \times \dfrac{4}{5} \times \dfrac{5}{6} = \dfrac{\overset{1}{\cancel{2}}}{3} \times \dfrac{4}{\cancel{5}} \times \dfrac{\overset{1}{\cancel{5}}}{\cancel{6}} = \dfrac{1 \times 4 \times 1}{3 \times 1 \times 3} = \dfrac{4}{9}$

There can be more than one way to cancel. In example c., the illustration shows the 2 in $\frac{2}{3}$ being cancelled. The final answer is still $\frac{4}{9}$ if you cancel a 2 in the 4 of $\frac{4}{5}$.

c. $\dfrac{2}{3} \times \dfrac{4}{5} \times \dfrac{5}{6} = \dfrac{2}{3} \times \dfrac{\overset{2}{\cancel{4}}}{\cancel{5}} \times \dfrac{\overset{1}{\cancel{5}}}{\cancel{6}} = \dfrac{2 \times 2 \times 1}{3 \times 1 \times 3} = \dfrac{4}{9}$

Multiplying a Whole Number by a Fraction

A whole number like 5 can be written as the fractions $\frac{5}{1}$, $\frac{10}{2}$, $\frac{15}{3}$, etc. The simplest fraction equal to 5 is $\frac{5}{1}$. Refer to the steps below to learn how to multiply a whole number by a fraction (for example, $5 \times \frac{3}{4}$).

Steps to Multiply a Whole Number by a Fraction

1. Write the whole number as a fraction by making the whole number the numerator and 1 the denominator.
2. Multiply the fractions.
3. Write the product as a mixed number in lowest terms.

---

d. Suppose that 5 gold prospectors each have $\frac{3}{4}$ ounce of gold. What is the total amount of gold that they have together? You can solve this problem by adding all of the numbers:

$$\frac{3}{4} + \frac{3}{4} + \frac{3}{4} + \frac{3}{4} + \frac{3}{4} = \frac{15}{4} = 3\frac{3}{4} \text{ oz.}$$

By using multiplication as a shortcut, the problem would be solved as follows:

$$5 \times \frac{3}{4} \overset{\text{Step 1}}{=} \frac{5}{1} \times \frac{3}{4} \overset{\text{Step 2}}{=} \frac{5 \times 3}{1 \times 4} = \frac{15}{4} \overset{\text{Step 3}}{=} 3\frac{3}{4} \text{ oz.}$$

The Word "of" and Multiplication of Fractions

When fractions are multiplied, the word *of* very often means to "multiply." It works that way whether the other number is a whole number or a fraction.

e.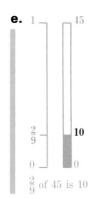

What is two-ninths $(\frac{2}{9})$ of forty-five (45)?

$$\frac{2}{9} \text{ of } 45 = \frac{2}{9} \times 45 = \frac{2}{9} \times \frac{45}{1} = \frac{2}{9} \times \frac{\overset{5}{\cancel{45}}}{\cancel{1}} = \frac{2 \times 5}{1 \times 1} = \frac{10}{1} = 10$$

A restaurant has written all of its recipes to feed 100 people. A recipe for meat sauce says to use $\frac{3}{4}$ tablespoon of red pepper powder. The restaurant wants to modify the recipe to use for only 50 people. 50 is $\frac{1}{2}$ of 100. They need to use $\frac{1}{2}$ of each ingredient. In other words, $\frac{1}{2}$ of the red pepper powder would be $\frac{1}{2}$ of $\frac{3}{4}$ tablespoon:

$$\frac{1}{2} \text{ of } \frac{3}{4} = \frac{1}{2} \times \frac{3}{4} = \frac{1 \times 3}{2 \times 4} = \frac{3}{8} \text{ tbsp. of red pepper powder}$$

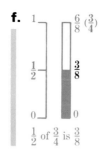

Multiplication with Mixed Numbers

If any of the numbers in a multiplication problem is a mixed number, certain steps must be taken. Refer to the steps below for instructions to multiply a fraction with mixed numbers.

Steps to Multiply Fractions with Mixed Numbers

1. Change the mixed numbers to improper fractions.
2. Multiply fractions (cancel if possible).
3. Write the product as a mixed number in lowest terms.

g.

$$\frac{2}{5} \text{ of } 5\frac{3}{4} = \frac{2}{5} \times 5\frac{3}{4} = \frac{2}{5} \times \frac{23}{4} = \frac{\overset{1}{\cancel{2}}}{5} \times \frac{23}{\underset{2}{\cancel{4}}} = \frac{1 \times 23}{5 \times 2} = \frac{23}{10} = 2\frac{3}{10}$$

$$\frac{1}{4} \times 3 \times 2\frac{2}{3} = \frac{1}{4} \times \frac{3}{1} \times \frac{8}{3} = \frac{1}{\underset{1}{\cancel{4}}} \times \frac{\overset{1}{\cancel{3}}}{1} \times \frac{\overset{2}{\cancel{8}}}{\underset{1}{\cancel{3}}} = \frac{1 \times 1 \times 2}{1 \times 1 \times 1} = \frac{2}{1} = 2$$

$$3\frac{3}{5} \times 3\frac{3}{4} = \frac{18}{5} \times \frac{15}{4} = \frac{\overset{9}{\cancel{18}}}{\underset{1}{\cancel{5}}} \times \frac{\overset{3}{\cancel{15}}}{\underset{2}{\cancel{4}}} = \frac{9 \times 3}{1 \times 2} = \frac{27}{2} = 13\frac{1}{2}$$

COMPLETE ASSIGNMENT 6-1

DIVISION WITH FRACTIONS

You already have solved one application that could involve division with fractions. When the recipe for meat sauce was changed to feed 50 instead of 100 people, it was divided in half (or divided by 2). The instruction calling for $\frac{3}{4}$ tablespoon of red pepper powder, therefore, needed to be divided in half. In the above example, we multiplied by $\frac{1}{2}$. But if we divide by 2 we know we will get $\frac{1}{2}$ of the amount: $\frac{1}{2}$ of $\frac{3}{4}$.

We know: $\frac{3}{4} \times \frac{1}{2} = \frac{3}{8}$ We also know: $\frac{3}{4} \div 2 = \frac{3}{8}$ or: $\frac{3}{4} \div \frac{2}{1} = \frac{3}{8}$

From this example, we can see a rule for division with fractions. Refer to the steps below for instructions on dividing fractions.

Steps to Divide Fractions

1. Write the divisor as a fraction if it is a whole or mixed number.
2. Invert the divisor (exchange the numerator and denominator).
3. Change the divide symbol to multiply.
4. Solve the multiplication problem, reducing where possible.

h.

$$\underset{\text{Step 1}}{\quad} \quad \underset{\text{Steps 2 \& 3}}{\quad} \quad \underset{\text{Step 4}}{\quad}$$

$$\frac{3}{4} \div 4 = \frac{3}{4} \div \frac{4}{1} = \frac{3}{4} \times \frac{1}{4} = \frac{3 \times 1}{4 \times 4} = \frac{3}{16}$$

$$\underset{\text{Steps 2 \& 3}}{\quad} \qquad \underset{\text{Step 4}}{\quad}$$

$$\frac{3}{10} \div \frac{2}{5} = \frac{3}{10} \times \frac{5}{2} = \frac{3}{\underset{2}{\cancel{10}}} \times \frac{\overset{1}{\cancel{5}}}{2} = \frac{3 \times 1}{2 \times 2} = \frac{3}{4}$$

$$\underset{\text{Step 1}}{\quad} \qquad \underset{\text{Steps 2 \& 3}}{\quad} \qquad \underset{\text{Step 4}}{\quad}$$

$$\frac{7}{12} \div 2\frac{2}{3} = \frac{7}{12} \div \frac{8}{3} = \frac{7}{12} \times \frac{3}{8} = \frac{7}{\underset{4}{\cancel{12}}} \times \frac{\overset{1}{\cancel{3}}}{8} = \frac{7 \times 1}{4 \times 8} = \frac{7}{32}$$

Division of a Whole or Mixed Number by a Fraction or Mixed Number

In each of the previous examples, the dividend was a proper fraction. However, the stated procedure works perfectly well when the dividend is a whole or mixed number and the divisor is a fraction or mixed number.

Steps to Divide a Whole or Mixed Number by a Fraction or Mixed Number

1. Change the dividend to an improper fraction.
2. If necessary, change the divisor to an improper fraction.
3. Invert (the divisor) and multiply.

i.

$$\underset{\text{Step 1}}{\quad} \qquad \underset{\text{Step 3}}{\quad}$$

$$9 \div \frac{3}{5} = \frac{9}{1} \div \frac{3}{5} = \frac{9}{1} \times \frac{5}{3} = \frac{\overset{3}{\cancel{9}}}{1} \times \frac{5}{\underset{1}{\cancel{3}}} = \frac{3 \times 5}{1 \times 1} = \frac{15}{1} = 15$$

$$\underset{\text{Step 1}}{\quad} \qquad \underset{\text{Step 3}}{\quad}$$

$$2\frac{2}{5} \div \frac{3}{4} = \frac{12}{5} \div \frac{3}{4} = \frac{12}{5} \times \frac{4}{3} = \frac{\overset{4}{\cancel{12}}}{5} \times \frac{4}{\underset{1}{\cancel{3}}} = \frac{4 \times 4}{5 \times 1} = \frac{16}{5} = 3\frac{1}{5}$$

$$\underset{\text{Steps 1 \& 2}}{\quad} \qquad \underset{\text{Step 3}}{\quad}$$

$$3\frac{3}{4} \div 1\frac{1}{2} = \frac{15}{4} \div \frac{3}{2} = \frac{15}{4} \times \frac{2}{3} = \frac{\overset{5}{\cancel{15}}}{\underset{2}{\cancel{4}}} \times \frac{\overset{1}{\cancel{2}}}{\underset{1}{\cancel{3}}} = \frac{5 \times 1}{2 \times 1} = \frac{5}{2} = 2\frac{1}{2}$$

ALIQUOT PARTS

When a number (whole or mixed) can be divided by another with no remainder, the divisor is known as an *aliquot part* of the first number. For example, $12\frac{1}{2}$ cents is called an aliquot part of \$1; that means that $12\frac{1}{2}$ cents divides evenly into \$1 with no remainder (exactly 8 times). Using aliquot parts gives you a shortcut method for estimating or for checking calculations.

What follows are common aliquot part relationships when calculating money. For a more complete table showing aliquot relationships see the Appendix titled Aliquot Parts.

50 cents = \$$\frac{1}{2}$	75 cents = \$$\frac{3}{4}$	$12\frac{1}{2}$ cents = \$$\frac{1}{8}$
$33\frac{1}{3}$ cents = \$$\frac{1}{3}$	60 cents = \$$\frac{3}{5}$	$37\frac{1}{2}$ cents = \$$\frac{3}{8}$
$66\frac{2}{3}$ cents = \$$\frac{2}{3}$	$16\frac{2}{3}$ cents = \$$\frac{1}{6}$	$62\frac{1}{2}$ cents = \$$\frac{5}{8}$
25 cents = \$$\frac{1}{4}$	$83\frac{1}{3}$ cents = \$$\frac{5}{6}$	$87\frac{1}{2}$ cents = \$$\frac{7}{8}$

Examples j. and k. show aliquot parts used as shortcuts for multiplication. Example l. shows a division shortcut. Remember, the rule for division is to invert the divisor and multiply.

j. Determine the total cost of 56 stainless steel bolts priced at $12\frac{1}{2}$ cents each. One way to calculate the answer is simply $56 \times 12\frac{1}{2}$ cents. However, since $12\frac{1}{2}$ cents = \$$\frac{1}{8}$, using the aliquot shortcut simplifies your computation:

$$56 \times 12\frac{1}{2}\cancel{c} = \frac{56}{1} \times \frac{25}{2}\cancel{c} = \frac{56 \times 25\cancel{c}}{1 \times 2} = \frac{1400\cancel{c}}{2} = \frac{700\cancel{c}}{1} = 700\cancel{c} = \$7 \text{ total cost}$$

or: $\quad 56 \times 12\frac{1}{2}\cancel{c} = 56 \times \frac{\$1}{8} = \frac{\overset{7}{\cancel{56}}}{1} \times \frac{\$1}{\cancel{8}} = \frac{7 \times \$1}{1 \times 1} = \frac{\$7}{1} = \$7 \text{ total cost}$

k. What is the total cost of 600 items priced at 50 cents each?

Since $50\cancel{c} = \$\frac{1}{2}$: $\quad 600 \times \$\frac{1}{2} = \frac{\overset{300}{\cancel{600}}}{1} \times \$\frac{1}{\cancel{2}} = \frac{300 \times \$1}{1 \times 1} = \frac{\$300}{1} = \$300 \text{ total cost}$

l. The wholesale price of solvent is 75 cents a pint. How many pints can you buy for \$60?

Since $75\cancel{c} = \$\frac{3}{4}$: $\quad \$60 \div 75\cancel{c} = 60 \div \frac{3}{4} = \frac{60}{1} \times \frac{4}{3} = \frac{\overset{20}{\cancel{60}}}{1} \times \frac{4}{\cancel{3}} = \frac{20 \times 4}{1 \times 1}$

$$= \frac{80}{1} = 80 \text{ pints}$$

NOTE: When dividing money by money, the money signs are eliminated.

Chapter terms for review

aliquot part
cancel (cancellation)
of

Assignment 6-1: Multiplication of Fractions

A (20 points) — Multiply the fractions, cancelling where possible. Reduce products to lowest terms (2 points for each correct answer).

1. $\frac{2}{5} \times \frac{3}{8} =$

2. $\frac{3}{4} \times \frac{5}{6} \times \frac{1}{2} =$

3. $\frac{5}{8} \times \frac{4}{9} =$

4. $\frac{7}{8} \times \frac{10}{21} \times \frac{3}{5} =$

5. $\frac{5}{8} \times \frac{14}{15} =$

6. $\frac{2}{3} \times \frac{4}{5} \times \frac{3}{10} =$

7. $\frac{2}{3} \times \frac{3}{4} =$

8. $\frac{5}{18} \times \frac{4}{9} \times \frac{3}{10} =$

9. $\frac{9}{10} \times \frac{5}{6} =$

10. $\frac{5}{12} \times \frac{5}{6} \times \frac{27}{50} =$

Score for A (20)

B (40 points) — Solve the following problems, replacing the word "of" by a multiplication symbol. Reduce products to lowest terms (4 points for each correct answer).

11. $\frac{1}{2}$ of $\frac{3}{4} =$

12. $\frac{2}{3}$ of $\frac{7}{8} =$

13. $\frac{2}{5}$ of $\frac{2}{3} =$

14. $\frac{1}{8}$ of $\frac{4}{5} =$

Chapter 6   Fractions: Multiplication and Division

69

15. $\frac{1}{4}$ of $\frac{3}{10}$ =

16. $\frac{4}{5}$ of $\frac{25}{26}$ =

17. $\frac{2}{3}$ of 12 =

18. $\frac{2}{5}$ of $3\frac{1}{3}$ =

19. $\frac{5}{8}$ of 20 =

20. $\frac{9}{10}$ of $4\frac{1}{6}$ =

C (40 points) — Change whole or mixed numbers to improper fractions and multiply. Write answers as mixed numbers in lowest terms (4 points for each correct answer).

21. $2\frac{1}{2} \times 2\frac{1}{3}$ =

22. $1\frac{1}{2} \times 1\frac{1}{5} \times 3\frac{1}{3}$ =

23. $3\frac{1}{4} \times 8$ =

24. $2\frac{1}{4} \times \frac{5}{6} \times 4\frac{2}{3}$ =

25. $3\frac{1}{3} \times 2\frac{1}{4}$ =

26. $2\frac{1}{2} \times 1\frac{5}{6} \times 2\frac{2}{5}$ =

27. $6 \times 4\frac{2}{3}$ =

28. $1\frac{7}{8} \times 12 \times \frac{3}{10}$ =

29. $1\frac{3}{5} \times 3\frac{3}{4}$ =

30. $2\frac{2}{3} \times 3\frac{3}{4} \times 1\frac{4}{5}$ =

Assignment 6-2: Division of Fractions

A (20 points) — Divide fractions. Cancel where possible. Write quotients as mixed numbers or proper fractions in lowest terms (2 points for each correct answer).

1. $\dfrac{2}{3} \div \dfrac{3}{4} =$

2. $\dfrac{3}{8} \div \dfrac{7}{10} =$

3. $\dfrac{5}{8} \div \dfrac{2}{3} =$

4. $\dfrac{7}{10} \div \dfrac{8}{15} =$

5. $\dfrac{1}{8} \div \dfrac{1}{5} =$

6. $\dfrac{5}{12} \div \dfrac{1}{6} =$

7. $\dfrac{3}{10} \div \dfrac{2}{7} =$

8. $\dfrac{5}{6} \div \dfrac{2}{3} =$

9. $\dfrac{7}{15} \div \dfrac{5}{8} =$

10. $\dfrac{15}{16} \div \dfrac{5}{24} =$

Score for A (20)

B (48 points) — Change the mixed/whole numbers to improper fractions and divide. Cancel where possible. Write quotients as mixed numbers or proper fractions in lowest terms (3 points for each correct answer).

11. $2\dfrac{2}{3} \div \dfrac{4}{5} =$

12. $\dfrac{3}{8} \div 1\dfrac{1}{4} =$

13. $2\dfrac{5}{6} \div \dfrac{7}{12} =$

14. $1\dfrac{5}{6} \div \dfrac{1}{3} =$

15. $1\frac{3}{4} \div \frac{3}{8} =$

16. $3\frac{3}{5} \div \frac{3}{10} =$

17. $\frac{9}{10} \div 3\frac{3}{5} =$

18. $4\frac{2}{3} \div \frac{2}{3} =$

19. $2\frac{2}{3} \div 1\frac{1}{4} =$

20. $6\frac{1}{4} \div 1\frac{7}{8} =$

21. $1\frac{3}{4} \div 1\frac{3}{5} =$

22. $2\frac{1}{2} \div 2\frac{3}{4} =$

23. $3\frac{3}{4} \div 1\frac{7}{15} =$

24. $1\frac{7}{12} \div 3\frac{5}{6} =$

25. $2\frac{4}{5} \div 3\frac{3}{4} =$

26. $4\frac{4}{5} \div 1\frac{3}{5} =$

Score for B (48)

C (16 points) — Use aliquot parts to solve the following problems. Use the values from Chapter 6 or the table in the Aliquot Parts Appendix (2 points for each correct answer).

27. What is the total cost of 640 items priced at 25¢ each?

　　　　　　　　　　　　　　　　　　　　Part Two　Fractions and Decimals

28. What is the total cost of 200 items priced at 75¢ each?

_____

29. What is the total cost of 1,200 items priced at $66\frac{2}{3}$¢ each?

_____

30. What is the total cost of 800 items priced at $37\frac{1}{2}$¢ each?

_____

31. How many items priced at $62\frac{1}{2}$¢ each can be purchased for $250?

_____

32. How many items priced at $16\frac{2}{3}$¢ each can be purchased for $50?

_____

33. How many items priced at 60¢ each can be purchased for $180?

_____

34. How many items priced at $87\frac{1}{2}$¢ each can be purchased for $350?

_____

D (16 points) — Use fractions and mixed numbers to solve each of the following applications (4 points for each correct answer).

35. Scobel Machine Shop wants to cut 20-foot steel bars into pieces that are 1 foot, 3 inches long. How many whole pieces can they get out of each bar? (Hint: 1 foot, 3 inches is equal to $1\frac{1}{4}$ feet.)

_____

36. There are $3\frac{3}{4}$ gallons of paint remaining in a five gallon paint can. A paint contractor thinks it will take $\frac{2}{3}$ of the remaining paint to paint one room. If the paint contractor is correct, how much paint will be left over after painting the room?

_____

37. A wheelbarrow holds $3\frac{1}{3}$ cubic feet of dirt. How many cubic feet of dirt would there be in $5\frac{1}{2}$ wheelbarrows?

_____

38. Hammerstrom Pest Control Company buys concentrated insect spray in 55 gallon barrels. They dilute the concentrate with water in smaller containers, pouring $3\frac{1}{3}$ gallons of spray into each container. How many containers of mixture can be filled with one barrel of concentrated insect spray?

_____

Chapter 7
Decimals: Addition and Subtraction

OBJECTIVES
After completing this chapter, you should be able to:

- Read decimal numbers
- Add and subtract decimal numbers
- Round decimal numbers

DECIMALS AND MONEY

One system of measurement is common to every business, government agency, nonprofit organization, and individual — the money system. We use the money system to measure profit, loss, cost, selling price, productivity, inflation, etc. The money system contains many fractions, but they are not written in the same way as the fractions explained in Chapters 5 and 6. For example, a dime is a fraction of a dollar. There are ten dimes in one dollar, but no one writes $\$\frac{1}{10}$ for a dime. Either we write 10¢ or we write \$0.10. We say that \$0.10 is the *decimal representation* of a dime.

PHOTO 7-1

We use the decimal system because of the advantage in calculating. The following example illustrates the use of decimals in calculations.

As fractional parts of $1, a quarter is $\frac{1}{4}$, a dime is $\frac{1}{10}$, a nickel is $\frac{1}{20}$, and a penny is $\frac{1}{100}$. But we never add these coins by writing:

$$\frac{1}{4} + \frac{1}{4} + \frac{1}{4} + \frac{1}{4} + \frac{1}{10} + \frac{1}{10} + \frac{1}{20} + \frac{1}{20} + \frac{1}{100} + \frac{1}{100} = \frac{132}{100}$$

Instead, we use the decimal representation of each coin:

$$0.25 + 0.25 + 0.25 + 0.25 + 0.10 + 0.10 + 0.05 + 0.05 + 0.01 + 0.01 = 1.32$$

Just as there are mixed numbers in fractions, there are also *mixed decimals*. For example, $1.32 is a mixed decimal. In $1.32, the period between the 1 and the 3 is the *decimal point*. The 1 is the whole-number part, and .32 is the decimal part. If there is no whole-number part, the number is a *pure decimal*. For example, $0.25 is a pure decimal.

When you enter . 2 5 on your calculator, the calculator automatically writes a 0 (zero) to the left of the decimal point. We will use the same rule in this book.

DECIMALS AND OTHER MEASUREMENTS

Today, most fractions are written in decimal form because of the development of electronic digital display. Displays like the one on your calculator are used frequently in electronic measuring equipment and tools.

PHOTO 7-2

Three examples are shown with the digital displays reproduced in Photo 7-2. The grocery store scale shown in the photo displays weight in pounds. Fractional parts of a pound are written as decimals accurate to $\frac{1}{10,000}$ of a pound. In the photo, the scale shows a weight of 0.0170 pounds.

The gasoline pump shown in the photo displays fractional parts of a gallon as decimals accurate to $\frac{1}{1,000}$ of a gallon. The gas pump displays a purchase of 12.661 gallons of gasoline.

The last device shown in the photo is used by contractors to estimate the height, width, and length of rooms in a home or office building. It functions like an "electronic tape measure" and displays length measured to the nearest $\frac{1}{10}$ of a foot. It cannot measure any more accurately than to the nearest inch and is only used to make estimates. It would not be used, for example, to measure the exact length of a door to fit into a doorway. In the photo, the length shown is 28.4 feet.

READING DECIMALS

The system for reading decimals is just like the system for reading whole numbers: each column represents a different value. Reading from right to left, the columns to the left of the decimal point are ones (or units), tens, hundreds, thousands, ten thousands, hundred thousands, etc. Reading from left to right, the columns to the right of the decimal place represent tenths, hundredths, thousandths, ten-thousandths, hundred-thousandths, etc.

Figure 7-1 illustrates the number system for both sides of the decimal point. The number is 607,194.35824. The place value of each digit is given by the column heading.

FIGURE 7-1   Number System for Both Sides of the Decimal Point

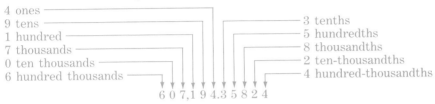

```
4 ones ─────────────────────┐                  ┌───── 3 tenths
9 tens ────────────────────┐│                 ┌│───── 5 hundredths
1 hundred ────────────────┐││                 ││┌──── 8 thousandths
7 thousands ─────────────┐│││                 │││┌─── 2 ten-thousandths
0 ten thousands ────────┐││││                 ││││┌── 4 hundred-thousandths
6 hundred thousands ───┐│││││                 │││││
                       ▼▼▼▼▼▼  ▼▼ ▼ ▼ ▼ ▼ ▼ ▼
                      6 0 7,1 9 4.3 5 8 2 4
```

Therefore, the 28.4 on the electronic tape measure in Photo 7-2 is read as "twenty-eight and four tenths." The decimal point is read as the word "and." The 12.661 on the gasoline pump in Photo 7-2 is read as "twelve and six hundred sixty-one thousandths." The 0.0170 on the grocery store scale in Photo 7-2 is more interesting because it ends in 0 (zero). Some people would read it as "one hundred seventy ten-thousandths;" others would ignore the zero at the end and would say "seventeen thousandths." Both are correct and can be used interchangeably.

In Figure 7-1, the whole-number part of the number is 607,194, and the decimal part is .35824. From the decimal part .35824, consider the decimal numbers 0.3, 0.35, 0.008, 0.0082, and 0.35824. The equivalent fractional forms of these decimals are $\frac{3}{10}$, $\frac{35}{100}$, $\frac{8}{1,000}$, $\frac{82}{10,000}$, and $\frac{35,824}{100,000}$. Whether they are written as decimals or fractions, they are read as follows:

Decimal	Words	Fraction
0.3	three tenths	$\frac{3}{10}$
0.35	thirty-five hundredths	$\frac{35}{100}$
0.008	eight thousandths	$\frac{8}{1,000}$
0.0082	eighty-two ten-thousandths	$\frac{82}{10,000}$
0.35824	thirty-five thousand eight hundred twenty-four hundred-thousandths	$\frac{35}{100,000}$

Thus, the number 607,194.35824 is read as "six hundred seven thousand one hundred ninety-four *and* thirty-five thousand eight hundred twenty-four hundred-thousandths." Because of the large number of words it takes to say such a number, an alternate method is used for reading long decimals.

1. Read the digits from left to right.
2. Use the word "point" for the decimal point when it appears.

a. *Decimal*   *Read*

0.35824	zero *point* three five eight two four
607,194.35824	six zero seven one nine four *point* three five eight two four

NOTE: There is no comma used to separate groups of three digits to the right of the decimal point.

ADDITION OF DECIMALS

Finding the sum of a series of decimals is a simple procedure. To learn how to add decimals, refer to the steps below.

Steps to Add a Series of Decimals

1. Arrange the numbers in columns with the decimal points in a vertical line.
2. Add each column from right to left as you would with any numbers.

NOTE: As an option, you may want to write zeros in the right-hand columns of decimals so that each number appears to have the same number of decimal places.

b. Add 3.42, 218.6004, 9.423, 32, and 0.87782

		Step 1		Step 2 (& option)
3.42		3.42		3.42000
218.6004		218.6004		218.60040
9.423	then ⟶	9.423	then ⟶	9.42300
32		32.		32.00000
+ 0.87782		+ 0.87782		+0.87782
				264.32122

SUBTRACTION OF DECIMALS

To find the difference between two decimals, certain steps must be followed. To learn how to subtract a series of decimals, refer to the steps below.

Steps to Subtract Decimals

1. Arrange the numbers in columns, with the decimal points in a vertical line. Write the *subtrahend* (number being subtracted) below the *minuend* (number from which the subtraction is being made).
2. The two numbers may not have the same number of decimal places. Write enough extra zeros so that both have the same number of decimal places.
3. Subtract each column from right to left as you would do with any numbers.

c. Subtract 4.935 (subtrahend) from 12.8 (minuend)

Step 1	Steps 2 & 3
12.8	12.800
− 4.935	− 4.935
	7.865

Subtract 9.4 (subtrahend) from 82.113 (minuend)

Step 1	Steps 2 & 3
82.113	82.113
− 9.4	− 9.400
	72.713

COMPLETE ASSIGNMENT 7 1

ROUNDING NUMBERS

In business transactions involving money, the smallest amount of money that can be paid is 1 cent. It is impossible to pay the amount $5.268. The amount to be paid can have at most two decimal places. Sometimes businesses will pay the amount to the nearest cent, which is called *rounding off* or just *rounding* the number. For example, $5.268 would be rounded to $5.27.

Decimals that are not dollars and cents can be rounded to any number of decimal places. The procedure is the same whether the number is representing money or not.

Steps for Rounding Decimals

1. Find the last place, or digit, to be retained. If the digit immediately to its right is equal to or greater than 5, the digit to be retained is increased by 1. All digits to the right of the one retained are then dropped.
2. If the digit immediately to the right of the last place to be retained is less than 5, the digit to be retained remains unchanged. All digits to the right of the ones retained are then dropped.

d. The decimals shown in this example are rounded to the number of places indicated:

Numbers to be rounded:	7.3951	35.2149
Round to the nearest tenth	7.3951 ⟶ 7.4	35.2149 ⟶ 35.2
Round to the nearest hundredth	7.3951 ⟶ 7.40	35.2149 ⟶ 35.21
Round to the nearest thousandth	7.3951 ⟶ 7.395	35.2149 ⟶ 35.215

Rounding Up

Retail businesses, such as grocery stores, often use a different method of rounding to a whole number of cents. Suppose a grocery store has lemons priced at "3 for $1.00." Usually the store will charge $0.34 for one lemon even though $1.00 divided by 3 is $0.3333 (to four places). The store has *rounded up* to the next larger whole cent. (See Chapter 8 for division of decimals.) Thus, to round up monetary amounts, always increase any partial cent to the next whole cent. For example, $27.842 would round up to $27.85.

Chapter terms for review

decimal point

decimal representation

minuend

mixed decimal

pure decimal

rounding

rounding off (rounding)

rounding up

subtrahend

Assignment 7-1: Addition and Subtraction of Decimals

A (24 points) — Use digits to write each number that is expressed in words. Use words to write each number that is expressed in digits (2 points for each correct answer).

1. Six hundredths _____
2. Three hundred twenty-five thousandths _____
3. Twelve ten-thousandths _____
4. Nineteen and sixty-five thousandths _____
5. Two thousand fifty and twenty-eight ten-thousandths _____
6. Three hundred two and seven hundred twelve thousandths _____
7. 0.005 _____
8. 0.38 _____
9. 0.03877 _____
10. 2,006.8 _____
11. 407.085 _____
12. 30.0004 _____

Score for A (24)

B (36 points) — Write the following numbers in columns, and then add (3 points for each correct answer).

13. 3.468, 14.8, 320.88

_____

14. 142.06, 0.2407, 52.8

_____

15. 0.008, 0.23, 0.0387

_____

16. 13.6209, 21.681, 72.99

_____

17. 402.62, 0.0332, 83.619, 2.5

_____

18. 6.4406, 72.419, 1,952.8, 246

_____

19. 28.0013, 4.07, 12.254, 7.44

_____

20. 3.766, 496.63, 14.9, 0.3949

_____

21. 14.72, 3.974, 100.29, 77.743

_____

22. 84.029, 6.9705, 298.66, 9.84

_____

23. 47.37, 482.088, 5.9767, 73.36

_____

24. 949.7, 3.869, 17.59, 82.948

_____

C (40 points) — Subtract the following (2 points for each correct answer).

25.
  0.204
− 0.173

26.
  0.351
− 0.26

27.
  0.84
− 0.369

28.
  0.4578
− 0.09

29.
  0.28
− 0.1474

30.
  0.34852
− 0.03963

31.
  0.82352
− 0.6836

32.
  0.581
− 0.00037

33.
  0.904832
− 0.008266

34.
  0.4
− 0.30587

35.
  13.804
− 8.908

36.
  45.436
− 26.3

37.
  58.4
− 9.075

38.
  26.
− 0.67

39.
  71.205
− 70.836

40.
  793.25
− 495.36

41.
  820.0453
− 755.8

42.
  415.27
− 0.35822

43.
  8,243.557
− 538.96426

44.
  1,000.
− 0.0001

Assignment 7-2:   Fundamentals of Decimals in Business

A   (21 points) — In Problems 1-7, round each number to the nearest tenth; in Problems 8-14, round amounts to the nearest cent; in Problems 15-21, round numbers to the nearest thousandth (1 point for each correct answer).

Nearest Tenth		*Nearest Cent*		*Nearest Thousandth*	
1. 0.24 ft.	_____	**8.** $0.048	_____	**15.** 5.46346 in.	_____
2. 0.455 mi.	_____	**9.** $8.252	_____	**16.** 83.9185 pt.	_____
3. 7.1499 gal.	_____	**10.** $10.125	_____	**17.** 0.00351 lb.	_____
4. 12.95 qt.	_____	**11.** $483.1249	_____	**18.** 0.02449 oz.	_____
5. 426.37 ft.	_____	**12.** $0.3751	_____	**19.** 99.9995 yd.	_____
6. 8.667 qt.	_____	**13.** $29.45499	_____	**20.** 8.36451 oz.	_____
7. 3.7259 in.	_____	**14.** $1.5009	_____	**21.** 1.00949 yd.	_____

Score for A (21)

B   (39 points) — Round each decimal as indicated by the column heading, and then add or subtract as indicated (3 points for each correct answer).

Tenths		*Hundredths*		*Thousandths*	
22. 12.3923 + 8.7489	_____	**27.** 4.8738 + 25.3575	_____	**31.** 18.11077 − 9.22249	_____
23. 394.656 − 89.849	_____	**28.** 9.3249 − 7.8251	_____	**32.** 7.91846 + 8.86655	_____
24. 3.2499 + 28.3501	_____	**29.** 44.0089 − 38.0147	_____	**33.** 0.517977 + 0.038241	_____
25. 0.0486 − 0.0395	_____	**30.** 48.6766 + 58.8009	_____	**34.** 0.037499 − 0.007501	_____
26. 71.0496 − 68.0998	_____				

Score for B (39)

C (40 points) — Work the following business applications. Do not round off your final answers (5 points for each correct answer).

35. Mary Wright sold three apples that weighed 6.7, 6.3, and 5.8 ounces. What was the total weight of the apples?

———————————

36. Beefy World Market sold 4.9 pounds of steak, 8.4 pounds of roast, and 13.7 pounds of ground beef to Ann Walters. What was the total weight of the meat products that Ann purchased?

———————————

37. David Wayne had 49.5 feet of rope. He cut off a piece 12.75 feet long. How much did he have left?

———————————

38. A jeweler had only 2.8 ounces of gold on hand. So, he bought 12.5 ounces more to make Christmas items. He used 8.6 ounces for gold rings. How much gold did he have left?

———————————

39. Inez Toya reads meters for the electric company. She walked 2.4 miles on Monday; 3.8 miles, Tuesday; 2.9 miles, Wednesday; 3.25 miles, Thursday; and 2.7 miles, Friday. What was her total distance for the week?

———————————

40. Four drivers bring their cars in to a service station to buy gasoline. Individually they buy 10.4, 8.3, 12.8, and 15.9 gallons. How much did they purchase all together?

———————————

41. Village Jewelers had 50.8 ounces of gold on hand. After they received 120 ounces and used 68.9 ounces, how much gold was on hand?

———————————

42. Walt's Paving Co. delivered 7.3 tons of asphalt. They used 5.2 tons for a parking lot in a shopping center and 1.5 tons for an access road. How many tons of asphalt were left?

———————————

———————————
Score for C (40)

Chapter 8
Decimals: Multiplication and Division

OBJECTIVES
After completing this chapter, you should be able to:

- Multiply numbers containing decimals
- Divide a decimal by a whole number
- Divide a decimal by another decimal
- Multiply and divide by powers of ten
- Change decimals to fractional equivalents
- Change fractions to decimal equivalents
- Approximate products and quotients

MULTIPLICATION WITH DECIMALS

Every business owner and employee multiplies decimal numbers. If an employee is paid \$8.40 per hour and works 6.5 hours, the total pay is calculated by multiplication: $6.5 \times \$8.40 = \$54.60$. Multiplication with one or more decimals is the same as multiplication with whole numbers except that you need to put the decimal point in the correct position in the product.

Steps to Multiply with Decimals

1. Multiply the two numbers as if they were whole numbers.
2. Count the **total** number of decimal places in the two numbers.
3. In the product, place the decimal point so that the number of decimal places is the same as the number in Step 2. (Count from right to left.)

a. 3.764×21

$$
\begin{array}{rl}
3.764 & \text{(3 places)} \\
\times\ 21 & \text{(0 places)} \\
\hline
\text{Step 1}\quad 3\ 764 & \\
75\ 28 & \underline{\qquad\text{Step 2}\qquad} \\
\text{Step 3}\quad 79.044 & (3 + 0 = 3 \text{ places})
\end{array}
$$

3.764×2.1

$$
\begin{array}{rl}
3.764 & \text{(3 places)} \\
\times\ 2.1 & \text{(1 place)} \\
\hline
\text{Step 1}\quad 3764 & \\
7\ 528 & \underline{\qquad\text{Step 2}\qquad} \\
\text{Step 3}\quad 7.9044 & (3 + 1 = 4 \text{ places})
\end{array}
$$

When the product in Step 1 has fewer digits than the total places counted in Step 2, insert zeros between the last digit counted and the decimal point.

b. 3.764 × 0.0021   0.3764 × 0.21

           3.764 (3 places)   0.3764 (4 places)

      × 0.0021 (4 places)   × 0.21 (2 places)

Step 1   3764   Step 1   3764

        7528   Step 2   7528   Step 2

Step 3 0.0079044 (3 + 4 = 7 places;   Step 3 0.079044 (4 + 2 = 6 places;

                   insert 2 zeros)   insert 1 zero)

In business applications, zeros that come at the right end of the decimal part of the product are often omitted (example c.). Do not omit zeros that come at the end of the whole-number part (example d.). When the product is written in dollars and cents, two decimal places are written, including zeros at the end (example e.).

c. 0.76 × 0.5   **d.** 12.5 × 0.8   **e.** $8.40 × 6.5

   0.76 (2 places)   12.5 (1 place) $8.40 (2 places)

× 0.5 (1 place)   × 0.8 (1 place)   × 6.5 (1 place)

0.380 (3 places)   10.00 (2 places) $54.600 (3 places)

written as 0.38   written as 10   written as $54.60

DIVISION WITH DECIMALS

Dividing a Decimal by a Whole Number

Division is the same as with two whole numbers except for placement of the decimal. Three steps may be required to divide correctly.

Steps to Divide a Decimal by a Whole Number

1. Write the decimal point in the quotient directly above the decimal point in the divisor.
2. If necessary, insert zeros in the quotient, between the decimal point and the other digits (example g.).
3. Divide as you would for whole numbers.

---

f. Step 1   Step 3   **g.** Step 1   Steps 2 & 3

$$12)\overline{40.8} = 12)\overline{40.8}$$

$$\begin{array}{r} 3.4 \\ 12)\overline{40.8} \\ \underline{36} \\ 4\ 8 \\ \underline{4\ 8} \\ 0 \end{array}$$

$$\begin{array}{r} 0.014 \\ 4)\overline{0.056} \\ \underline{4} \\ 16 \\ \underline{16} \\ 0 \end{array}$$

To complete the division process or to carry it out to more places, it may be necessary to add zeros to the right end of the dividend (examples h., i., and j.).

For a large divisor and small dividend, it might be necessary to insert zeros in the quotient between the decimal point and the other digits (example i.).

When the dividend is also a whole number, the procedure is the same because the decimal point is at the right end of the dividend (example j.).

h. Step 1   Steps 2 & 3   **i.**   Step 1   Steps 2 & 3   **j.**   Step 1   Steps 2 & 3

$$
\begin{array}{r}
3.05 \\
8\overline{)24.4} = 8\overline{)24.40} \\
\underline{24} \\
40 \\
\underline{40} \\
0
\end{array}
\qquad
\begin{array}{r}
0.0024 \\
25\overline{)0.06} = 25\overline{)0.0600} \\
\underline{50} \\
100 \\
\underline{100} \\
0
\end{array}
\qquad
\begin{array}{r}
0.35 \\
20\overline{)7} = 20\overline{)7.00} \\
\underline{6\,0} \\
1\,00 \\
\underline{1\,00} \\
0
\end{array}
$$

Remainders

In decimal division there are no remainders as there are in whole number division. Instead of remainders, the process carries the quotient to one or more places to the right of the decimal. Example j. shows how a remainder of 10 can be $(7 \div 20 = 3R10)$ further divided.

Dividing by a Decimal

When the divisor is a decimal, change the divisor into a whole number before doing the division. Refer to the steps below to learn how to divide by a decimal.

Steps to Divide by a Decimal

1. Move the decimal point in the divisor to the right until the divisor is a whole number.
2. Move the decimal point in the dividend to the right exactly the same number of decimal places as were moved in Step 1. Place the decimal point in the quotient directly above the new decimal point in the divisor.
3. Divide. If necessary, add zeros on the right end of the divisor (example k.), or add zeros in the quotient between the decimal point and the other digits (example l).

---

k. Steps 1 & 2   Step 3   **l.**   Steps 1 & 2   Step 3

$$
\begin{array}{r}
3.5 \\
1.2\overline{)4.2} = 12.\overline{)42.0} \\
\underline{36} \\
6\,0 \\
\underline{6\,0} \\
0
\end{array}
\qquad
\begin{array}{r}
0.092 \\
0.5\overline{)0.0.46} = 5.\overline{)0.460} \\
\underline{45} \\
10 \\
\underline{10} \\
0
\end{array}
$$

MULTIPLICATION AND DIVISION BY POWERS OF TEN

The numbers 10, 100, 1,000, etc. are called *powers of 10*. To multiply or divide by a power of 10, move the decimal point to the right or left.

Rule: To multiply, move the decimal point in the multiplicand to the right the same number of places as the number of zeros in the multiplier.

m. $0.7492 \times 10 = 0.7\,492 = 7.492$ $205.704 \times 100 = 205.70\,4 = 20{,}570.4$

                        1 place   2 places

$3.15 \times 1{,}000 = 3.150. = 3{,}150$

                        3 places

Rule: To divide, move the decimal point in the dividend to the left the same number of places as the number of zeros in the divisor.

n. $0.7492 \div 10 = 0.7492 = 0.07492$ $205.704 \div 100 = 2.05.704 = 2.05704$

1 place   2 places

$3.15 \div 1,000 = .003.15 = 0.00315$

3 places

DECIMAL AND FRACTIONAL EQUIVALENTS

Every decimal number can be changed into its *fractional equivalent*. The numerator is the decimal number without a decimal point. The denominator is the correct power of ten (10, 100, 1,000, etc.).

o. $0.6 = \frac{6}{10} = \frac{3}{5}$ $0.013 = \frac{13}{1,000}$ $1.25 = \frac{125}{100} = \frac{5}{4}$

Every fraction can be changed into its *decimal equivalent* by dividing the numerator by the denominator.

p. $\frac{3}{4} = 4\overline{)3.00}^{\,0.75}$ $\frac{13}{8} = 8\overline{)13.000}^{\,1.625}$ $\frac{11}{16} = 16\overline{)11.0000}^{\,0.6875}$

Sometimes the division does not end evenly. In the problems shown in example q. below, the division is carried to five places and the quotient is rounded to four places.

q. $\frac{1}{3} = 3\overline{)1.00000}^{\,0.33333}$ $\frac{8}{3} = 3\overline{)8.00000}^{\,2.66666}$ $\frac{5}{12} = 12\overline{)5.00000}^{\,0.41666}$

$0.33333 \longrightarrow 0.3333$ $2.66666 \longrightarrow 2.6667$ $0.41666 \longrightarrow 0.4167$

It is important to learn equivalents because some problems are easier to solve using decimals, while others are easier to solve using fractions. When using a calculator, it is necessary to first change fractions to their decimal equivalents.

r. Solve $8\frac{3}{4} - 3\frac{1}{3}$ using both fractions and decimals.

Decimals	*Fractions*
$8\frac{3}{4} = \quad 8.7500$	$8\frac{3}{4} = \quad 8\frac{9}{12}$
$- 3\frac{1}{3} = -3.3333$	$- 3\frac{1}{3} = -3\frac{4}{12}$
$\qquad\qquad 5.4167$	$\qquad\qquad 5\frac{5}{12}$

s. Solve 3.75×1.8 using both fractions and decimals.

Decimals

$\begin{array}{r} 3.75 \\ \times\ 1.8 \\ \hline 3\ 000 \\ 3\ 75\ \ \\ \hline 6.750 \end{array}$

Fractions

$3.75 = 3\frac{3}{4};\quad 1.8 = 1\frac{8}{10} = 1\frac{4}{5}$

$3\frac{3}{4} \times 1\frac{4}{5} = \frac{15}{4} \times \frac{9}{5} = \frac{3}{4} \times \frac{9}{1} = \frac{27}{4} = 6\frac{3}{4}$

APPROXIMATING THE PRODUCT AND QUOTIENT

Today, business persons use calculators extensively in their work. To find a calculator error, make a simple mental calculation to check whether the original answer is reasonable. The objective of the check is to determine whether the answer is approximately the right size. The correct placement of the decimal point is most important. Note that the check is only an approximation of the correct answer.

Steps to Estimate a Multiplication Problem

1. Round off each factor to the nearest single, non-zero digit.
2. Multiply and correctly position the decimal point.

t. 3.764×7.1 61.18×0.089

		Step 1				Step 1	
	3.764 $\longrightarrow$	4.000	(3 places)	61.18 $\longrightarrow$	60.00	(2 places)
	$\times$ 7.1 $\longrightarrow$	$\times$ 7.0	(1 place)	$\times$ 0.089 $\longrightarrow$	$\times$ 0.090	(3 places)
	Step 2	28.0000	(4 places)	Step 2	5.40000	(5 places)

The estimates shown in example t. are approximately equal to the actual answers, 26.7244 and 5.44502.

For division, the mental arithmetic is easier if you round off the numbers so that the division will end in only one step.

Steps to Estimate a Division Problem

1. Round off the divisor to the nearest non-zero digit.
2. Round off the dividend to two non-zero digits, so that the divisor divides exactly into the dividend.
3. Divide and correctly position the decimal point.

u.

$$\text{Steps 1 \& 2} \qquad \text{Step 3}$$

$$7.1\overline{)3.764} \longrightarrow 7.0\overline{)3.5} \longrightarrow 7.0\overline{)3.5}^{\;0.5}$$

$$\text{Steps 1 \& 2} \qquad \text{Step 3}$$

$$0.089\overline{)61.18} \longrightarrow 9.0\overline{)6,300} \longrightarrow 9.0\overline{)6,300.}^{\;700.}$$

The estimates shown in example u. are approximately equal to the actual answers, 0.5301 and 687.4157 (rounded to four decimal places).

COMPLETE ASSIGNMENTS 8-1 AND 8-2

Chapter terms for review

decimal equivalents
fractional equivalents
powers of ten

Assignment 8-1: Multiplication and Division of Decimals

A **(30 points) — Multiply. Round off monetary products to the nearest cent. Do not round off non-monetary products ($2\frac{1}{2}$ points for each correct answer).**

1. $12.20
   $\times\ 35$

_____

2. 15.25
   $\times\ 3.6$

_____

3. $53.60
   $\times\ 0.25$

_____

4. 320.00
   $\times\ 0.305$

_____

5. 83.45
   $\times\ 7.2$

_____

6. $18.61
   $\times\ 0.82$

_____

7. 205.45
   $\times\ 0.96$

_____

8. $ 720.06
   $\times\ 0.304$

_____

9. 36.409238
   $\times\ 0.08$

_____

10. $4.06
   $\times\ 0.25$

_____

11. 30.504
   $\times\ 0.024$

_____

12. 0.00766
   $\times\ 0.053$

_____

Score for A (30)

B **(36 points) — Divide. Round off monetary quotients to the nearest cent. Round off non-monetary quotients to three decimals places (3 points for each correct answer).**

13. $7\overline{)\$12.95}$

14. $1.2\overline{)\$54.30}$

15. $23\overline{)5.911}$

16. $2.5\overline{)7.506}$

_____   _____   _____   _____

17. $0.06\overline{)1.023}$ **18.** $0.075\overline{)0.0642}$ **19.** $0.36\overline{)\$6.75}$ **20.** $2.25\overline{)\$18.36}$

21. $1.5\overline{)\$2.57}$ **22.** $0.09\overline{)0.7888}$ **23.** $0.11\overline{)0.6735}$ **24.** $0.007\overline{)0.003548}$

Score for B (36)

C (34 points) — For each of the following problems, underline the estimate that is most nearly correct (2 points for each correct answer).

25. 3.8×68.758	(a) 0.28	(b) 2.8	(c) 28	(d) 280
26. 7.65×0.8599	(a) 0.064	(b) 0.64	(c) 6.4	(d) 64
27. 0.8388×0.5503	(a) 0.0048	(b) 0.048	(c) 0.48	(d) 4.8
28. 278.25×93.99	(a) 27,000	(b) 2,700	(c) 270	(d) 27
29. 0.00867×642	(a) 0.054	(b) 0.54	(c) 5.4	(d) 54
30. 0.079×0.053	(a) 4.0	(b) 0.4	(c) 0.04	(d) 0.004
31. 0.00389×0.0957	(a) 0.04	(b) 0.004	(c) 0.0004	(d) 0.00004
32. $0.21 \times 5,987$	(a) 120	(b) 1,200	(c) 12,000	(d) 120,000
33. 0.00058×0.0049	(a) 0.000003	(b) 0.00003	(c) 0.0003	(d) 0.003
34. $43.85 \div 6.397$	(a) 70	(b) 7	(c) 0.7	(d) 0.07
35. $3.865 \div 873.12$	(a) 0.004	(b) 0.04	(c) 0.4	(d) 4
36. $7.958 \div 0.0544$	(a) 16	(b) 160	(c) 1,600	(d) 16,000
37. $83.72 \div 0.6186$	(a) 0.14	(b) 1.4	(c) 14	(d) 140
38. $0.5447 \div 0.00585$	(a) 900	(b) 90	(c) 9	(d) 0.9
39. $0.02655 \div 0.09481$	(a) 300	(b) 30	(c) 3	(d) 0.3
40. $0.00612 \div 0.00358$	(a) 0.15	(b) 1.5	(c) 15	(d) 150
41. $0.000738 \div 0.0082$	(a) 0.009	(b) 0.09	(c) 0.9	(d) 9

Score for C (34)

Part Two Fractions and Decimals

Assignment 8-2:   Fractional Equivalents and Business Applications

A **(24 points) — For each fraction, find the decimal equivalent to four decimals places (2 points for each correct answer).**

1. $\frac{3}{4}$ = _____   **2.** $\frac{2}{7}$ = _____   **3.** $\frac{5}{8}$ = _____   **4.** $\frac{1}{9}$ = _____

5. $\frac{1}{12}$ = _____   **6.** $\frac{5}{11}$ = _____   **7.** $\frac{4}{3}$ = _____   **8.** $\frac{2}{15}$ = _____

9. $\frac{13}{5}$ = _____   **10.** $\frac{5}{16}$ = _____   **11.** $\frac{3}{8}$ = _____   **12.** $\frac{1}{30}$ = _____

Score for A (24)

B **(12 points)** — A decimal can be written as a fraction by writing the decimal part without the decimal point as the numerator. The denominator is the appropriate power of 10. Use the same procedure for mixed decimals. Convert the following decimals to fractions or mixed numbers, and reduce to lowest terms (1 point for each correct answer).

Examples: $0.8 = \frac{8}{10} = \frac{4}{5}$ $\qquad$ $1.04 = \frac{104}{100} = 1\frac{4}{100} = 1\frac{1}{25}$ $\qquad$ $0.235 = \frac{235}{1,000} = \frac{47}{200}$

13. 0.35 _____ $\qquad$ **14.** 0.08 _____ $\qquad$ **15.** 0.16 _____

16. 1.75 _____ $\qquad$ **17.** 4.6 _____ $\qquad$ **18.** 0.12 _____

19. 0.64 _____ $\qquad$ **20.** 2.54 _____ $\qquad$ **21.** 0.875 _____

22. 0.525 _____ $\qquad$ **23.** 0.888 _____ $\qquad$ **24.** 3.625 _____

_____
Score for B (12)

C **(40 points)** — Work each of the following problems twice, once using fractions and once using decimals. A partial table of decimal equivalents is shown below ($2\frac{1}{2}$ points for each correct answer).

$\frac{1}{2}$ 0.5	$\frac{1}{3}$ 0.3333*	$\frac{2}{3}$ 0.6667*	$\frac{1}{4}$ 0.25	$\frac{3}{4}$ 0.75	$\frac{1}{5}$ 0.2
$\frac{3}{5}$ 0.6	$\frac{4}{5}$ 0.8	$\frac{1}{6}$ 0.1667*	$\frac{5}{6}$ 0.8333*	$\frac{1}{8}$ 0.125	$\frac{3}{8}$ 0.375
$\frac{5}{8}$ 0.625	$\frac{7}{8}$ 0.875	$\frac{1}{10}$ 0.1	$\frac{3}{10}$ 0.3	$\frac{7}{10}$ 0.7	$\frac{1}{12}$ 0.0833*

* Indicates that the decimal is rounded off to 4 decimal places.

Decimals _____ *Fractions* _____ $\qquad$ *Fractions* _____ *Decimals* _____

25. $\quad$ 12.7
$\quad$ + 9.75

26. $\quad 3\frac{2}{3} =$
$\quad + 2\frac{4}{5} =$

_____ $\quad$ _____ $\qquad$ _____ $\quad$ _____

	Decimals	_Fractions_		_Fractions_	_Decimals_
27.	14.3333		**28.**	$7\frac{1}{2} =$	
	$-$ 9.75			$- 4\frac{2}{3} =$	

_____ _____   _____ _____

	Decimals	_Fractions_		_Fractions_	_Decimals_
29.	1.6667		**30.**	$3\frac{1}{8} \times 3\frac{3}{5} =$	
	$\times$ 1.25				

_____ _____   _____ _____

	Decimals	_Fractions_		_Fractions_	_Decimals_
31.	$2.1\overline{)4.375}$		**32.**	$3\frac{1}{2} \div 5\frac{1}{4} =$	

_____ _____   _____ _____

D (24 points) — Solve the following business problems. Whenever necessary, round monetary amounts to the nearest cent (6 points for each correct answer).

33. Larson's Landscape Supplies sells irrigation pipe. Plastic pipe costs $0.18 per foot, and copper pipe is $1.68 per foot. A customer needs 136.5 feet of pipe for her new lawn. How much will she save in the cost of pipe alone if she uses plastic pipe?

———————————

34. Four drivers bring their cars in to a service station to buy gasoline. Two drivers buy 10.35 and 8.43 gallons of unleaded gasoline at $1.419 per gallon. The other two buy 12.83 and 15.92 gallons of super unleaded at $1.679 per gallon. How much is the total amount they spent for gasoline?

———————————

35. One share of Joe's computer stock is priced at $34\frac{3}{8}$. This means that one share will cost $34.375. One share of Joyce's computer stock is priced at $102\frac{5}{8}$. What would be the difference in price between 15 shares of Joe's computer stock and 5 shares of Joyce's computer stock?

———————————

36. As a weekend special, Fairfield Market is selling certain types of beef for $4.60 per pound. A customer has $12.50 to spend on beef. How many pounds can he buy (calculate to the nearest tenth of a pound)?

———————————

———————————
Score for D (24)

Part Three
Banking and Payroll Application

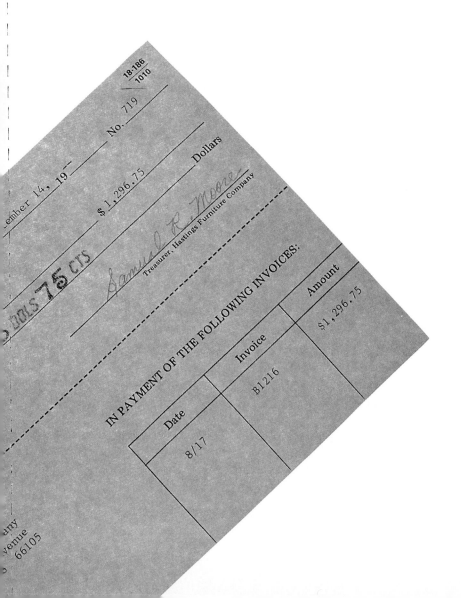

Chapter 9
Bank Records

OBJECTIVES

After completing this chapter, you should be able to:

• Understand checking accounts
• Reconcile bank statements

Practically all people and businesses deal with banks, savings and loan associations, or credit unions (all called "banks" in this chapter). Most bank customers have accounts in which they deposit cash and checks. They then draw checks (or drafts) or make withdrawals against their balances on deposit to pay their bills and other obligations.

CHECKS AND CHECK RECORDS

Checks are written orders directing the bank to pay a certain sum to a designated party, called a *payee*. Banks sometimes provide checkbooks to their members. (*Checkbooks* include check stubs to record deposits, withdrawals, check numbers, dates of transactions, other additions or subtractions, and the account balance.)

a. The copy of a check and check stub in Figure 9-1 shows that check number 2506 was written against the account of Hart Furniture Co. on September 24 to Ace Auto Repair for $124.35 for repairs to the delivery truck. The stub shows a balance brought forward ("Bal Bro't Fwd") of $1,332.80, a deposit on September 24 of $1,160.49, the amount of this check, and a balance carried forward ("Bal Car'd Fwd") of $2,368.94.

FIGURE 9-1   Check and Check Stub

No. 2506 $ 124.35		Hart Furniture Co.	No. 2506

No. 2506 $ 124.35
September 24   19 --
To Ace Auto Repair
For Delivery truck

	$	¢
Balance Bro't Fwd	1,332	80
Amount Deposited	1,160	49
Total	2,493	29
Amount This check	124	35
Balance Car'd Fwd	2,368	94

Hart Furniture Co.
1039 Broadway
Houston, TX 77079-3035

No. 2506

September 24   19 --   35-6686 / 3130

Pay to the order of Ace Auto Repair $ 124.35

One hundred twenty-four and 35/100   DOLLARS

For Classroom Use Only

★HOUSTON STATE BANK

For Delivery truck repair   Robert S. Hart

⑆31306686⑆ 506" 117"020"8

Figure 9-2 illustrates the *check register*, which, like the check stub, provides a place for recording important information about each transaction.

FIGURE 9-2   Check Register

CHECK REGISTER		DEDUCT ALL PER CHECK OR SERVICE CHARGES THAT APPLY			BALANCE
DATE	CHECK NUMBER	CHECKS ISSUED TO OR DEPOSITS RECEIVED FROM	AMOUNT OF CHECK	AMOUNT OF DEPOSIT	$1,332.80
Sept 24		Deposit cash receipts		1,160.49	2,493.29
24	2506	Ace Auto Repair	124.35		2,368.94
24	2507	Morton Window Decorators	450.00		1,918.94
24	2508	Donation to Guide Dogs	100.00		1,818.94
25	2509	Secure Alarm Systems	150.00		1,668.94
Oct 19	2517	Best Janitorial Service	325.00		855.94
20		Deposit cash receipts		980.00	1,835.94

RECONCILIATION OF A BANK STATEMENT

A depositor receives a *statement of account*, or *bank statement*, from the bank at regular intervals, usually once a month. This statement shows an opening balance, all deposits and credits, all checks paid, withdrawals recorded, bank service charges, general information about the account, and the balance at the end of the period. (See figure 9-3 on page 100.)

b. The October 20 statement sent to Hart Furniture Co. by the bank is shown in Figure 9-3. To check for possible errors, the bookkeeper compares the check stubs or check register for Hart Furniture Co. with the bank statement. Such a comparison is called a *reconciliation of the bank balance*.

FIGURE 9-3   Bank Statement

HOUSTON STATE BANK

★HOUSTON
STATE
BANK

HART FURNITURE CO.
1039 BROADWAY
HOUSTON, TX 77079-3035

THIS STATEMENT COVERS: 9/21/9- THROUGH 10/20/9-

SUMMARY

PREVIOUS BALANCE	$1,332.80
DEPOSITS	1,160.49
WITHDRAWALS	1,081.23
INTEREST	6.30
SERVICE CHARGES	13.00
NEW BALANCE	$1,405.36

CHECKS AND WITHDRAWALS	CHECK	DATE PAID	AMOUNT
	2506	9/26	124.35
	2507	9/26	450.00
	2508	9/26	100.00
	2509	9/27	150.00
	2510	10/03	50.00
	2511	10/10	132.50
	2512	10/20	74.38

DEPOSITS	CUSTOMER DEPOSIT	DATE POSTED	AMOUNT
	CUSTOMER DEPOSIT	9/25	1,160.49

YOUR HOUSTON STATE BANK STATEMENT

NOTE: The date shown on the check stub or check register is usually earlier than the date the check or deposit is posted on the bank statement. The date on this statement is the date the transaction was processed by the bank. (See Figure 9-3.)

The balance shown in the checkbook (stub or register) is usually different from the balance on the bank statement. Reasons for the difference are as follows:

Outstanding checks—Some checks may have been written and recorded by the depositor, but they have not yet been presented to the bank for payment and charged to the depositor's account.

Bank charges to the depositor—The depositor may have been charged for service fees, for printing checks, for automatic transfers to a savings account, for bad checks returned, or for other services. The depositor would not know the amounts of these charges until the bank statement arrived. Therefore, these charges would not yet be deducted from the checkbook balance by the depositor.

Credits to depositor's account—The bank may have credited the depositor's account for an item, such as interest on a checking account. The depositor would not know the amount of this credit until the bank statement arrived. Therefore, this deposit would not yet be entered on the depositor's check stubs or register.

Outstanding deposits—A deposit made near the end of the statement period may have been recorded by the depositor in the check register, but not yet recorded by the bank and credited to the depositor's account.

NOTE: On the back of most bank statements is a printed form that can be used to reconcile your checkbook and statement balances.

Steps to Reconcile the Bank Balance

1. Determine the *adjusted bank statement balance*:
   a. Starting with the balance on the bank statement, add any deposits not yet recorded by the bank.
   b. Compare the checks cashed and listed on the bank statement with the checks written; list and total the checks still outstanding and subtract these from the total in Step 1a.
2. Determine the *adjusted checkbook balance*:
   a. Starting with the balance from the last check stub or check register entry, subtract any charges made by the bank, such as service charges or returned-check charges, that have not already been subtracted in the checkbook.
   b. Add to the difference calculated in Step 2a any bank statement credits, such as interest earned, that have not been recorded in the checkbook.
3. Compare the adjusted bank balance and the adjusted checkbook balance calculated in Steps 1 and 2. These two should agree (thus the balance is "reconciled"). If they do not, an error has been made by the bank or the depositor.

---

c. When Hart Furniture Co. received the monthly bank statement, the bookkeeper noted that the ending balance was $1,405.36, but the balance in the company checkbook was $1,835.94. The bookkeeper noted the following differences: a service charge of $13.00 had been subtracted from the bank account; interest of $6.30 had been added to and deposited in the company account by the bank; an October 20 deposit of $980.00 had not yet been recorded on the bank statement; and the checks listed below had not yet reached the bank.

Check Number	Amount
2513	$ 27.92
2514	10.00
2515	48.95
2516	144.25
2517	325.00

Taking these items into account, the bookkeeper prepared the following reconciliation statement:

HART FURNITURE CO.
Reconciliation of Bank Statement
October 30, 19—

Bank balance on statement	$1,405.36
Plus deposit not recorded by bank	980.00
	$2,385.36

Minus outstanding checks:

#2513	=	$ 27.92
#2514	=	10.00
#2515	=	48.95
#2516	=	144.25
#2517	=	325.00 . . . .

	556.12
Adjusted bank balance	$1,829.24
Checkbook balance	$1,835.94
Minus unrecorded bank charges	13.00
	$1,822.94
Plus bank interest	6.30
Adjusted checkbook balance	$1,829.24

COMPLETE ASSIGNMENTS 9-1, 9-2, AND 9-3

Chapter terms for review

adjusted bank statement balance
adjusted checkbook balance
bank statement (statement of
  account)
check register

checkbooks
checks
payee
reconciliation of the bank balance

Assignment 9-1: Check Register and Check Stubs

A (20 points) — In the check register below, fill in the cash balance resulting from each transaction (2 points for each correct answer).

CHECK REGISTER			DEDUCT ALL PER CHECK OR SERVICE CHARGES THAT APPLY			BALANCE
DATE		CHECK NUMBER	CHECKS ISSUED TO OR DEPOSITS RECEIVED FROM	AMOUNT OF CHECK	AMOUNT OF DEPOSIT	$ 980.00
Apr 04		842	Central Mortgage Company	775.00		
04		—	Deposit weekly cash receipts		3,987.50	
05		843	Internal Revenue Service	1,743.00		
06		844	State Income Tax	990.00		
07		845	Olympic Telephone	45.00		
08		846	Cash Register Repair Service	72.00		
12		—	Deposit weekly cash receipts		2,995.75	
12		847	Central Utilities	87.00		
12		848	Central Advertising, Inc.	850.00		
12		849	Tax Services, Inc.	425.00		

Score for A (20)

B (30 points) — Fill in the total and balances on the check stubs, carrying each balance forward to the next numbered check stub (10 points for each correct stub balance).

No. 1 $ 65.00
May 1   19--
To Citizens News
For Advertising

	$	¢
Balance Bro't Fwd	890	00
Amount Deposited		
Total		
Amount This check	65	00
Balance Car'd Fwd		

No. 2 $ 79.00
May 4   19--
To District Utilities
For Gas + electric

	$	¢
Balance Bro't Fwd		
Amount Deposited		
Total		
Amount This check	79	00
Balance Car'd Fwd		

No. 3 $ 25.00
May 5   19--
To U.S. Postal Service
For Stamps

	$	¢
Balance Bro't Fwd		
Amount Deposited	100	00
Total		
Amount This check	25	00
Balance Car'd Fwd		

Score for B (30)

C (20 points) — According to the check register of the Centerville Advertising Company, the cash balance on July 22 was $1,072.16. During the remainder of the month, deposits were made of $129.67, $681.10, and $100.50. Checks were recorded for the following amounts: $98.99, $307.53, $19.56, $212.40, $4.77, and $88.62. (15 points for a correct answer in a., and 5 points for a correct answer in b.)

1. What was the cash balance shown in the check register on July 31?

_____

2. After entering all of the items in the check register, the bookkeeper found that the check recorded as $212.40 was actually written $224.20. What should be the correct cash balance?

_____

D (30 points) — The following problems show the deposits and checks that were recorded on a series of check stubs. In each problem, find the bank balance after each deposit or check (2 points for each correct answer).

3.

Balance	$4,300	00
Check #1	279	10
Balance		
Check #2	148	20
Balance		
Deposit	976	80
Balance		
Check #3	814	00
Balance		
Check #4	285	17
Balance		

4.

Balance	$ 205	55
Check #21	25	00
Balance		
Deposit	876	43
Balance		
Check #22	188	14
Balance		
Check #23	314	82
Balance		
Check #24	72	38
Balance		

5.

Balance	$1,401	36
Deposit	277	00
Balance		
Check #31	136	41
Balance		
Check #32	364	18
Balance		
Deposit	1,124	85
Balance		
Check #33	775	10
Balance		

Assignment 9-2: Check Stubs and Bank Statements

A **(40 points)—Solve the following problems (points for correct answers are marked).**

1. On October 31, the balance of the account of Toyland, Inc. at the Citizens Bank was $922.10. This amount was also the balance on the check register at that time. Company checks written and deposits made during November are shown on the check register. Fill in the cash balance for each transaction (22 points; 2 points for each correct transaction).

CHECK REGISTER			DEDUCT ALL PER CHECK OR SERVICE CHARGES THAT APPLY			BALANCE
DATE		CHECK NUMBER	CHECKS ISSUED TO OR DEPOSITS RECEIVED FROM	AMOUNT OF CHECK	AMOUNT OF DEPOSIT	$922.10
Nov	01	551	Muni. Water, Inc. (2 mos)	119.60		
	06	552	Columbia Gas	49.60		
	07	553	Olympia Telephone	74.19		
	07	—	Deposit cash receipts		225.50	
	21	554	City Trash Disposal (3 mos)	112.32		
	21	555	Jack's Janitorial Service	33.33		
	24	556	United Fund	12.00		
	24	557	Guide Dogs for the Blind	67.77		
	26	558	Wilson Insurance	212.00		
	28	559	Security Systems, Inc.	138.00		
	28	—	Deposit cash receipts		94.00	

2. On December 3, Toyland, Inc., whose check register you completed in Problem 1, received the bank statement shown below. Reconcile the balance on the check register at the end of the month with the final balance on the bank statement. In reconciling the bank statement, you can find which of the checks are outstanding by comparing the list of checks on the statement with the register. Interest and a service charge were recorded on the statement (18 points).

CITIZEN'S BANK

STATEMENT OF ACCOUNT

TOYLAND, INC.
4617 GILMORE ROAD
WHEATLAND, WI 54828-6075

ACCOUNT NUMBER
072 4736

11/30/--

DATE OF STATEMENT

Balance From Previous Statement	Number of Debits	Amount of Checks and Debits	No. of Credits	Amount of Deposits and Credits	Service Charge	Statement Balance
922.10	8	594.81	2	229.70	9.00	547.99

DATE	CHECKS DEBITS		CHECKS DEBITS	DEPOSITS CREDITS	BALANCE
11/03	119.60				802.50
11/05	49.60				752.90
11/09	9.00 SC				743.90
11/09	74.19				669.71
11/09				225.50 ATM	895.21
11/23	112.32		33.33		749.56
11/26	67.77				681.79
11/30	138.00				543.79
11/30				4.20 INT	547.99

PLEASE EXAMINE AND REPORT ANY DISCREPANCIES WITHIN 10 DAYS   DM – Debit Memo ATM – Automated Teller CM – Credit Memo
OD – Overdraft   INT – Interest Paid   SC – Service Charge

Score for A (40)

B (60 points)—Solve the following problems (12 points for each correct answer).

3. Compute the reconciled balance for each of the problems from the information given.

	Bank Statement Balance	Checkbook Balance	Other Information	Reconciled Balance
a.	$ 956.15	$ 974.30	Outstanding checks, $8.75; $29.10 Automatic transfer to savings, $50.00	_____
b.	$1,559.39	$1,617.94	Automatic charge, safety deposit box, $6.00 Outstanding checks, $84.62; $14.20; $55.00 Outstanding deposit, $224.70	_____
c.	$ 893.17	$1,007.13	Automatic transfer to savings, $25.00 Bank interest credited, $37.33 Outstanding checks, $7.50; $4.18 Outstanding deposits, $12.32; $120.00	_____
d.	$ 984.32	$ 944.39	Bank interest credited, $24.18 Charge for printing new checks, $17.50 Outstanding check, $42.00	_____
e.	$ 797.65	$1,259.83	Deposit of $76.89 shown in check register as $78.96 Outstanding checks, $150.00; $37.82 Outstanding deposit, $325.00 Deposit of $325.00 shown twice in check register	_____

Assignment 9-3: Reconciliation Statement

A (30 points) — Using the data provided, prepare a bank reconciliation statement in each of the following problems. Space is provided for your solutions (15 points for each correct reconciliation).

1. The balance shown in the bank statement of Central Heating, Inc., on November 13, 19—, was $1,132.46. The balance shown on the check register was $896.91. The following checks were outstanding:

No. 148 ...... $ 26.62
No. 156 ...... 100.16
No. 161 ...... 77.17
No. 165 ...... 29.10

There was a bank interest credit of $12.00 and a service charge of $9.50 that had not been entered on Central Heating, Inc.'s check register.

2. This month's bank statement balance for Franklin Chemical Company shows that a customer's bad check in the amount of $960 was returned and charged against the Franklin Chemical Company's account by the bank. This is the first knowledge Franklin Chemical Company has that one of the checks deposited was no good.

The balance shown on the bank statement of the Franklin Chemical Company on June 30, 19—, was $22,367.14. The balance shown on the check register was $24,696.83. The following checks were outstanding:

No. 336 ...... $1,066.20
No. 387 ...... 972.81
No. 395 ...... 2,389.60
No. 396 ...... $544.14
No. 397 ...... 383.26

The following items required adjustment on the bank reconciliation statement:

a. Outstanding deposit $3,001.87
b. Automatic transfer to note payment 4,000.00
c. Bad check returned and charged to Franklin Chemical Company's account by the bank 960.00
d. Bank interest credit 276.17

B (40 points) — Using the data provided, prepare a bank reconciliation statement in each of the following problems. Space is provided for your solutions (20 points for each correct reconciliation).

3. The balance shown on the bank statement of Davis and Davis, Inc., July 31, 19—, was $17,464.54. The balance shown by the check register was $17,940.44. A deposit of $2,004.35 had not been credited by the bank. The following checks were outstanding:

No. 730	$ 78.60
No. 749	2,765.23
No. 753	556.25
No. 757	271.84
No. 761	97.73
No. 768	958.60

The following items require adjustment on the bank reconciliation statement:

a. Charge for printing checks	$ 18.00
b. Interest on bank account credited by the bank.	83.20
c. Check deposited by Davis and Davis, Inc., returned to bank as bad check	1,500.00
d. Automatic insurance payment charged to depositor's account by the bank	1,765.00

4. The balance shown on the bank statement of Melody Music, Inc. on March 31, 19—, was $9,686.56. The balance shown on the check register was $6,855.74. The following checks were outstanding:

No. 1243	.....	$ 640.70
No. 1258	.....	1,225.20
No. 1267	.....	87.30
No. 1268	.....	221.12
No. 1270	.....	143.90
No. 1272	.....	462.70

The following items were listed on the bank statement:

a. Charge made by the bank for safety deposit box . . . . $ 13.86

b. Harris Realty Co.'s check incorrectly charged to the account of Melody Music, Inc. by the bank 65.00

c. Interest on bank account credited by the bank 128.76

Score for B (40)

C (30 points)—Solve the following problems (points for correct answers as marked).

5. Johnson Hardware Company has just received the monthly bank statement. The statement alerts the customer to outstanding checks by placing an asterisk beside any check number that is not in exact sequence. Midtown Bank provides a bank reconciliation form on the back of each monthly statement, as do most banks. The check register for Johnson Hardware Company is shown below.

a. Determine the adjusted balance on the check register (10 points).

CHECK REGISTER			DEDUCT ALL PER CHECK OR SERVICE CHARGES THAT APPLY			BALANCE
DATE		CHECK NUMBER	CHECKS ISSUED TO OR DEPOSITS RECEIVED FROM	AMOUNT OF CHECK	AMOUNT OF DEPOSIT	$304.36
Mar	27	123	Replenish petty cash	$ 20.00		284.36
	31	124	Jiffy Janitorial Service	100.00		184.36
Apr	01	125	Sun County Water District	132.50		51.86
	03	—	Deposit weekly receipts		$2,470.80	2,522.66
	03	126	Midtown Mortgage Co.	475.00		2,047.66
	03	127	Sun Gas and Electric Co.	48.32		1,999.34
	04	128	Midtown Weekly Advertiser	29.80		1,969.54
	04	129	Trash Disposal, Inc.	60.00		1,909.54
	04	130	Pacific Plumbing Supplies	1,743.00		166.54
	10	—	Deposit weekly receipts		2,942.50	3,109.04
	10	131	Western Tool Supplies, Inc.	1,947.00		1,162.04
	12	132	Ace Advertising Company	183.00		979.04
	15	—	Deposit weekly receipts		2,687.35	3,666.39
	15	133	Jiffy Janitorial Services	100.00		3,566.39
	15	134	Salary – John R. Johnson	1,500.00		2,066.39
	15	135	Salary – Mary L. Johnson	1,500.00		566.39
	24	—	Deposit weekly receipts		2,010.29	2,576.68

b. Use the bank reconciliation form (which usually appears on the back of the bank statement) provided on the following page to figure the adjusted bank balance. The adjusted balances on the check register and the bank statement should be the same (20 points).

3782-946130

MIDTOWN BANK

MIDTOWN
B A N K

JOHNSON HARDWARE COMPANY
346 POPLAR STREET
MIDTOWN, CA 94872

THIS STATEMENT COVERS: 3/27/9- THROUGH 4/25/9-

SUMMARY
PREVIOUS BALANCE $ 304.36
DEPOSITS   8,100.65+
WITHDRAWALS   7,546.12-
INTEREST   5.60+
SERVICE CHARGES   7.00-

NEW BALANCE $ 857.49

CHECKS AND WITHDRAWALS	CHECK	DATE PAID	AMOUNT	CHECK	DATE PAID	AMOUNT
	123	3/29	20.00	130*	4/06	1,743.00
	124	4/02	100.00	131	4/12	1,947.00
	126*	4/03	475.00	132	4/14	183.00
	127	4/05	48.32	134*	4/17	1,500.00
	128	4/05	29.80	135	4/17	1,500.00

DEPOSITS	CUSTOMER DEPOSIT	DATE POSTED	AMOUNT
	CUSTOMER DEPOSIT	4/05	2,470.80
	CUSTOMER DEPOSIT	4/12	2,942.50
	CUSTOMER DEPOSIT	4/19	2,687.35

Y O U R   M I D T O W N   B A N K   S T A T E M E N T

THIS WORKSHEET IS PROVIDED TO HELP YOU BALANCE YOUR ACCOUNT

1. Go through your register and mark each check, withdrawal, payment, deposit, or other credit listed on this statement. Be sure that your register shows any interest paid into your account and any service or other charges withdrawn from your account during this statement period.

2. ENTER the New Balance shown on this statement. .... $ |

3. ADD any deposits listed in your register that are not shown on this statement.

   _____
   _____
   _____
   Total _____ .... $ |

4. CALCULATE THE SUBTOTAL. .... $ |

5. Using the chart below, list any outstanding check or other withdrawals (including any from previous months) that are listed in your register but are not shown on this statement. SUBTRACT the total outstanding checks.

Number	Amount
_____	_____
_____	_____
_____	_____
_____	_____
Total _____	.... $

6. CALCULATE THE ENDING BALANCE. This amount should be the same as the current balance shown in your check register. .... $ |

Score for C (30)

Chapter 10
Percents in Business

OBJECTIVES
After completing this chapter, you should be able to:

- Change among percents, fractions, and decimals
- Find base, rate, and percentage
- Understand the use of percentages in business
- Allocate overhead costs

Percents are used often in business. For example, payment for the use of money, called *interest*, is expressed as a percent: "The interest rate is 10%." Special discounts may be given for large purchases or for early payment of debt. Commonly, these discounts are calculated as a percentage of the retail price or of the debt amount. A real estate agent may be paid a commission that is a percentage of the selling price of the property. Sales taxes, income taxes, and property taxes are calculated using percents. Percentages also are used to help owners and managers analyze how well a company has performed this year as compared to the previous year's results.

PERCENTS, FRACTIONS, AND DECIMALS

A *percent* is a number equal to a fraction whose denominator is 100. For example, 15 percent = 15% = $\frac{15}{100}$ = 0.15. It is helpful to understand how to change among percents, fractions, and decimals.

Steps to Change a Decimal Into a Percent

1. Move the decimal point two places to the right (add zeros if needed).
2. Write a percent sign at the right end of the new number.

a.

Step 1	Step 2		Step 1	Step 2		Step 1	Step 2
$0.75 \rightarrow 0.75.$	$= 75\%$		$0.005 \rightarrow 0.00.5$	$= 0.5\%$		$0.3 \rightarrow 0.30.$	$= 30\%$

Use the same rule if the number is a mixed decimal or a whole number.

b.

Step 1	Step 2		Step 1	Step 2		Step 1	Step 2
$2.375 \rightarrow 2.37.5$	$= 237.5\%$		$3.5 \rightarrow 3.50.$	$= 350\%$		$4 \rightarrow 4.00.$	$= 400\%$

1. Change the fraction to a decimal.
2. Move the decimal point two places to the right.
3. Write a percent sign at the right end of the new number.

c.
$$\frac{2}{5} = \overset{\text{Step 1}}{0.4} \to \overset{\text{Step 2}}{0.40.} = \overset{\text{Step 3}}{40\%} \qquad 2\frac{5}{8} = \overset{\text{Step 1}}{2.625} \to \overset{\text{Step 2}}{2.62.5} = \overset{\text{Step 3}}{262.5\%}$$

Steps to Change a Percent Into a Decimal

1. Delete the percent sign.
2. Move the decimal point two places to the left (insert zeros if needed).

d.
$$35\% \to \overset{\text{Step 1}}{35} \to \overset{\text{Step 2}}{.35.} = 0.35 \qquad 1.5\% \to \overset{\text{Step 1}}{1.5} \to \overset{\text{Step 2}}{.01.5} = 0.015 \qquad 200\% \to \overset{\text{Step 1}}{200} \to \overset{\text{Step 2}}{2.00.} = 2$$

Steps to Change a Percent Containing a Fraction Into a Decimal

1. Convert the fraction in the percent to its decimal equivalent.
2. Drop the percent sign.
3. Move the decimal point two places to the left.

e.
$$\frac{1}{2}\% = \overset{\text{Step 1}}{0.5\%} \to \overset{\text{Step 2}}{0.5} \to \overset{\text{Step 3}}{.00.5} = 0.005 \qquad 2\frac{3}{4}\% = \overset{\text{Step 1}}{2.75\%} \to \overset{\text{Step 2}}{2.75} \to \overset{\text{Step 3}}{.02.75} = 0.0275$$

BASE, RATE, AND PERCENTAGE

In percentage problems, there are always three elements: the Rate (R), the Base (B) amount, and the Percentage (P) amount. The *Rate* is the percent (%). The *Base* is the whole quantity or 100% of an amount. The *Percentage* is a portion of the Base. Thus, both B and P are always the *same* type of measurement unit. For example, both will be dollars, both will be feet, or both will be pounds, etc.

f. 80% of $5 = $4   25% of 12 ft. = 3 ft.   50% of 40 lb. = 20 lb.

80% is the Rate   25% is the Rate   50% is the Rate
$5 is the Base   12 ft. is the Base   40 lb. is the Base
$4 is the Percentage   3 ft. is the Percentage   20 lb. is the Percentage

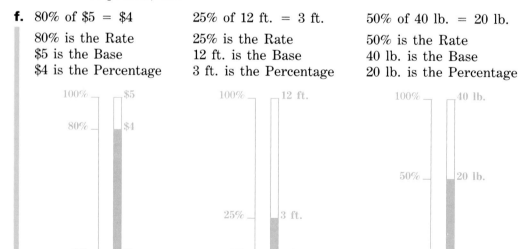

80% of $5 is $4   25% of 12 ft. is 3 ft.   50% of 40 lb. is 20 lb.

The word "of" appears in almost every percentage problem (notice the previous examples). "*Of*" means "multiply" when it is preceded by the Rate and followed by the Base. The fundamental formula for calculating the Percentage is:

Rate times Base equals Percentage   or   R × B = P

Using this formula, the previous examples could be written as shown below.

80% of \$5 = \$4	25% of 12 ft. = 3 ft.	50% of 40 lb. = 20 lb.
R × B = P	R × B = P	R × B = P
80% × \$5 = \$4	25% × 12 ft. = 3 ft.	50% × 40 lb. = 20 lb.
0.80 × \$5 = \$4	0.25 × 12 ft. = 3 ft.	0.50 × 40 lb. = 20 lb.

Solving for P, or B, or R

Rule: When any two elements are known, you can solve for the third element. The table below will help you calculate the missing amount or percent.

To find	You must know	Use this formula
P	R and B	R × B = P
R	P and B	P ÷ B = R
B	P and R	P ÷ R = B

g. Find P, when

R = 50% and B = 200 qt.

Find R, when

B = \$50 and P = \$10

Find B, when

P = 60 yd. and R = 75%

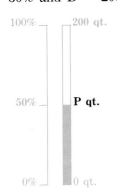

50% of 200 qt. is P qt.

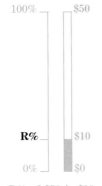

R% of \$50 is \$10

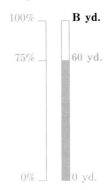

75% of B yd. is 60 yd.

R × B = P	P ÷ B = R	P ÷ R = B
50% × 200 qt. = P	\$10 ÷ \$50 = R	60 yd. ÷ 75% = B
0.5 × 200 qt. = P	0.20 = R	60 yd. ÷ 0.75 = B
100 qt. = P	or 20% = R	80 yd. = B

h. Write the three examples above using the word "of."

50% of 200 qt. = P   R(%) of \$50 = \$10   4% of B yd. = 60 yd.

COMPLETE ASSIGNMENT 10-1

The following examples illustrate some of the business situations in which percent calculations are important. These also provide you with additional word problems to study.

i. James Smythe is a secretary. In December he received a $150 bonus. $150 was 10% of his monthly salary. What was his monthly salary?

P = amount of bonus = $150; R = rate of bonus = 10%; B = monthly salary = ?

B = P ÷ R = $150 ÷ 10% = $150 ÷ 0.10 = $1,500 monthly salary

j. Last year Warner Video Store had total expenses of $250,000. $150,000 of that total was the expense for employee salaries. At Warner, employee salary expense is what percent of total expenses?

P = employee salaries = $150,000; R = ?; B = total expenses = $250,000
R = P ÷ B = $150,000 ÷ $250,000 = 0.60 = 60%

Rate of Increase and Rate of Decrease

Business applications using percents often measure changes (increases or decreases) from a base value. "10% more" means a "10% increase;" "10% less" or "10% fewer" means a "10% decrease." The 10% is called the *rate (percent) of increase* or the *rate (percent) of decrease*.

Steps to Determine the New Value after an Increase or Decrease

1. Calculate the *amount of increase* (or *amount of decrease*). Multiply the rate of increase (or decrease) times the base amount.
2. Depending on the type of calculation, do one of the following steps:
   a. For an increase, add the amount of change (from Step 1) to the base amount.
   b. For a decrease, subtract the amount of change (from Step 1) from the base amount.

---

k. Lorance Construction Company built 20% more homes this year than it did last year (i.e., it had a 20% increase). Lorance built 120 homes last year. How many did it build this year?

Step 1   P = B × R = 120 × 20% = 24 more homes this year
Step 2a   120 homes + 24 increase = 144 homes built this year

l. This year Thrift Builders had a 10% decrease in number of homes built (i.e., this year it built 10% fewer homes than last year). Last year Thrift built 150 homes. How many did it build this year?

Step 1   P = B × R = 150 × 10% = 15 fewer homes built this year
Step 2b   150 homes − 15 decrease = 135 homes built this year

Finding the Rate of Increase or Decrease

The amount in the first year (or month) is the *base value*. To find the rate of change (increase or decrease), compare the base value and the later value and follow the steps described on the next page.

1. Subtract one value from the other to find the amount of change.
2. Divide the amount of the change by the base value.

m. In August, Kingsley and Rigik each used 30 gallons of paint. In July, Kingsley had used 40 gallons and Rigik had used 20 gallons. What are the rates of change for Kingsley and Rigik during August?

Kingsley: Step 1   40 gal. (July) − 30 gal. (Aug.)
             = 10 gal. decrease in August
        Step 2   10 gal. decrease ÷ 40 gal. (July)
             = 0.25 or 25% decrease in August

Rigik: Step 1   30 gal. (Aug.) − 20 gal. (July)
             = 10 gal. increase in August
        Step 2   10 gal. increase ÷ 20 gal. (July)
             = 0.50 or 50% increase in August

COMPLETE ASSIGNMENTS 10-2 AND 10-3

DISTRIBUTION OF OVERHEAD COSTS

Many businesses are separated into departments or divisions. It is helpful to the owners and management of a company to assign costs in order to measure the profitability of each department/division. Some costs are directly related to the department/division. For example, Burke's Clothing Store has a children's department, a women's department, and a men's department. The store records the revenue that it earns from the sales in each department. It is easy to assign the cost it paid for each item sold to the appropriate department.

More general costs, such as rent, electricity, and insurance, are not directly related to sales merchandise. These are called *overhead costs*. For example, Burke's monthly rental cost is $6,000 for the entire building. How can that single amount be allocated to each department? Should each of the departments be assigned $\frac{1}{3}$, or $2,000, of the total cost?

Most businesses *allocate*, or distribute, the rent based on a measurement that is related to the total cost. Since rent is a cost of using the building, it could be allocated on the basis of floor space since each department occupies some of that space.

Steps to Allocate an Overhead Cost Based on Total Floor Space (or Some Other Measurement)

1. Find the total square feet of floor space.
2. Divide the floor space of each department by the total floor space and change to percents.
3. Multiply each percent times the total rent (or other overhead value).

n. This is the amount of rent to allocate to the respective departments.

Department	Step 1 Floor Space	Step 2 Percent of Total	Step 3 Distribution of Rent
Children's	25 × 20 = 500 sq. ft.	500 ÷ 2,500 = 20%	$6,000 × 20% = $1,200
Women's	25 × 50 = 1,250 sq. ft.	1,250 ÷ 2,500 = 50%	6,000 × 50% = 3,000
Men's	25 × 30 = 750 sq. ft.	750 ÷ 2,500 = 30%	6,000 × 30% = 1,800
Total	2,500 sq. ft.	100%	$6,000

This same method is used for many other business expenses, such as utilities, fire insurance, salaries of office personnel, etc. Examples of other bases that may be used for allocation are number of employees, hours worked, and units produced.

COMPLETE ASSIGNMENT 10-4

Chapter terms for review

allocate	overhead costs
amount of decrease	percent
amount of increase	Percentage (P)
Base (B)	rate of decrease
base value	rate of increase
interest	Rate (R)
of	

Assignment 10-1: Base, Rate, and Percentage

A (20 points) — Change the percents to decimals, fractions, or whole numbers. Change the decimals, fractions, or whole numbers to percents (1 point for each correct answer).

1. 12% = _____

2. 100% = _____

3. $3\frac{1}{3}\% =$ _____

4. 0.96 = _____

5. 250% = _____

6. $0.16\frac{2}{3} =$ _____

7. 0.03 = _____

8. 0.3 = _____

9. $1\frac{1}{2} =$ _____

10. 21% = _____

11. 3.0 = _____

12. 0.000075 = _____

13. 3.2% = _____

14. 475.5% = _____

15. 0.0004% = _____

16. 0.375 = _____

17. 7 = _____

18. $33\frac{1}{3}\% =$ _____

19. 0.5% = _____

20. 1,000% = _____

Score for A (20)

B (30 points) — Solve each of the following problems for the Percentage (2 points for each correct answer).

21. 6% of 120 = _____

22. 15% of 0.06 = _____

23. 50% of 284 = _____

24. 25% of 0.72 = _____

25. 250% of $24 = _____

26. 62.5% of 16 = _____

27. 1.5% of $96 = _____

28. 0.5% of 560 = _____

29. 262.5% of 16 = _____

30. 0.25% of 1,200 = _____

31. 100% of 17.19 = _____

32. 0.375% of 96 = _____

33. 120% of $42 = _____ **34.** 7.5% of $200 = _____ **35.** 75% of $0.08 = _____

C (50 points) — Solve each of the following for the Percentage, the Rate, or the Base. Round dollars and percents to the nearest two decimal places, where necessary (2 points for each correct answer).

36. 37.5% of _____ = 15 **37.** 250% of _____ = 14.4

38. 0.25% of _____ = 30 **39.** 2.5% of $2,460 = _____

40. 80% of _____ = $0.12 **41.** _____ of 625 = 12.5

42. 100% of _____ = 21.47 **43.** 0.025% of $12,800 = _____

44. 150% of _____ = $36 **45.** _____ of 0.048 = 0.012

46. _____ of $24 = $4.80 **47.** $33\frac{1}{3}$% of _____ = 38

48. _____ of 150 = 120 **49.** 120% of $91 = _____

50. _____ of 0.72 = 0.036 **51.** 120% of _____ = $39

52. _____ of 26.9 = 26.9 **53.** _____ of 0.12 = 0.48

54. _____ of 120 = 150 **55.** 0.75% of _____ = 1.8

56. 19% of $210 = _____ **57.** _____ of $46,800 = $2,340

58. 18% of _____ = 2.7 **59.** 175% of _____ = $560

60. _____ of 2.1 = 0.336

Part Three   Banking and Payroll Applications

Assignment 10-2:   Rate of Increase and Rate of Decrease

A   (40 points) — Calculate the missing value (2½ points for each correct answer).

1. Base value = 65; increase = 20%; new (final) value = _____

2. Base value = 1,000; decrease = 35%; new (final) value = _____

3. Start with 92; increase by 40%; end up with _____

4. Start with 20; decrease by 12%; end up with _____

5. _____ is 30% greater than 36.

6. _____ is 50% smaller than 120.

7. Increasing the base value 180 by 100% yields the new (final) value _____

8. Decreasing the base value 180 by 100% yields the new (final) value _____

9. Sales were $2,000 last month. There was a 10% increase this month. Sales were _____ this month.

10. Profits were $1,200 last month. There was a 6% decrease this month. Profits were _____ this month.

11. An increase of $18 is 15% of the base value _____

12. A decrease of 40 units is 25% of the base value _____

13. The price decreased from $160 to $120; the percent decrease was _____

14. Production increased from 600 units to 690 units; the percent increase was _____

15. Sales were $2,100 last month and $2,000 the previous month. The rate of increase was _____

16. Profits were $150,000 in June, but only $75,000 in July. The rate of decrease was _____

B (30 points) — The table below shows the volumes of various items sold by Clyde's Automotive during the past two years. Calculate the amount of change and the rate of change between this year and last year. Calculate the rates to the nearest $\frac{1}{10}$ of a percent. Write the amount and the rate in the correct columns (1 point for each correct number; $\frac{1}{2}$ point for each correct column).

CLYDE'S AUTOMOTIVE   VOLUME SOLD (number of units)

	Description of Item	This Year	Last Year	Amount of Increase	Amount of Decrease	Rate of Increase	Rate of Decrease
17.	Batteries	310	250	_____	_____	_____	_____
18.	Headlight lamps	768	1,200	_____	_____	_____	_____
19.	Mufflers	98	80	_____	_____	_____	_____
20.	Shock absorbers	474	440	_____	_____	_____	_____
21.	Tires, Auto	1,105	884	_____	_____	_____	_____
22.	Tires, Truck	440	320	_____	_____	_____	_____
23.	Wiper blades	636	612	_____	_____	_____	_____
24.	Brake fluid (pt.)	155	410	_____	_____	_____	_____
25.	Coolant (gal.)	374	720	_____	_____	_____	_____
26.	Oil (qt.)	3,032	4,202	_____	_____	_____	_____

C (30 points) — During July and August, Norman's Paint Store sold the amounts shown in the table below. Calculate the amount of change and the rate of change between July and August. Calculate the rates of change to the nearest $\frac{1}{10}$ of a percent. If the amount and rate are increases, write a "+" sign in front of them; if they are decreases, then write a "−" sign in front of them (1 point for each correct number; $\frac{1}{2}$ point for each correct sign).

NORMAN'S PAINT STORE   VOLUME SOLD (in dollars)

	Description of Item	August	July	Amount of Change	Rate of Change
27.	Brush, 2″ wide	$ 121.68	$ 116.34	_____	_____
28.	Brush, 3″ wide	228.88	215.19	_____	_____
29.	Brush, 4″ wide	81.28	84.37	_____	_____
30.	Drop cloth, 9 × 12	20.73	21.86	_____	_____
31.	Drop cloth, 12 × 15	47.59	49.77	_____	_____
32.	Paint, latex (gal.)	25,406.24	24,382.19	_____	_____
33.	Paint, latex (qt.)	845.20	864.12	_____	_____
34.	Paint, oil (gal.)	479.16	504.91	_____	_____
35.	Paint, oil (qt.)	1,540.05	1,483.24	_____	_____
36.	Paint scraper	19.66	17.48	_____	_____

Assignment 10-3: Business Applications

A (50 points) — Solve the following problems. Round percents to the nearest $\frac{1}{10}$ of a percent and dollar amounts to the nearest cent (5 points for each correct answer).

1. Harris Equipment Corp. is in a state that has a 4% sales tax. What would be the sales tax on a purchase of $658.42 worth of equipment from Harris Corp.?

   _____

2. Suppose that Harris Corp. (above) pays sales tax of $33.70 on another order. What is the price of just the merchandise?

   _____

3. Jolene Hoover is a salesperson. For every sale that she makes, Jolene is paid 7% of the sale amount (excluding sales tax). (Jolene's pay is called a commission and the 7% is called the commission rate.) What would be Jolene's commission for a month when she makes sales totaling $31,650?

   _____

4. Jolene (above) receives no other pay besides the 7% commission. In one month, her total pay was $2,415. How much were her sales for that month?

   _____

5. Jane Lee is another salesperson who is paid only by commissions. On one sale of $640 worth of merchandise, Jane received a commission of $41.60. What is Jane's commission rate?

   _____

6. George Roggero owns a automobile body repair shop. 83% of his business is paid by insurance companies. In a month George does $168,000 worth of business, how much (in dollars) is NOT paid by insurance companies?

_____

7. Karen Ijichi works for the newspaper and is paid $3,000 per month. Every month money is deducted for taxes, social security, insurance, and credit union savings. If her check is for $1,650, what percent of her salary has been deducted?

_____

8. Robins Department Store employs 27 sales clerks. If 60% of all of Robins' employees are sales clerks, how many persons total does Robins employ?

_____

9. A competing department store, Devlin's, has a sales force that consists of 55% females. If Devlin's employs 22 female sales clerks, how many male sales clerks does it employ?

_____

10. Cain Corp. employs 34 full-time employees and 21 part-time employees. What percent of all Cain Corp. employees are employed part-time?

_____

B **(50 points) — Solve the following problems. Round percents to the nearest $\frac{1}{10}$ of a percent and dollar amounts to the nearest cent (5 points for each correct answer).**

11. Mel's Fish Company sold $248,000 worth of fish this month. If Mel wants to sell 5% more next month, how much will he have to sell?

_____

12. Peterson Plumbing had 4% fewer hours of weekend emergency repairs in April as compared with March. If they had 150 hours of weekend emergency repairs in March, how many hours of weekend emergency repairs did they have in April?

_____

13. Spurgeon Trucking had 128 trucks in 1992 and 144 trucks in 1993. What was the percent increase in Spurgeon's number of trucks between 1992 and 1993?

_____

14. Titus Quality Graphics generates 15% more revenue on its color graphics than it does on black and white graphics. If Titus has $12,800 revenue on black and white graphics, how much revenue does it have on its color graphics?

_____

15. Titus Graphics (above) does work for both businesses and individuals. However, only 15% of Titus's total revenue comes from individuals. If Titus has revenue of $4,275 from individuals, how much revenue do they get from businesses?

_____

16. McCombs Appliance priced a vacuum cleaner at $78.50 during December. In January, they reduce the price by 20%. What is the price in January?

_____

17. Beginning in July, Patnode Pharmacy has to pay 2.5% more for shampoo. If they paid $22.80 a case for shampoo in June, how much do they have to pay in July?

_____

18. In September, the price of a table saw at Larsen's Saw Shop increased from $475 to $525. What is the percent increase?

_____

19. Ellen Blenz saved $28 on a portable telephone because the price was decreased by 25% for a special pre-Christmas promotion at McBride Electronics. What was the original price before the promotion?

_____

20. Because of Valentine's Day, Hazel's Candy Shoppe sold 152 fewer pounds of dark chocolates in March than they did in February. In March they sold 483 pounds of dark chocolates. What is the percent decrease in the sale of dark chocolates between February and March?

_____

Score for B (50)

Assignment 10-4: Distribution of Overhead

A **(20 points) — Complete the square feet, percent, and distribution columns below. Round percents to the nearest whole number (1 point for each correct answer in Column 1; 2 points for each correct answer in Columns 2 and 3).**

1. Silvana's Pasta Co. has stores in four communities: Millington, Eastside, Englewood, and Bunker Hill. The company office, located at Santa Maria, has monthly expenses of $6,000. Silvana distributes the $6,000 among the four shops based on the floor space of each.

		Column 1	Column 2	Column 3
			Percent	*Distribution*
Store	*Space Occupied*	*Square Feet*	*of Total*	*of Expense*
Millington	40 ft. × 60 ft.	_____	_____	_____
Eastside	30 ft. × 40 ft.	_____	_____	_____
Englewood	40 ft. × 45 ft.	_____	_____	_____
Bunker Hill	30 ft. × 70 ft.	_____	_____	_____

Score for A (20)

B **(16 points) — Complete the percent and distribution columns below. Before calculating the distribution, round each percent to the nearest whole number (2 points for each correct answer).**

2. Hackett Landscaping does four basic types of projects: industrial parks, residential, apartment complexes, and city park maintenance. Hackett rents space for offices and his corporate grounds. Total monthly rent is $4,200, and Hackett distributes it among the four project groups according to the number of employees.

	Number of Employees	*Percent of Total*	*Distribution of Rent*
Industrial Parks	12	_____	_____
Residential	9	_____	_____
Apartment Complexes	18	_____	_____
City Parks	21	_____	_____

Score for B (16)

C (64 points) — The following situations provide practice in distributing monthly overhead expenses to each of four locations. From the information given in the table, complete the distributions indicated in Problems 3 through 6 (4 points for each correct answer).

MONTHLY OVERHEAD EXPENSES		BASIS OF DISTRIBUTION	LOCATION				
			Idaho	Iowa	Maine	Ohio	TOTAL
Mgmt Salaries	$15,000	Number of Employees	60	45	90	55	250
Utilities	$ 4,200	Square Feet	12,000	7,200	19,200	9,600	48,000
Insurance	$ 6,000	Machine Hours Worked	11,200	6,400	12,800	9,600	40,000
Advertising	$10,800	Units Produced	15,600	11,400	20,400	12,600	60,000

3. Distribute management salaries based on the number of employees at each location.

Idaho: _____; Iowa: _____; Maine: _____; Ohio: _____

4. Distribute utility expenses based on the number of square feet at each location.

Idaho: _____; Iowa: _____; Maine: _____; Ohio: _____

5. Distribute insurance expenses based on the number of machine hours worked in each location.

Idaho: _____; Iowa: _____; Maine: _____; Ohio: _____

6. Distribute advertising expenses based on the units produced at each location.

Idaho: _____; Iowa: _____; Maine: _____; Ohio: _____

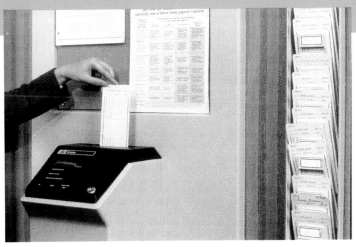

Chapter 11
Payroll Records

OBJECTIVES
After completing this chapter, you should be able to:

- Prepare a weekly payroll report
- Prepare a payroll register
- Calculate FICA and income tax withholding
- Complete an employee's earnings record

All businesses must keep payroll records. The form of the payroll records varies with different businesses. They are more detailed if there are many employee benefits or if employees are paid by the hour. The payroll records in this chapter are typical.

Today, almost all organizations have their payroll records computerized. However, the processes in this chapter are common to all payroll records and need to be understood by anyone working with payroll management.

WEEKLY PAYROLL REPORT

A typical weekly payroll report showing regular and overtime hours is illustrated in Figure 11-1. The total number of hours worked each week is entered in the Total Hours column. Then the number of hours in a regular work week (usually 40) is entered in the Regular Earnings Hours Worked column. Any difference is subtracted and is entered in the Overtime Earnings Hours Worked column.

The base rate per hour is multiplied by the number of regular earnings hours worked, and this amount is entered in the Regular Earnings Amount column. The overtime rate is multiplied by the number of hours in the Overtime Hours Worked column, and the amount is entered in the Overtime Amount column. The sum of the amounts in the Regular and the Overtime Amount columns is entered in the Total Earnings column.

FIGURE 11-1 Weekly Payroll Report

MARTIN PRODUCE FARM
Week Ending March 29, 19--

Name	Total Hours	Regular Earnings				Overtime Earnings			Total Earnings
		Hours Worked	Rate Per Hour	Amount		Hours Worked	Rate Per Hour	Amount	
Allen, H.	48	40	$11.00	$ 440.00		8	$16.50	$132.00	$ 572.00
Garcia, F.	48	40	8.20	328.00		8	12.30	98.40	426.40
Parker, M.	33	33	6.80	224.40		0	10.20	–	224.40
Thomas, R.	46	40	9.40	376.00		6	14.10	84.60	460.60
Weber, J.	20	20	8.20	164.00		0	12.30	–	164.00
TOTALS				**$1,532.40**				**$315.00**	**$1,847.40**

PAYROLL REGISTER

A *payroll register* is a summary of wages earned, payroll deductions, and final take-home pay. Whether done manually or by computer, some form of the register is created and maintained for all employers.

A business firm frequently deducts a series of items from an employee's gross pay. These include such items as federal taxes, state taxes, local taxes, group medical insurance premiums, group dental insurance premiums, charitable contributions, pension benefits, union dues, and others. The employer submits the amounts deducted for these items to the appropriate recipient. All of this is summarized on a register.

The register includes columns to show employee data, gross earnings, deductions, and net pay. The register illustrated in Figure 11-2 shows employee data, gross earnings, various deductions, and net pay for the group of employees included in Figure 11-1.

FIGURE 11-2 Weekly Payroll Register

NAME	MARITAL STATUS	WITHHOLDING ALLOWANCES	W = WEEKLY H = HOURLY	RATE	EARNINGS			DEDUCTIONS							
					REGULAR TIME	OVER TIME	GROSS EARNINGS	FICA	FEDERAL INCOME TAX	GROUP MED. INS.	GROUP DENTAL INS.	OTHER	TOTAL DEDUCTIONS	NET PAY
ALLEN, H	M	4	H	11.00	$ 440.00	$132.00	$ 572.00	$ 43.76	$ 52.40	$13.00	$4.50	$15.00	$128.66	$ 443.34
GARCIA, F	M	2	H	8.20	328.00	98.40	426.40	32.62	42.38			12.00	87.00	339.40
PARKER, M	S	1	H	6.80	224.40		224.40	17.17	24.30				41.47	182.93
THOMAS, R	M	3	H	9.40	376.00	84.60	460.60	35.24	41.60	13.00	4.50	15.00	109.34	351.26
WEBER, J	S	1	H	8.20	164.00		164.00	12.55	15.24			7.50	35.29	128.71
TOTALS					$1,532.40	$315.00	$1,847.40	$141.34	$175.92	$26.00	$9.00	$49.50	$401.76	$1,445.64

PAYROLL COMPUTATIONS: FICA TAX (SOCIAL SECURITY)

Howard Allen, the first employee listed on the payroll register in Figure 11-2, is employed on an hourly basis at the rate of $11 per hour. His base of 40 hours provided regular earnings of $440. He worked overtime and earned an extra $132 for a total of $572.

Howard's first deduction is for Social Security. This tax is identified on payroll records by the abbreviation *FICA* (Federal Insurance Contributions Act).

For FICA, the federal government requires the employer to withhold a certain percentage of each employee's wages up to a maximum fixed by law. Both the percent and the maximum are subject to change, based on legislation by Congress. In the illustrations and problems in this book, 7.65% will be the rate used, and $51,300 will be the maximum yearly earnings on which the tax is paid. Thus, Howard Allen, who had gross earnings of $572 and who has not yet earned the maximum of $51,300 this year, will have 7.65% of $572, or $43.76, deducted for FICA tax. This deduction is based on total wages and is not affected by the employee's marital status or the number of dependents.

a.

$572.00 = gross earnings
× 0.0765 = FICA contribution rate
$ 43.76 = amount of FICA deduction

The 7.65% withheld from the employee's salary is a tax on the employee. In addition, the employer is required to match the employee's percentage. After the employer matches the employee's 7.65%, the employer then sends the total 15.30% to the Internal Revenue Service (IRS). The purpose of the FICA tax is to secure revenue so employees may receive monthly Social Security benefits after they retire.

PAYROLL COMPUTATIONS: FEDERAL INCOME TAX

The federal income tax is another type of payroll tax that the employer is required to withhold from the employee's pay and turn over to the IRS. The amount of the deduction varies with the amount of earnings, the employee's marital status, and the number of withholding allowances claimed.

A withholding allowance is an amount exempted from gross earnings and not subject to federal income tax. Generally, one withholding allowance is taken by the employee, and additional withholding allowances are taken for each of the employee's family dependents. To inform the government of one's marital status and to claim withholding allowances, every employee must fill out a W-4 form. The W-4 form for Howard Allen is shown in Figure 11-3. He gives his marital status and claims four allowances.

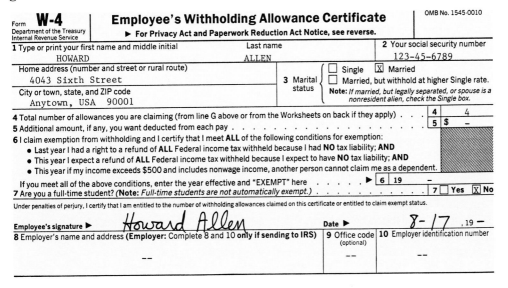

FIGURE 11-3
Employee's Withholding Allowance Certificate (W-4 Form)

The regulations and procedures for computing and withholding FICA and income tax deductions for employees are provided in a booklet published by the IRS. The booklet is entitled "Employer's Tax Guide." A new edition is printed each calendar year.

The "Employer's Tax Guide" gives employers two primary methods to figure how much income tax to withhold from their employees. The two primary methods are the *percentage method* and the *wage-bracket method*.

In Figure 11-2, Howard Allen's federal income tax withholding amount was $52.40. This was computed by the percentage method.

The percentage method starts by granting a deduction for each withholding allowance claimed. The amount for each withholding allowance is provided by the IRS in a table called "Income Tax Withholding Percentage Method Table." A recent table is illustrated below in Figure 11-4. This table shows that for weekly pay, a deduction of $39.42 is allowed for each withholding allowance. It shows that for monthly pay, a deduction of $170.83 is allowed for each withholding allowance.

FIGURE 11-4
Income Tax Withholding Percentage Method Table

Income Tax Withholding — Percentage Method

If you do not want to use the wage bracket tables to figure how much income tax to withhold, you can use a percentage computation based on the table below and the appropriate rate table. This method works for any number of withholding allowances the employee claims.

Percentage Method Income Tax Withholding Table

Payroll Period	One with-holding allowance
Weekly	$39.42
Biweekly	78.85
Semimonthly	85.42
Monthly	170.83
Quarterly	512.50
Semiannually	1,025.00
Annually	2,050.00
Daily or miscellaneous (each day of the payroll period)	7.88

After the total withholding allowance is subtracted from an employee's gross earnings, the amount to be withheld is determined by taking a percentage of the balance. The percentage to be used is given by the IRS in the "Tables for Percentage Method of Withholding." A recent table for weekly and monthly payroll periods is illustrated in Figure 11-5.

Using the two tables in Figures 11-4 and 11-5, the steps listed below can be followed to figure the amount of federal income tax an employer withholds for an employee.

Steps Used to Figure the Amount of Federal Income Tax Withholdings

1. Determine the employee's gross earnings.
2. Multiply the appropriate (weekly-monthly) "one withholding allowance amount" from the "Withholding Table" by the number of allowances the employee claims.
3. Subtract that amount from the employee's gross earnings.
4. Determine the amount to withhold from the appropriate (weekly/ monthly and single/married) "Percentage Method" table.

FIGURE 11-5   Tables for Percentage Method of Withholding

TABLES FOR PERCENTAGE METHOD OF WITHHOLDING

TABLE 1—If the Payroll Period With Respect to an Employee is Weekly

(a) SINGLE person—including head of household:

If the amount of wages (after subtracting withholding allowances) is: The amount of income tax to be withheld shall be:

Not over $23 0

Over—	But not over —		of excess over—
$23	—$397	15%	—$23
$397	—$928	$56.10 plus 28%	—$397
$928	—$2,121	$204.78 plus 33%	—$928
$2,121		$598.47 plus 28%	—$2,121

(b) MARRIED person—

If the amount of wages (after subtracting withholding allowances) is: The amount of income tax to be withheld shall be:

Not over $65 0

Over—	But not over—		of excess over—
$65	—$689	15%	—$65
$689	—$1,573	$93.60 plus 28%	—$689
$1,573	—$3,858	$341.12 plus 33%	—$1,573
$3,858		$1,095.17 plus 28%	—$3,858

TABLE 4—If the Payroll Period With Respect to an Employee is Monthly

(a) SINGLE person—including head of household:

If the amount of wages (after subtracting withholding allowances) is: The amount of income tax to be withheld shall be:

Not over $100 0

Over—	But not over —		of excess over—
$100	—$1,721	15%	—$100
$1,721	—$4,021	$243.15 plus 28%	—$1,721
$4,021	—$9,192	$887.15 plus 33%	—$4,021
$9,192		$2,593.58 plus 28%	—$9,192

(b) MARRIED person—

If the amount of wages (after subtracting withholding allowances) is: The amount of income tax to be withheld shall be:

Not over $283 0

Over—	But not over—		of excess over—
$283	—$2,988	15%	—$283
$2,988	—$6,817	$405.75 plus 28%	—$2,988
$6,817	—$16,718	$1,477.87 plus 33%	—$6,817
$16,718		$4,745.20 plus 28%	—$16,718

b. Using the four steps listed above, Howard Allen's $52.40 withholding is computed as follows:

Step 1 $572.00 = gross earnings from payroll register

Step 2 $ 39.42 = one withholding allowance
         × 4 = withholding allowances claimed
     $157.68 = total allowances claimed

Step 3 $572.00 = gross earnings
    − 157.68 = total allowances claimed
     414.32 = amount subject to withholding

Step 4 $414.32 = amount subject to withholding
    − 65.00 = less "excess" per "married" table
     $349.32 = amount subject to 15% tax
     × 0.15 = 15% computation
     $ 52.40 = amount of tax withheld

The second method of figuring the amount of tax to be withheld from an employee's pay is the "Wage-Bracket Table" method. This method uses a series of wage-bracket tables published by the IRS. The table for married persons paid on a weekly payroll period is illustrated in Figure 11-6.

FIGURE 11-6
A Partial Wage-
Bracket Table

WEEKLY Payroll Period—Employee MARRIED

And the wages are		And the number of withholding allowances claimed is—						
At least	But less than	0	1	2	3	4	5	6
		The amount of income tax to be withheld shall be—						
$0	$70	$0	$0	$0	$0	$0	$0	$0
70	75	1	0	0	0	0	0	0
75	80	2	0	0	0	0	0	0
80	85	3	0	0	0	0	0	0
85	90	3	0	0	0	0	0	0
90	95	4	0	0	0	0	0	0
95	100	5	0	0	0	0	0	0
100	105	6	0	0	0	0	0	0
105	110	6	0	0	0	0	0	0
110	115	7	1	0	0	0	0	0
115	120	8	2	0	0	0	0	0
120	125	9	3	0	0	0	0	0
125	130	9	3	0	0	0	0	0
130	135	10	4	0	0	0	0	0
135	140	11	5	0	0	0	0	0
530	540	70	65	59	53	47	41	35
540	550	72	66	60	54	48	42	36
550	560	73	68	62	56	50	44	38
560	570	75	69	63	57	51	45	39
570	580	76	71	65	59	53	47	41
580	590	78	72	66	60	54	48	42
590	600	79	74	68	62	56	50	44
600	610	81	75	69	63	57	51	45
610	620	82	77	71	65	59	53	47
620	630	84	78	72	66	60	54	48

Using the table from Figure 11-6, we see that an employee earning a weekly wage between $570 and $580 and claiming 4 withholding allowances will be taxed $53. It is important to note that the amount of federal income tax withheld from Howard Allen's pay by using the wage-bracket method is approximately the same amount as by using the percentage method — $53.00 versus $52.40, respectively. The small difference is due to using wage-brackets of $10 amounts and rounding the withholding amount to the nearest dollar.

For illustrations and problems in this book, we consistently use the percentage method.

PAYROLL COMPUTATIONS: MISCELLANEOUS DEDUCTIONS

Most employers today provide some form of group medical insurance for their employees. Frequently, the employee is asked to pay a portion of the premium charged for such insurance. The portion the employee is asked to pay is usually based on the number of dependents the employee has named to be insured. For the payroll register displayed in Figure 11-2, we assumed the following weekly rates for medical and dental plans.

	Weekly Medical Plan Premium Paid by Employee	Weekly Dental Plan Premium Paid by Employee
Employee only	$ 4.00	$1.80
Employee plus 1 dependent	$ 9.00	$3.20
Employee plus 2 or more dependents	$13.00	$4.50

In the payroll register in Figure 11-2, we see that Howard Allen subscribed to both the medical and dental programs. Because of his 3 dependents, the amount of his deductions were $13.00 and $4.50, respectively.

Frequently, employees will arrange to have special payroll deductions made by the employer for the convenience of paying union dues, putting money into special retirement or savings plans, or making contributions to charitable organizations.

The payroll register illustrated in Figure 11-2 reflects a $15 weekly deduction Howard Allen has requested be made for payment of his union dues.

EMPLOYEE'S EARNINGS RECORD

An employer is required to turn over to the federal and state governments the amounts withheld from employees' earnings for taxes and to file certain quarterly and annual tax reports. To obtain this information, most employers keep an *employee's earnings record* for each employee. The Cumulative Total column will indicate when the employee's earnings have reached the FICA taxable wage base ($51,300) for the year (the amount after which FICA tax is no longer deducted from earnings). The employee's earnings record summarizes by quarter the employee's gross earnings, deductions, and net pay.

The employee earnings record in Figure 11-7 shows that Howard Allen is married, claims 4 allowances, and for the first quarter of the year earned total wages of $6,952. His net take-home pay was $5,389.05 after first quarter FICA taxes of $531.88, federal income tax withholdings of $608.57, and "other" deductions of $422.50.

Name Howard Allen   Social Security No. 123-45-6789

Address 4043 Sixth Street   No. of Allowances 4   Marital Status Married

| Period Ending | Total Wages | Cumulative Total | Deductions | | | | Net Pay |
			FICA Tax	Federal Inc. Tax	Other Deductions	Total	
1/4	$ 440.00	$ 440.00	$ 33.66	$ 32.60	$ 32.50	$ 98.76	$ 341.24
1/11	440.00	880.00	33.66	32.60	32.50	98.76	341.24
3/29	572.00	$6,952.00	43.76	52.40	32.50	128.66	443.34
Quarter Total	$6,952.00		$531.83	$608.57	$422.50	$1,562.95	$5,389.05

FIGURE 11-7
Employee Earnings Record

EMPLOYER'S QUARTERLY FEDERAL TAX RETURN

Every employer who withholds federal income tax or FICA tax must file a quarterly return (Form 941) with the IRS within one month after the end of the quarter. The information below shows the data that the employer is required to include for Form 941. The FICA amount is obtained by multiplying the total wages by 0.1530 (employees' 7.65% plus employer's 7.65%).

Total wages subject to withholding	$60,138.12
Total income tax withheld from wages	8,306.14
Total FICA tax paid ($60,138.12 × 0.1530)	9,201.13
Total taxes ($8,306.14 + $9,201.13)	17,507.27
Total deposits for quarter (sent to qualified bank depository)	17,450.00
Undeposited taxes due IRS	57.27

As displayed on page 135, the total taxes due to the IRS consist of $8,306.14 (employees' federal income tax) and $9,201.13 (employees' and employer's share of FICA tax). Although the employer files Form 941 with the IRS quarterly, the amount of the withheld income and FICA taxes, along with the employer's own share of FICA taxes, is usually deposited in a qualified bank depository or a Federal Reserve bank on a monthly basis. The frequency of the deposits depends on the amount of the deposits. Each deposit must be accompanied by a federal tax deposit form. Any undeposited taxes due at the time of filing Form 941 must be paid either directly to the IRS (if less than $500) or deposited in a qualified bank depository (if more than $500).

COMPLETE ASSIGNMENTS 11-1, 11-2, AND 11-3

Chapter terms for review

employee's earnings record
FICA
payroll register
percentage method
wage-bracket method

Assignment 11-1: Payroll Problems

A **(30 points)—Complete the payroll (1 point for each correct answer).**

1. In this company, the workers are paid for any time worked in excess of 40 hours a week at a rate of $1\frac{1}{2}$ times their regular hourly rate.

| Name | Total Hours | Regular Earnings | | | | Overtime Earnings | | | Total Earnings |
		Hours Worked	Rate Per Hour	Amount		Hours Worked	Rate Per Hour	Amount	
Berry, Lori	49	40	$7.00			9	$10.50		
Calhoun, Robert	38	38	8.20			–	12.30		
Davis, Adele	52	40	6.40			12	9.60		
Farmer, Ralph	47	40	7.20			7	10.80		
Grey, Jack	48	40	6.50			8	9.75		
Holt, Fred	49	40	6.10			9	9.15		
Huber, Lynn	51	40	9.20			11	13.80		
Jacobs, Tom	51	40	6.60			11	9.90		
Lloyd, Sara	46	40	6.60			6	9.90		
TOTALS									

Score for A (30)

B **(40 points)—Complete the payroll (1 point for each correct answer).**

2. In this company, employees are paid $1\frac{1}{2}$ times their regular rate for overtime hours between 40 and 48 and 2 times their regular rate for overtime hours over 48.

| Name | Total Hours | Regular Rate Per Hour | Regular Earnings | | Time and a Half | | Double Time | | Total Earnings |
			Hours	Amount	Hours	Amount	Hours	Amount	
Abrams, John	52	9.00	40		8		4		
Aguilar, Ralph	40	8.00	40		–	–	–	–	
Kula, Mary	50	7.50	40		8		2		
Murphy, Tom	45	9.00	40		5		–	–	
Norton, Alice	40	8.80	40		–	–	–	–	
Payton, Alan	40	8.00	40		–	–	–	–	
Perry, Lance	47	8.00	40		7		–	–	
Polar, Barbara	41	9.00	40		1		–	–	
Quinn, Carl	49	8.80	40		8		1		
Reston, Sally	40	8.80	40		–	–	–	–	
Sacco, Dom	50	7.50	40		8		2		
Warren, Bill	44	8.80	40		4		–	–	
TOTALS									

Score for B (40)

C **(30 points)—Solve the following problems (points for correct answers as marked).**

3. Joy Agliano is employed at a monthly salary of $5,000. How much is deducted from her November salary for FICA tax? She has been employed the entire calendar year (7 points).

_____

4. Coleen Klein is employed by a company that pays her $2,900 a month. She is single and claims one withholding allowance. What is her net pay after FICA and income tax withholding (9 points)?

_____

5. On April 1, the company in Problem 4 changed its pay plan from monthly to weekly and began paying Coleen $700 per week. What is her weekly pay after FICA and income tax deductions (7 points)?

_____

6. James Cox is married and claims six withholding allowances. His monthly wages are $3,800. Using the percentage method of withholding for federal income tax, find his net pay on August 31 (7 points).

_____

_____
Score for C (30)

Assignment 11-2:   Payrolls

A **(50 points)—Solve the following problems (points for correct answers as marked).**

1. Complete the following payroll register. Workers receive overtime pay for any time worked in excess of 40 hours per week at the rate of time and a half. There is a 7.65% deduction for FICA tax. Use the percentage method for federal income tax withholding. Be sure to use the correct withholding table based on the marital status of each employee (40 points; 1 point for each correct answer in the Total Wages column and 3 points for each correct answer in the Net Pay column).

Name	Marital Status	W/H Allow.	Total Hours	Regular Earnings Rate Per Hour	Regular Earnings Amount	Overtime Earnings Hours Worked	Overtime Earnings Rate Per Hour	Overtime Earnings Amount	Total Wages	FICA Tax	Fed. Inc. Tax	Med. Ins.	Total	Net Pay
Black, J.	M	3	40	$ 8.10		–	–	–				$ 15.00		
Burns, E.	S	0	45	8.80		5						12.00		
Dawson, R.	M	2	40	9.20		–	–	–				15.00		
Frey, W. R.	M	5	40	10.50		–	–	–				21.00		
Muldez, T.	S	1	44	9.80		4						12.00		
Nations, B.	M	2	41	8.10		1						15.00		
Odell, L. O.	M	4	40	9.80		–	–	–				18.00		
Rayder, D.	M	4	48	10.50		8						18.00		
Ridem, G.	S	1	40	8.80		–	–	–				12.00		
TOTALS														

2. The total weekly wages of four employees are listed below. Determine the amount of the deductions and the net pay due to each employee. Use 7.65% for FICA tax withholding and the percentage method for federal income tax withholding. Determine the total of the payroll and the deductions (10 points; 2 points for each correct answer in the Net Pay column).

Name	Marital Status	W/H Allow.	Total Wages	Deductions FICA Tax	Deductions Federal Income Tax	Deductions Total	Net Pay
Alvarez, George	S	1	$ 450.00				
Coburn, Carol	M	3	480.00				
Garnett, Mildred	S	1	505.00				
Kline, Marvin	M	2	430.00				
TOTALS			$1,865.00				

Score for A (50)

B (50 points)—Complete the payroll registers (points for correct answers as marked).

3. In this payroll register, the regular time is calculated at 40 hours a week. Time in excess of 40 hours per week is overtime, paid at time and a half. Use 7.65% to determine the amount of FICA tax. For federal income tax withheld, use the percentage method (25 points; 1 point for each correct answer in the Total Wages column and 4 points for each correct answer in the Net Pay column).

Name	Marital Status	W/H Allow.	Total Hours	Regular Earnings Rate Per Hour	Amount	Overtime Earnings Hours Worked	Rate Per Hour	Amount	Total Wages	Deductions FICA Tax	Fed. Inc. Tax	Total	Net Pay
Baldwin, S.	M	2	42	$9.20		2							
Conklin, J.	M	2	42	7.58		2							
Kempf, L.	M	5	47	7.82		7							
Masjid, M.	M	7	45	9.00		5							
TOTALS													

4. In this payroll register, the employees make a monthly salary plus commission. Determine the month's gross earnings. Compute the FICA tax. Compute the income tax withholding using the percentage method. Add in the medical insurance premiums. Calculate the final monthly net pay (25 points; 1 point for each answer in the Gross Earnings column and 4 points for each correct Net Pay answer).

Name	Marital Status	W/H Allowances	Monthly Salary	Commission	Monthly Gross Earnings	Deductions FICA	Federal Income Tax	Group Medical Insurance	Total Deductions	Net Pay
Barnes, M.	S	0	$2,100.00	$ 386.00				$ 38.50		
Johnson, F.	M	5	2,700.00	1,013.00				74.00		
Maddox, L.	S	2	1,850.00	444.00				74.00		
Minor, R.	M	2	2,000.00	585.00				74.00		
TOTALS			$8,650.00	$2,428.00						

Score for B (50)

Assignment 11-3: Employee's Earnings Record and Payroll Tax Returns

A **(60 points)—Solve the following problems (points for correct answers as marked).**

1. Complete the employee's earnings records for J. R. Collins. Use 7.65% for FICA taxes. Use the percentage method for federal income tax withholdings (40 points; 3 points for each correct weekly answer in the Net Pay column, and 1 point for the quarter total of that column).

Name **J. R. Collins**   Social Security No. **125-11-3290**
Address **7821 Oak Ave.**   No. of Allowances **2** Marital Status **Married**

Period Ending	Total Wages	Cumulative Total	FICA Tax	Federal Inc. Tax	United Fund	Total	Net Pay
1/6	$ 286.50	$ 286.50			$ 4.00		
1/13	318.40	604.90			4.00		
1/20	318.40	923.30			4.00		
1/27	309.00	1,232.30			4.00		
2/3	320.50	1,552.80			4.00		
2/10	322.40	1,875.20			4.00		
2/17	318.60	2,193.80			4.00		
2/24	318.00	2,511.80			4.00		
3/3	320.14	2,831.94			4.00		
3/10	361.00	3,192.94			4.00		
3/17	305.00	3,497.94			4.00		
3/24	316.20	3,814.14			4.00		
3/31	306.50	4,120.64			4.00		
Quarter Totals	$4,120.64				$52.00		

2. Shown below is a summary of quarterly earnings of employees. Determine the information requested for the employer's quarterly federal tax return (20 points; 4 points for each correct answer).

		Taxes Withheld	
Name	Total Wages	Fica Tax	Fed. Inc. Tax
Collins, J.	$4,120.64	$315.24	$337.58
Doyle, L.	4,828.00	369.34	400.18
Gordon J.	4,772.60	365.10	317.80
McBride, C.	4,748.70	363.28	412.90
Taggert, L.	4,787.00	366.21	500.24
Walton, N. D.	4,791.90	366.58	319.80
TOTALS			

a. Total earnings paid.................................... _____

b. Federal income tax withheld .... _____

c. Total FICA tax paid (15.30% of total taxable earnings) ...... _____

d. Employees' contribution of FICA tax....................... _____

e. Total taxes... _____ _____

B (40 points)—Solve the following problems (points for correct answers as marked).

3. The quarterly earnings of the employees of the Zulu Company are listed below. You are to determine the information needed for the employer's quarterly federal tax return (Form 941) (20 points; 4 points for each correct answer).

Name	Total Wages	Taxes Withheld	
		FICA Tax	Federal Income Tax
Caldwell, Janice	$ 3,420.00	$ 261.63	$ 423.90
Dorman, J. A.	3,600.00	275.40	473.67
Eagle, T. W.	4,016.50	307.26	433.33
Fortune, Mark	3,774.90	288.78	410.05
Morris, Regina	3,605.40	275.81	399.83
Tracy, Joseph	4,111.60	314.54	360.17
TOTALS			

a. Total earnings paid.......................... _____
b. Employee's contribution of FICA tax.......... _____
c. Total FICA tax paid .... _____
d. Federal income tax withheld from wages....... _____
e. Total taxes .... _____

4. The Primo Company had a total payroll of $148,600.34 for the first quarter of the current year. It has withheld $28,531.27 from the employees for federal income tax during this quarter. The company has made the following deposits in a qualified bank depository for the amount of the income and FICA taxes withheld from the employees and for the company's contribution to FICA tax: $17,050 on February 6; $17,050 on March 4; and $17,050 on April 5. Primo Company is now filling out Form 941 (quarterly return), which is due by the end of April. Complete the following to determine the amount of the check that the company must send to the IRS for the undeposited taxes due (20 points; 5 points for each correct answer).

a. Total FICA tax to be paid for quarter.......................... _____

b. Total taxes .... _____

c. Total deposits for quarter (sent to qualified bank depository) ...... _____

d. Undeposited taxes due IRS .... _____

Chapter 12
Commissions

Commission is payment to an employee or to an agent for performing or helping to perform a business transaction or service. The most familiar type of commission is that received by a salesperson. Many companies have employees who are either totally or partially paid on a commission basis. Persons that sell insurance, real estate, and automobiles typically are in this category. For a business owner, the advantage of using the commission method to pay employees is that commission is an incentive. Employees are paid on the basis of the volume of business that they produce for the company. The advantage to the employee is that he or she can earn more by being more productive.

Commission merchants and *brokers* perform services of buying and/or selling for which they are paid a commission. In this case, the person (client) for whom the service is performed is called the *principal*. Normally, a commission merchant takes actual possession of merchandise and makes the sales transaction in his or her own name. A broker, however, usually makes the transaction in the principal's name and does not take possession of the merchandise.

SALES COMMISSIONS

A sales commission paid to a salesperson is usually a stated percent of the dollar value of the goods or services sold. Whether the commission is based upon the wholesale or retail value of the goods will depend upon the type of business and merchandise sold. The rate that is used to calculate the commission will also vary among different businesses. In some companies, the salesperson will receive both a salary and a commission.

Steps to Calculate Commission and Total Pay

1. Multiply the amount sold by the commission rate to get the commission amount.
2. If there is a salary, add it to the commission to get the total gross pay.

a. Helen Davis works for Independent Office Furniture. She receives a base salary of $1,500 per month and earns a commission that is 3% of the value of all furniture that she sells during the month. Find her commission and total pay during September, a month in which she sold $92,000 worth of office furniture.

Step 1 $3\% \times \$92,000 = 0.03 \times \$92,000 = \$2,760$ commission
Step 2 $\$2,760$ commission $+ \$1,500$ base salary $= \$4,260$ total pay

Commissions normally are paid only on actual sales. Thus, goods that are returned or orders that are canceled are not eligible for commission. The reason for this is to protect the business owner. Suppose Independent Office Furniture in the preceding example pays the 3% commission whether or not the goods are returned. When Helen Davis gets an order for $10,000, her commission would be $3\% \times \$10,000 = \$300$. If the goods are all returned, but the commission is still paid, then the owner would have to pay $300 to Helen. Since no goods are sold, the owner actually would lose $300 on this transaction.

Steps to Calculate Commission When Sale Involves Returned Goods

1. Subtract the value of the returned goods from the total ordered to determine the amount sold.
2. Multiply the amount sold by the commission rate to get the commission amount.

b. Norm Brewer is a salesperson for Worthy Electrical Connectors. He works on a "commission-only" basis. He receives a commission of 2.5% on his monthly sales, but no base salary. What is his commission and total pay during a month when he sold $165,000 worth of connectors, but one of his customers canceled an entire order of $12,500 and returned the connectors?

Step 1 $\$165,000 - \$12,500 = \$152,500$
Step 2 $2.5\% \times \$152,500 = 0.025 \times \$152,500 = \$3,812.50$ commission
              Total pay $= \$3,812.50$ since he is paid on a commission-only basis

As described earlier, a commission payment plan provides an incentive for the employee. The basic concept is that an employee can earn more money by selling more goods. However, by using a system of *graduated commission rates*, the company can give even more incentive to the employee. Graduated commissions increase as the level of sales increases.

Steps to Calculate Commission Under a Graduated Rates Plan

1. Calculate the dollar amount at each rate level by using subtraction.
2. Multiply each level's sales dollars by the level's commission rate.
3. Add the products calculated in Step 2 to determine the total commission.

c. Travis Brown has a monthly commission plan under which he receives 2% on the first $40,000 of sales during the month and 3% on sales above $40,000 for the month. If Travis has sales of $73,000 during a month, calculate his commission for that month.

Step 1 $ 73,000 total sales   Step 2 $40,000 × 0.02   = $ 800
         − 40,000 at 2%   33,000 × 0.03   =   990
         $ 33,000 at 3%   Step 3   Total Commission = $1,790

d. Assume Travis has a monthly commission plan under which he receives 2% on the first $40,000 of sales during the month, 3% on sales between $40,000 and $80,000, and 4% on all sales over $80,000. If Travis has sales of $106,500 during a month, calculate his commission for that month.

Step 1 $106,500 total sales   Step 2 $40,000 × 0.02   = $ 800
         − 40,000 at 2%   40,000 × 0.03   =   1,200
         $ 66,500   26,500 × 0.04   =   1,060
         − 40,000 at 3%
         $ 26,500 at 4%   Step 3   Total Commission = $3,060

The same graduated incentive plan can be defined in terms of bonus rates. The calculations are quite similar.

e. Lydia Green has a monthly commission plan in which she receives 2% on all sales during the month. If she has sales over $40,000, she receives a bonus of 1% of everything over $40,000. If she sells more than $80,000, she receives a "super bonus" of an additional 1% of everything over $80,000. What is her commission for a month during which she sold $96,500?

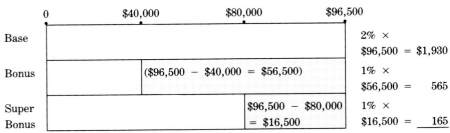

           0         $40,000 $80,000 $96,500

Base   2% × $96,500 = $1,930

Bonus   ($96,500 − $40,000 = $56,500)   1% × $56,500 =   565

Super Bonus $96,500 − $80,000 = $16,500   1% × $16,500 =   165

Total Commission (add the three commission amounts) = $2,660

SALES AND PURCHASES FOR PRINCIPALS

A producer may send goods to a commission merchant for sale at the best possible price. Such a shipment is a *consignment*. The party who sends the shipment is the *consignor*; the party to whom it is sent—that is, the commission merchant—is the *consignee*.

Whatever price the commission merchant gets for the consignment is the *gross proceeds*. The commission is generally a certain percent of the gross proceeds. Sometimes it is a certain amount per unit of weight or measure of the goods sold. The commission, and any other sales expenses such as transportation, advertising, storage, insurance, etc., are the *charges*. The charges are deducted from the gross proceeds. The resulting amount, which is sent to the consignor, is the *net proceeds*.

f. First Quality commissions Thoren Sales to sell some excess paper stock. 300 units are sold at $7.50 per unit, and 225 units are sold at $4.10 per unit. Thoren Sales charges a 6% commission of the gross proceeds. Thoren Sales also pays $43.28 in freight charges. What are the net proceeds due to First Quality from the sale of the paper?

300 units × $7.50 = $2,250.00 $3,172.50 × 6% = $190.35 commission
225 units × $4.10 =   922.50   + 43.28 freight
gross proceeds   = $3,172.50 $233.63 charges

$3,172.50 gross proceeds − $233.63 charges = $2,938.87 net proceeds

Along with the net proceeds, the commission merchant sends the consignor a form known as an *account sales*. This is a detailed statement of the amount of the sales and the various deductions. Figure 12-1 is a typical account sales.

FIGURE 12-1   Account Sales

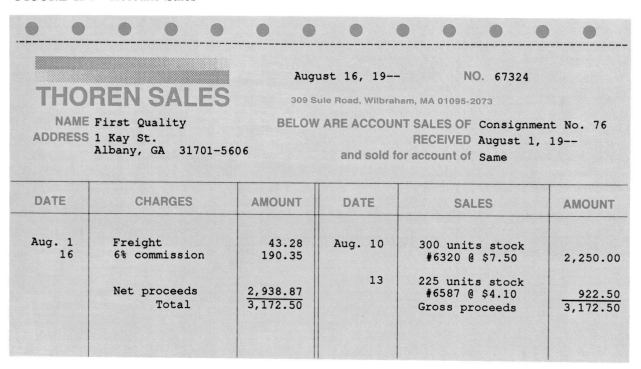

THOREN SALES
309 Sule Road, Wilbraham, MA 01095-2073

August 16, 19--   NO. 67324

NAME First Quality
ADDRESS 1 Kay St.
        Albany, GA   31701-5606

BELOW ARE ACCOUNT SALES OF Consignment No. 76
RECEIVED August 1, 19--
and sold for account of Same

DATE	CHARGES	AMOUNT	DATE	SALES	AMOUNT
Aug. 1 16	Freight 6% commission	43.28 190.35	Aug. 10	300 units stock #6320 @ $7.50	2,250.00
	Net proceeds Total	2,938.87 3,172.50	13	225 units stock #6587 @ $4.10 Gross proceeds	922.50 3,172.50

When commission merchants purchase goods for their principals, the price that they pay for the merchandise is the *prime cost*. The prime cost and all charges are the *gross cost*, or the cost that the principal pays.

g. Town Marketing is commissioned by Catena Ltd. to purchase 10,000 canvas tote bags that will be labeled and used as promotional items. For this size of an order, Town Marketing is able to purchase these tote bags for $4.29 each. Charges include the commission, which is 6% of the prime cost; storage, $42.50; and freight, $24.40. What is the gross cost that Catena Ltd. should pay to Town Marketing?

   $4.29 $42,900 prime cost
× 10,000 units   × 0.06
 $42,900 prime cost $ 2,574 commission

$2,574 commission + $42.50 storage + $24.40 freight = $2,640.90 charges
$42,900 prime cost + $2,640.90 charges = $45,540.90 gross cost

An *account purchase* is a detailed statement from the commission merchant to the principal. It shows the cost of goods purchased, including charges. Figure 12-2 is a typical account purchase using the same information as in example g.

FIGURE 12-2 Account Purchase

TOWN MARKETING
4563 Bauer Road
Ft. Wayne, IN 46806-6055

ACCOUNT PURCHASE

NO. **1311**

October 26 ____ 19 __

Bought on Consignment for

Catena, Ltd.

10 Allen Road

Muncie, IN 47303-0095

DATE		CHARGES	AMOUNT
Oct. 23	10,000 units stock #T805 @ $4.29		42,900.00
23	6% commission	2,574.00	
	Storage	42.50	
	Freight	24.40	2,640.90
	Gross Cost		45,540.90

COMPLETE ASSIGNMENTS 12-1 AND 12-2

Chapter terms for review

account purchase
account sales
broker
charges
commission
commission merchant
consignee
consignment

consignor
graduated commission rates
gross cost
gross proceeds
net proceeds
prime cost
principal

Assignment 12-1: Commission

A (24 points) — Find the commission and the total gross pay (2 points for each correct commission; 1 point for each correct gross pay).

	Employee	Monthly Salary	Commission Rate	Monthly Sales	Commission	Gross Pay
1.	Palo, M.	$1,500	5.0%	$30,000	_____	_____
2.	Chard, P.	1,250	4.0%	25,000	_____	_____
3.	Wilson, R.	0	8.0%	40,000	_____	_____
4.	Ednie, J.A.	1,000	6.0%	32,000	_____	_____
5.	Barner, J.	750	7.0%	50,000	_____	_____
6.	Jenkins, G.	1,800	3.5%	28,000	_____	_____
7.	Rice, B.	2,500	2.5%	38,000	_____	_____
8.	Millet, S.	900	7.5%	42,000	_____	_____

Score for A (24)

B (28 points) — Calculate the total commission for the following commission payment plans (4 points for each correct answer).

	Graduated Commission Rates	Sales	Commission
9.	2% on sales to $80,000 3% on sales above $80,000	$ 92,400.00	_____
10.	1.5% on sales to $100,000 3% on sales above $100,000	$158,150.00	_____
11.	4% on sales to $40,000 5% on sales above $40,000	$ 62,560.00	_____
12.	3% on sales to $45,000 4% from $45,000 to $60,000 5% on sales above $60,000	$ 82,750.00	_____
13.	2% on sales to $50,000 3% from $50,000 to $100,000 4% on sales above $100,000	$123,800.00	_____
14.	4% on sales to $30,000 5.5% from $30,000 to $50,000 7% on sales above $50,000	$ 42,300.00	_____

15. 1% on sales to $75,000 $130,500.00 _____
    3% from $75,000 to $125,000
    5% on sales above $125,000

C (24 points) — Find the commission and gross cost for the following purchases (1 point for each correct commission; 2 points for each correct gross cost).

	Prime Cost	Commission Rate	Commission	Trucking & Delivery	Storage	Air Freight	Gross Cost
16.	$ 4,850	5.00%	_____	$250.00	$ 413.00	$ 0.00	_____
17.	3,216	4.50%	_____	89.50	0.00	259.00	_____
18.	15,600	6.00%	_____	204.00	0.00	1,211.00	_____
19.	6,540	3.75%	_____	0.00	0.00	358.75	_____
20.	2,536	8.00%	_____	46.20	90.00	107.15	_____
21.	11,380	5.25%	_____	385.00	1,450.00	0.00	_____
22.	9,488	5.50%	_____	486.75	350.00	0.00	_____
23.	36,965	4.00%	_____	0.00	650.00	2,845.00	_____

D (24 points) — Find the commission and net proceeds for each sale on consignment (1 point for each correct commission; 2 points for each correct net proceeds).

	Gross Sales	Commission Rate	Commission	Trucking & Delivery	Storage	Air Freight	Net Proceeds
24.	$ 3,530	3.50%	_____	$173.80	$ 215.00	$ 0.00	_____
25.	22,400	5.00%	_____	942.85	0.00	1,482.12	_____
26.	6,737	2.00%	_____	0.00	800.00	688.00	_____
27.	8,560	4.25%	_____	382.91	650.00	0.00	_____
28.	14,636	6.50%	_____	495.00	0.00	1,525.00	_____
29.	38,409	4.00%	_____	0.00	1,850.00	1,075.00	_____
30.	6,725	7.75%	_____	85.00	175.00	785.00	_____
31.	1,100	1.50%	_____	64.75	0.00	0.00	_____

Assignment 12-2: Applications with Commission

A (45 points) — Solve each of the following applications (5 points for each correct answer).

1. Dwayne Gregory sells office furniture. He receives a monthly salary of $2,100 plus a commission of 1.5% on all sales. What would be Dwayne's pay for a month in which he sold $78,000 worth of furniture?

   _____

2. Dwayne does not get a commission for furniture he sells that is later returned. If an item is returned, its price is deducted from Dwayne's total sales to get "net sales," and Dwayne is paid a commission of 1.5% of his net sales. From Problem 1, what would be Dwayne's total monthly pay if $13,450 worth of the $78,000 of furniture had been returned?

   _____

3. Marco Boschiazzo is paid $1,750 monthly salary by Johnson Business Products. For commission, he receives 1% on his net sales up to $30,000 and 2% on net sales over $30,000. What is his total pay in a month when he sells $74,000?

   _____

4. Judy Moore is paid by a "straight commission" (i.e., she gets no salary at all). She is paid 4% for her net sales up to $75,000. For the next $40,000 of net sales, she is paid 4.5%. For any net sales above $115,000, she gets 5%. How much commission would she earn in a month when she sells $122,780?

   _____

5. Using the information from Problem 4, suppose that $8,420 worth of merchandise sold by Judy Moore has been returned. What would be her commission with this additional information?

   _____

6. Jenny Chu sells office equipment for New CompuCorp. She is paid a monthly salary of $2,400 and is expected to sell a minimum of $50,000 each month (the minimum is called a "quota"). If she sells more than her $50,000 quota in a month, she is paid a bonus of 2% on her net sales above $50,000. What would be Jenny's total pay in a month when she has net sales of $62,500?

_____

7. Using the information from Problem 6, what would be Jenny's total pay for the month if $13,000 worth of her total sales had been returned?

_____

8. Tom McIntosh is a telemarketing salesman for magazine subscriptions. He is paid 20 cents for each telephone call that he completes and talks for more than 30 seconds. In addition, if a person signs up and pays for a one-year magazine subscription, Tom receives 4.5% of the subscription price. How much would Tom earn if he made 619 telephone calls that lasted more than 30 seconds and if the total value of the one-year subscriptions that he sold was $3,150?

_____

9. Magazine publishers prefer subscribers to take longer subscriptions. To encourage longer subscriptions, they offer lower rates for longer subscriptions. Also, the telemarketers are paid a higher commission rate for selling longer subscriptions: 4.5% for a one-year subscription, 5.5% for a two-year subscription, and 7.0% for a three-year subscription. What would be Tom McIntosh's pay if he made 857 telephone calls that lasted more than 30 seconds (see Problem 8) and had sales of $2,820 of one-year subscriptions, $1,940 of two-year subscriptions, and $1,795 of three-year subscriptions?

_____

_____
Score for A (45)

B (35 points) — Solve each of the following applications (5 points for each correct answer).

10. Stan McCulloch paints ceramic tiles for decorative use in kitchens and bathrooms. He sells his tiles primarily at arts and crafts shows. He gives the tiles on consignment to a commission merchant, Sandy Keefer, to sell for him at different "street fairs" in various cities and towns around the state. Sandy charges 15% on all sales, plus the fees to operate a booth and transportation expenses. What would be Stan's net proceeds for the month if Sandy sells $7,600 worth of Stan's tiles at four different street fairs? (Each fair charged a booth fee of $125, and Stan's total transportation expense for the month was $160.)

_____

11. Stan could also give his tiles to a competing commission merchant, Alice Wood. Alice charges a commission rate of 20%. However, Alice sells for three different artists from only one booth. She charges each artist only $\frac{1}{3}$ of the booth fees and $\frac{1}{3}$ of her transportation costs. (Assume that Alice's costs are the same as Sandy's above.) What would be Stan's net proceeds if Alice sells $7,600 worth of tiles for him?

_____

12. Suppose the volume of tiles sold in Problem 11 had been $8,800. Which commission merchant would have given Stan the greater net proceeds, and by how much?

_____

13. Thompson Foods is planning to open a new restaurant. To buy furniture and other decorative items they hire an agent, Martin Interiors. Martin will charge Thompson 5% of the purchase price of the items acquired. In addition, Thompson will have to pay for any freight costs and for storage costs if the items arrive much before they are needed. What will be the gross cost to Thompson if Martin spends $55,700 for furniture, another $1,380 for shipping, and $463 for one month's storage?

_____

14. What would be the gross cost to Thompson (see Problem 13) if Martin charged 5.5%, but stored the furniture at no cost to Thompson during the month?

_____

15. Thompson (above) talks with another firm, Atchison Representatives, who will charge a flat rate of $4,000, plus expenses. Atchison will try to find the furniture selected at the lowest price for Thompson. Atchison finds the furniture for only $50,127. However, it must come from a dealer located 1,500 miles further away, so the shipping expense will be $1,790. Storage is still $463. What will be Thompson's gross cost if they hire Atchison Representatives to do its purchasing?

_____

16. Gary Wells is a commission merchant. He has taken some merchandise on consignment because he knows of a person who would be willing to pay him a commission to buy it. The price is set at $5,000. Gary is paid a commission of 5% by the seller to sell the merchandise. Gary is also paid a commission of 4% by the buyer to buy the merchandise. How much does Gary earn from the two persons combined?

_____

Score for B (35)

C (20 points) — Solve each of the following applications (5 points for each correct answer).

17. Rick Oxford wants to sell his house. He selects Linda Morrow, an agent of the VanCalcar Real Estate Agency, to be his real estate agent. Linda tells him that VanCalcar Realty charges a commission of 6% of the selling price and that Rick would have to pay another $700 in various fees. If his home were to sell for $100,000, how much net proceeds would Rick receive?

_____

18. Sharon Dalton wants to buy a home so she goes to see Don Sumpter, a real estate agent of the Houston Realty Company. Don takes Sharon to see Rick Oxford's house (above). Sharon purchases Rick's house for a price of $100,000. Because Don found the buyer, the Houston Realty got one half of the commission earned by VanCalcar Realty (see Problem 17). How much commission would each real estate firm receive?

_____

19. The two real estate companies each pay their employees by the same method: The employee gets one half of whatever revenue his/her agency receives from the transaction. How much would Linda and Don (see Problem 18) each earn?

_____

20. Linda is the agent who Rick hires to sell his house for $100,000. Rick pays a total commission of 6%. Using the information from Problems 17-19, what rate of commission of the selling price did Linda herself actually receive?

_____

Score for C (20)

Part Four
Additional
Percentage
Applications

Chapter 13
Trade and Cash Discounts

OBJECTIVES
After completing this chapter, you should be able to:

- **Compute straight discounts**
- **Compute a series of discounts and equivalent single discounts**
- **Understand difference between cash and trade discounts**

When one business sells merchandise to another business it is usual to offer discounts. A discount is an important tool for the seller. Two common types of discounts are trade discounts and cash discounts. Trade discounts affect the agreed-upon selling price **before** the sale happens. Cash discounts affect the amount actually paid **after** the transaction.

TRADE DISCOUNTS

Businesses that sell products want to attract and keep customers who make repeated large volume purchases. Manufacturers, distributors and wholesalers frequently offer *trade discounts* to buyers who are "in the trade." These discounts generally are based on the quantity purchased. For example, a distributor of electrical supplies might give a large discount of 40% to an electrical contractor who works on hotels and shopping centers; but the discount might be only 25% for a self-employed electrician who rewires houses. The customer who does not work "in the trade" probably would not receive any special discount, and therefore would pay *list price*, which is the amount listed in the catalog.

There are two methods to calculate trade discounts. Both can be used to find the *net price* that the distributor will charge to his customer after the discount. The *discount method* is useful when you want to know both the net price and the actual amount of the trade discount. The other method, called the *complement method*, is used to find only the net price. It gets its name because you use the *complement rate*, which is 100% minus the discount rate. Each method has only two calculation steps:

1. Discount = Trade discount rate × List price
2. Net price = List price − Trade discount

Steps for Calculating Net Price (Complement Method)

1. Complement rate = 100% − Trade discount rate
2. Net price = Complement rate × List price

a. Kavner Electrical Supply Co. sells electrical wiring material to Cassady Electric. The list price is $240 and Cassady Electric qualifies for a 25% trade discount. Calculate the net price.

Discount Method

Step 1   Discount   = 25% × $240 = $60
Step 2   Net price = $240 − $60 = **$180**

Complement Method

Step 1   Complement rate = 100% − 25% = 75%
Step 2   Net price   = 75% × $240 = **$180**

Series of Trade Discounts

A distributor or manufacturer may give additional discounts to those customers who actually buy the largest volumes. Two electricians each get a 25% discount for being "in the trade." But if one of them buys twice as much from the distributor, he possibly will be rewarded with additional discounts. For example, after an electrician buys $50,000 worth of products, he may receive an additional 20% discount; if he buys $100,000 worth he may receive another 10% discount on top of that. Therefore, that electrician would have discounts of 25%, 20% and 10%. This is called a *series of discounts*.

Both the discount method and the complement method can be used to calculate the net price with a series of discounts. *The two methods are the same as shown above except the steps are repeated for each discount in the series.* For example, if there are three discounts, repeat the steps three times. Apply the first discount rate to the list price. For the second and third discounts, calculate "intermediate prices" and then apply the discount rates to them.

b. An electrical generator has a list price of $480. Cassady Electric qualifies for a series of discounts: 25%, 20% and 10%. Calculate the net price.

	1st discount	*2nd discount*	*3rd discount*
Discount Method:			
Step 1	25% × $480 = $120	20% × $360 = $72	10% × $288 = $28.80
Step 2	$480 − $120 = $360	$360 − $72 = $288	$288 − $28.80 = $259.20
Complement Method:			
Step 1	100% − 25% = 75%	100% − 20% = 80%	100% − 10% = 90%
Step 2	75% × $480 = $360	80% × $360 = $288	90% × $288 = $259.20

It is possible to modify the complement method and make it much quicker by not calculating the intermediate prices.

Steps for Calculating Net Price (Modified Complement Method)

1. Determine all of the complement rates.
2. Net price = List price times the product of the complement rates.

c. Use the *modified complement method* to calculate the net price in the previous example. The list price was $480 and the trade discounts were 25%, 20% and 10%.

Step 1 1st Complement rate = 100% − 25% = 75%
2nd Complement rate = 100% − 20% = 80%
3rd Complement rate = 100% − 10% = 90%
Step 2 Net price   = $480 × 75% × 80% × 90% = **$259.20**

NOTE: Remember that there should be NO ROUNDING until the final net price. It should be rounded to the nearest cent.

Equivalent Single Discount Rate

Suppose that another distributor offers Cassady Electric a single discount of 45% on purchases. How does that compare with the series of discounts: 25%, 20%, 10%? To answer the question, Cassady can calculate the *equivalent single discount rate*.

The most efficient method to find the single discount rate that is equivalent to a series of discounts is almost like the modified complement method above:

Steps for Calculating the Equivalent Single Discount Rate

1. Determine the complement of each rate.
2. Calculate the product of the complements by multiplying all complement rates together.
3. Determine the equivalent single discount rate by subtracting the product (Step 2) from 100%.

d. Find the equivalent single discount rate for Cassady Electric's series of discounts: 25%, 20%, 10%.

Step 1 1st Complement rate   = 100% − 25% = 75%
2nd Complement rate   = 100% − 20% = 80%
3rd Complement rate   = 100% − 10% = 90%
Step 2 Product of complements = 75% × 80% × 90% = 54%
Step 3 Single discount   = 100% − 54% = **46%**

COMPLETE ASSIGNMENT 13-1

CASH DISCOUNTS

When one business buys from another, the buyer orders the merchandise and the seller ships it, or orders it to be shipped. Then, the seller's office sends a document requesting payment to the buyer's office. This document is called an *invoice*. It lists each item purchased, its cost and the total cost. If there are additional costs, such as packaging or freight, these are included.

Sellers want their customers to pay the invoices quickly. To encourage prompt payment, the seller may offer the buyer a *discount rate*, such as 1% or 2%, for paying the invoice within the *discount period*, a certain number of days after the *invoice date*. This discount is called a *cash discount*, or simply *terms of payment*.

One common cash discount is "two ten, net thirty." It may be written as 2/10, n/30; or 2-10, n-30; or 2/10, net 30. A discount of 2/10, net/30 means the buyer can deduct 2% from the portion of the invoice amount that is paid within 10 days of the invoice date.

e. If the invoice date is May 25, the discount is available through June 4 (the *discount date*). (Reminder: May has 31 days.) Any unpaid remainder (the "net," or "unpaid balance") is due within 30 days of the invoice date. After that date (the *due date*), an interest penalty would be charged to the buyer. With a May 25 invoice date, the due date would be June 24. Figure 13-1 illustrates the time periods involved and shows the placement of the key dates for this example.

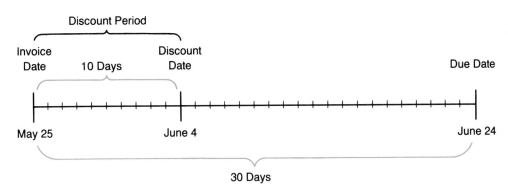

FIGURE 13-1
Cash Discount
Time Line

There can be more than one discount rate and discount period. For example, "2/5, 1/15, n/30" means that the buyer can get a 2% discount by paying within 5 days or a 1% discount by paying within 6 to 15 days. The net invoice is due within 30 days. After 30 days a penalty will be assessed.

The amount that a buyer actually pays after deducting the cash discount is called the *remittance*. There are two methods used to calculate the remittance, the *discount method* and the *complement method*. Some people prefer the complement method because it is faster. However, with it, you never actually calculate the amount of the cash discount. For this reason, the discount method is useful. The *net purchase* is the price of the merchandise actually purchased. This is the price after the cost of returned merchandise and any freight charges have been subtracted. Additional information about returned merchandise and freight charges is provided below.

Steps for Calculating the Remittance (Discount Method)

1. Discount = Discount rate × Net purchase
2. Remittance = Net purchase − Cash discount

Steps for Calculating the Remittance (Complement Method)

1. Complement rate = 100% − Discount rate
2. Remittance = Complement rate × Net Purchase

f. Northern Supply sells merchandise for $480 to Washington Cleaners. The invoice is dated August 23 and lists terms of 2/10, n/30.

1. What is the last date on which the cash discount may be taken (i.e., the discount date)?

Invoice Date + 10 days = August 23 + 10 days = September 2

2. What is the date on which the net payment is due (i.e., the due date)?

Invoice Date + 30 days = August 23 + 30 days = September 22

3. If the entire invoice is paid within ten days, how much actually is paid? Use both methods.

Discount Method

Step 1   Cash discount = 2% × $480 = $9.60
Step 2   Remittance   = $480 − $9.60 = **$470.40**

Complement Method

Step 1   Complement Rate = 100% − 2% = 98%
Step 2   Remittance   = 98% × $480 = **$470.40**

Each method gives the same result: $470.40. The cash discount method also gives the actual cash discount: $9.60. One method can be used as a check on the other.

FIGURE 13-2
Sales Invoice

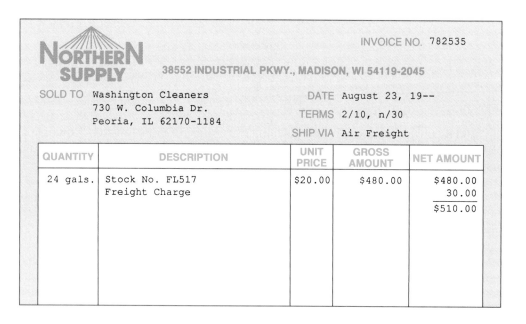

Returned Goods and Freight Charges

The seller only gives the buyer a discount on the merchandise that actually is purchased. Suppose that Washington Cleaners buys $480 worth of merchandise and then returns $200 worth. Northern Supply would only give a discount on the remaining $280 that Washington keeps.

Similarly, suppose that Washington Cleaners requests that the merchandise be sent by air freight, and that Northern Supply prepays a freight charge of $30. On the invoice, Northern will charge Washington for the merchandise and for the freight. Northern can offer a discount on the merchandise, but not on the freight. Northern does not make any profit on the $30 freight, so it cannot offer any discount on it.

Part Four   Additional Percentage Applications

To calculate the cash discount and remittance when there is a return of merchandise and, perhaps, a freight charge, first calculate the net purchases by subtracting returns and the freight charge from the invoice amount.

Steps for Calculating the Remittance When Merchandise Returns and/or Freight Charges Exist:

1. Net purchase = Invoice amount − Merchandise returns − Freight
2. Cash discount = Discount rate × Net purchase
3. Cost of merchandise = Net purchase − Cash discount
4. Remittance = Cost of merchandise + Freight, if any

g. Northern Supply sells merchandise to Washington Cleaners. The invoice amount is $510 which includes $30 freight charges. The invoice date is August 13 and the terms are 2/10, n/30. Washington Cleaners returns $200 worth of merchandise and pays the entire remaining invoice before August 23. Calculate the cash discount and the remittance.

Discount Method
Step 1 Net purchase = $510 − $200 − $30 = $280
Step 2 Cash discount = 2% × $280 = $5.60
Step 3 Cost of merchandise = $280 − $5.60 = $274.40
Step 4 Remittance = $274.40 + $30 freight = **$304.40**

Complement Method:*
Step 1 Actual purchase = $510 − $200 − $30 = $280
Step 2 Complement rate = 100% − 2% = 98%
Step 3 Cost of merchandise = $280 × 98% = $274.40
Step 4 Remittance = $274.40 + $30 freight = **$304.40**

*(does not determine the cash discount)

Partial Payment of Invoice

Sometimes a buyer wants to take some advantage of the cash discount, but can only afford to pay part of the invoice within the discount period. The invoice will be reduced by the amount paid (remittance) plus the amount of the discount. The total of the amount paid plus the amount of cash discount is called the *amount credited* to the buyer's account.

NOTE: The steps for calculating the unpaid balance are almost the reverse of the complement method, using division instead of multiplication.

Steps for Calculating the Unpaid Balance

1. Determine the complement of the discount rate (100% − discount rate).
2. Calculate the amount credited by dividing the amount paid (remittance) by the complement rate.
3. Calculate the unpaid balance by subtracting the amount credited (Step 2) from the invoice amount.

h. Neta Gentry buys $392 worth of materials to use in her picture framing shop. The terms are 2/10, n/60. Within 10 days, she sends in a check for $200. How much credit should she receive? What is her unpaid balance?

Step 1 Complement rate = 100% − 2% = 98%
Step 2 Amount credited = $200 ÷ 98% = $204.0816 or $204.08
Step 3 Unpaid balance = $392.00 − $204.08 = **$187.92**

Notice that in the example, Ms. Gentry receives $1.00 credit for every $0.98 paid. In other words, the $200 actually remitted is 98% of the total amount credited. Check your work by multiplication:

Cash discount $= 2\% \times \$204.08 = \$4.0816$ or $\$4.08$
Remittance $= \$204.08 - \$4.08 = \mathbf{\$200.00}$

A slightly different situation, and less frequently used, is when the buyer decides in advance the total amount she wants to have credited to the account. This problem is exactly like the original cash discount problems.

i. Neta Gentry buys $392 worth of materials to use in her framing shop. The terms are 2/10, n/60. She wants to pay some money within 10 days in order to reduce her account by exactly $200. How much should she remit now? What is the unpaid balance?

Discount Method

Step 1 Cash discount $= 2\% \times \$200 = \$4$
Step 2 Remittance $= \$200 - \$4 = \$196$
Step 3 Unpaid balance $= \$392 - \$200 = \mathbf{\$192}$

Complement Method

Step 1 Complement rate $= 100\% - 2\% = 98\%$
Step 2 Remittance $= 98\% \times \$200 = \$196$
Step 3 Unpaid balance $= \$392 - \$200 = \mathbf{\$192}$

COMPLETE ASSIGNMENT 13-2

Chapter terms for review

amount credited	invoice
cash discount	invoice date
complement method	list price
complement rate	modified complement method
discount date	net price
discount method	net purchase
discount period	remittance
discount rate	series of discounts
due date	terms of payment
equivalent single discount rate	trade discount

Assignment 13-1: Trade Discounts

A   (20 points) — Problems 1-5: Find the dollar amount of the trade discount and the net price using the discount method. Problems 6-10: Find the complement rate and the net price using the complement method (1 point for each correct answer).

	List Price	Trade Discount	Discount Amount	Net Price
1.	$900	35%		
2.	330	20%		
3.	96	25%		
4.	765	40%		
5.	500	32%		

	List Price	Trade Discount	Complement Rate	Net Price
6.	$642	35%		
7.	450	20%		
8.	185	25%		
9.	808	40%		
10.	295	32%		

Score for A (20)

B   (25 points) — Find the amounts of discounts (enter an "*" where none exist) and the net price (1 point for each correct discount; 2 points for each correct net price).

	List Price	Trade Discounts	Trade Discount Amounts			Net Price
			First	Second	Third	
11.	$1,520	45%, 20%				
12.	$842.50	20%, 10%				
13.	$1,200	30%, 25%, 20%				
14.	$720	25%, 20%, 10%				
15.	$420	20%, 10%, 5%				

Score for B (25)

C (35 points) — Find the complement rates (enter an "*" where none exist) and the net price, using the complement method (1 point for each correct complement rate; 2 points for each correct net price).

	List Price	Trade Discounts	Complement Rates First	Second	Third	Net Price
16.	$842.50	20%, 10%	____	____	____	____
17.	$465	25%, 15%	____	____	____	____
18.	$1,115	30%, 20%	____	____	____	____
19.	$1,200	30%, 25%, 20%	____	____	____	____
20.	$420	20%, 10%, 5%	____	____	____	____
21.	$748.65	25%, 20%, 10%	____	____	____	____
22.	$1,550.80	30%, 20%, 10%	____	____	____	____

D (20 points) — Find each of the complement rates and the equivalent single discount rate, to the nearest $\frac{1}{10}$ of a percent (1 point for each correct answer).

	Trade Discounts	Complement Rates First	Second	Third	Equivalent Single Discount
23.	30%, 25%, 20%	____	____	____	_____
24.	20%, 10%, 5%	____	____	____	_____
25.	30%, 20%, 10%	____	____	____	_____
26.	20%, 15%, 10%	____	____	____	_____
27.	40%, 25%, 10%	____	____	____	_____

Assignment 13-2: Cash Discounts

A (20 points) — For the following problems, calculate the discount date, due date, amount of discount if the entire invoice is paid within the discount period, and amount of the remittance (2 points for each correct discount amount; 1 point for all other correct answers).

1. Terms: 2/10, n/30   Invoice amount: $485.72   Discount date: _____

   Invoice date: August 29   Due date: _____   Remittance: _____

   Discount amount: _____

2. Terms: 1.5/10, n/60   Returned goods: $51.99   Discount amount: _____

   Invoice date: July 23   Discount date: _____   Remittance: _____

   Invoice amount: $390.48   Due date: _____

3. Terms: 2/5, n/20   Freight included: $79.57   Discount amount: _____

   Invoice date: December 28   Discount date: _____   Remittance: _____

   Invoice amount: $1,480.50   Due date: _____

4. Terms: 1/10, n/45   Freight included: $34.90   Due date: _____

   Invoice date: June 27   Returned goods: $124.75   Discount amount: _____

   Invoice amount: $926.33   Discount date: _____   Remittance: _____

Score for A (20)

B (20 points) — For the following problems, calculate the discount date, due date, amount of discount if the entire invoice is paid within the discount period, and amount of the remittance (2 points for each correct discount amount; 1 point for all other correct answers).

5. Martinez Mfg. purchased $807.58 worth of material on terms of 1-15, net-45. The invoice was dated March 19. Calculate the required information.

   Discount date: _____   Discount amount: _____

   Due date: _____   Remittance: _____

6. Bodley Financial Services bought a new desk and filing cabinet for $683.21 with terms of 2/10, n/30. The invoice was dated October 24. The next day, they returned the filing cabinet, which cost $102.44. Calculate the required information.

Discount date: _____   Discount amount: _____

Due date: _____   Remittance: _____

7. Johannsen Lumber Company gives terms of 1.5-10, net-30, but do not give a discount on delivery charges. One of their invoices is dated April 14, in the amount of $239.40 and includes $18.35 for delivery. Calculate the required information.

Discount date: _____   Discount amount: _____

Due date: _____   Remittance: _____

8. Prefontaine's Paint Store gives terms of 3/10, net/25 to contractors. On January 25, Jerry Weekly, a contractor, ordered paint and supplies and had his order delivered. The invoice total was $318.42 and included $28.19 for freight.

Weekly returned five gallons of paint, which cost $58.04. Calculate the required information.

Discount date: _____   Discount amount: _____

Due date: _____   Remittance: _____

Score for B (20)

C   (20 points) — For the following problems, calculate the discount date, the due date and the complement rate. Use the complement method to find the remittance (2 points for each correct remittance; 1 point for all other correct answers).

9. Terms: 1/15, net/30   Discount date: _____   Remittance: _____

Invoice date: May 20   Due date: _____

Invoice amount: $2,338.45   Complement rate: _____

10. Terms: 3-5, net-25   Returned goods: $63.23   Complement rate: _____

Invoice date: March 30   Discount date: _____   Remittance: _____

Invoice amount: $811.79   Due date: _____

11. Terms: 2.5/10, net/20   Freight included: $124.90   Complement rate: _____

      Invoice date: December 26   Discount date: _____   Remittance: _____

      Invoice amount: $2,258.99   Due date: _____

12. Terms: 1/10, n/60   Freight included: *$64.35*   Due date: _____

      Invoice date: August 27   Returned goods: *$98.00*   Complement rate: _____

      Invoice amount: $715.82   Discount date: _____   Remittance: _____

Score for C (20)

D (20 points) — For the following problems, calculate the discount date, the due date and the remittance. Use the complement method to find the remittance (2 points for each correct remittance; 1 point for all other correct answers).

13. Shutter Marine Supply purchased goods from their wholesaler with terms of 2/10, n/60. The invoice was for $742.91 and was dated July 22. Find the required information.

      Discount date: _____   Complement rate: _____

      Due date: _____   Remittance: _____

14. Knowles Equipment Co. bought several different power saws on October 23. The total invoice amount was $1,723.62 and terms were 1.5-10, n-45. On October 25 Knowles returned a small saw that had a price of $288.38. Calculate the required information.

      Discount date: _____   Complement rate: _____

      Due date: _____   Remittance: _____

15. Smith & Treat Stationery ordered additional school supplies. An August 24 invoice was for $867.76, which included $43.75 freight, offered terms of 2/10, net/30. Calculate the required information.

      Discount date: _____   Complement rate: _____

      Due date: _____   Remittance: _____

16. Doty Delivery Service bought 4 different bicycles to use for package delivery in the downtown area. The invoice, dated June 15, offered terms of 2-10, n-30 and was for $370.51, including $31.25 freight. One bicycle, costing $84.68, was defective, so they returned it on June 20. Calculate the required information.

Discount date: _____   Complement rate: _____

Due date: _____   Remittance: _____

E **(20 points) — The following problems involve partial payments within the discount period. Solve for either the amount of the remittance, or the amount credited to the account, and for the unpaid balance (2 points for each correct answer).**

17. Terms: 2/10, net/30   Remittance: $250.00

Invoice date: September 9   Amount credited: _____

Invoice amount: $524.90   Unpaid balance: _____

18. Terms: 1/15, n/40   Remittance: $1,000.00

Invoice date: November 18   Amount credited: _____

Invoice amount: $1,853.39   Unpaid balance: _____

19. Terms: 2/10, net/30   Amount credited: $1,200.00

Invoice date: February 14   Remittance: _____

Invoice amount: $2,380.25   Unpaid balance: _____

20. Palo Plumbing bought $745.29 worth of material on April 18 with terms of 3-5, n-25. They paid $375 on April 20. Calculate the amount credited and the unpaid balance.

Amount credited: _____   Unpaid balance: _____

21. Chard Custom Cabinetry buys lumber with terms of 1/15, n/45. On September 10, Chard bought lumber for $892.54. On September 18 they wanted to pay enough cash to reduce the balance by a total of $492.54. Calculate the amount credited and the unpaid balance.

Remittance: _____   Unpaid balance: _____

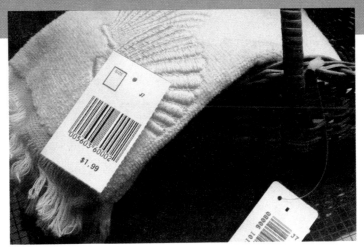

Chapter 14
Markup

OBJECTIVES
After completing this chapter, you should be able to:

- **Determine markup based on cost and on selling price**
- **Understand and use markup methods**

In any business that buys and sells merchandise, the selling price of the goods must be high enough to cover the cost of the goods sold and to cover all operating expenses and provide a profit for the owner.

MARKUP

Gross profit is the term used by accountants to describe the difference between the sales price (*sales*) and the cost of the sold goods (*cost of goods sold*). Gross profit is simply the total sales minus the cost of goods sold.

Sales − Cost of goods sold = Gross profit

The gross profit of a profitable business pays all the additional costs of operating the business (*operating expenses*) and leaves a return for the owner. This return to the owner is known as *net profit*.

Gross profit − Operating expenses = Net profit

When merchants set the selling prices of their goods they add a *markup*. The markup in dollars is the amount added to the cost of the goods in order to have a gross profit high enough to cover operating expenses and to make a net profit.

Operating expenses + Net profit = *Dollar markup*

Calculation of the markup is based on either the cost of the goods for sale or the selling price of those goods.

MARKUP BASED ON COST

When markup is based on the cost of the goods for sale, it is expressed as a *percent of cost*.

Calculating Markup Percent

When the dollar cost and the dollar markup are known, the *markup percent* based on cost is calculated by dividing the dollar markup by the cost.

Dollar markup ÷ Cost = Markup percent

a. Using cost-based markup, what is the markup percent when the cost is $40 and the dollar markup is $10?

$10 Markup ÷ $40 Cost = 0.25 or **25% Markup**

When the selling price and the cost are known, the markup percent based on cost is calculated by determining the markup in dollars and then dividing the dollar markup by the cost.

b. Using cost-based markup, what is the markup percent when the selling price is $50 and the cost is $40?

$50 Selling price − $40 Cost = $10 Markup
$10 Markup ÷ $40 Cost = 0.25 or **25% Markup**

Calculating Dollar Markup

When both the dollar cost and the markup percent are known, the amount of markup in dollars is calculated by multiplying the cost by the markup percent.

Cost × Markup percent = Dollar markup

c. Using cost-based markup, what is the dollar markup on a good that costs $40 and has a markup percent of 25%?

$40 Cost × 25% Markup (0.25) = **$10 Markup**

Calculating Selling Price

The selling price of a good is the cost plus the amount of markup in dollars.

Dollar markup + Cost of goods = Selling price

d. Using cost-based markup, what is the selling price on a good that costs $40 and has a markup percent of 25%?

$40 Cost × 25% Markup (0.25) = $10 Markup
$40 Cost + $10 Markup = **$50 Selling price**

The selling price of a good also can be calculated by adding the markup percent to 100% and then multiplying the sum times the cost.

100% + Markup percent × Cost = Selling price

e. Using cost-based markup, what is the selling price of a good that cost $40 and has a markup of 25%?

100% + 25% Markup = 125%
125% × $40 Cost = **$50 Selling price**

MARKUP BASED ON SELLING PRICE

For many years almost all businesses based their markup on cost. Today, markup based on a *percent of selling price* is more common in retail businesses.

Calculating Markup Percent
When both the selling price and the dollar markup are known the markup percent is found by dividing the dollar markup by the selling price.

Dollar markup ÷ Selling price = Markup percent

f. Using price-based markup, what is the markup percent when the selling price is $80 and the dollar markup is $32?

$32 Markup ÷ $80 Selling price = 0.40 or **40% Markup**

When the selling price and the cost are known, the markup percent based on selling price is calculated by determining the dollar markup and then dividing it by the selling price.

g. Using price-based markup, what is the markup percent when the selling price is $80 and the cost is $48?

$80 Selling price − $48 Cost = $32 Markup
$32 Markup ÷ $80 Selling price = 0.40 or **40% Markup**

Calculating Dollar Markup
When both the selling price and the markup percent are known, the dollar markup is calculated by multiplying the selling price by the markup percent.

Selling price × Markup percent = Dollar markup

h. Using price-based markup, what is the dollar markup when the item sells for $80 and has a markup of 40%?

$80 Selling price × 40% Markup (0.40) = **$32 Markup**

Calculating Cost
In selling price-based markup, as in cost-based markup, the cost of the good is simply the selling price less the dollar markup.

Selling price − Dollar markup = Cost

i. What is the cost of an item that sells for $80 and has a markup of 40% based on selling price?

$80 Selling price × 40% Markup (0.40) = $32 Markup
$80 Selling price − $32 Markup = **$48 Cost**

The cost of a good also can be calculated by subtracting the markup percent from 100% and then multiplying the selling price times the difference.

100% − Markup percent × Selling price = Cost

j. What is the cost of an item if the markup is 40% of the selling price and the selling price is $80?

100% − 40% Markup percent = 60%
60% × $80 Selling price = **$48 Cost**

COMPLETE ASSIGNMENT 14-1

RELATIONSHIP BETWEEN COST-BASED AND PRICE-BASED METHODS

Rule: Given equal cost and dollar markup the markup percent for the cost-based method *will always be higher* than for the price-based method.

k. If an item costs $40, is marked up $10, and sells for $50, what will be the markup percent based on cost and what will be the markup percent based on selling price?

Markup Based on Cost *(Cost-Based Method)*	*Markup Based on Selling Price* *(Price-Based Method)*
$10 Markup ÷ $40 Cost = 25% Markup (**more**)	$10 Markup ÷ $50 Selling price = 20% Markup (**less**)

Sometimes merchants decide they want to have a certain percent of sales to cover operating expenses and to return a net profit. As shown earlier in this chapter, the dollar markup can be easily determined. But what if only the cost of the good and the price-based markup percent are known? How can the selling price be determined?

Assume the desired markup percent is 40% of the selling price. This means the cost of the good would be 60% (100% − 40%) of the selling price. Thus, the dollar cost divided by 60% (*price-based cost percent*) equals the selling price needed to have the dollar markup equal 40% of the selling price.

l. AD Corporation has decided that it wants a price-based markup of 40% for every radio it sells. If each radio costs the company $48 what should be the selling price for one radio?

100% Selling price − 40% Price-based markup = 60% Price-based cost
$48 Cost ÷ 60% Cost = **$80 Selling price**

Check: $80 Selling price − $48 Cost = $32 Markup
$32 Markup ÷ $80 Selling price = 40% Price-based markup

DISCOUNTED AND SPECIAL SALE ITEMS

Some businesses want to discount all of the merchandise in their stores. For example, a merchant might want to attract customers by taking 20% off the "original" price. At the same time, the merchant might want to have a 40% *price-based markup* **after** selling the goods at the discounted price. The "original" and the discounted prices can be calculated using the information already covered in this chapter.

Price-Based Markups

m. The merchandise in the Anderson Store, a retail outlet, contains a markup based on selling price. One item for sale in the store costs $90. The store's owner, R. K. Anderson, wants to offer the item at a 20% discount off the "original" price and still have a 40% markup based on the discounted sales price. What would be the discounted sales price and what would be the "original" price?

100% Discount sales price − 40% Markup = 60% Cost
$90 Cost ÷ 60% Price-based cost = $150 Discount sales price

100% "Original" price − 20% Discount = 80%
$150 Discount sales price ÷ 80% = **$187.50 "Original" price**

Check: 20% Discount on $187.50 = $187.50 × 20% = $37.50
      $187.50 − $37.50 = $150 Discount sales price
      $150 × 60% Price-based cost = $90 Cost

Cost-Based Markups

n. To calculate example m. when a *40% cost-based markup* is desired, the following steps can be used to determine the discount sales price and the "original" price.

$90 Cost × 40% Markup = $36 Markup
$90 Cost + $36 Markup = $126 Discount sales price
100% "Original" price − 20% Discount = 80%
$126 Discount sales price ÷ 80% = **$157.50 "Original" price**

Check: 20% Discount on $157.50 = $157.50 × 20% = $31.50
      $157.50 − $31.50 = $126 Discount sales price
      100% Cost + 40% Markup = 140% (1.40)
      $126 ÷ 140% = $90 Cost

COMPLETE ASSIGNMENTS 14-2 AND 14-3

Chapter terms for review

cost-based markup
cost of goods sold
dollar markup
gross profit
markup
markup percent
net profit

operating expenses
percent of cost
percent of selling price
price-based cost percent
price-based markup
sales

Assignment 14-1: Markup 1

A **(20 points)** — Calculate the markup in dollars and the selling price (1 point for each correct answer).

	Cost	Markup Based on Cost	Markup in Dollars	Selling Price			Cost	Markup Based on Cost	Markup in Dollars	Selling Price
1.	$200	20%	_____	_____	**6.**	$ 84	50%	_____	_____
2.	300	25%	_____	_____	**7.**	760	15%	_____	_____
3.	595	30%	_____	_____	**8.**	300	22%	_____	_____
4.	810	40%	_____	_____	**9.**	90	16.5%	_____	_____
5.	946	60%	_____	_____	**10.**	3,172	27%	_____	_____

Score for A (20)

B **(20 points)** — Calculate the selling price and the markup in dollars (1 point for each correct answer).

	Cost	Markup Based on Selling Price	Selling Price	Markup in Dollars			Cost	Markup Based on Selling Price	Selling Price	Markup in Dollars
11.	$200	20%	_____	_____	**16.**	$ 84	50%	_____	_____
12.	300	25%	_____	_____	**17.**	760	15%	_____	_____
13.	595	30%	_____	_____	**18.**	300	22%	_____	_____
14.	810	40%	_____	_____	**19.**	90	16.5%	_____	_____
15.	946	60%	_____	_____	**20.**	3,172	27%	_____	_____

Score for B (20)

C **(30 points)** — Round percents and dollar amounts to two places ($3\frac{1}{3}$ points for each correct answer).

21. The markup is $8 which is 20% of selling price:
  a. What is the selling price?   b. What is the cost?

_____   _____

22. The markup is $144 which is 45% of cost:
   a. What is the cost?   b. What is the selling price?

   _____   _____

23. The selling price is $90; the cost is $60:
   a. What is the markup in dollars?   b. What is the markup percent based on cost?

   _____   _____

   c. What is the markup percent based on selling price?

   _____

24. The markup is 30% of cost; the selling price is $182:
   a. What is the cost?   b. What is the markup percent based on selling price?

   _____   _____

D (30 points) — Calculate the markup in dollars based on selling price, cost, and markup percent based on cost. Round decimals to two places (1 point for each correct answer).

	Selling Price	Markup % Based on Selling Price	Markup In Dollars	Cost	Markup % Based on Cost
25.	$ 420.00	20%			
26.	700.00	35%			
27.	850.00	37.5%			
28.	1,204.80	40%			
29.	1,684.50	50%			
30.	66.00	$33\frac{1}{3}\%$			
31.	318.40	10%			
32.	160.00	20%			
33.	160.00	30%			
34.	160.00	40%			

Assignment 14-2:   Markup 2

A   (60 points) — Calculate the missing items. Round percents and dollar amounts to two places (2 points for each correct answer).

	Selling Price	Cost	Markup in Dollars	Markup % Based on Selling Price	Markup % Based on Cost
1.			$ 100	20%	
2.	560				$33\frac{1}{3}$%
3.		910		35%	
4.	420	300			
5.			90		50%
6.		1,200	400		
7.	96		16		
8.	900			40%	
9.		3,800			30%
10.	19.95	12.60			

Score for A (60)

B   (40 points) — Round percents to two decimal places (points for each correct answer as marked).

11. Bikes Around, Inc. sells a bicycle that costs $120 at a markup of 50% of selling price. The cost increased to $150. What would be the new markup percent based on selling price to earn the same amount of dollar profit (10 points)?

_____

12. The cost of the inventory in the hardware store is $470,250. The selling price of this merchandise totals $639,540 (2 points each).

a. What is the markup in dollars?

_____

b. What is the store's markup percent based on cost?

_____

c. What is the store's markup percent based on selling price?

_____

13. The Bilt Rite Company built five duplex apartments at a total cost of $525,000. The company sells them for $155,000 each. What is the markup percent based on selling price (6 points)?

_____

14. A boating store buys flags for $4 each and marks them up 150% of the cost price. What percent of the selling price does the supplier of the flags receive (6 points)?

_____

15. Western Sports buys imported soccer balls for $100 a dozen. What must be the selling price of each soccer ball in order for the store to make a profit (markup) of $33\frac{1}{3}$% based on selling price (6 points)?

_____

16. Clothing which cost $45,880 originally was priced at $82,000. It was damaged by smoke from a fire and discounted 20%. The store sold the entire stock. What was the percent of markup based on cost of the damaged goods (6 points)?

_____

Assignment 14-3:   Markup 3

A   (60 points) — Calculate each of the missing items. Round percents to two places (2 points for each correct answer).

	Selling Price	Markup Percent— Selling Price	Dollar Markup	Markup Percent on Cost	Cost
1.	$100	20%	_____	_____	____
2.	100	25%	_____	_____	____
3.	100	40%	_____	_____	____
4.	100	50%	_____	_____	____
5.	100	60%	_____	_____	____
6.	_____	_____	_____	25%	100
7.	_____	_____	_____	50%	100
8.	_____	_____	_____	60%	100
9.	_____	_____	_____	100%	100
10.	_____	_____	_____	125%	100

Score for A (60)

B   (40 points) — Round amounts and percents to two places (5 points for each correct answer).

11. At what price should an article costing $400 be marked so as to provide a markup of 25% on cost and allow for a 15% discount on its original price?

_____

12. The original price of a bicycle would have yielded a gain of 45% of selling price, but it had to be marked down to $130 in order to sell, which reduced the profit to 25% of selling price. What was the original marked price?

_____

13. A shoe store manager knows from experience that operating expenses are 35% over and above the cost of the shoes. If a profit of one-third of selling price is desired, what will be the selling price of a pair of shoes that cost $30?

_____

14. A watch costs a jeweler $120. The cost of covering store operations to buy and sell the watch is $16. If a profit (markup) of 30% of selling price is desired, what must be the marked price?

_____

15. The total cost of purchasing and stocking a small calculator is $12.40. At what price must the calculator be sold in order to have a gross profit (markup) of 30% on these costs and also allow 12% of the selling price for selling expense?

_____

16. A jobber sold one lot of goods at a profit (markup) of $160, which was 8% of cost. A second lot, costing the same, was sold for $2,500. What was the percent of markup on cost on the second lot?

_____

17. To decrease inventory, a clothier marked down a line of $120 men's jackets by 20%. This resulted in an increase in average daily sales from 5 to 8 jackets. By what percent did sales income increase?

_____

18. A department store bought 80 women's scarves for $560. At what price should each be marked in order to show a markdown of 20% and still make a profit (markup) of 25% on cost?

Original price   _____
Marked-down price _____

Part Four   Additional Percentage Applications

Chapter 15
Simple Interest

OBJECTIVES
After completing this chapter, you should be able to:

- **Understand simple interest concepts**
- **Compute interest using the ordinary interest method**
- **Compute interest using the exact interest method**
- **Approximate simple interest**

USING CREDIT IN BUSINESS

Much modern business is done on a credit basis. The buyer gains immediate possession and use of the seller's merchandise in exchange for a promise to pay within a given period. The purchase price on credit terms is equal to the cash price plus a fee called *interest*. The amount that is borrowed using credit is called the *principal*. Sometimes a buyer can save money by borrowing the principal, at a lower interest rate, from a bank and then paying cash to the seller.

The promise to pay for merchandise or repay a loan may be oral or written. If it is written, it may be in the form of a letter, or it could be a special form called commercial paper. *Short-term credit* or loans are normal transaction arrangements between one day and one year in length. *Long-term credit* transactions are usually those loans that are longer than one year. Normally they are used for major items such as new equipment or building improvements.

COMPUTING SIMPLE INTEREST

Interest is a percent of the principal for a specific period of time. Interest rates normally are stated in terms of one year. A rate of 10% means that the interest for one year would be 10% of the principal. To calculate simple interest multiply the principal times the rate times the time (stated in terms of years).

$$\text{Interest} = \text{Principal} \times \text{Rate} \times \text{Time} \quad \text{or} \quad I = P \times R \times T \quad \text{or} \quad I = PRT$$

When the time is exactly one year, Interest = Principal $\times$ Rate $\times$ 1 year.

a. Find the simple interest on a purchase of $450 if the rate is 10% and the time period is one year.

$$I = P \times R \times T = \$450 \times 0.10 \times 1 = \$45$$

When the time is different than one year, the method is exactly the same.

b. Find the simple interest on a loan of $1,000 when the rate is 8% and the loan period is:

One-half year	*3 years*
$I = P \times R \times T$	$I = P \times R \times T$
$= \$1,000 \times 0.08 \times \frac{1}{2}$	$= \$1,000 \times 0.08 \times 3$
$= \$40$	$= \$240$

The time period often will be measured in months or days instead of years. Before calculating the interest, change the time into years. When the time period is stated in months, divide the number of months by 12 (the number of months in one year).

c. Calculate the interest on a credit purchase of $2,000 at 10% for:

9 months	*18 months*
$I = P \times R \times T$	$I = P \times R \times T$
$= \$2,000 \times 0.10 \times \frac{9}{12}$	$= \$2,000 \times 0.10 \times \frac{18}{12}$
$= \$2,000 \times 0.10 \times \frac{3}{4}$	$= \$2,000 \times 0.10 \times \frac{3}{2}$
$= \$150$	$= \$300$

Ordinary Interest and Exact Interest

If the term of the loan is stated as a certain number of days, divide the number of days by the number of days in one year—either 360 or 365. Before computers and calculators, interest was easier to calculate by assuming that every year had 360 days and that every month had 30 days. The 360-day method, called the *ordinary interest method*, is still used by many businesses and individuals.

Banks, savings and loan institutions, credit unions and the federal government have a 365-day year (366 days for leap years) to calculate interest. This method is called the *exact interest method*. The calculations are the same except 365 days is used instead of 360 days.

d. Calculate the ordinary interest and the exact interest on $800 at 9% for:

60 days, ordinary interest	*60 days, exact interest*	*90 days, ordinary interest*	*90 days, exact interest*
$I = P \times R \times T$	$I = P \times R \times T$	$I = P \times R \times T$	$I = P \times R \times T$
$= \$800 \times 0.09 \times \frac{60}{360}$	$= \$800 \times 0.09 \times \frac{60}{365}$	$= \$800 \times 0.09 \times \frac{90}{360}$	$= \$800 \times 0.09 \times \frac{90}{365}$
$= \$800 \times 0.09 \times \frac{1}{6}$	$= \$800 \times 0.09 \times \frac{12}{73}$	$= \$800 \times 0.09 \times \frac{1}{4}$	$= \$800 \times 0.09 \times \frac{18}{73}$
$= \$12$	$= \$11.8356$ or **$11.84**	$= \$18$	$= \$17.7534$ or **$17.75**

The dollar amount of the interest will always be smaller using the exact interest method. The difference may not seem like very much. In examples d. and e. (90 days), the difference is only 25¢ ($18.00 − $17.75). However, when businesses borrow money, the principal is often large, and then the difference between ordinary interest and exact interest can be significant.

e. Find the difference between ordinary interest and exact interest on $8,000,000 at 9% for 90 days.

Ordinary Interest	Exact Interest
$I = P \times R \times T$	$I = P \times R \times T$
$= \$8,000,000 \times 0.09 \times \dfrac{90}{360}$	$= \$8,000,000 \times 0.09 \times \dfrac{90}{365}$
$= \$8,000,000 \times 0.09 \times \dfrac{1}{4}$	$= \$8,000,000 \times 0.09 \times \dfrac{18}{73}$
$= \$180,000$	$= \$177,534.2466$ or $\$177,534.25$

The difference is **$2,465.75** ($180,000 − $177,534.25).

Use of Calculators

Today, calculators or computers are used in almost every interest application. The numbers are often large, and important. The calculator steps are performed in the same order as written in the formula.

f. Write the calculator steps to calculate the exact interest on $8,000,000 at 9% for 90 days.

$$I = P \times R \times T = \$8,000,000 \times 0.09 \times \frac{90}{365}$$

$$8,000,000 \quad \times \quad 0.09 \quad \times \quad 90 \quad \div \quad 365 \quad = \quad 177,534.2466$$

Using the Percent Key % , the steps would be

$$8,000,000 \quad \times \quad 9 \quad \% \quad \times \quad 90 \quad \div \quad 365 \quad = \quad 177,534.2466$$

Cancellation

When a calculator is not available, it may be possible to simplify the multiplication by cancellation. This is especially true with 360-day interest and loan periods such as 30, 60, 90 and 120 days. Example d. is solved again, this time using cancellation.

g. Calculate the ordinary interest on $800 at 9% for:

60 days	90 days
$I = P \times R \times T$	$I = P \times R \times T$
$= \$800 \times 0.09 \times \dfrac{60}{360}$	$= \$800 \times 0.09 \times \dfrac{90}{360}$
$= \overset{\$400}{\cancel{\$800}} \times \overset{0.03}{\cancel{0.09}} \times \dfrac{\overset{1}{\cancel{60}}}{\underset{\underset{1}{\cancel{3}}}{\cancel{360}}}$	$= \overset{\$200}{\cancel{\$800}} \times 0.09 \times \dfrac{\overset{1}{\cancel{90}}}{\underset{1}{\cancel{360}}}$
$= \$12$	$= \$18$

Cancellation is not as useful in exact interest because 365 does not reduce very easily. Only 5 and 73 divide evenly into 365.

APPROXIMATING INTEREST

Although calculators are used to compute interest, approximation remains as useful as ever. The following calculator solution requires 19 key entries.

$$8,000,000 \times 0.09 \times 90 \div 365 = 177,534.2466$$

If any one of the 19 keys is pressed incorrectly, there will be a large error. Making an estimate of the interest in advance can help you spot a significant calculator error.

Combinations of Time and Interest that Yield 1%

To make simple mental approximations, the principal, rate and time should be rounded to numbers that are easy to compute mentally. For ordinary interest, several combinations of rate and time are easier to use because their product is 1%. For example, $12\% \times \frac{30}{360} = 12\% \times \frac{1}{12} = 1\%$ and $6\% \times \frac{60}{360} = 6\% \times \frac{1}{6} = 1\%$.

h. Approximate the ordinary interest on $1,475 at 6.25% for 59 days.

Round $1,475 to $1,500; 6.25% to 6%; and 59 days to 60 days.

Estimate: $\qquad \$1,500 \times 0.06 \times \dfrac{60}{360} = \$1,500 \times 0.01 = \$15$

Actual Interest: $\$1,475 \times 0.0625 \times \dfrac{59}{360} = \$15.1085$ or $\$15.11$

Other Rates and Times

Listed below are several other combinations of rate and time whose products are useful for estimating interest.

$$8\% \times \frac{45}{360} = 8\% \times \frac{1}{8} = 1\% \qquad 10\% \times \frac{36}{360} = 10\% \times \frac{1}{10} = 1\%$$

$$9\% \times \frac{40}{360} = 9\% \times \frac{1}{9} = 1\% \qquad 18\% \times \frac{20}{360} = 18\% \times \frac{1}{18} = 1\%$$

$$12\% \times \frac{60}{360} = 12\% \times \frac{1}{6} = 2\% \qquad 12\% \times \frac{90}{360} = 12\% \times \frac{1}{4} = 3\%$$

$$8\% \times \frac{90}{360} = 8\% \times \frac{1}{4} = 2\% \qquad 9\% \times \frac{120}{360} = 9\% \times \frac{1}{3} = 3\%$$

Estimation of Exact Interest

The goal in approximating interest is to get a close estimate. Even though exact interest requires 365 days in a year, you can make a good estimate by assuming that the number of days in a year is 360.

i. Estimate the exact interest on $1,025 at 11.5% for 61 days.

First, round $1,025 to $1,000, 11.5% to 12% and 61 days to 60 days. Second, assume that a year has 360 days.

Estimate: $\qquad \$1,000 \times 0.12 \times \dfrac{60}{360} = \$1,000 \times 0.02 = \$20$

Actual Interest: $\$1,025 \times 0.115 \times \dfrac{61}{365} = \$19.6997$ or $\$19.70$

COMPLETE ASSIGNMENTS 15-1 AND 15-2

Chapter terms for review

exact interest method	ordinary interest method
interest	principal
long-term credit	short-term credit

Assignment 15-1:   Simple Interest

A (48 points) — Calculate both the ordinary interest and exact interest for the following problems. Round answers to the nearest cent (2 points for each correct answer).

Principal, Rate and Time	Ordinary Interest	Exact Interest
$1,000 at 11% for 30 days	1. _____	2. _____
$600 at 15% for 60 days	3. _____	4. _____
$1,250 at 8% for 90 days	5. _____	6. _____
$3,600 at 12% for 20 days	7. _____	8. _____
$750 at 9% for 45 days	9. _____	10. _____
$2,400 at 7.5% for 75 days	11. _____	12. _____
$400 at 13% for 120 days	13. _____	14. _____
$2,700 at 20% for 15 days	15. _____	16. _____
$4,000 at 8.25% for 180 days	17. _____	18. _____
$1,720 at 14.5% for 240 days	19. _____	20. _____
$820 at 16% for 270 days	21. _____	22. _____
$100 at 20% for 5 years	23. _____	24. _____

Score for A (48)

B (26) points) — In each problem, (1) calculate the actual ordinary interest; and (2) estimate the interest by rounding the principal to the nearest hundred dollars. Also, for each estimate, use the given suggestion to create a shortcut. Round answers to the nearest cent (3$\frac{1}{4}$ points for each correct answer).

Principal, Rate and Time	Actual Ordinary Interest	Estimated Interest
$820 at 11.75% for 30 days	**25.** _____	**26.** _____ (let I = 12%)
$1,575 at 12% for 61 days	**27.** _____	**28.** _____ (let T = 60 days)
$580 at 12.25% for 90 days	**29.** _____	**30.** _____ (let I = 12%)
$2,540 at 6% for 58 days	**31.** _____	**32.** _____ (let T = 60 days)

C (26 points) — In each problem, (1) calculate the actual exact interest; and (2) estimate the interest by rounding the principal to the nearest hundred dollars. For each estimate, assume that a year has 360 days and use the given suggestion to create a shortcut. Round answers to the nearest cent (3$\frac{1}{4}$ points for each correct answer).

Principal, Rate and Time	Actual Exact Interest	Estimated Interest
$735 at 6% for 57 days	**33.** _____	**34.** _____ (let T = 60 days)
$1,965 at 12.3% for 60 days	**35.** _____	**36.** _____ (let I = 12%)
$3,280 at 12% for 28 days	**37.** _____	**38.** _____ (let T = 30 days)
$440 at 5.75% for 120 days	**39.** _____	**40.** _____ (let I = 6%)

Assignment 15-2: Simple Interest Applications

A (50 points) — Solve each of the following ordinary simple interest problems using a 360-day year. Calculate both the interest and the total amount of the loan: i.e., principal plus interest (5 points for each correct answer).

1. Mary Wallis borrowed $1,400 at 11% simple interest for 270 days. What is the total amount that she will be required to pay on the due date?

Interest _____

Amount _____

2. Nancy and Doug Olson want to borrow money for a trip to Europe. They estimate that they should borrow $5,000 and that they will pay it back in two years. If the simple interest rate is 12%, how much will they need to pay on the due date?

Interest _____

Amount _____

3. Bill Chan has a radio and television repair shop. One of his favorite customers borrowed $1,200 cash for an emergency. Bill charged him 5% simple interest for 75 days. How much will the customer be required to pay at the end of the 75 days?

Interest _____

Amount _____

4. In January, David Smith, owner of River's Edge Boat Dock, wanted a short-term loan to buy material to repair his dock before summer. He borrowed $2,800 for 180 days at a rate of 18% simple interest. How much will he need to pay at the end of the term of the loan?

Interest _____

Amount _____

5. Jack White loaned $300 to his best friend, Dale, and charged him 6% simple interest. Dale repaid everything, interest and principal, to Jack 120 days later. How much did Dale pay on the due date?

Interest _____

Amount _____

Score for A (50)

B (50 points) — Solve each of the following exact simple interest problems using a 365-day year. Calculate both the interest and the total amount of the loan: i.e., principal plus interest (5 points for each correct answer).

6. Jorge Salizar owns and operates a computer store. To make the payment on new equipment that is soon to be shipped to him, he borrowed $40,000 at 12.5% simple interest for 45 days. How much will Jorge owe on this short-term loan at the end of the 45 days?

Interest _____

Amount _____

7. Betty Kiker of Kiker CopCo owns a small copying and printing business. She gives her customers credit at a simple interest rate of 15% from the time of purchase. If a customer with a printing job costing $220 charges the entire amount and pays for it 17 days later, how much will the customer have to pay to Betty?

Interest _____

Amount _____

8. When Ken Nishimura graduated from high school, he went to work on a fishing boat. After three years, he has saved almost enough money to buy his own fishing boat, a used one his boss wants to sell. He needs an additional $8,500. His boss agreed to loan him the additional money for 250 days, which would permit Ken to complete a season of fishing before having to pay the loan. How much will Ken need to pay on this loan if the boss charged a simple interest rate of 9%?

Interest _____

Amount _____

9. Olga Rocza's younger sister lived with Olga while she attended school. When school finished, she got a job and wanted to move into an apartment. Olga loaned her sister $2,500 and said that she did not have to pay anything for 300 days. If Olga charged 8% simple interest, how much will her sister need to pay when the 300 days expire?

Interest _____

Amount _____

10. Harriet Sanders of Sanders Heating Co. wishes to purchase a new truck for her company, and she needs to borrow part of the money. Rather than make monthly payments to a bank, she wants to make a private loan where she pays back all interest and principal in one lump sum at the end of 3 years. How much in total will Harriet pay back if she borrows $10,000 at 11.2% simple interest for three years?

Interest _____

Amount _____

Score for B (50)

Part Five

Applications of
Simple Interest

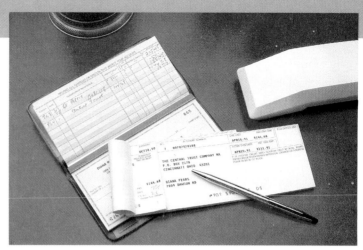

Chapter 16
Notes and Interest Variables

OBJECTIVES
After completing this chapter, you should be able to:

- **Understand promissory notes**
- **Calculate the number of days between two dates**
- **Determine due dates**
- **Complete interest variables**

PROMISSORY NOTES

Businesses use many different methods or instruments to charge interest. Perhaps the most fundamental instrument is the *promissory note*, which is defined by the Uniform Commercial Code as an unconditional promise made in writing by one party to another. The maker of the promise agrees to pay on demand, or at a particular time, a certain sum of money to the bearer. It is called a *negotiable promissory note* when it may be sold to a third party.

The dollar amount written on the note is called the *face value* of the note. The face value is the same as the *principal (P)*, or amount borrowed. Promissory notes may be either interest-bearing or non-interest-bearing. If a note is interest-bearing, the sum of the face value and the *interest dollars (I)* is the *maturity value (MV)*. It is the total amount that must be paid by the borrower when the note becomes due. Figure 16-1 shows an example of a promissory note.

FIGURE 16-1   Promissory Note

$ *2,000⁰⁰* _____ ATLANTA, GEORGIA *March 15* _____ 19____

— *Sixty days* — AFTER DATE _____ *I* _____ PROMISE TO PAY TO

THE ORDER OF *Mary Low Pastorino* _____

PAYABLE AT MERCHANT'S BANK

Two thousand ⁰⁰/100 _____ DOLLARS

VALUE RECEIVED WITH INTEREST AT *16 %* _____

NO. *47* _____ DUE *May 14, 19--*

Nathaniel Rothman _____

DETERMINING DUE DATE AND NUMBER OF INTEREST DAYS

The interest period of a promissory note may be defined either by specifying the due date of the note or by stating the number of interest days. When the due date is specified you must calculate the number of interest days. When the number of interest days is given you must determine the due date. To make either calculation, you need to know the number of days in each month.

Month	Number of Days	Month	Number of Days	Month	Number of Days
January	31 days	May	31 days	September	30 days
February	28 days	June	30 days	October	31 days
March	31 days	July	31 days	November	30 days
April	30 days	August	31 days	December	31 days

This old rhyme may help you remember the number of days: Thirty days has September, April, June and November. When short February's done, all the rest have thirty-one.

February has 29 days in a leap year. A leap year is a year that can be evenly divided by 4. However, a year ending in 00 is not a leap year unless it can be evenly divided by 400. 1900 was not a leap year, but 2000 will be a leap year. (Note: Exact interest is calculated using 366 days in a leap year.)

Steps for Calculating the Number of Days Between Two Dates

1. Determine the number of interest days in the beginning month.
2. Determine the number of interest days in the middle months.
3. Add the numbers from Steps 1 and 2 and the number of interest days in the final month. For the final month the number of interest days is equal to the due date number.

a. A promissory note is made on July 25. The due date is October 8. Determine the number of interest days between July 25 and October 8.

Step 1	Step 3
31 days in July	6 days in July
− 25 date of note	31 days in August
6 days of interest in July	30 days in September
	+ 8 days in October
Step 2	75 total interest days in the promissory note
August has 31 days	
September has 30 days	

Steps for Determining the Due Date

1. Determine the number of interest days in the beginning month.
2. Determine the number of interest days which remain after the first month.
3. Determine the number of interest days remaining at the end of each succeeding month. Continue until less than one month remains. The due date number is the same as the remaining number of interest days in the final month.

b. A promissory note is made on July 25. The note is for 75 days. Determine the due date.

Step 1	Step 3
31 days in July	69 days of interest left after July
− 25 date of note	− 31 days in August
6 days of interest in July	38 days of interest left after August
	− 30 days in September
Step 2	8 days of interest left after September
75 days of interest in the note	
− 6 days left in July	
69 days left in term after July	The due date is October 8.

When the length of the interest period is expressed in months, the date is advanced by the number of months given. The same day of the month is the due date. For example, a 3-month note dated July 3 will be due on October 3. The exact number of interest days must then be calculated, as shown previously. If the note is dated the 31st of some month and the month of maturity is April, June, September or November, then the due date is the 30th.

c. Find the due date of a 3-month note dated January 31 (the last day of the month).

Maturity month	April (count "February, March, April")
Last day	30 (last day of April)
	Therefore, the due date is April 30.

COMPUTING THE INTEREST VARIABLES

A simple interest problem has four variables: Interest, Principal, Rate and Time. In Chapter 15, we solved for the amount of Interest (I) when the Principal (P), Rate (R), and Time (T) were all given. However, as long as any three variables are given, the fourth always may be computed by just changing the formula $I = P \times R \times T$ into one of its possible variations that are shown below.

You should assume the use of ordinary interest (a 360-day year) unless the use of exact interest (a 365-day year) is indicated. The stated or calculated interest *rate (R)* is the rate for one full year. Also, the length of *time (T)* used for calculating the interest dollars must be stated in terms of all or part of a year.

Finding the Interest Amount, Principal, Rate, or Time

RULE: When any three variables are known, you can solve for the fourth variable.

This table will help you calculate the missing value:

To find	You must know	Use this formula
I	P, R, and T	$I = P \times R \times T$
P	I, R, and T	$P = \dfrac{I}{R \times T}$
R	I, P, and T	$R = \dfrac{I}{P \times T}$
T	I, P, and R	$T = \dfrac{I}{P \times R}$

d. Find the Principal if the Interest is $45, the Rate is 9%, and the Time is 60 days.

$P = ?$ $R = 9\%$ $I = \$45$ $T = 60$ days

$$P = \frac{I}{R \times T} = \frac{\$45}{0.09 \times \frac{60}{360}} = \frac{\$45}{0.015} = \$3,000$$

e. Find the Rate if the Interest is $22, the Principal is $2,000, and the Time is 30 days.

$R = ?$ $P = \$2,000$ $I = \$22$ $T = 30$ days

$$R = \frac{I}{P \times T} = \frac{\$22}{\$2,000 \times \frac{30}{360}} = \frac{\$22}{\$166.67} = 0.13 \text{ or } 13\%$$

f. Find the Time if the Interest is $54, the Principal is $1,800, and the Rate is 12%. Express Time in days, based on a 360-day year.

$T = ?$ $P = \$1,800$ $I = \$54$ $R = 12\%$

$$T = \frac{I}{P \times R} = \frac{\$54}{\$1,800 \times 0.12} = \frac{\$54}{\$216} = 0.25 \text{ year}$$

Based on a 360-day year, 0.25 year = 0.25 × 360 days = 90 days

Calculating the Maturity Value

As stated earlier, the maturity value of a note is the face value (principal) plus the interest, or $MV = P + I$. The interest-bearing, 90-day note in Figure 16-1 has a face value of \$1,500 and 12% annual interest rate. The exact interest (using a 365-day year) is: $I = P \times R \times T = \$1,500 \times 0.12 \times \frac{90}{365} = \$44.38$. The maturity value is: \$1,500 + \$44.38 = \$1,544.38.

COMPLETE ASSIGNMENTS 16-1 AND 16-2

Chapter terms for review

face value	principal (P)
interest dollars (I)	promissory note
maturity value (MV)	rate (R)
negotiable promissory note	time (T)

Assignment 16-1: Dates, Time and Interest

A (20 points) — Find the number of days upon which interest would be computed in the following situations. Check for leap years (2 points for each correct answer).

From	To	Number of Days
1. September 13, 1996	December 6, 1996	_____
2. August 10, 1995	October 30, 1995	_____
3. January 12, 1996	March 12, 1996	_____
4. June 9, 1994	September 19, 1994	_____
5. March 5, 1997	August 15, 1997	_____
6. December 3, 1999	March 13, 2000	_____
7. April 15, 1998	October 15, 1998	_____
8. November 10, 1995	January 25, 1996	_____
9. May 20, 1996	September 20, 1996	_____
10. January 2, 1998	April 15, 1998	_____

Score for A (20)

B (20 points) — Determine the maturity date for each of the following notes. Consider leap years where necessary (2 points for each correct answer).

Date of Note	Time	Maturity Date
11. July 24, 1997	75 days	_____
12. August 26, 1995	60 days	_____
13. January 14, 1998	120 days	_____
14. June 7, 1996	180 days	_____
15. December 8, 1995	90 days	_____
16. October 4, 1999	45 days	_____
17. October 31, 1995	6 months	_____
18. June 30, 1994	2 months	_____
19. November 30, 1995	3 months	_____
20. February 29, 1996	1 year	_____

Score for B (20)

C (60 points) — Compute the amount of interest due at maturity on each of the following notes. On problems 21-26, use a 360-day year. On problems 27-32, use a 365-day year and consider leap years if necessary. Fill in the missing entries for Time or Maturity Date (2 points for each correct Time or Maturity Date; 3 points for each correct Interest amount).

Face Value (360-day year)	Date	Time	Due Date	Rate	Interest
21. $12,400	September 24, 1996	_____	December 23, 1996	10%	_____
22. $4,250	August 4, 1995	45 days	_____	8%	_____
23. $860	April 28, 1997	75 days	_____	11%	_____
24. $450	December 15, 1995	_____	February 13, 1996	9%	_____
25. $8,200	March 21, 1994	_____	July 19, 1994	13%	_____
26. $25,000	July 23, 1997	180 days	_____	10%	_____

(365-day year)					
27. $5,820	May 28, 1998	45 days	_____	7%	_____
28. $14,825	January 18, 1996	_____	March 18, 1996	12%	_____
29. $640	December 18, 1997	_____	March 18, 1998	9%	_____
30. $21,500	July 20, 1995	75 days	_____	11%	_____
31. $1,800	February 28, 2000	90 days	_____	10%	_____
32. $925	October 28, 1994	_____	December 12, 1994	8%	_____

Score for C (60)

Assignment 16-2: Solving for Interest Variables

A   (60 points) — Determine the missing variable from the basic interest formula. **Express Time in days. Use a 360-day year (6 points for each correct answer).**

	Principal	Rate	Time	Interest
1.	$4,230	8%	60 days	_____
2.	_____	14%	225 days	$101.50
3.	$680	_____	45 days	$8.50
4.	$8,460	10%	105 days	_____
5.	_____	15%	120 days	$60
6.	$10,000	12%	_____	$200
7.	$15,400	12%	_____	$154
8.	$12,680	_____	135 days	$285.30
9.	$1,200	_____	75 days	$22.50
10.	$25,000	12%	_____	$2,000

Score for A (60)

B   (40 points) — **Solve each of the following problems for the missing variable. Express fractions of years in days and base all calculations on a 360-day year. Round dollar amounts to the nearest cent and percents to the nearest $\frac{1}{10}$ of a percent (8 points for each correct answer).**

11. Cindy Warner wants to purchase a new set of bedroom furniture for her two children. She borrowed $1,500 for 120 days from a friend and agrees to pay interest equivalent to what her friend could otherwise earn in 120 days. If she pays her friend $47.50 in interest, what simple interest rate would Cindy pay?

_____

12. Ken Carrera borrows $800. At the end of the loan period, Ken will pay a total of $836. The lender, Fitzwalter Finance Company, charges 18% simple interest. What is the length of the loan period?

_____

13. Michael Moore needs a new furnace for his store. Brown Heating and Air Conditioning will sell and install a new furnace for $3,000 cash. Brown told Michael that he could choose to pay 20% of the price now, and the balance in 75 days. For this financing, Brown charges 16% simple interest on the unpaid amount. How much will Michael save by paying all cash at the time of purchase?

_____

14. Gomez Appliance Center sold a freezer to a customer who paid one-half the cash price at the time of purchase. The customer will pay the other half, plus 12% simple interest, in 60 days. If the amount of the interest is $4.75, what is the cash price?

_____

15. Walter Mayberry made an emergency loan of $2,000 to a relative, with the agreement that the relative will repay a total of $2,300 in 270 days. What rate of simple interest is Walter charging to his relative?

_____

Chapter 17
Borrowing by Business

OBJECTIVES
After completing this chapter, you should be able to:

- Calculate interest using the single-payment method
- Calculate interest using the unpaid-balance method
- Choose between borrowing to take advantage of a cash discount and foregoing the discount to avoid the loan cost
- Calculate the proceeds from discounting an interest-bearing note
- Calculate the proceeds from discounting a non-interest-bearing note
- Determine the proceeds of a bank discount

While businesses, like individuals, may use loans that are longer than one year to purchase new equipment or buildings, they also borrow cash for very short periods of time, even for just a few days. A business that buys and then resells merchandise usually will have to pay its supplier for the goods before it has had sufficient time to sell and collect payment from customers. During this time period, the business may need to borrow money from a bank in order to pay the supplier's bill, called an *invoice*.

LOANS FROM FINANCIAL INSTITUTIONS

Financial institutions offer a wide variety of loans, each with several variations. It is important to become familiar with some of them.

Single-Payment Interest
Single-payment interest is the most direct method of computing interest on loans. This method is popular for loans over a short period of time. For example, as you studied in Chapter 15, the interest on $2,500 at 11% for 45 days, based upon a 365-day year, is calculated using the basic formula $I = P \times R \times T$.

$$I = P \times R \times T = \$2,500 \times 0.11 \times \frac{45}{365} = \$33.9041 \text{ or } \$33.90$$

The loan principal, $2,500, plus the interest due at maturity, $33.90, would be paid in a single amount, $2,533.90, on the due date, called the *maturity date*, of the loan.

Unpaid-Balance Interest

Lenders charge interest on the *principal*, which is the amount of money that the borrower owes to the lender. A borrower often repays a loan by making regular, usually monthly, payments that may be equal in amount. (The period of time from one payment to the next is called the *payment period*.) Part of each payment pays the lender the interest owed for the period and the rest repays part of the principal. Therefore, with each payment the remaining principal not yet repaid, called the *unpaid balance*, decreases. Frequently a lender uses the *unpaid-balance interest method* to recalculate a new interest amount each payment period. (Note: In this chapter interest will be calculated each month on an annual basis, using a 365-day year, unless stated otherwise.)

Steps for Calculating Interest and the New Unpaid Balance (Unpaid-Balance Interest Method)

1. Determine the number of interest days covered by the payment.
2. Calculate the interest for the current payment period:
   a. Multiply the unpaid balance amount as of the beginning of the interest period times the annual interest rate times the number of interest days in the payment period (from Step 1);
   b. Divide the product from Step 2a by 365 days (or 360 days if stated).
3. Determine the amount of the principal payment by subtracting the interest calculated in Step 2 from the payment amount.
4. Determine the new unpaid balance by subtracting the amount of the principal payment (from Step 3) from the unpaid balance at the beginning of the interest period (see Step 2a).

a. A loan of $2,000 at 10% for 3 months is made on June 10. Two payments of $675 each are made on July 10 and August 10. The remaining unpaid balance and interest is paid on September 10. Exact interest is calculated and paid on the unpaid balance each month.

		First Month	*Second Month*
Step 1	Days of interest:	30 days (June 10 to July 10)	31 days (July 10 to Aug. 10)
	Unpaid balance:	$2,000 on June 10	$1,341.44 on July 10
Step 2	Month's interest:	$I = P \times R \times T$	$I = P \times R \times T$
		$= \$2,000 \times 0.10 \times \frac{30}{365}$	$= \$1,341.44 \times 0.10 \times \frac{31}{365}$
		$= \$16.44$	$= \$11.39$
	Total payment:	$675 paid (July 10)	$675 paid (Aug. 10)
Step 3	Paid on principal:	$675.00 − $16.44 = $658.56	$675.00 − $11.39 = $663.61
Step 4	New unpaid balance:	$2,000 − $658.56 = $1,341.44	$1,341.44 − $663.61 = $677.83

		Last Month
Step 1	Days of interest:	31 days (Aug. 10 to Sept. 10)
	Unpaid balance:	$677.83 on Aug. 10
Step 2	Month's interest:	$I = P \times R \times T$
		$= \$677.83 \times 0.10 \times \frac{31}{365}$
		$= \$5.76$
	Total payment:	$683.59 paid (Sept. 10)
		($677.83 unpaid balance
		+ $5.76 interest)
Step 3	Paid on principal:	$677.83 (the unpaid balance)
Step 4	New unpaid balance:	$0.00

BORROWING MONEY TO MAKE A CASH DISCOUNT

As you learned in Chapter 11, a business may receive purchase terms such as 2-10, net 30 which means that it will receive a discount of 2% if it pays cash for its merchandise within 10 days. Often, however, the business may not have sufficient cash on hand to pay for the merchandise to qualify for the discount. An important question is whether the business can save money by borrowing cash to be able to pay the invoice within the discount period. Frequently a business finds the answer by determining which costs less: (1) the full cost of the invoice paid at the due date, or (2) the cost of the invoice minus the discount plus the loan interest.

b. Popplewell Corp. purchased $10,000 worth of merchandise on September 17 at terms of 2-10, net 30. Thus, Popplewell Corp. must pay $10,000 on October 17, but if it pays before September 27, it will receive a discount of 2%.

Assume Popplewell will have the cash on the October 17 deadline, but not before. If it chooses to, it is able to borrow the cash it needs from the bank at an annual interest rate of 18%.

Choice #1: Wait until October 17 to pay the invoice.
Total cost to Popplewell: the $10,000.00 invoice amount

Choice #2: Borrow money and pay by September 27 (within the discount period):

Total invoice amount:	$10,000.00
Cash discount: 2% × $10,000 =	− 200.00
Total cash needed to pay by Sept. 27	$ 9,800.00

Interest cost to borrow the $9,800 from September 27 to

October 17: $I = P \times R \times T = \$9,800 \times 0.18 \times \frac{20}{365} =$ + 96.66

    Total cost of Choice #2 to Popplewell $ 9,896.66

Therefore, even at 18% interest, Popplewell Corp. will save $103.34 ($10,000.00 − $9,896.66) if it borrows $9,800 for just 20 days in order to receive the $200 discount.

NOTE: Do not conclude that borrowing and paying off the invoice within the discount period will always be the better choice. Factors such as the bank interest rate and the discount percentage may change and could cause the calculations to change.

COMPLETE ASSIGNMENT 17-1

DISCOUNTING NOTES

In Chapter 16 you learned about negotiable promissory notes. The *face value* of the note is the principal; the *maturity value* is the face value plus the interest on the maturity date; this type of note is an *interest-bearing note.*

c. On September 20, Eickworth Engineering ("Ike") lent $1,200 to FitzCo Products ("Fitz") for 90 days at a 10% rate of interest. In return, Fitz gave Ike an interest-bearing negotiable promissory note. Calculate the due date and the maturity value of the note. (Assume a 360-day year.)

Due date: September 20 + 90 days = December 19

Maturity value
(two computations):

(a) Interest:
$$= P \times R \times T$$
$$= \$1,200 \times 0.10 \times \frac{90}{360} = \$30$$

(b) Maturity value:
$$= Principal + Interest$$
$$= \$1,200 + \$30 = \$1,230$$

Discounting an Interest-Bearing Note

A *negotiable note* is one that can be sold by the lender. In example c. the note has a value of $1,230 on December 19 because Eickworth Engineering will receive $1,230 from FitzCo on that date. If Ike needs cash on November 19, it can sell the note to someone who will receive the $1,230 from Fitz on December 19. Of course, they will give Ike less than the maturity value of $1,230. Selling a note before maturity is called *discounting the note* and is calculated using percents.

When someone buys the note before maturity there is a fee (the *discount*) that is the product of the percent (the *discount rate*) the buyer is charging times the maturity value of the note. The amount the seller receives from the buyer (the *proceeds*) is the difference between the maturity value and the discount amount. The time between the date of sale (the *discount date*) and maturity date is called the *discount period*. Note that the formula for the discount calculation is similar to the interest formula:

Discount = Maturity value × Discount rate × Discount period
(or D = MV × R × T)

FIGURE 17-1
Discounting Notes
Time Line

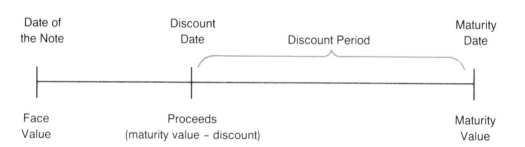

Steps for Discounting an Interest-Bearing Note

1. Determine the maturity (due) date of the note.
2. Calculate the number of days in the discount period.
3. Calculate the maturity value of the note (face value + interest to the maturity date).
4. Calculate the amount of the discount (maturity value × discount rate × time).
5. Calculate the proceeds by subtracting the discount amount (Step 4) from the maturity value (Step 3).

d. Suppose on November 19 Rocky Mountain Finance Company ("RMF") agrees to buy from Eickworth the FitzCo Products note and charges Ike 18% of the maturity value of the note. Calculate the due date of the note, the number of days in the discount period, the maturity value, the amount of the discount, and the proceeds. (Assume a 360-day year.)

Step 1   Due date: December 19 (from example c.)
Step 2   Discount period: = November 19 to December 19 = 30 days
Step 3   Maturity value: = $1,230 (from example c.)
Step 4   Discount amount: = MV × R × T = $1,230 × 0.18 × $\frac{30}{360}$
                                   = $18.45
Step 5   Proceeds: = $1,230 − $18.45 = $1,211.55

$1,200	$1,211.55	$1,230
Fitz ←——— Ike	Ike ←——— RMF	RMF ←——— Fitz
Note	Note	Note
Fitz ———→ Ike	Ike ———→ RMF	RMF ———→ Fitz
September 20	November 19	December 19
Original loan with note to Ike	RMF buys note from Ike, at a discount	Fitz repays loan to note holder (RMF)

Discounting a Non-Interest-Bearing Note

If the maturity value of a note equals its face value it is a *non-interest-bearing note*. Perhaps the lender asked the borrower to pay the interest in advance or did not charge interest for the loan. Whatever the arrangement, the steps for discounting a non-interest-bearing note are almost the same as for an interest-bearing one.

Steps for Discounting a Non-Interest-Bearing Note

1. Determine the maturity (due) date of the note.
2. Calculate the number of days in the discount period.
3. Calculate the amount of the discount (maturity value × discount rate × time).
4. Calculate the proceeds by subtracting the discount amount (Step 3) from the maturity value.

e. A 45-day non-interest-bearing note for $500 is dated April 2. Calculate the proceeds if the note is discounted at 15% on April 11. (Assume a 360-day year.)

Step 1   Due date: April 2 + 45 days = May 17
Step 2   Discount period: = April 11 to May 17 = 36 days
Step 3   Discount amount: = MV × R × T = $500 × 0.15 × $\frac{36}{360}$
                                   = $7.50
Step 4   Proceeds: = $500 − $7.50 = $492.50

Bank Discount

Suppose that a bank agrees to a 60-day 9% note for $800. The bank charges $800 × 0.09 × $\frac{60}{360}$ = $12. Generally, banks give the borrower $800 and collect $812 on the due date. Sometimes, however, banks collect the interest in advance. Instead of giving the borrower $800, they deduct $12 and only give $788 on the date of the note.

The $800 is the face value of the note and the $788 is the proceeds. The $12 is the amount of the discount and the 9% is the discount rate. The 60 days is the discount period. The concept and the terms are identical to discounting the note explained on the previous page.

Discount Rate Versus Interest Rate

When a bank uses the discount method, the "discount rate" is not the "interest rate." In the example of discounting above, the "discount rate" was 9%, and the borrower had to pay $12 to borrow $788 for 60 days. To calculate the actual "interest rate" that exists, use the formula $R = \frac{I}{P \times T}$ from Chapter 16, and let $I = \$12$, $P = \$788$ and $T = \frac{60}{360}$ (based on a 360-day year).

$$R = \frac{I}{P \times T} = \frac{\$12}{\$788 \times \frac{60}{360}} = 0.09137 \text{ or } 9.14\%$$

The interest rate is actually 9.14%. Since the two rates do not represent the same thing, a borrower must understand which rate is used in the loan.

COMPLETE ASSIGNMENT 17-2

Chapter terms for review

discount	maturity value
discount date	negotiable note
discount period	non-interest-bearing note
discount rate	payment period
discounting a note	principal
face value	proceeds
interest-bearing note	single-payment interest method
invoice	unpaid balance
maturity date	unpaid-balance interest method

Assignment 17-1: Borrowing by Business

A **(28 points)** — Compute the amount of single payment interest and the amount due at maturity on each of the following loans. Use a 365-day year (3 points for each correct interest amount; 1 point for each correct amount due at maturity).

	Loan Amount	Interest Rate	Time	Amount of Interest	Due at Maturity
1.	$2,850	12.5%	75 days	_____	_____
2.	$1,200	8.4%	60 days	_____	_____
3.	$875	10%	45 days	_____	_____
4.	$400	7.25%	120 days	_____	_____
5.	$8,500	11%	90 days	_____	_____
6.	$3,650	9%	270 days	_____	_____
7.	$2,100	15%	30 days	_____	_____

Score for A (28)

B **(32 points)** — Complete the tables. Use a 365-day year and compute the exact interest on the unpaid balance each month. Reduce the principal accordingly and compute the new unpaid balance (1 point for each correct answer).

8. Smith Corporation borrows $5,000 on July 30 at 13% interest. On August 30, they will pay $2,800 which will include interest due during the first month, the remainder to principal. On September 30, they will pay the month's interest that is due plus all of the remaining principal.

First month:

Days of interest: _____

Beginning unpaid balance: _____

Total payment: $2,800

Month's interest: _____

Paid on principal: _____

New unpaid balance: _____

Last month:

Days of interest: _____

Beginning unpaid balance: _____

Total payment: _____

Month's interest: _____

Paid on principal: _____

New unpaid balance: _____

9. Sandy McCulloch borrows $3,200 on June 1 at 11% interest. On the first of July, August and September, she will make a payment of $850 which will include interest due during the month, and the remainder to principal. On October 1, she will pay the month's interest due, plus all of the remaining principal.

First month:

Days of interest: _____

Beginning unpaid balance: _____

Total payment: $850

Month's interest: _____

Paid on principal: _____

New unpaid balance: _____

Second month:

Days of interest: _____

Beginning unpaid balance: _____

Total payment: $850

Month's interest: _____

Paid on principal: _____

New unpaid balance: _____

Third month:

Days of interest: _____

Beginning unpaid balance: _____

Total payment: $850

Month's interest: _____

Paid on principal: _____

New unpaid balance: _____

Last month:

Days of interest: _____

Beginning unpaid balance: _____

Total payment: $722.12

Month's interest: _____

Paid on principal: _____

New unpaid balance: _____

Score for B (32)

C (40) — How much will the Shangle Company save if they borrow money to pay the following invoices to get the cash discount? Use a 360-day year. Assume that the number of interest days is the time between the due date and the last date to take advantage of the cash discount (2 points for each correct answer).

	Invoice	Terms	Cash Discount	Interest Rate on Loan	Days of Interest	Amount of Interest	Savings
10.	$800	2/10, n/30	_____	10%	_____	_____	_____
11.	$1,250	1/20, n/60	_____	8%	_____	_____	_____
12.	$1,800	3/5, n/30	_____	12%	_____	_____	_____
13.	$625	2/10, n/60	_____	11%	_____	_____	_____
14.	$1,000	1.5/15, n/45	_____	9%	_____	_____	_____

Score for C (40)

Assignment 17-2: Bank Discount and Discounting Notes

A (16 points) — Calculate the amount of discount interest, the proceeds and the actual interest rate based upon the proceeds rather than the face value. Use a 360-day year and calculate actual rates to the nearest $\frac{1}{100}$ of a percent (1 point for each discount and proceeds; 2 points for each actual rate).

	Face Value	Discount Rate	Time	Discount Amount	Proceeds	Actual Interest Rate
1.	$3,000	10%	30 days	_____	_____	_____
2.	$840	9%	60 days	_____	_____	_____
3.	$1,650	12%	90 days	_____	_____	_____
4.	$3,600	15%	45 days	_____	_____	_____

Score for A (16)

B (8 points) — Calculate the missing information for the following non-interest-bearing notes discounted at Trey Financial Services. Use a 360-day year (2 points for each discount amount; 1 point each for all other correct answers).

5. Face value: $2,000
   Date of note: November 12
   Time to run: 90 days
   Discount date: December 12
   Discount rate: 15%

Maturity date: _____

Days of discount: _____

Discount amount: _____

6. Face value: $1,200
   Date of note: July 8
   Time to run: 60 days
   Discount date: August 22
   Discount rate: 12%

Maturity date: _____

Days of discount: _____

Discount amount: _____

Score for B (8)

7. Pat Key held an $800, 30-day, non-interest-bearing note dated May 25. On June 4, she took the note to a finance company which discounted the note at 13%.

Maturity date: _____

Days of discount: _____

Discount amount: _____

Proceeds: _____

8. Brenda Walliard held an $1,850, 45-day, non-interest-bearing note dated March 18. On March 31, she took the note to a bank which discounted the note at 12.5%.

Maturity date: _____

Days of discount: _____

Discount amount: _____

Proceeds: _____

9. Keith Smith held a $480, 75-day, non-interest-bearing note dated July 9. On August 19, he took the note to a bank which discounted the note at 18%.

Maturity date: _____

Days of discount: _____

Discount amount: _____

Proceeds: _____

10. Ken Chard held a $2,200, 60-day, non-interest-bearing note dated October 3. On November 3, he took the note to a finance company which discounted the note at 16%.

Maturity date: _____

Days of discount: _____

Discount amount: _____

Proceeds: _____

Score for C (20)

D (28 points) — Calculate the missing information for the following interest-bearing notes discounted at Bay Villages Thrift & Finance. Use a 360-day year (2 points for each discount amount; 1 point each for all other correct answers).

11. Face value: $1,500
    Date of note: October 22
    Interest rate: 8%
    Time to run: 45 days
    Discount date: November 6
    Discount rate: 12%

Interest amount: _____

Maturity value: _____

Maturity date: _____

Days of discount: _____

Discount amount: _____

Proceeds: _____

12. Face value: $960
    Date of note: June 28
    Interest rate: 10%
    Time to run: 60 days
    Discount date: August 12
    Discount rate: 15%

Interest amount: _____

Maturity value: _____

Maturity date: _____

Days of discount: _____

Discount amount: _____

Proceeds: _____

13. Face value: $620
    Date of note: August 2
    Interest rate: 12%
    Time to run: 90 days
    Discount date: September 1
    Discount rate: 18%

Interest amount: _____

Maturity value: _____

Maturity date: _____

Days of discount: _____

Discount amount: _____

Proceeds: _____

14. Face value: $3,750
    Date of note: April 21
    Interest rate: 9%
    Time to run: 75 days
    Discount date: May 21
    Discount rate: 13%

Interest amount: _____

Maturity value: _____

Maturity date: _____

Days of discount: _____

Discount amount: _____

Proceeds: _____

E (28 points) — Calculate the missing information for the following problems involving interest-bearing notes. Use a 365-day year (2 points for each discount amount; 1 point each for all other correct answers).

15. Wanda Hubbell held a $730, 30-day note dated January 15, bearing interest of 9.75%. On February 1 she took the note to a bank which discounted the note at 16%.

Interest amount: _____

Maturity value: _____

Maturity date: _____

Days of discount: _____

Discount amount: _____

Proceeds: _____

16. Rich Hughes held a $2,820, 90-day note dated May 19, bearing interest of 12%. On June 25 he took the note to a finance company which discounted the note at 20%.

Interest amount: _____

Maturity value: _____

Maturity date: _____

Days of discount: _____

Discount amount: _____

Proceeds: _____

17. Don Fleming held a $1,460, 75-day note dated March 1, bearing interest of 10.2%. On March 15 he took the note to a finance company which discounted it at 17%.

Interest amount: _____

Maturity value: _____

Maturity date: _____

Days of discount: _____

Discount amount: _____

Proceeds: _____

18. Patti McCue held a $910, 60-day note dated October 23, bearing interest of 8.5%. On November 23 she took the note to a bank which discounted it at 14%.

Interest amount: _____

Maturity value: _____

Maturity date: _____

Days of discount: _____

Discount amount: _____

Proceeds: _____

Chapter 18
Charges for Credit—Part I

OBJECTIVES
After completing this chapter, you should be able to:

- **Calculate simple interest on a monthly basis**
- **Calculate retail finance charges**
- **Understand a loan payment schedule**
- **Approximate effective interest rates**
- **Distinguish between effective rates and stated rates**

Businesses and individuals without the necessary cash to purchase an item may borrow the money from a bank. Another alternative is for the seller to permit the buyer to have the item and to pay for it at some time in the future. The seller is effectively a lender and is "selling on credit."

FINANCE CHARGES

The fee that the seller charges for the privilege of buying on credit often is called a *finance charge* instead of interest. The fee may include other charges in addition to any interest that is assessed. For example, there could be a carrying charge, an administration fee, or a premium for insurance on the merchandise. Lending institutions may have other finance charges for some of their loans. The term finance charge will be discussed further in the next chapter.

Monthly Interest
In modern business, interest rates are quoted as either monthly or annual rates. To a borrower, 1.5% per month may sound like a lower rate than 18% per year. When simple interest is calculated these rates are identical.

A simple rule for changing between monthly and annual rates is: Divide the annual rate by 12 to find the equivalent monthly rate; multiply the monthly rate by 12 to find the equivalent annual rate.

a. Change 15% per year to the monthly rate and change 1.5% per month to the annual rate.

15% per year ÷ 12 = 1.25% per month
1.5% per month × 12 = 18% per year

To calculate simple interest, the rate and time need to be either both annual or both monthly. To change time from months to years, divide the number of months by 12.

b. $1,000 is borrowed for two months at 18% per year. Calculate the simple interest on an annual and a monthly basis.

Annual: Rate—18% per year; Time—2 months $= \frac{2}{12}$ year

$I = P \times R \times T = \$1,000 \times 0.18$ per year $\times \frac{2}{12}$ year $= \$30$

Monthly: Rate—18% per year $= \frac{18\%}{12} = 1.5\%$ per month; Time—2 months

$I = P \times R \times T = \$1,000 \times 0.015$ per month $\times 2$ months $= \$30$

Truth in Lending

To assist consumers in knowing the total cost of credit, the federal *Truth in Lending Act* was passed. This act requires businesses to tell customers the exact total of the finance charges, including interest, carrying charges, insurance and special fees; and the *annual percentage rate* (APR) of the total finance charge. If an unpaid balance of $1,000 is subject to a total finance charge of $15.00 for one month, the monthly rate is 1.5%, and the annual percentage rate is 18% (1.5% × 12).

In order to conform to the Truth in Lending regulations, retail stores state their credit terms precisely and print them on monthly statements. Although the format of statements vary, the same basic information must be given on all of them.

Figure 18-1 is the lower portion of a typical statement of a retail store. Note in this case the finance charge is based on the previous balance before deducting payments and credits.

c. The finance charge is $9.36 (1.5% of $624), even though there was a payment of $500 and a credit $62.95. The new balance is computed as shown

$\$624.00 + \$9.36 - \$500.00 - \$62.95 + \$364.57 = \$434.98$

FIGURE 18-1
Retail Statement of
Account

PREVIOUS BALANCE	FINANCE CHARGE	PAYMENTS	CREDITS	PURCHASES	NEW BALANCE	MINIMUM PAYMENT	CLOSING DATE
624.00	9.36	500.00	62.95	364.57	434.98	45.00	10-16-93

IF WE RECEIVE PAYMENT OF THE FULL AMOUNT OF THE NEW BALANCE BEFORE THE NEXT CYCLE CLOSING DATE, SHOWN ABOVE, YOU WILL AVOID A FINANCE CHARGE NEXT MONTH. THE FINANCE CHARGE, IF ANY, IS FIGURED ON THE PREVIOUS BALANCE BEFORE DEDUCTING ANY PAYMENTS OR CREDITS SHOWN ABOVE. THE PERIODIC RATES USED ARE 1 1/2% OF THE BALANCE ON AMOUNTS UNDER $1,000 AND 1% OF AMOUNTS IN EXCESS OF $1,000 WHICH ARE ANNUAL PERCENTAGE RATES OF 18% AND 12% RESPECTIVELY.

COMPLETE ASSIGNMENT 18-1

EFFECTIVE INTEREST RATES

When a credit purchase is completed, the terms of the contract may be negotiated by the buyer and seller. The entire amount plus the finance charge may be paid all at once, or there may be a series of payments. With a series of payments, the payments may or may not all be equal. An interest rate usually will be stated, but the *stated interest rate* may not be the same as the *effective* (actual, or true) *interest rate*. The effective rate more closely tells what you really are paying for the money you have borrowed. Whether you are the buyer or the seller, you should be able to distinguish between the stated rate and the effective rate.

Suppose you borrow $2,400 for four months at a stated simple interest rate of 15%. From the formula, $I = P \times R \times T = \$2,400 \times 0.15 \times \frac{4}{12} = \$120$. If you repay $2,520 ($2,400 + $120) at the end of the four months, you are paying $120 to use the entire $2,400 for the entire four months. In this situation, the effective interest rate is also 15%.

But, if you pay $120 interest and do not have the entire $2,400 for the entire four months, the effective rate of interest will be higher than 15%. For example, suppose you agree to pay $600 of principal and $30 of interest each month. In the four months, you will repay the $2,400 principal and $120 in interest (4 × $600 = $2,400; 4 × $30 = $120). During the first month you have the use of all $2,400; the second month you have only $1,800; in the third month you have $1,200; and in the last month, only $600 is available. On the average, you have $1,500 per month [($2,400 + $1,800 + $1,200 + $600 = $6,000) ÷ 4 = $1,500]. If it costs $120 to borrow $1,500 for the four months, the effective interest rate is 24%, as shown below.

$$R = \frac{I}{P \times T} = \frac{\$120}{\$1,500 \times \frac{4}{12}} = \frac{\$120}{\$500} = 0.24 \text{ or } 24\%$$

Interest on the Unpaid Balance

As you learned in Chapter 17, finance (interest) charges may be determined using the unpaid-balance interest method. This method is used frequently throughout the business community.

In the problem above, the $120 interest paid over the four months is not really simple interest because multiple payments are made, each containing payment of both principal and interest. Tables 18-1 and 18-2 show monthly *loan payment schedules* in which the interest is calculated on the unpaid principal balance at the beginning of each month. (The calculations follow the same steps as those in Chapter 17 on page 200 except that a 360-day year with 30 days each month is assumed.) Thus, beginning unpaid balance × monthly rate = interest payment; total payment − interest payment = principal payment; unpaid balance − principal payment = new balance. While the stated interest of 15% is used in Table 18-1, the total interest calculated is only $75.00. However, the total interest shown in Table 18-2 on page 214 is $120 when the effective interest rate of 24% is used.

Month	Unpaid Balance	Interest Payment	Principal Payment	Total Payment	New Balance
1	$2,400	$30.00	$ 600.00	$ 630.00	$1,800
2	1,800	22.50	600.00	622.50	1,200
3	1,200	15.00	600.00	615.00	600
4	600	7.50	600.00	607.50	0
		$75.00	$2,400.00	$2,475.00	

TABLE 18-1
Monthly Loan Payment Schedule
(15% annual; 1.25% monthly)

TABLE 18-2
Monthly Loan Payment Schedule
(24% annual; 2% monthly)

Month	Unpaid Balance	Interest Payment	Principal Payment	Total Payment	New Balance
1	$2,400	$ 48.00	$ 600.00	$ 648.00	$1,800
2	1,800	36.00	600.00	636.00	1,200
3	1,200	24.00	600.00	624.00	600
4	600	12.00	600.00	612.00	0
		$120.00	$2,400.00	$2,520.00	

NOTE: Whenever (1) the interest is calculated on the unpaid balance every month and (2) the amount paid on the principal is exactly the same every month, you can use the following formula as a short-cut for calculating the total interest paid (n = number of months):

$$\text{Total interest} = \frac{\text{First month's interest} \times (n + 1)}{2}$$

$$= \frac{P \times R \times T \times (n + 1)}{2}$$

Therefore, to compute the total interest in Tables 18-1 and 18-2, the calculations would be:

$$\text{Total interest (15\%)} = \frac{\$30 \times (4 + 1)}{2} = \frac{\$30 \times 5}{2} = \frac{\$150}{2} = \$75$$

$$\text{Total interest (24\%)} = \frac{\$48 \times (4 + 1)}{2} = \frac{\$48 \times 5}{2} = \frac{\$240}{2} = \$120$$

Approximating the Effective Rate

Consumers and business persons make decisions about credit purchasing and borrowing based upon several factors. One of the most important factors is the interest rate. However, as you have learned, the rate that actually is paid may not be the rate that is stated. The effective rate is more important than the stated rate. However, with many loans and credit purchases the effective rate may be difficult or impossible to calculate. When that is the case a reasonable approximation of the effective rate should be made.

Steps for Approximating the Effective Interest Rate

1. Calculate I, the total amount of the finance charge, by:
   a. subtracting the cash price from the total payments, including any down payment, or
   b. calculating total interest and adding all additional charges to it.
2. Calculate R, the approximate effective interest rate, using the formula
   $$R = \frac{2 \times M \times I}{P \times (n+1)}$$

   where
   R = approximate effective annual interest rate
   M = number of payment periods in one year (e.g., 12 months)
   I = total finance charge (interest plus additional fees, if any)
   P = amount of the loan, or amount of the purchase that is on credit
   n = number of payments in the credit plan

d. Kristin Jorgensen can purchase office furniture for $2,900 cash, or for $100 down payment and six monthly payments of $500 each. Calculate (1) the total finance charge; (2) the approximate effective rate; and (3) the stated rate.

Step 1 $500 × 6 = $3,000 total of six monthly payments
$3,000 + $100 down payment = $3,100 total cost using credit plan
$3,100 − $2,900 cash price = $200 total finance charge = I

Step 2   It is not clear how much of each payment is interest and how much is principal. Since it is impossible to actually calculate the true effective rate a reasonable approximation should be made using the formula.
M = 12 months (payment periods) in one year
I = $200 total finance charge (Step 1)
P = $2,900 cash price − $100 down payment
   = $2,800 amount financed
n = 6 monthly payments

$$R = \frac{2 \times M \times I}{P \times (n + 1)} = \frac{2 \times 12 \times \$200}{\$2,800 \times (6 + 1)} = \frac{\$4,800}{\$19,600}$$
= 0.2449 or 24.5%, effective rate

NOTE: This approximation formula works with loans just as it does with credit purchases. With a loan there will not be a down payment, and P will be the amount of the loan instead of the amount of the purchase that has been financed.

Step 3   Calculate the stated rate using $R = \frac{I}{P \times T}$ where I = the total finance charge; T = time in years; and P = total amount financed on credit.

I = $200 finance charge; T = $\frac{6}{12}$ year; P = $2,900 − $100
   = $2,800

$$R = \frac{I}{P \times T} = \frac{\$200}{\$2,800 \times \frac{6}{12}} = \frac{\$200}{\$1,400}$$

= 0.1429 or 14.3%, stated rate

COMPLETE ASSIGNMENT 18-2

Chapter terms for review

annual percentage rate (APR)
finance charge
effective interest rate

loan payment schedule
stated interest rate
Truth in Lending Act

Assignment 18-1: Finance Charges

A **(22 points)** — In Problem 1, change the rates from monthly to annual. In Problem 2, change the rates from annual to monthly (1 point for each correct answer).

1. a. 1.5% = _____ **b.** 1.25% = _____ **c.** 1.75% = _____ **d.** $1\frac{1}{3}$% = _____

    e. $1\frac{2}{3}$% = _____ **f.** $1\frac{1}{6}$% = _____ **g.** 1% = _____ **h.** 0.75% = _____

    i. 0.5% = _____ **j.** 2% = _____ **k.** $\frac{2}{3}$% = _____

2. a. 12% = _____ **b.** 8% = _____ **c.** 15% = _____ **d.** 9% = _____

    e. 21% = _____ **f.** 16% = _____ **g.** 18% = _____ **h.** 20% = _____

    i. 10% = _____ **j.** 24% = _____ **k.** 6% = _____

_____
Score for A (22)

B **(39 points)** — Calculate the finance charge and the new balance for Problems 3–8, using the stated credit terms. Note that in no month was full payment made within the 25-day limit (3 points for each correct answer).

TERMS: The finance charge, if any, is based on the previous balance before payments or credits are deducted. The rates are 1.5% per month up to $1,000 and 1.25% per month on amounts in excess of $1,000. These are annual percentage rates of 18% and 15%, respectively. There is no finance charge if the full amount of the new balance is paid within 25 days after the cycle closing date.

	Cycle Closing	Previous Balance	Finance Charge	Payments	Purchases	Credits	New Balance
3.	5/25/9-	$1,450.26	_____	$1,000.00	$755.91	$215.95	_____
4.	12/20/9-	$1,018.50	_____	$1,018.50	$421.50	$0.00	_____
5.	7/15/9-	$742.24	_____	$0.00	$587.80	$72.59	_____
6.	10/10/9-	$2,648.25	_____	$1,500.00	$0.00	$191.15	_____

Problems 7 and 8 are the payment and purchase history of one customer for two consecutive months.

	Cycle Closing	Previous Balance	Finance Charge	Payments	Payment Date	Purchases	Credits	New Balance
7.	03/25	$1,420.35	_____	$1,200	04/20	$372.58	25.00	_____
8.	04/25	_____	_____	$500	05/15	$284.14	0	_____

Score for B (39)

C   (39 points) — Calculate the missing amounts in the retail charge accounts in Problems 9–12. The credit terms for all are stated (3 points for each correct answer).

Terms: Finance charge is based upon the net balance if payment is made within 30 days of the billing date. If payment is made after 30 days, then the finance charge is based on the previous balance. Net balance equals previous balance less payments/credits. In either case, the monthly rate is 1.4% on the first $500 of the balance and 1.2% on any amount over $500.

9.
Billing date	05/15/94
Previous balance	$742.58
Date of payment	06/16/94
Payments/credits	$600.00
Net balance	_____
Finance charge	_____
Purchases	$320.09
New balance	_____

10.
Billing date	09/10/93
Previous balance	$1,071.82
Date of payment	10/10/93
Payments/credits	$850.00
Net balance	_____
Finance charge	_____
Purchases	$739.75
New balance	_____

Problems 11 and 12 are for consecutive months for the same customer.

11.
Billing date	06/20/93
Previous balance	$818.91
Date of payment	07/20/93
Payments/credits	$250.00
Net balance	_____
Finance charge	_____
Purchases	$241.80
New balance	_____

12.
Billing date	07/20/93
Previous balance	_____
Date of payment	08/21/93
Payments/credits	$250.00
Net balance	_____
Finance charge	_____
Purchases	$145.24
New balance	_____

Score for C (39)

Assignment 18-2:   Charges for Credit 1

A   (12 points) — Problems 1 and 2 assume the following information: Joe Johnson plans to borrow $1,200 for four months at 18% interest. He plans to make four equal payments, one at the end of each of the four months (4 points for each correct answer).

1. a. What is the total simple interest amount?

_____

b. What is the amount of each payment?

_____

2. Calculate the effective annual rate of interest using the formula $R = \dfrac{2 \times M \times I}{P \times (n+1)}$ where P is the amount of the loan, I is amount of interest, M is the number of months in a year and n is the number of actual payments.

_____

_____
Score for A (12)

B   (40 points) — Joe Johnson borrowed $1,200. He agreed to pay the principal in four monthly installments of $300 each. For interest, he agreed to pay 18% (annual rate) on the unpaid balance each month. Complete the table (2 points for each correct answer).

	Month	Unpaid Balance	Interest Payment	Principal Payment	Total Payment	New Balance
3.	1	_____	_____	_____	_____	_____
4.	2	_____	_____	_____	_____	_____
5.	3	_____	_____	_____	_____	_____
6.	4	_____	_____	_____	_____	_____

_____
Score for B (40)

C   (15 points) — For Problems 7 and 8, assume the same information as B. Use the formulas provided and the information from the loan table in B to calculate your answers (points for correct answers as marked).

7. a. What is the average principal amount (P)? (4 points)

_____

b. What is the total interest amount (I)? (3 points)

_____

c. Calculate the effective annual interest rate using the formula $R = \dfrac{I}{P \times T}$. (4 points)

_____

8. Calculate the effective annual rate of interest using the formula $R = \dfrac{2 \times M \times I}{P \times (n + 1)}$ where P is the amount of the loan, I is total amount of interest, M is the number of months in a year and n is the number of actual payments (4 points).

Effective Rate: _____

D (33 points) — Approximate the effective rate of interest using the formula $R = \dfrac{2 \times M \times I}{P \times (n + 1)}$ where P is the amount of the purchase that is charged, I is total finance charge, M is the number of months in a year and n is the number of actual payments. Give the rate to the nearest $\dfrac{1}{100}$ of a percent (11 points for each correct answer).

9. Bill Starnes has the option of buying a motor scooter for $2,200 cash or $200 down payment and 24 payments of $100. If he chooses to use the credit option what is the approximate effective rate of interest?

_____

10. Fay Merrit owns an appliance store that offers a time payment plan for the merchandise it sells. A $380 washing machine can be purchased for $32 down and $32 a month for one year. Calculate the approximate effective rate.

_____

11. Burch Video and Stereo Store advertises a large-screen television for $1,800 cash, or 5% down and 36 monthly payments of only $65 each. Calculate the approximate effective rate of interest.

_____

Chapter 19
Charges for Credit—Part II

OBJECTIVES
After completing this chapter, you should be able to:

- Approximate an effective interest rate (when additional fees are involved)
- Locate amortization payment factors
- Determine monthly loan payments using the amortization payment factors
- Understand an amortization schedule

Borrowers and credit purchasers often consider the interest rate before they make the loan or purchase. If one lender offers a rate of 12% and another offers a rate of 15%, it might be assumed that the 12% is the better rate for the borrower.

RAISING THE EFFECTIVE RATE

As you learned in Chapter 18, the interest rate that is stated may not be the same as the effective rate. By altering other terms of the agreement, such as how quickly the principal is to be repaid, the lender can change the effective rate.

Another way that the lender can raise the effective rate is by charging additional fees to the borrower or to the credit purchaser. A bank may do this by charging a *loan initiation fee*, which is a fee to cover the cost of processing the loan application. The bank also may charge a fee based on the size of the loan. A merchant may charge a loan administration fee, a credit fee, or a fee for insurance on the merchandise. All of these fees are finance charges, and the effective interest rate should be calculated with all fees considered, not just the actual interest. To approximate the effective rate, without using a computer or financial calculator, use the formula introduced in Chapter 18:

$$R = \frac{2 \times M \times I}{P \times (n+1)}$$

where

R = approximate effective annual interest rate
M = number of payment periods in one year
I = total finance charge (interest plus any extra borrowing fees)
P = amount of the loan, or amount of the purchase that is on credit
n = number of payments in the credit plan

a. Wright, Inc., an appliance dealer, sells a home entertainment center for a cash price of $3,000. She will also sell it on the following credit plan: $300 cash down payment, 10 monthly payments consisting of $270 on the principal plus interest of 1.5% of the unpaid balance that month, and a monthly credit fee of $3.00 which is to cover both paperwork and an insurance premium on the merchandise. What is the approximate effective rate of interest?

Because the monthly interest is calculated on the unpaid balance and the principal payments are equal each month, you can calculate the total interest using the short-cut formula from Chapter 18:

$$\text{Total interest} = \text{First month's interest} \times \frac{(n+1)}{2} = P \times R \times T \times \frac{(n+1)}{2}$$

$$= (\$3,000 \text{ cash price} - \$300 \text{ down}) \times 1.5\% \times 1 \text{ month} \times \frac{(10+1)}{2}$$

$$= \$2,700 \times 1.5\% \times 1 \times \frac{11}{2} = \frac{\$445.50}{2} = \$222.75$$

Thus, I = $222.75 interest + ($3.00 × 10 months) credit fee = $252.75

Approximate the effective rate using the formula: $R = \frac{2 \times M \times I}{P \times (n+1)}$

M = 12 monthly payment periods in one year
I = $252.75 total finance charge
P = $2,700 amount of purchase that is financed
n = 10 payments in the credit plan

$$R = \frac{2 \times M \times I}{P \times (n+1)} = \frac{2 \times 12 \times \$252.75}{\$2,700 \times (10+1)} = \frac{\$6,066}{\$29,700} = 0.2042 \quad \text{or} \quad 20.4\%$$

Notice that the stated rate is 1.5% per month (nominal annual percentage rate of 18% (1.5% × 12)). It is the addition of the $30 in loan fees that increases the effective rate to approximately 20.4% annual rate.

With the credit plan used by Wright, Inc., the monthly payments will be different every month. The principal payment is always $270 and the loan fee is always $3. However, the interest decreases each month because the unpaid balance is always decreasing.

b. Calculate the first two monthly payments for the previous example.

	First Month	*Second Month*
Unpaid balance	$3,000 cash − $300 down = $2,700 (the amount financed)	$2,700 − $270 = $2,430 (previous balance − principal payment)
Month's interest	$2,700 × 1.5% monthly × 1 month = $40.50	$2,430 × 1.5% monthly × 1 month = $36.45
Month's payment	$270.00 principal + $3.00 loan fee + $40.50 interest = $313.50	$270.00 principal + $3.00 loan fee + $36.45 interest = $309.45

AMORTIZED LOANS

In example b. with interest calculated on the unpaid balance, the monthly payments were not equal. By using a computer, financial calculator, or special tables such as Table 19-1, it is possible to have the monthly payments always be equal and still have the interest calculated on the unpaid balance. This is called *amortizing* the loan and often is done with loans for homes, cars and other longer-term, high cost items. In a credit purchase, the buyer may make a down payment and finance the balance.

The amount borrowed or financed is paid in equal monthly payments. Each of the equal monthly payments includes the interest on the unpaid balance of the loan and a payment on the principal. With each successive payment, the unpaid balance decreases. Thus, subsequent interest payments will be smaller, and the corresponding payment on the principal will be larger.

TABLE 19-1   Monthly Payments Required to Repay Principal and Interest on a $1,000 Loan

| Term of Loan | Annual Interest Rate | | | | |
	12%	*13%*	*14%*	*15%*	*16%*
1 month	$1,010.00	$1,010.83	$1,011.67	$1,012.50	$1,013.33
2 months	507.51	508.14	508.77	509.39	510.02
3 months	340.02	340.58	341.14	341.70	342.26
4 months	256.28	256.81	257.33	257.86	258.39
5 months	206.04	206.55	207.05	207.56	208.07
6 months	172.55	173.04	173.54	174.03	174.53
5 years	$ 22.24	$ 22.75	$ 23.27	$ 23.79	$ 24.32
10 years	14.35	14.93	15.53	16.13	16.75
15 years	12.00	12.65	13.32	14.00	14.69
20 years	11.01	11.72	12.44	13.17	13.91
25 years	10.53	11.28	12.04	12.81	13.59
30 years	10.29	11.06	11.85	12.64	13.45

Computing the Monthly Payment

Companies that amortize loans calculate the monthly payment by using computers, financial calculators, or special tables. Table 19-1 has only five interest rates (columns) and twelve loan time periods (rows), but it can be used as an example. For a $1,000 loan, the monthly payment is found at the intersection of the appropriate column and row.

Steps for Determining the Payment When the Loan is $1,000

1. Locate the correct percentage column and the row showing the right time length of the loan.
2. Read the number in the space where the right row and column intersect. For a loan of exactly $1,000 this number is the payment amount.

c. Find the monthly payment for a $1,000 loan at 13% for 15 years.

Step 1   Find the 13% column and 15 year row.
Step 2   Read the payment of $12.65 at the intersection.

When the loan amount is not exactly $1,000, the table is still easy to use, but the number in the table is not the final answer. It now is called the *amortization payment factor*, and some additional calculation is required.

Steps for Calculating the Payment When the Loan is not $1,000

1. Locate the factor in the proper column and row of the table.
2. Divide the amount borrowed (or financed) by $1,000.
3. Multiply the quotient (Step 2) by the factor from the table (Step 1). The product is the monthly payment.

---

d. Find the monthly payment to amortize a loan of $2,400 over four months with interest at 15% (1.25% per month).

Step 1 The factor for $1,000 at 15% for 4 months = $257.86
Step 2 $2,400 ÷ $1,000 = 2.4
Step 3 2.4 × $257.86 = $618.86 per month

Amortization Schedule

After determining the amount of the monthly payment, a lending company usually prepares a schedule of payments called an *amortization schedule*. Table 19-2 illustrates the amortization of the loan in the previous example: $2,400 at 15% for four months. The key difference between Table 19-2 and Table 18-1 in the prior chapter is that the total payment amounts in the amortization schedule are the same.

In this example all payments except the last one are $618.86; the last payment is $618.89, three cents larger. Because of rounding, the final payment almost always will be slightly larger or smaller than the other payments.

TABLE 19-2   Amortization Schedule

Month	A Unpaid Balance	B ($= A \times \% \times \frac{1}{12}$) Interest Payment	C Total Payment	D ($= C - B$) Principal Payment	E ($= A - D$) New Balance
1	$2,400.00	$30.00	$618.86	$588.86	$1,811.14
2	1,811.14	22.64	618.86	596.22	1,214.92
3	1,214.92	15.19	618.86	603.67	611.25
4	611.25	7.64	618.89	611.25	0

COMPLETE ASSIGNMENTS 19-1 AND 19-2

Chapter terms for review

amortization payment factor
amortization schedule
amortizing
loan initiation fee

Assignment 19-1: Charges for Credit 2

A **(50 points)** — In most problems below, there are other finance charges in addition to the interest. Calculate the approximate effective interest rate two times: Once when only those charges called interest are included, and once when the additional charges have been included. Use the formula $R = \frac{2 \times M \times I}{P \times (n+1)}$. Give the rate to the nearest $\frac{1}{100}$ of a percent (10 points for each correct answer).

1. Lew Roderick is selling a metal lathe for $3,200 cash or for $200 down and 24 equal payments. Principal each month is $125, plus $25 interest and $2.50 insurance on the lathe.

    a. What is the approximate effective interest rate when you do not consider the insurance fee to be a finance charge?

    _____

    b. What is the approximate interest rate when the insurance fee is included as a finance charge?

    _____

2. Judy Taylor is selling camcorders for a cash price of $650. To attract new customers and to make money on financing she offers the camcorder for 10% down and $58.50 per month for 10 months. In addition to the $58.50 principal each month, there is a monthly interest fee of $4.50 and a carrying charge of $2.00.

a. What is the approximate effective interest rate when you do not consider the carrying charge to be a finance charge?

_____

b. What is approximate interest rate when the carrying charge is included as a finance charge?

_____

3. Lew Roderick is selling a metal lathe for $3,200 cash or for $400 down and 24 equal payments of $150 each, which includes principal and all interest charges. Calculate the approximate effective interest rate. (Compare this problem, and its solution, to those in number 1a.)

_____

B (50 points) — Solve the following amortization problems (points as stated).

4. Lyon Lending Corp. amortizes the loans it makes. Use Table 19-1 to determine the monthly payments for the following loans (3 points for each correct answer).

a. $2,600 at 16% for 6 months _____

b. $10,375 at 15% for 10 years _____

c. $6,250 at 14% for 5 years _____

d. $56,825 at 12% for 20 years _____

5. Sharon Wilder borrows $1000 from Lyon Lending Corp, which amortizes the loan at 15% over 4 months.

a. Complete the amortization table below. Use Table 19-1 to determine the total monthly payment for the first three months. $1,000 loan amortized at 15% for 4 months: Payment = $257.86 (1 point for each correct answer).

Month	Unpaid Balance	Interest Payment	Total Payment	Principal Payment	New Balance
1					
2					
3					
4					

b. Calculate the approximate stated interest rate using $R = \dfrac{I}{P \times T}$ where P is the average principal over the four months and I is the total interest charge (9 points).

_____

c. Calculate the approximate effective annual rate of interest using the formula $R = \dfrac{2 \times M \times I}{P \times (n+1)}$ where P is the amount of the loan, I the total amount of interest, M is the number of months in a year and n is the actual number of payments (9 points).

_____

Assignment 19-2: Amortization

A (56 points) — Amortization problems (1 point for each correct answer in Problems 1 and 2; 11 points each for Problems 3 and 4).

1. Amortize a loan for $1,600 at 12% for four months. Using Table 19-1, the monthly payment = 1.6 × $256.28 = $410.05. Complete the amortization table below.

	Month	Unpaid Balance	Interest Payment	Total Payment	Principal Payment	New Balance
a.	1	_____	_____	$410.05	_____	_____
b.	2	_____	_____	$410.05	_____	_____
c.	3	_____	_____	$410.05	_____	_____
d.	4	_____	_____	_____	_____	_____

2. Follow exactly the same procedure to complete this table that you used in the above table, EXCEPT use a payment of $300 in months 1, 2 and 3.

   In all months: Interest payment = Unpaid balance × $\frac{0.12}{12}$ (i.e., 0.01)

   In months 1-3: Principal payment = $300 − Interest payment
                    New balance = Unpaid balance − Principal payment
   In month 4: Total payment = Unpaid balance + Interest payment
                 Principal payment = Unpaid balance
                 New balance = 0

	Month	Unpaid Balance	Interest Payment	Total Payment	Principal Payment	New Balance
a.	1	_____	_____	$300.00	_____	_____
b.	2	_____	_____	$300.00	_____	_____
c.	3	_____	_____	$300.00	_____	_____
d.	4	_____	_____	_____	_____	_____

3. Calculate the approximate stated interest rate in Problem 2 using $R = \frac{I}{P \times T}$ where P is the average principal over the four months and I is the total interest (11 points).

   _____

4. Calculate the approximate effective annual rate in Problem 2 using the formula $R = \dfrac{2 \times M \times I}{P \times (n + 1)}$ where P is the amount of the loan, I the total amount of interest, M is the number of months in a year and n is the actual number of payments (11 points).

_____

B **(44 points) — Problems involving amortization. In each problem use Table 19-1 to determine the monthly payment. Then make one or two rows of the amortization table (4 points for each correct answer except Problem 7 which is worth 12 points).**

5. After one year on a new job, Carole Payne buys a new car. She borrows $8,600, and the loan is amortized at 15% for 5 years.

a. What is her monthly payment? _____

b. In the first month, how much will she pay in interest? _____

c. In the first month, how much will she pay on the principal? _____

d. After the first payment, how much will she still owe on the loan? _____

6. Greg Monahan needs a new warehouse for his company. The bank will lend him $200,000 for 10 years, amortizing the loan at 15%.

a. What is the company's monthly payment? _____

b. In the first month, how much will the company pay in interest? _____

c. In the first month, how much will they pay on the principal? _____

d. After the first payment, how much will the company still owe on the loan? _____

7. Louise Messerle plans to buy a new minicomputer for her equipment company. A bank will lend her $70,000 for 5 years, amortizing the loan at 12%. After two payments, how much will Louise's company still owe on the loan?

_____

Part Six
Taxes and Insurance

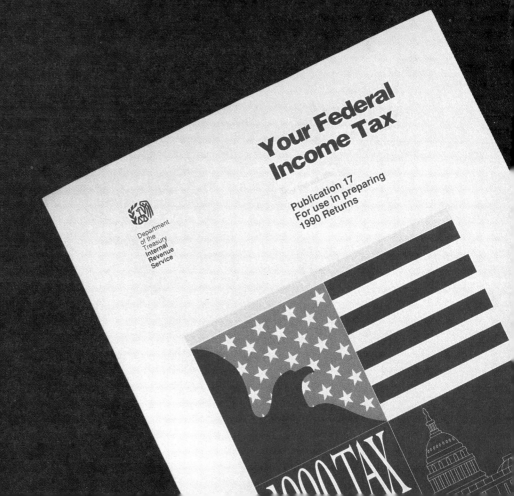

Your Federal Income Tax

Publication 17
For use in preparing
1990 Returns

Department
of the
Treasury
Internal
Revenue
Service

1990 TAX

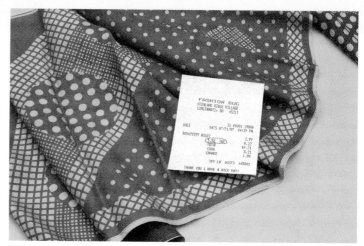

Chapter 20
Sales and Property Taxes

OBJECTIVES
After completing this chapter, you should be able to:

- **Calculate sales taxes**
- **Equalize different assessed values among communities**
- **Find property tax rates and calculate property tax amounts**

Many businesses must collect a sales tax from customers when a sale occurs. At certain times the tax money must be turned over to the government. Companies owning property usually pay taxes on the property's value. This chapter explains sales and property taxes. Chapter 21 covers a third tax, federal income tax.

SALES TAXES

A *sales tax* is a government *levy*, or charge, on retail sales of certain goods and services. Most states and many cities and counties levy sales taxes. The state *tax rate*, the percent used to calculate the tax, currently may be as low as 3% or as high as 8%, and city and county rates range from 0.925% to 6%.

Sales Tax as a Percentage of Price
Sales taxes generally are rounded to the nearest cent. For example, sales taxes of 4% and 5% may be charges on amounts as shown in Table 20-1. Often the sales tax is stated on the sales receipt.

TABLE 20-1
Sales Taxes

4% Sales Tax		5% Sales Tax	
1¢ to 12¢	none	1¢ to 10¢	none
13¢ to 29¢	1¢	11¢ to 25¢	1¢
30¢ to 58¢	2¢	26¢ to 45¢	2¢
59¢ to 81¢	3¢	46¢ to 65¢	3¢
82¢ to 99¢	4¢	66¢ to 85¢	4¢
$1.00	4¢	86¢ to 99¢	5¢
		$1.00	5¢

Steps for Calculating Sales Tax on an Uneven Dollar Amount

1. Multiply the number of whole dollars by the tax rate on $1.
2. Use the rate table to determine the tax on the partial dollar amount.
3. Determine the total tax by adding the amounts calculated in the first two steps.

a. If a sale totals $50.65 in a state with a 4% sales tax, the calculation is:

0.04 × $50	$2.00
Tax on 65¢ (see Table 20-1)	0.03
Total sales tax	$2.03

Sales Tax as an Amount Per Unit

All of the states and the District of Columbia levy special sales taxes on gasoline and cigarettes, which usually are stated in cents per unit. State taxes on gasoline are generally 11¢ or more per gallon, plus a federal tax that was 9¢ per gallon at the beginning of the 1990's, but this tax is scheduled to increase significantly during the decade. State taxes on cigarettes range from 2¢ to 24¢ a pack; the federal tax is 16¢ a pack.

COMPLETE ASSIGNMENT 20-1

PROPERTY TAXES

A *property tax* for a business is a tax on real estate or other property, such as machinery, owned by the business. Sometimes separate bills are supplied, but often several taxing units combine their taxes into one bill that is payable semiannually or quarterly. Taxes are based on a value, known as the *assessed valuation*, determined by a representative of the local or state government.

Assessed Valuations

Assessed valuation ordinarily is based on the current market value of the property. While in many states it is fixed by law at 100%, it is a fraction of that value in other states. Thus, a particular community may use 60% of property values as the basis for tax billing. In most instances, land and buildings are assessed separately.

In assessing a property, the assessor may take into consideration a number of factors, such as size and shape of the lot, front footage on the street, type of neighborhood, square and cubic footage of the building, and deterioration.

Assessed valuation often is increased by improvements to the property, such as the addition of an enclosed porch or expensive shrubbery. Ordinary maintenance costs, like a new coat of paint or repairs to the roof, are not justification for an increased assessment.

Equalization

When larger governmental units, such as counties and states, levy taxes on properties in smaller units, like towns, the smaller unit's assessed valuation often is used. Different towns in a county, however, may not be assessed at the same percentage of value. An *equalization*, or adjustment, of the assessments must be done so that each town pays its fair share of the county tax. Table 20-2 shows the assessments in the four townships of a particular county. The equalized value of 100% is obtained by dividing each assessment by its own rate. For example, $20,000,000 ÷ 0.4 (40%) = $50,000,000. County property taxes then are based on the equalized valuations.

TABLE 20-2
Property Tax
Equalization

Township	Local Valuation	Rate	Equalized Valuation (100%)
A	$ 20,000,000	40%	$ 50,000,000
B	150,000,000	60%	250,000,000
C	30,000,000	30%	100,000,000
D	60,000,000	50%	120,000,000
Total	$260,000,000		$520,000,000

Tax Rate

The tax rate is found by dividing the amount of taxes to be raised by the total assessed valuation of a particular governmental unit. A tax rate may be expressed in mills. A *mill* is one tenth of one cent or $0.001. To convert mills into cents, divide by 10; for example, 30 mills equals 3¢. To convert cents into mills, multiply by 10. Thus, a rate of 15¢ on $1 is 150 mills. Rates of 100 mills or more are better expressed as cents on $1 or as dollars and cents on $100.

b. The town of Murphysville has a total assessed valuation of $570,000,000. The amount to be raised by taxation is $9,975,000. The tax rate is:

$9,975,000 ÷ $570,000,000 = 0.0175 or 1.75%

This rate may be written as 17.5 mills, or 1.75% on $1, or $1.75 on $100.

c. If property in Murphysville is assessed for $20,000, the tax is found by multiplying that amount by the rate.

$20,000 × 1.75% (0.0175) = $350

Tax Payment

Residential property usually is purchased with a down payment, followed by monthly installment payments. Such installments may include an amount to cover taxes as well as principal and interest. This is to insure that the property will not be sold for unpaid taxes, which would jeopardize the interest of the lending agency.

Special assessments can be levied for improvements in a community, such as sewers, roads, or sidewalks. Sometimes the cost may be spread over a period of years and added to the annual property tax bill of the owner. If so, any unpaid balance represents a lien that must be assumed by the purchaser unless the seller pays it in full. Tax liens have priority over other claims.

Whenever property is sold, it is customary to *prorate*, or distribute, the taxes between seller and buyer as of the date of the settlement.

In almost all states, property used exclusively by nonprofit organizations, such as schools, churches, governments and charities, is exempt from taxation. In some states, partial exemptions are allowed for veterans and elderly persons.

COMPLETE ASSIGNMENT 20-2

Chapter terms for review

assessed valuation	property tax
equalization	prorate
levy	sales tax
mill	tax rate

Assignment 20-1: Sales Taxes

A **(25 points) — Solve the following problems ($\frac{1}{2}$ point for each correct answer).**

1. Paiolies fast-food restaurant is in a state with a tax rate of 5%. Using Table 20-1, calculate the amount of tax, total sale, and change given for each transaction listed below (15 points).

Amt. of Sale	Sales Tax	Total	Cash Paid	Amt. of Change
$ 5.89	_____	_____	$10.00	_____
3.07	_____	_____	4.00	_____
14.12	_____	_____	20.00	_____
7.97	_____	_____	10.37	_____
0.85	_____	_____	1.00	_____
23.15	_____	_____	30.00	_____
9.60	_____	_____	20.08	_____
28.35	_____	_____	50.00	_____
13.21	_____	_____	15.00	_____
17.49	_____	_____	19.00	_____

2. Giramonte's clothing store is in a city where the state tax is 3% and the city tax is 1%. Using the table for 4% (Table 20-1), determine the tax on each sale, the total of each sale, and the amount of change given in each transaction. Then calculate the total taxes and total sales (10 points).

Amt. of Sale	Sales Tax	Total	Cash Paid	Amt. of Change
$317.20	_____	_____	$350.00	_____
29.30	_____	_____	31.00	_____
72.85	_____	_____	80.00	_____
9.95	_____	_____	20.35	_____
109.40	_____	_____	120.00	_____
299.95	_____	_____	500.00	_____
Total	_____	_____	—	

_____
Score for A (25)

B **(50 points) — Use Table 20-1 to solve Problems 3 and 4 (points for correct answers as marked).**

3. A chain store, operating in a state with a sales tax of 4%, made the following sales: 868 sales at 10¢; 946 sales at 45¢; 457 sales at 50¢; 921 sales at 75¢; 815 sales at 90¢. How much did the store receive in taxes (6 points)?

_____

4. If the chain store (Problem 3) calculated the amount of state sales tax submitted to the state based on 4% of gross sales, what would be the difference between the amount of tax the store calculated and the amount it submitted to the state (6 points)?

_____

5. Gems, Inc. and Jewelry Co. each bought a new car. Gems, located in a state that has a 4% sales tax, paid the regular price of $12,487 plus tax. Jewelry is located in a state that has a 5% sales tax and got a special discount of $150 off the regular $12,487 price.

a. Including sales tax, which company paid more for its car (6 points)?

_____

b. How much more (4 points)?

_____

6. Sunshine Retirement Home is located in a state in which the sales tax rate is 8%. Sunshine Retirement Home is located 50 miles from the state border. The bordering state has a sales tax of 3%. An employee of Sunshine Retirement Home drove a company vehicle across the state line and 5 miles into the bordering state to purchase the following items: 4 dozen blankets at $14 per blanket; 6 dozen towels at $5 per towel; 3 dozen sheets at $9 per sheet; a set of cooking utensils for $39; and 8 gallons of disinfectant at $7.50 per gallon.

a. Assuming the prices were the same in both states, how much did Sunshine Retirement Home save in state sales taxes (8 points)?

_____

b. The vehicle of Sunshine Retirement Home costs $0.45 per mile to operate. The driver is paid $9 per hour. The round trip took two and one half hours. In the home state the merchandise would have been delivered at no additional charge. Considering all expenses, how much did Sunshine Retirement Home save by purchasing in another state (8 points)?

_____

7. State X had a sales tax of 6% and needed more revenue. Taxable sales last year were $973,000,000. The sales tax rose to 7% this year. Taxable sales fell by 11% as people went to other states for large purchases. How many dollars of increased revenue resulted from the increase in sales tax? Figure all sales as fully taxable (6 points).

_____

8. If a bordering state with a 3% sales tax received all of the sales lost by state X, how much increased revenue did the bordering state receive (6 points)?

_____

C (25 points) — Solve the following problems (points for correct answers as marked).

9. Pianos Plus has stores in 4 states. Sales tax rates for the four states are: State A = 8%; State B = $6\frac{1}{2}$%; State C = $5\frac{1}{2}$%; State D = 3%. Annual sales for the four states last year were: State A = $742,000; State B = $837,000; State C = $491,000; State D = $987,000.

a. How much did Pianos Plus collect in sales taxes during the year (8 points)?

_____

b. If all 4 states had the same low sales tax rate of 3%, how much would Pianos Plus have collected in sales taxes during the year (4 points)?

_____

c. If all 4 states had the same high sales tax rate of 8%, how much would Pianos Plus have collected in sales taxes during the year (3 points)?

_____

10. A gas station owner sold 7,814 gallons of gasoline at $1.25 a gallon on the day before a holiday. The price included a state tax of 11¢ a gallon and a federal tax of 9¢ a gallon. In addition, the seller was required to pay a state tax of 3% of the retail price (selling price minus federal and state tax) of the gasoline. What was the total tax on the day's business (10 points)?

_____

_____
Score for C (25)

Assignment 20-2: Property Taxes

A (30 points) — Solve the following problems (points for correct answers as marked).

1. Find the assessed valuation for each of the following towns (2 points for each correct answer).

Town	Property Value	Basis for Tax Billing	Assessed Valuation
A	$940,000,000	100%	_____
B	515,625,000	80%	_____
C	424,000,000	75%	_____
D	730,000,000	60%	_____
E	980,000,000	50%	_____

2. Find the tax rate for each of the following towns. Show your answer as a percent (2 points for each correct answer).

Town	Assessed Valuation	Amount to Be Raised	Tax Rate
F	$940,000,000	$16,920,000	_____
G	412,500,000	7,095,000	_____
H	876,000,000	11,826,000	_____
I	345,000,000	5,520,000	_____
J	97,000,000	1,406,500	_____

3. Convert the following percentage tax rates into dollars and cents per $100 of assessed valuations (1 point for each correct answer).

Tax Rate	Dollars and cents
1.8%	_____
1.75%	_____
1.6%	_____
1.35%	_____
1.2%	_____

4. Convert the following percentage tax rates into mills per $1 of assessed valuation (1 point for each correct answer).

Tax Rate	Mills
1.8%	_____
1.75%	_____
1.6%	_____
1.35%	_____
1.2%	_____

B (30 points) — Solve the following problems (points for correct answers as marked).

5. The Parson Company is located in a state in which assessed valuation is 100% of market value. The tax rate this year is $1.35 on each $100 of market value. The market value of the company building is $190,000. How much property tax will Parson pay this year (5 points)?

_____

6. If the tax rate in Parson's area increases next year to $1.42 on each $100 of market value, how much more property tax will Parson pay next year than it paid this year (5 points)?

_____

7. Raulston Corporation is located in an area in which assessed valuation is 70% of market value. The tax rate this year is 1.6%. The market value of Raulston's property is $310,000. How much property tax will Raulston pay this year (5 points)?

_____

8. Next year the assessed valuation in Raulston's area will decrease to 65% of market value and the tax rate will remain the same as this year. How much less tax will Raulston pay next year than it paid this year (5 points)?

_____

9. Perez Inc. is headquartered in an area in which assessed valuation is 80% of market value. The tax rate this year is $1.40 on each $100 of assessed valuation. Its property has a market value of $320,000. How much property tax will Perez pay this year (5 points)?

_____

Part Six   Taxes and Insurance

10. Perez is planning on moving to a new area in which the assessed valuation is only 60% of market value. The tax rate is $1.90 on each $100 of assessed valuation. The new property also has a market value of $320,000. Will Perez pay more or less property tax next year (1 point)?

_____

How much is the increase or decrease? (4 points)?

_____

C   (40 points) — Solve the following problems (points for correct answers as marked).

11. Clay County is divided into five communities whose assessed valuations, determined individually, are shown in the table below, along with the percent of assessed value to true value.

a. In the right-hand column below, show what each one's equalized assessment should be for the fair sharing of the county's overhead expenses (8 points, 2 points for each correct answer).

Community	Local Valuation	Rate	Equalized Valuation
Chatham	$ 24,560,000	50%	_____
Dover	100,276,000	55%	_____
Lafayette	276,008,000	60%	_____
Newton	88,476,000	75%	_____

b. If a house in Dover has an assessed value of $181,500, what should an identical house in Newton be assessed for equalization (4 points)?

_____

c. If a house in Newton has an assessed value of $290,000, what should an identical house in Dover be assessed for equalization (4 points)?

_____

12. In a certain development, the houses sell for $92,500, and they are located on both sides of a street which is the boundary line between Madison and Monroe townships. Madison assesses at 60% of market value and has a tax rate of $5.80 per $100. Monroe assesses at 80%, but with a rate of $4.20 per $100. On which side of the street would a buyer have lower taxes, and by how much (8 points)?

_____

13. Julia Horton Ltd. purchased a building for $240,000. Payments of principal and interest on the mortgage are $1,670 per month. The same bank also handles insurance and tax payments on all commercial mortgages. Horton pays the bank $90 per month for fire and liability insurance. If the area has an assessment valuation of 60% and a tax rate of $1.50 per $100 of assessed valuation, what will be Horton's total monthly payment to its bank for principal, interest, insurance, and taxes (8 points)?

_____

14. The assessed valuation in Brownville is 60% and the tax rate is 1.7%. More revenue is needed. Two methods on increasing taxes are being considered: a. raising assessed valuation to 70% and leaving the tax rate at 1.7%, or b. leaving the assessed valuation at 60% and raising the tax rate to 1.9%

Which would result in greater revenue, a or b (4 points)?

_____

How much more per $100 of market value (4 points)?

_____

Chapter 21
Federal Income Tax

OBJECTIVES
After completing this chapter, you should be able to:

- Understand basic income tax terms
- Understand the basic makeup of taxable income
- Compute a simple individual income tax
- Compute a simple corporate income tax

Federal income tax calculation can be a very complex process. The purpose of this chapter is for you to become familiar with some of the basic structure of the calculation. The general principal of an income tax is to charge a percent of the taxable income of the taxpayer according to a graduated scale.

Revisions of the Internal Revenue Code periodically make changes in the income tax laws and adjustments in the graduated scale. For 1990, the graduated scale for individual taxpayers was comprised of three brackets, 15%; 28%; and 33% as shown in Table 21-1. These figures are the latest available for inclusion in this book.

TABLE 21-1
1990 Tax Rate Structure

	Taxable Income			
Tax Rate	Joint Returns	Heads of Households	Single	Married Filing Separately
15%	Up to $32,450	Up to $26,050	Up to $19,450	Up to $16,225
28%	Over $32,450 Up to $78,400	Over $26,050 Up to $67,200	Over $19,450 Up to $47,050	Over $16,225 Up to $39,200
33%	Over $78,400 Up to $162,770	Over $67,200 Up to $134,930	Over $47,050 Up to $97,620	Over $39,200 Up to $123,570

Taxable income in excess of the highest bracket in Table 21-1 is figured on a separate schedule attached to the tax return.

INDIVIDUAL FILINGS

Determining the federal income tax amount requires basic understanding of the meaning of certain important tax terms and the process of calculating the tax.

Basic Tax Term Definitions

1. *Gross income* consists of all income received—such as wages, salaries, commissions, bonuses, tips, dividends, and interest—as well as income from businesses, professions, farming, partnerships, rents, royalties, estates, trusts, and other sources. A portion of social security benefits and pensions also may need to be included as income. Losses are subtracted.

   The following are not included as income—gifts, inheritances, and bequests; interest on tax-exempt state and municipal bonds; life insurance proceeds at death; workers' compensation benefits; dividends from veterans' insurance; and bonuses and pensions to veterans and their families.

2. *Adjusted gross income* is found by subtracting from gross income any adjustments to income, such as certain business expenses not paid by the employer.

3. *Itemized deductions* are deductions allowed for certain payments made during the tax year. These deductions consist of charitable contributions to approved church and public organizations; certain interest payments; taxes paid on real estate; some state and local taxes; a portion of medical and dental expenses; and a few miscellaneous deductions.

   No federal taxes of any kind are deductible. Expenses such as life and fire insurance premiums, rent for a home, and maintenance of a personal residence are not deductible. If property is rented to a tenant, however, certain insurance and maintenance costs would be deductible by the owner as business expenses, but not as itemized deductions. (For problems in this section, assume that all taxes and interest on the home, all state income taxes, and all donations to charity are deductible.)

4. *Standard deductions* are set amounts found in a table and may be claimed by those individuals who do not itemize their deductions. The standard deduction amounts for 1990 are shown in Table 21-2.

TABLE 21-2
Standard Deductions for 1990

Filing Status	Standard Deduction
Married Filing Joint	$5,450
Head of Household	$4,750
Single Individual	$3,250
Married Filing Separately	$2,725

Additional standard deductions are allowed for any person over 65 years old or blind who does not itemize deductions. These additional deductions for 1990 are shown in Table 21-3.

TABLE 21-3
Additional Standard Deductions for 1990

Filing Status	Over 65	Blind	Over 65 & Blind
Single individual	$800	$800	$1,600
Married individual	$650	$650	$1,300

5. An *exemption* is a reduction of adjusted gross income that is allowed for each taxpayer and qualifying spouse. (A spouse qualifies on a joint tax return as long as s/he is not a dependent of another taxpayer.) In 1990 each exemption is $2,050. This amount will be adjusted for inflation annually. The taxpayer is also allowed an exemption for each dependent who meets all of the following requirements for the tax year:

   i. Income—The dependent must have an income of less than $2,050 (adjusted annually for inflation), unless the dependent is under 19 or a full-time student.

   ii. Support—The dependent must have received more than half of his or her support from the taxpayer.

   iii. Married Dependents—If married, the dependent must not file a joint return.

   iv. Citizenship—The dependent must be a citizen or resident of the United States, a citizen of Canada or Mexico, or an alien child adopted by and living with a U.S. citizen in a foreign country.

   v. Relationship—The dependent must be related to the taxpayer or a member of the household for the entire year.

6. *Taxable income* is the amount of income upon which the income tax is determined. For most individual taxpayers it is figured by one of the following methods:

If deductions are itemized:
Taxable income = Adjusted gross income − Itemized deductions
                 − Exemptions

If deductions are not itemized:
Taxable income = Adjusted gross income − Standard deduction
                 − Exemptions

7. *Form 1040* is the basic income tax return form filed by the majority of taxpayers. Special schedules provided with this form are used to account for interest and dividend income earned and itemized deductions. (See Figure 21-2 on pages 248 and 249 for an example of Form 1040.)

8. *Form W-2*, the wage and tax statement sent to each employee by the employer at the end of the year, must be attached to Form 1040. (See Figure 21-1 on page 247 for an example of Form W-2.)

Tax Calculations

a. Larry Erickson, a single taxpayer, has an adjusted gross income of $25,500; a salary of $25,000, plus interest income of $500. He itemizes the following deductions: $500 to the Salvation Army, $500 to his church, $2,100 interest on his house, and $1,200 state taxes, for a total of $4,300. He claims one exemption. Calculate his federal income tax amount.

Adjusted gross income	$25,500
Minus itemized deductions	4,300
	$21,200
Minus one exemption.....................................	2,050
Taxable income..	$19,150
Income tax ($19,150 × 15%)	$2,872.50

b. Robert and Rosemary Waligore file a joint return. Their adjusted gross income is $52,000 (his salary of $38,000 plus her part-time earnings of $14,000). They have three children and claim five exemptions, two for themselves and three for their children. Calculate their federal income tax amount.

Adjusted gross income	$52,000
Minus standard deduction	5,450
	$46,550
Minus 5 exemptions @ $2,050 each	10,250
Taxable income	$36,300

Income tax calculation:

$32,450 × 15%	=	$4,867.50
($36,300 − $32,450 = $3,850) × 28%	=	1,078.00
Total income tax		$5,945.50

Therefore, the Waligore's 1990 income tax (rounded to the nearest dollar) would be $5,946.

BUSINESS FILINGS

For a *sole proprietorship*, a business that has only one owner and is not incorporated, the owner includes the net income or loss from the business on his/her Form 1040 and attaches a special schedule giving the details.

Taxpayers in a *partnership*, a business that is not incorporated and has more than one owner, must include their share of the income or loss on each one's individual Form 1040.

Corporations (basically businesses whose owners are stockholders) that are subject to income tax must file their special corporate returns regardless of their amount of taxable income or whether any tax is due. For 1990 corporate income is taxed at the following graduated rates:

Taxable Income	1990 Corporate Tax Rates
$0–$50,000	15%
$50,001–$75,000	25%
$75,001–$100,000	34%
$100,001–$335,000	39%
Over $335,000	34%

c. Steel Structures Corporation had a taxable income of $110,000.

15%	×	$ 50,000	=	$ 7,500	
25%	×	$ 25,000	=	$ 6,250	
34%	×	$ 25,000	=	$ 8,500	
39%	×	$ 10,000	=	$ 3,900	
		$110,000		$26,150	

Therefore, the company's total income tax for the year is $26,150.

FIGURE 21-1
Form W-2

1 Control number 016876-19	22222	For Paperwork Reduction Act Notice, see separate instructions OMB No. 1545-0008	For Official Use Only ▶							
2 Employer's name, address, and ZIP code

Reliable Accounting, Inc.
482 North Avenue
Midtown, CA 94976 | | | 6 Statutory employee ☐ Deceased ☐ Pension plan ☐ Legal rep. ☐ 942 emp. ☐ Subtotal ☐ Deferred compensation ☐ Void ☐ | | | | | | | |
			7 Allocated tips				8 Advance EIC payment			
			9 Federal income tax withheld $3,200				10 Wages, tips, other compensation $38,000			
3 Employer's identification number 94-1234567	4 Employer's state I.D. number 910-7001		11 Social security tax withheld $2,907				12 Social security wages $38,000			
5 Employee's social security number 474-22-1234			13 Social security tips				14 Nonqualified plans			
19a Employee's name (first, middle, last) Robert R. Waligore			15 Dependent care benefits				16 Fringe benefits incl. in Box 10			
1496 Spruce Road Midtown, CA 94976			17 See Instr. for Forms W-2/W-2P				18 Other			
19b Employee's address and ZIP code										
20		21			22				23	
24 State income tax $2,300	25 State wages, tips, etc. $38,000	26 Name of state CA		27 Local income tax		28 Local wages, tips, etc.		29 Name of locality		

Copy A For Social Security Administration   Dept. of the Treasury—Internal Revenue Service

Form **W-2 Wage and Tax Statement 1990**

COMPLETE ASSIGNMENTS 21-1 AND 21-2

Chapter terms for review

adjusted gross income
corporation
exemption
Form 1040
Form W-2
gross income

itemized deductions
partnership
sole proprietorship
standard deductions
taxable income

FIGURE 21-2 Form 1040 (page 1)

Form 1040 Department of the Treasury—Internal Revenue Service
U.S. Individual Income Tax Return **1990**

For the year Jan.–Dec. 31, 1990, or other tax year beginning _____ , 1990, ending _____ , 19 ____ | OMB No. 1545-0074

Label
(See Instructions on page 8.)

Use IRS label. Otherwise, please print or type.

Your first name and initial	Last name	Your social security number
Robert R.	Waligore	474 : 22 : 1234

If a joint return, spouse's first name and initial	Last name	Spouse's social security number
Rosemary S.	Waligore	474 : 22 : 5678

Home address (number and street). (If you have a P.O. box, see page 9.) | Apt. no.
1496 Spruce Road

City, town or post office, state, and ZIP code. (If you have a foreign address, see page 9.)
Midtown, CA 94976

For Privacy Act and Paperwork Reduction Act Notice, see Instructions.

Presidential Election Campaign (See page 9.)

Do you want $1 to go to this fund? . . . . [X] Yes [ ] No
If joint return, does your spouse want $1 to go to this fund? . . [X] Yes [ ] No

Note: Checking "Yes" will not change your tax or reduce your refund.

Filing Status

Check only one box.

1. [ ] Single. (See page 10 to find out if you can file as head of household.)
2. [X] Married filing joint return (even if only one had income)
3. [ ] Married filing separate return. Enter spouse's social security no. above and full name here. ▶ _____
4. [ ] Head of household (with qualifying person). (See page 10.) If the qualifying person is your child but not your dependent, enter this child's name here. ▶ _____
5. [ ] Qualifying widow(er) with dependent child (year spouse died ▶ 19 ___). (See page 10.)

Exemptions

(See Instructions on page 10.)

If more than 6 dependents, see Instructions on page 11.

6a [X] **Yourself** If your parent (or someone else) can claim you as a dependent on his or her tax return, do not check box 6a. But be sure to check the box on line 33b on page 2 .
b [X] **Spouse** . . . .

c **Dependents:** (1) Name (first, initial, and last name)	(2) Check if under age 2	(3) If age 2 or older, dependent's social security number	(4) Dependent's relationship to you	(5) No. of months lived in your home in 1990
Susan T. Waligore	X	: :	daughter	12
Robert P. Waligore		582 : 93 : 9876	son	12
Barbara A. Waligore		431 : 82 : 5432	daughter	12
		: :		
		: :		

d If your child didn't live with you but is claimed as your dependent under a pre-1985 agreement, check here ▶ [ ]
e Total number of exemptions claimed . . . .

No. of boxes checked on 6a and 6b: **2**
No. of your children on 6c who:
• lived with you: **3**
• didn't live with you due to divorce or separation (see page 11)
No. of other dependents on 6c: ___
Add numbers entered on lines above ▶ **5**

Income

Attach Copy B of your Forms W-2, W-2G, and W-2P here.

If you do not have a W-2, see page 8.

Attach check or money order on top of any Forms W-2, W-2G, or W-2P.

7	Wages, salaries, tips, etc. (attach Form(s) W-2)	7	52,000
8a	**Taxable** interest income (also attach Schedule B if over $400)	8a	
b	**Tax-exempt** interest income (see page 13). DON'T include on line 8a 8b		
9	Dividend income (also attach Schedule B if over $400)	9	
10	Taxable refunds of state and local income taxes, if any, from worksheet on page 14	10	
11	Alimony received	11	
12	Business income or (loss) (attach Schedule C)	12	
13	Capital gain or (loss) (attach Schedule D)	13	
14	Capital gain distributions not reported on line 13 (see page 14). . . .	14	
15	Other gains or (losses) (attach Form 4797)	15	
16a	Total IRA distributions . |16a|	16b Taxable amount (see page 14)	16b	
17a	Total pensions and annuities |17a|	17b Taxable amount (see page 14)	17b	
18	Rents, royalties, partnerships, estates, trusts, etc. (attach Schedule E)	18	
19	Farm income or (loss) (attach Schedule F)	19	
20	Unemployment compensation (insurance) (see page 16) . . .	20	
21a	Social security benefits . |21a|	21b Taxable amount (see page 16)	21b	
22	Other income (list type and amount—see page 16) ------------------	22	
23	Add the amounts shown in the far right column for lines 7 through 22. This is your **total income** ▶	23	52,000

Adjustments to Income

(See Instructions on page 17.)

24a	Your IRA deduction, from applicable worksheet on page 17 or 18	24a	
b	Spouse's IRA deduction, from applicable worksheet on page 17 or 18	24b	
25	One-half of self-employment tax (see page 18)	25	
26	Self-employed health insurance deduction, from worksheet on page 18	26	
27	Keogh retirement plan and self-employed SEP deduction	27	
28	Penalty on early withdrawal of savings	28	
29	Alimony paid. Recipient's SSN ▶ ___ : ___ : ___	29	
30	Add lines 24a through 29. These are your **total adjustments** . . . . . ▶	30	

Adjusted Gross Income

31 Subtract line 30 from line 23. This is your **adjusted gross income**. If this amount is less than $20,264 and a child lived with you, see page 23 to find out if you can claim the "Earned Income Credit" on line 57 . . . . . . ▶ | 31 | 52,000 |

FIGURE 21-2 Form 1040 (page 2)

Form 1040 (1990)

Page **2**

Tax Computation

If you want IRS to figure your tax, see Instructions on page 19.

32	Amount from line 31 (adjusted gross income)	32	52,000

33a Check if: ☐ **You** were 65 or older ☐ Blind; ☐ **Spouse** was 65 or older ☐ Blind.
Add the number of boxes checked above and enter the total here . . . ▶ 33a [ ]

b If your parent (or someone else) can claim you as a dependent, check here . . . ▶ 33b ☐

c If you are married filing a separate return and your spouse itemizes deductions, or you are a dual-status alien, see page 19 and check here . . . . ▶ 33c ☐

34 Enter the **larger** of:
- Your **standard deduction** (from the chart (or worksheet) on page 20 that applies to you), **OR**
- Your **itemized deductions** (from Schedule A, line 27).
  If you itemize, attach Schedule A and check here . . ▶ ☐

		34	5,450
35	Subtract line 34 from line 32	35	46,550
36	Multiply $2,050 by the total number of exemptions claimed on line 6e . . .	36	10,250
37	**Taxable Income.** Subtract line 36 from line 35. (If line 36 is more than line 35, enter -0-.) . .	37	36,300

38 Enter tax. Check if from: **a** ☐ Tax Table, **b** ☐ Tax Rate Schedules, or **c** ☐ Form 8615 (see page 21)
(If any is from Form(s) 8814, enter that amount here ▶ **d** _____ .)

		38	5,946
39	Additional taxes (see page 21). Check if from: **a** ☐ Form 4970 **b** ☐ Form 4972 . . .	39	
40	Add lines 38 and 39 . . . . ▶	40	5,946

Credits
(See Instructions on page 21.)

41	Credit for child and dependent care expenses (attach Form 2441)	41		
42	Credit for the elderly or the disabled (attach Schedule R) . . .	42		
43	Foreign tax credit (attach Form 1116)	43		
44	General business credit. Check if from: **a** ☐ Form 3800 or **b** ☐ Form (specify) _____	44		
45	Credit for prior year minimum tax (attach Form 8801)	45		
46	Add lines 41 through 45		46	
47	Subtract line 46 from line 40. (If line 46 is more than line 40, enter -0-.) . . . . ▶		47	5,946

Other Taxes

48	Self-employment tax (attach Schedule SE)	48	
49	Alternative minimum tax (attach Form 6251)	49	
50	Recapture taxes (see page 22). Check if from: **a** ☐ Form 4255 **b** ☐ Form 8611 . .	50	
51	Social security tax on tip income not reported to employer (attach Form 4137)	51	
52	Tax on an IRA or a qualified retirement plan (attach Form 5329)	52	
53	Advance earned income credit payments from Form W-2	53	
54	Add lines 47 through 53. This is your **total tax** . . . . ▶	54	5,946

Payments

Attach Forms W-2, W-2G, and W-2P to front.

55	Federal income tax withheld (**If any is from Form(s) 1099, check** ▶ ☐).	55	3,200	
56	1990 estimated tax payments and amount applied from 1989 return	56		
57	**Earned income credit** (see page 23)	57		
58	Amount paid with Form 4868 (extension request)	58		
59	Excess social security tax and RRTA tax withheld (see page 24)	59		
60	Credit for Federal tax on fuels (attach Form 4136)	60		
61	Regulated investment company credit (attach Form 2439) . .	61		
62	Add lines 55 through 61. These are your **total payments** . . . . ▶		62	3,200

Refund or Amount You Owe

63	If line 62 is more than line 54, enter amount **OVERPAID** . . . . ▶	63	
64	Amount of line 63 to be **REFUNDED TO YOU** . . . . ▶	64	
65	Amount of line 63 to be **APPLIED TO YOUR 1991 ESTIMATED TAX** ▶	65	
66	If line 54 is more than line 62, enter **AMOUNT YOU OWE**. Attach check or money order for full amount payable to "Internal Revenue Service." Write your name, address, social security number, daytime phone number, and "1990 Form 1040" on it.	66	2,746
67	Estimated tax penalty (see page 25) 67		

Sign Here

Keep a copy of this return for your records.

Under penalties of perjury, I declare that I have examined this return and accompanying schedules and statements, and to the best of my knowledge and belief, they are true, correct, and complete. Declaration of preparer (other than taxpayer) is based on all information of which preparer has any knowledge.

Your signature *Robert R. Waligore* | Date 4-14-91 | Your occupation Accountant

Spouse's signature (if joint return, BOTH must sign) *Rosemary S. Waligore* | Date 4-14-91 | Spouse's occupation Decorator

Paid Preparer's Use Only

Preparer's signature ▶ | Date | Check if self-employed ☐ | Preparer's social security no.

Firm's name (or yours if self-employed) and address ▶ | E.I. No.
 | ZIP code

Assignment 21-1: Federal Income Tax 1

A (52 points) — Complete all problems using the 1990 exemptions, deductions, and tax rates located in Chapter 21. Round all amounts to the nearest dollar. Decimal amounts of fifty cents or more should be rounded to the next highest dollar. This is allowed as long as it is done consistently (points for correct answers as marked).

1. Determine the taxable income for each of the following taxpayers (20 points, 4 points for each correct answer).

	Adjusted Gross Income	Number of Exemptions	Type of Return	Deductions	Taxable Income
a.	$19,700	1	single	standard	_____
b.	$52,450	4	head of hh.	$5,650	_____
c.	$23,900	2	joint	standard	_____
d.	$12,464	1	single		_____
e.	$43,700	6	joint	$6,023	_____

2. Mary Rogers is a 70-year-old single person who lives alone. She takes the standard deduction. Her income during the year was $16,500.

   a. What is Mary's taxable income (12 points)? _____

   b. What is Mary's income tax (4 points)? _____

3. George Sampson is 82 years old, and his wife, Marcia, is 83. Marcia is blind. They have $19,000 taxable income, including dividends from investments. They file a joint return and take the standard deduction.

   a. What is the Sampsons' taxable income (12 points)? _____

   b. What is the Sampsons' income tax (4 points)? _____

Score for A (52)

B (48 points) — Solve the following problems (points for correct answers as marked).

4. John Paul is 66 years old, his wife, Ann, is 64, and they file a joint return. John's salary for the year was $30,000. Ann's salary was $24,500. They paid mortgage interest of $3,900 and property tax of $950 on their home. They paid state income tax of $3,200 during the year. They itemize their deductions.

a. What is their taxable income (12 points)? **b.** What is the Pauls' income tax (4 points)?

_____   _____

5. Walter Cross and his wife, Louise, have two children. Both Walter's and Louise's mothers live with them and have no income. Walter's salary for the year was $23,000. Louise's salary was $24,000. They received stock dividends of $1,200. They received $500 from a state bond. They take the standard deduction and file a joint return.

a. What is their taxable income (12 points)? **b.** What is their income tax (4 points)?

_____   _____

6. Arnold Stewart and his wife, Rita, have three children. Arnold's father lives with them and has no income. Arnold earned a salary of $36,000 during the year. Rita is not employed. They received cash dividends from stock of $3,000. They paid $3,100 property tax and $4,100 mortgage interest on their home. They paid $2,600 principal on their mortgage. They paid state income tax of $2,175. They donated $500 to their church and $500 to the Salvation Army. They spent $5,600 on groceries and $1,100 on utilities. They itemize their deductions.

a. What is their taxable income (12 points)? **b.** What is their income tax (4 points)?

_____   _____

Score for B (48)

Assignment 21-2:   Federal Income Tax 2

A   (55 points) — Solve the following problems (points for correct answers as marked).

1. Tara St. Clair, who is single, is employed at a salary of $15,500. She reported receiving tips amounting to $5,650. She collected $475 interest on her savings account and $2,000 interest on state bonds. She pays $350 a month rent for her apartment. Her itemized deductions total $2,280. During the year, her employer withheld $1,260 from her pay for income tax purposes. She had also made four estimated tax payments of $270 each within the year. How much more would she have to remit with her tax return (25 points)?

_____

2. Ben Hardy's salary is $24,000 a year, and his wife, Gail, earns $14,400 in a part-time job. They have two children, ages 13 and 15 (30 points, 3 points for each correct answer).

   a. If they file a joint return, what is their tax? _____

b. If they file separately and Ben takes both children as exemptions, how much tax would they pay?

Ben   _____

Gail   _____

Total   _____

c. If they file separately and each takes one child as an exemption, how much tax would they pay?

Ben   _____

Gail   _____

Total   _____

d. If they file separately and Gail takes both children as exemptions, how much tax would they pay?

Ben   _____

Gail   _____

Total   _____

B (45 points) — Solve the following problems (points for correct answers as marked).

3. The Allen and Day families live on the same street and work for the same company. Each has a salary of $32,000 a year. Allen also receives $5,000 a year as the village treasurer and $280 a year dividends from a veterans' insurance policy. The family consists of Mr. Allen, his wife, and a daughter, age 17. The Allens own their own home and pay real estate taxes of $2,900 annually. Interest payments on their mortgage total $2,200 for the year, and charitable contributions total $800.

The Days are the parents of five children, all below high school age. They pay $500 a month rent for their home and their charitable contributions are $900.

If each family files a joint return, which pays the higher federal income tax and by how much (25 points)?

_____

4. The Green Laundry Corporation had income of $169,400 and expenses of $134,300. How much income tax should it pay (8 points)?

_____

5. A corporation had taxable income of $85,000. During the year it paid $1,865 for social security and $1,245 for unemployment compensation tax. What was the total it paid in taxes (12 points)?

_____

_____
Score for B (45)

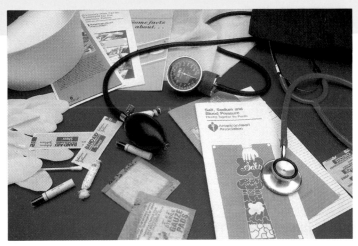

Chapter 22
Life and Health Insurance

OBJECTIVES

After completing this chapter, you should be able to:

- Determine life insurance premiums
- Determine cash surrender values, loan values, and settlement options from tables
- Determine medical insurance contributions and reimbursements

Insurance coverage has become a helpful, and often necessary, part of today's world. Life insurance provides a way for an individual to help protect his or her family and for a company to protect itself against the financial trouble caused by the death of the insured person. Likewise, health insurance helps protect against the high cost of medical care and encourage people to seek preventive medical attention.

LIFE INSURANCE

The most common policies issued by life insurance companies are straight life (ordinary), limited-payment life, term, endowment, and annuity.

On a *straight* (or *ordinary*) *life insurance* policy, a certain *premium*, or fee, is paid every year until the death of the insured person (called "the insured"). The policy then becomes payable to the beneficiary. A policy *beneficiary* is a person, a company, or an organization that benefits from the policy.

On a *limited-payment life insurance* policy, a certain premium is paid every year for a certain number of years specified at the time of insuring, or until the death of the insured, should that occur during the specified period. The policy is payable on the death of the insured, although there may be some options available at the end of the payment period.

A *term insurance* policy is insurance protection that is issued for a limited time. A certain premium is paid every year during the specified time period, or "term." The policy is payable only in case of death of the insured during the term. Otherwise, neither the insured nor the specified beneficiaries receive any payment, and the protection stops at the end of the term.

Because premiums for term policies are much lower than premiums for the same amount of coverage in policies having cash value many people choose to carry a term policy. Often people choose to carry term insurance in addition to their other policies during a period in their lives in which financial obligations are at their greatest, such as while their children are growing up.

An *endowment insurance* policy provides insurance payable upon the insured's death if it occurs within a specified period, and an endowment of the same amount as the policy, payable if the insured is alive at the end of that period.

An *annuity insurance* policy pays a certain sum of money to the insured every year after the insured reaches a specified age and until the insured's death.

Additional death benefit (*ADB*), sometimes referred to as accidental death benefit, is available with some policies. ADB allows the insured to purchase, at a low rate per thousand dollars of coverage, additional insurance up to the full face value of the policy. In case of death of the insured by accident, both the full value of the policy and the ADB would be paid to the beneficiaries of the insured. If death occurs other than by accident, the full value of the policy is paid but no ADB is paid.

Premiums

Table 22-1 shows typical annual, semiannual, and quarterly premiums (ages 25-28) for straight-life, 20-payment life, and 20-year endowment policies. Premiums vary from company to company due to such differences as the exact type of coverage and participation in dividends.

TABLE 22-1   Typical Premiums for $1,000 Life Insurance

	Straight Life			20-Payment Life			20-Year Endowment		
Age	Annual	Semiannual	Quarterly	Annual	Semiannual	Quarterly	Annual	Semiannual	Quarterly
25	$17.20	$ 8.94	$4.73	$31.20	$16.26	$8.26	$52.00	$27.04	$14.30
26	17.85	9.28	4.91	31.81	16.52	8.45	52.60	27.35	14.47
27	18.60	9.67	5.11	32.41	16.83	8.64	53.20	27.66	14.63
28	19.30	10.04	5.31	33.06	17.31	8.85	53.86	28.01	14.81

a. Using the premiums shown in Table 22-1, what are the yearly premiums for each of the following $50,000 life insurance policies purchased at the age of 26?

Type of Insurance	Method of Payment	Premium Computation
Straight Life	Annual	$17.85 × 50 = $892.50
20-Year Endowment	Quarterly	$14.47 × 4 × 50 = $2,894
20-Payment Life	Semiannual	$16.52 × 2 × 50 = $1,652
20-Year Endowment	Semiannual	$27.35 × 2 × 50 = $2,735
Straight Life	Quarterly	$4.91 × 4 × 50 = $982

Cash Surrender and Loan Values

Except for term insurance an insurance policy usually has a *cash surrender value,* which is the amount of cash that the company will pay the insured on the surrender, or "cashing-in," of the policy. The *loan value* of a policy is the amount that the insured may borrow on the policy from the insurance company. Interest is charged on such loans, but it is usually a lower rate than can be obtained elsewhere since the insurance policy has a cash value as great as the loan and there is no financial risk to the insurance company in granting the loan. The values, often quoted after the third year of the policy, are stated in the policy and increase every year. Typical cash surrender and loan values for policies issued at age 25 for $1,000 are shown in Table 22-2.

TABLE 22-2
Cash Surrender
and Loan Values
Policies Issued at
Age 25 for $1,000

Cash Surrender and Loan Values

End of Policy Year	Straight Life	20-Payment Life	20-Year Endowment
3	$ 10	$ 43	$ 88
4	22	68	130
5	35	93	173
10	104	228	411
15	181	380	684
20	264	552	1,000

b. Using the figures shown in Table 22-2, what would be the cash surrender and loan value for each of the following policies?

Policy Year	Type of Policy	Amount of Policy	Cash Surrender or Loan Value		
10	Straight Life	$ 30,000	$104 × 30	=	$ 3,120
5	20-Year Endow.	$ 15,000	$173 × 15	=	$ 2,595
10	20-Pay. Life	$ 10,000	$228 × 10	=	$ 2,280
4	Straight Life	$100,000	$ 22 × 100	=	$ 2,200
15	20-Year Endow.	$ 50,000	$684 × 50	=	$34,200

Life Insurance Settlement Options

Life insurance policies usually are settled by a lump-sum payment. However, other payment methods are available. These two optional payment methods are compared in Table 22-3.

Option 1: Regular monthly payments of a fixed amount are paid for a specified number of years. After this, no further payments are made.

Option 2: Regular installments of a fixed amount are paid for a guaranteed minimum number of years and as long as the beneficiary lives thereafter. If death occurs before all the guaranteed payments are made, the heirs receive the remaining payments. The amount of the payments is determined by the payee's age when payments begin, and this amount differs between male and female according to age.

TABLE 22-3 Options of Life Insurance Settlement—Monthly Payments Per $1,000

Option 1		Option 2				
Number of Years	Amount of Monthly Payment	Age of Payee at Date Payments Begin		Amt. of Monthly Payments Guaranteed for		
				10 Years	15 Years	20 Years
		Male	Female			
11	$8.53	41	46	$3.83	$3.77	$3.69
12	7.91	42	47	3.90	3.83	3.74
13	7.38	43	48	3.97	3.90	3.79
14	6.92	44	49	4.04	3.96	3.85
15	6.53	45	50	4.12	4.03	3.90
16	6.20	46	51	4.20	4.10	3.96
17	5.90	47	52	4.28	4.17	4.02
18	5.62	48	53	4.37	4.24	4.07
19	5.38	49	54	4.45	4.32	4.12
20	5.16	50	55	4.55	4.39	4.19

c. What would be the total cash payments to the beneficiaries in each of the following cases?

Amount of Insurance	Payee (Insured) Age: First Payment	Gender of Insured	Years to be Paid		Insured age at Death	Amount Paid
			No Guarantee	Guarantee		(1) (2) (3)
$10,000	52	M	15	—	70	$6.53 × 12 × 15 × 10 = $11,754
$20,000	55	F	—	10	70	$4.55 × 12 × 15 × 20 = $16,380
$30,000	47	M	—	15	49	$4.17 × 12 × 15 × 30 = $22,518
$50,000	46	F	—	20	68	$3.69 × 12 × 22 × 50 = $48,708

(1) Months in year   (2) Years to be paid   (3) $1,000's of insurance

COMPLETE ASSIGNMENTS 22-1 AND 22-2

HEALTH INSURANCE

As medical and hospital costs have soared in the past decade, the possibility of a long or serious illness has become an increasing threat to the financial stability of the individual and the family. *Group insurance* plans address this problem by providing medical insurance coverage to large numbers of people at lower premium rates than individuals could obtain separately.

Many companies subscribe to a group plan on behalf of any employees who choose to participate. Employer participation in paying part or all of the premiums for a group plan varies from company to company. Employers generally pay most of the premium for employees and participate to a lesser extent in paying premiums for family members of employees.

d. Employer A selected Blue Banner Health Plan to cover company employees. Monthly premiums are: single person = $200; single with one dependent = $300; single with multiple dependents = $360. The employer pays most of the premium, but employees pay a portion as follows: employee only = $20; employee with one dependent = $60; employee with multiple dependents = $90. What percent of the premium will be paid by 1) a single employee? 2) an employee with one dependent? 3) an employee with 7 dependents?

1) $20 ÷ $200 = 0.1 or 10%
2) $60 ÷ $300 = 0.20 or 20%
3) $90 ÷ $360 = 0.25 or 25%

Many group plans include a provision for a *deductible*, which is a cost that must be paid by the employee before any cost is paid by the insurance company. In these plans, the employee pays the first $200 to $500 medical charges each year and the insurance company participates in payment of charges above this deductible amount. Another frequent provision in group medical plans is the payment by the insurance company of a percent of costs over the deductible, usually 70% to 90%, with the remaining 10% to 30% paid by the insured.

e. Employer B provides group health coverage that includes a $300 annual deductible per family and payment of 80% of cost over the deductible. How much would an employee with two dependents pay if her year's medical bills were: self = $150; dependent one = $980; and dependent two = $90?

Total medical costs: $150 + $980 + $90 = $1,220
$1,220 less deductible of $300 = $920
$920 × 20% also paid by employee = $184
$300 deductible + $184 = $484 total cost paid by the employee

Premiums for most group insurance plans have soared recently. One way many companies have found to reduce costs is by seeking less expensive means of providing group coverage than the ordinary group plan provides. Another way is by lowering the percent of employer participation in paying premiums for employees and their dependents. Since the latter option would place an increasing financial burden on employees, many companies are turning to a relatively new and less expensive type of group plan known as a *health maintenance organization (HMO)*.

Health maintenance organizations generally offer the same medical and hospital protection as other group plans, but limit options of participants to a definite list of facilities, general practitioners, and specialists. Most health maintenance organization plans are structured so that each participant selects one physician from the list of general practitioners available. This physician is responsible for medical treatment of the patient or for any referral of the patient to a specialist.

In addition to a group medical plan, some employers offer a group dental or life insurance plan. Such additional plans would be similar in structure to the medical plan with the employer's participation in premium payments varying from company to company.

COMPLETE ASSIGNMENT 22-3

additional death benefit (ADB)
annuity insurance
beneficiary
cash surrender value
deductible
endowment insurance
group insurance
health maintenance organization
(HMO)

limited-payment life insurance
loan value
premium
straight life (ordinary life) insurance
term insurance

Assignment 22-1: Life Insurance

A (36 points) — Refer to Tables 22-1 and 22-2 in solving the following problems. Assume every year is a full 12 months long (1 point for each correct answer).

1. Find the premiums on the following policies.

Age	Type	Payments Made	Face of Policy	Rate Per $1,000	Premium Paid Each Year
28	Straight Life	Annually	$ 15,000	_____	_____
25	20-Payment Life	Quarterly	12,000	_____	_____
25	20-Year Endowment	Semi-annually	20,000	_____	_____
26	Straight	Quarterly	100,000	_____	_____
27	20-Payment Life	Semi-annually	50,000	_____	_____
28	20-Year Endowment	Annually	75,000	_____	_____

2. The Great Life Insurance Company wants to encourage customers to buy higher levels of insurance coverage. To do this, Great Life charges its regular premium plus a one-time $20 policy charge paid at the time of purchase. If the annual premium rate for a straight-life policy is $16 per $1,000, what is the actual charge per $1,000 for the first year if each of the following policies were purchased with the one-time $20 policy charge?

	Annual Premium Rate	Policy Charge	Total Charge	Charge Per $1,000
$ 1,000	_____	_____	_____	_____
10,000	_____	_____	_____	_____
25,000	_____	_____	_____	_____
50,000	_____	_____	_____	_____
60,000	_____	_____	_____	_____
100,000	_____	_____	_____	_____

Score for A (36)

B (64 points) — Refer to Tables 22-1 and 22-2 in solving the following problems. Assume every year is a full 12 months long (points for correct answers as marked).

3. When Alberto Perez was 27 years old, he took out a $20,000, 20-year endowment policy. He paid the premiums annually and survived the endowment period.

a. Did he receive more or less than he paid as annual premiums? In determining the amount paid, do not take into consideration any interest the premiums might have earned (3 points).

_____

b. How much more or less (5 points)?

_____

4. a. Jack Young purchased a $25,000, 20-payment life policy at the age of 28. He paid premiums annually. He died at the age of 48 after he had made the last payment. How much more did he pay in premiums during the 20 years than he would have paid for the same amount of ordinary life insurance (8 points)?

_____

b. If Jack Young had lived to the age of 78, what is the difference that he would have had to pay for the 20-payment life rather than the same amount of ordinary life (8 points)?

_____

5. When she was exactly 26 years old, Rhonda Fletcher purchased a straight life policy of $30,000. She paid annual premiums for 36 years. She died at the age of 62. How much more did her heirs receive than she actually paid in premiums (8 points)?

_____

6. At the age of 25, Jack Miller purchased a straight life policy of $30,000, premiums payable annually. He also purchased a 20-payment life policy of $20,000, premiums payable semiannually. At the end of 15 years, he decided to cash both policies.

a. How much did he receive for the straight life policy (4 points)?

_____

b. How much did he receive for the 20-payment life policy (4 points)?

_____

c. How much more did he pay in premiums than the total amount received for both policies (8 points)?

_____

7. **a.** What is the annual premium for a 20-year endowment policy of $15,000, purchased when the insured was 25 (2 points)?

_____

b. What would be the loan value of this policy after 10 years (2 points)?

_____

8. George Brown purchased an ordinary life policy of $20,000 and ADB for 50% of the value of the policy. In addition, he purchased a 5-year, $25,000 term policy. He died in an accident 3 years later.

a. How much money did George's beneficiaries receive (4 points)?

_____

b. How much money would George's beneficiaries have received if George Brown had died in an accident 7 years after purchasing the policies (4 points)?

_____

c. How much money would George's beneficiaries receive if George had died of natural causes 10 years after purchasing the policies (4 points)?

_____

_____
Score for B (64)

Assignment 22-2: Life Insurance Settlement Options

A **(48 points) — Refer to Table 22-3 in solving the following problems. Assume every year is a full 12 months long (8 points for each correct answer).**

1. Brenda Wyly was the beneficiary of a $50,000 life insurance policy when she was 51 years old. She decided to elect a method of settlement that would pay her a life income with monthly payments guaranteed for 15 years.

   a. How much would she receive monthly?

   _____

   b. How much would she receive monthly if she had selected a guaranteed period of 20 years instead of 15?

   _____

   c. If she lived to the age of 75, how much more would she have received under (a) than under (b)?

   _____

   d. How much would she receive monthly under Option 1 if she chose equal payments until she reached the age of 65?

   _____

   e. For how many years would she receive payments under Option 1 if she chose an income of approximately $258 monthly (compute to nearest year)?

   _____

   f. What is the exact total amount she would receive in (e) for that number of years?

   _____

                                                       _____
                                                       Score for A (48)

B **(52 points)** — **Refer to Tables 22-1, 22-2, and 22-3 in solving the following problems. Assume every year is a full 12 months long (points for correct answers as marked).**

2. Jeremy Bishop was the beneficiary of a $60,000 insurance policy. He was 50 years old at the time. He selected Option 1 for a 17-year period. He lived until he was 71 years old (28 points, 7 points for each correct answer).

a. How much did he receive monthly under the option he selected?

———————————

b. How much did he receive for the 17-year period?

———————————

c. How much would he have collected monthly if he had selected a 15-year guaranteed income under Option 2?

———————————

d. How much would he have received by the time of his death if he had selected Option 2 on a 20-year basis?

———————————

3. Jocelyn Hayes, the beneficiary of a $40,000 insurance policy, was undecided whether to choose Option 2 with a guaranteed period of 20 years, or Option 1 for 20 years. She was 49 years old at the time and lived to be 87 years old. How much did she lose by choosing Option 1 (12 points)?

———————————

4. Greg Wickham at age 25 bought a $100,000 straight life policy. After four annual payments, he lost his job and was unable to make the fifth payment. He borrowed from the insurance company, at 7% interest, enough to pay the premium due (12 points, 6 points for each correct answer).

a. What was the loan value of his policy after the fifth payment?

———————————

b. How much profit did his procedure net him?

———————————

———————————
Score for B (52)

Part Six Taxes and Insurance

Assignment 22-3: Health Insurance

A   (65 points) — Solve the following problems (points for correct answers as marked).

The Meyer Manufacturing Company subscribes to the American Family Medical Organization, an HMO. The Meyer Manufacturing Company pays a large part of the premiums. Participating employees have deducted from their paychecks every month $30 for an employee without dependents, $70 for an employee with one dependent, and $90 for an employee with multiple dependents.

The American Family Medical Organization has a deductible of $300 per year for an employee with no dependents, $420 per year for an employee with one dependent, and $500 for an employee with multiple dependents. The insurance company reimburses 80% of all medical expenses over the deductible.

Bob Smith is employed by Meyer Manufacturing Company. He chose to participate in the medical plan for himself, his wife, and their two children.

1. How much is deducted from Bob Smith's paycheck every month for medical insurance (4 points)?

_____

2. The Smith family has a total of $1,374 in medical expenses for the first year. How much money did the insurance company reimburse the Smith family for medical expenses for the first year (6 points)?

_____

3. At the beginning of the second year, Bob Smith's wife became employed and chose to use the health plan offered by her company for her own medical coverage. How much will be deducted every month of this second year from Bob Smith's paycheck for medical insurance (4 points)?

_____

4. If Bob Smith and his two dependents have medical expenses of $680 this second year, how much will he be reimbursed by the insurance company under his plan (6 points)?

_____

5. How much will Bob Smith spend this second year for medical expenses and medical insurance for himself and two dependents (8 points)?

_____

6. Bob Smith's wife's company medical plan has a $300 deductible for the insured without dependents, and reimburses 85% of all medical expenses over the deductible. Her employer deducts $40 from her monthly paycheck as her participation in payment of the premium.

a. How much will Mrs. Smith be reimbursed by her insurance company for this second year if her total medical expenses are $520 (6 points)?

_____

b. How much will she spend this year for her medical expenses and medical insurance (8 points)?

_____

7. What was the total amount paid this year for medical expenses and medical insurance by the four members of the Smith family using two medical plans (4 points)?

_____

8. If Mrs. Smith had remained under the medical plan at her husband's company this year:

a. How much would the four members of the Smith family have paid this year for medical expenses and medical insurance (11 points)?

_____

b. How much will the insurance company reimburse the Smith family of four under Bob Smith's insurance coverage this second year (4 points)?

_____

9. How much did the Smith family lose by using the two medical plans instead of one (4 points)?

_____

_____
Score for A (65)

B **(35 points) — Solve the following problems (5 points for each correct answer).**

10. A group medical plan charges a monthly premium of $300 for an insured employee without dependents, $450 for an employee with one dependent, and $535 for an employee with multiple dependents. Employees participate in monthly premium payments through payroll deductions of $30 for the insured employee, $60 for an employee with one dependent, and $80 for an employee with multiple dependents. An employee, a spouse, and three children in a family are insured.

a. How much does the insured employee have deducted from the paycheck for medical insurance coverage in one year?

_____

b. How much does the employer contribute towards medical insurance every month for the family of five?

_____

c. How much does the employer contribute toward medical insurance for the family of five over a 10 year period of employment?

_____

11. An insurance company charges for group insurance a premium of $425 for an employee without dependents, $550 for an employee with one dependent, and $610 for an employee with multiple dependents. The insurance company has a deductible of $350 for an employee without dependents, $450 for an employee with one dependent, and $500 for an employee with multiple dependents. The insurance company reimburses 85% of medical expenses over the deductible. The employer pays the entire premium. An employee and dependent spouse are insured.

a. What is the annual premium paid on behalf of the employee and spouse?

_____

b. If the employee and spouse have total medical expenses of $8,750 this year:

1. How much will the insurance company reimburse?

_____

2. How much will the employee and spouse pay toward medical expenses this year?

_____

3. How much money will the insurance company make or lose this year by insuring the employee and spouse?

_____

Chapter 23
Property and Auto Insurance

OBJECTIVES
After completing this chapter, you should be able to:

- Determine short-rate refunds
- Determine coinsurance losses

Both individuals and businesses are concerned about theft and damage to belongings. For businesses in particular, a loss of assets can cause serious delays in the production and delivery of products and can result in a great deal of extra expense. Therefore, it is wise for firms to purchase property insurance.

PROPERTY INSURANCE

Property insurance is insurance against loss of or damage to property. A policy can be written to protect the insured against one or more of the following: fire, casualty, liability, and theft. The most common property coverage is for fire.

The payment for an insurance policy is called a *premium*. Premium rates, which are quoted by the number of dollars per $1,000 of insurance, depend upon the nature of the risk, the location of the property, and the length of time covered by the policy.

Short Rates

Short rates are rates charged for less than a full term of insurance. If an insurance policy is canceled by the *insured* (the person who receives the benefit of the insurance) before the policy's full term is completed, the insured will receive a short-rate return of premium.

If a policy is canceled by the insurance company rather than by the insured, the company must refund the entire unused premium. In example a., the refund would be $246.50 for a half year.

a. Zephyr Corporation purchased a 1-year insurance policy to cover its building for $85,000 at a premium rate of $5.80 per $1,000. At the end of six months, the building was sold, and Zephyr canceled the insurance. The insurance company refunded the remaining half of the premium at the short rate, based on a penalty of 15% of the annual premium.

$$\frac{\$85,000}{\$1,000} \times \$5.80 = \$493 \text{ annual premium}$$

$$\$493 \times \tfrac{1}{2} \quad = \quad \$246.50 \text{ unused premium}$$

$$\$493 \times 15\% = \underline{-\ 73.95} \text{ penalty}$$

$$\$172.55 \text{ short-rate refund}$$

Adjustment of Losses

In an ordinary fire insurance policy, the insured will be paid the extent of the loss, sometimes *depreciated* (reduced in value due to use) up to the amount of the insurance. Policies may be obtained at lower rates, however, if they contain a *coinsurance clause*. This clause specifies that if a property is not insured up to a certain percentage of its value, the owner is the bearer of part of the insurance and will not be covered for the full amount of damages.

It is common for the coinsurance clause to be set at 80%. Under this clause, the full amount of the loss will not be paid by the insurance company unless the amount of the policy equals 80% of the property value. It is important to understand that the amount of the loss is not necessarily equal to the value of the property. For example, a building that is valued at $150,000 may be partly damaged in a fire. The loss would not be the entire value of the building; rather, it would be the cost of repairing the damage.

Steps for Determining the Owner's Share of Property Loss Under Coinsurance

1. Determine the amount of insurance required by multiplying the entire value of the property by the coinsurance percentage.
2. Determine the *recovery amount*, the maximum amount the insurance company will pay, by using the following formula:

$$\frac{\text{Amount of insurance carried}}{\text{Amount of insurance required}} \times \text{Loss} = \text{Recovery amount}$$

3. Compare the recovery amount with the amount of the insurance policy.
   a. If the recovery amount is greater than the amount of the policy, the insurance company will pay the amount of the policy.
   b. If the recovery amount is less than the amount of the policy, the insurance company will pay the recovery amount.
   NOTE: The insurance company will not pay more than the amount of the loss.
4. Determine the owner's share of the property loss by subtracting the amount the insurance company will pay from the loss amount.

b. Property valued at $300,000 was insured for $120,000, and the policy carried an 80% coinsurance clause. A fire caused $270,000 in damage. How much will the insurance company pay and how much must the owner pay if the building is repaired for $270,000?

Step 1 $\$300,000 \times 80\% = \$240,000$ amount of insurance required

Steps 2 & 3 $\dfrac{\$120,000}{\$240,000} \times \$270,000 = \$135,000$ (exceeds the $\$120,000$ insurance policy)

Step 4 $\$270,000$ damage $- \$120,000$ paid by insurance company $= \$150,000$ owner's share

If the amount of the loss was $\$200,000$ instead of $\$270,000$ the owner's share would be:

Steps 2 & 3 $\dfrac{\$120,000}{\$240,000} \times \$200,000 = \$100,000$ (less than the $\$120,000$ insurance policy)

Step 4 $\$200,000$ damage $- \$100,000$ paid by insurance company $= \$100,000$ owner's share

COMPLETE ASSIGNMENT 23-1

AUTO INSURANCE

Auto insurance falls into three classifications: liability and property damage; comprehensive; and collision. A policy that fully protects the insured will contain all three classifications.

Auto liability and property damage insurance protects the insured against claims resulting from personal injuries and property damage. Some states require all licensed drivers to carry auto liability and property damage insurance. Premium rates are based on the amount of protection, which generally ranges from $\$50,000$ to $\$1,000,000$ per accident.

Auto comprehensive insurance protects the vehicle of the insured against fire, water, theft, vandalism, falling objects, and other damage that is not caused by collision.

Auto collision insurance protects the vehicle of the insured against collision damage. Such collision damage may result from a collision with another vehicle or a one-car accident, such as hitting a tree.

Auto collision insurance policies usually contain a *deductible clause* which stipulates that the insured will pay the first portion of collision damage, usually $\$100$ to $\$500$, and the insurance company will pay the remainder up to the value of the insured vehicle. A deductible clause not only reduces the amount of damages for which the insurance company must pay, but also precludes the cost of paper work for small repairs costing under $\$100$. Therefore, a deductible clause lowers the premium for collision insurance.

c. A car was insured for collision damage with a $\$100$ deductible. The premium was $\$950$ per year. If an accident caused $\$1,500$ damage to the car, how much more did the insured receive than he paid in premiums for that year?

$\$1,500$ damage $- \$100$ deductible $= \$1,400$ paid by insurance company
$\$1,400 - \$950$ annual premium $= \$450$ more received than paid in premiums

No-Fault

No-fault insurance is a relatively new concept already mandatory in some states. No-fault coverage means that the driver of each vehicle involved in an injury accident submits a claim to his or her own insurance company to cover medical costs for injuries to the driver and passengers in that person's own vehicle. No-fault insurance was intended to preclude both delay in collecting coverage and the need to incur legal fees and court costs in deciding whose insurance company should pay for medical expenses. No-fault insurance does not cover damage to either vehicle involved in an accident.

Low Risk and High Risk

Auto insurance premium rates, as property insurance premium rates, reflect the type of risk. Premium rates may be adjusted according to the driving record of the insured. A driver with a clear record of long standing is considered to be a *low risk driver* and may be rewarded with a discount in the premium rate. Conversely, a driver with a record of numerous citations or accidents is considered to be a *high risk driver* and may pay double or triple the normal premium rate.

d. Drivers A and B have identical automobiles and amounts of insurance coverage. The normal premium rate for each is $890 per year. Driver A is a low-risk driver and receives a 10% discount on the premium rate. Driver B is a high risk driver and must pay double the normal rate. How much more does Driver B pay for insurance than Driver A?

Driver A pays: $890 $\times$ 90% = $801
Driver B pays: $890 $\times$ 2 = $1,780
Driver B pays: $1,780 $-$ $801 = $979 more

Short Rates

Short rates apply to auto insurance coverage as they do to property insurance coverage.

e. A driver paid an annual premium of $980 for auto insurance. After three months the vehicle was sold and insurance canceled. The insurance company refunded the remaining portion of the premium at the short rate, based on a 15% penalty.

Unused premium: $980 $\times \frac{3}{4}$ = $735

Penalty: $980 $\times$ 15% = $147
Short-rate refund: $735 $-$ $147 = $588

COMPLETE ASSIGNMENT 23-2

Chapter terms for review

auto collision insurance	insured
auto comprehensive insurance	low risk driver
auto liability and property	no-fault insurance
damage insurance	premium
coinsurance clause	property insurance
deductible clause	recovery amount
depreciated	short rates
high risk driver	

Assignment 23-1: Property Insurance

A **(40 points)— Solve the following problems (points for correct answers as marked.)**

1. $315 is the annual premium on insurance at the rate of $9 per $1,000. What is the amount of insurance (6 points)?

_____

2. $1,680 is the annual premium on insurance of $120,000. What is the premium rate per thousand (6 points)?

_____

3. An inventory of refrigerators was insured for $360,000 at $10 per $1,000. The policy was canceled by the insurance company at the end of 9 months. What was the amount of premium refunded (12 points)?

_____

4. A business carries $950,000 insurance on inventory at $10 per $1,000. The insured sells the business and cancels the insurance after 73 days. If the short-rate penalty is 15% of the annual premium, how much does it cost the insured for the 73 days of coverage (the insurance company uses a 365-day year) (16 points)?

_____

Score for A (40)

B **(60 points)— Solve the following problems (points for correct answers as marked).**

5. A home valued at $300,000 is insured by the owner under a 90% coinsurance clause for $180,000. A fire causes a loss of $60,000. How much does the insurance company pay (10 points)?

_____

How much of the fire damage does the insured pay (3 points)?

_____

6. A building valued at $400,000 is insured by the owner under an 80% coinsurance clause for $250,000. A fire causes a loss of $360,000. How much of the fire damage does the insured pay (10 points)?

_____

How much of the fire damage does the insurance company pay (3 points)?

_____

7. The owner of a building valued at $250,000 is purchasing an insurance policy with $150,000 coverage. She will pay a premium of $1,200 for a 90% coinsurance clause or a premium of $1,400 for an 80% coinsurance clause. Assuming a fire causes $100,000 damage (round all answers to nearest dollar):

a. How much of the fire damage would the insurance company pay with a 90% coinsurance clause (8 points)?

_____

How much would the insured pay (3 points)?

_____

b. How much of the fire damage would the insurance company pay with an 80% coinsurance clause (8 points)?

_____

How much will the insured pay (3 points)?

_____

c. How many more dollars of fire damage would the insured pay with the 90% coinsurance clause than with the 80% coinsurance clause (6 points)?

_____

d. Considering the difference in premium costs for the 80% coinsurance clause and the 90% coinsurance clause, how many dollars would the insured save by taking the 80% coinsurance clause (6 points)?

_____

Assignment 23-2: Auto Insurance

A **(50 points)— Solve the following problems (5 points for each correct answer).**

1. John Lewis has liability and property damage insurance coverage up to $50,000 per accident and comprehensive insurance. He does not have collision insurance. He fell asleep at the wheel and hit three parked cars, a fire hydrant, and a fence. Damage to the parked cars was $4,582, $7,947, and $5,633. Damage to the fire hydrant was $580. Damage to the fence was $24. Damage to his own car was $2,987.

a. How much did the insurance company pay for damages?

_____

b. How much would the insurance company have paid for this accident if John Lewis had collision insurance with a $500 deductible clause?

_____

c. If John Lewis had included in his policy collision insurance with a $500 deductible clause, and paid a total premium of $1,840, how much would this accident and his insurance cost John Lewis this year?

_____

d. How much more would the insurance company have paid if total damages, excluding the car of the insured, were $75,000?

_____

e. How much would the accident have cost John Lewis if total damages, excluding his own car, had been $90,000?

_____

2. Julie White carries liability and property damage insurance coverage up to $50,000 per accident, comprehensive insurance, and collision insurance with a $200 deductible clause. She lost control of her car and drove over a sidewalk and through the wall of a warehouse. Damage to the warehouse structure was $22,300. Damage to inventory stored in the warehouse was $27,150. Damage to a bike rack on the sidewalk and 4 bicycles in the rack was $3,200. Damage to her own car was $7,590.

a. What was the total property damage, excluding Julie White's car?

_____

b. How much did the insurance company pay for property damage, excluding Julie White's car?

_____

c. How much did the insurance company pay for Julie White's car?

_____

d. How much did the accident cost Julie White?

_____

e. If Julie White had been in a previous accident this year with property damage of $13,420 to a traffic signal, how much would the insurance company have paid for damages to everything in the current accident, including Julie White's car?

_____

_____
Score for A (50)

B **(50 points)— Solve the following problems (5 points for each correct answer).**

3. Alice Jones has auto collision insurance with a $100 deductible clause. Her brakes failed and she hit a tree. Damages to her car totaled $1,842. Her annual insurance premium was $1,230. How much did she save this year by having insurance?

_____

4. Jon Martin had full insurance coverage. His liability and property damage coverage was $100,000 per accident. His collision insurance had a $500 deductible clause. He struck two cars. Damages to the cars were $640 and $320. Damages to his car were $470. His annual insurance premium was $1,180.

a. What are the total costs to the insurance company for Jon Martin's accident?

_____

b. If this was the only accident Jon Martin had this year, how much money did the insurance company make from him?

_____

c. What are Jon Martin's total costs this year for insurance and accident?

_____

d. What would Jon Martin's total costs of the accident have been without insurance?

_____

5. Drivers A and B each have full insurance coverage with a $100 deductible clause for collision coverage. Driver A has an excellent driving record and receives a 15% discount on the standard premium as a low-risk driver. Driver B has a record of numerous citations and small accidents. Driver B, as a high-risk driver, pays double the standard rate for insurance. The standard rate for the insurance would be $1,240. How much more does Driver B pay for insurance than Driver A?

_____

6. Susan Smith received her driver's license one year ago. She has had three citations for speeding, but no accident. Her insurance premium last year was $1,350. This year her premium will be 40% higher, due to her driving record.

a. What will be the amount of her premium this year?

_____

b. Four months into the next year, Susan Smith has continued her unsafe driving habits. The insurance company is canceling her policy. What will be the amount of refund?

_____

c. Susan Smith has found an insurance company that will insure her as a high-risk driver at triple the standard annual rate of $1,350. What will be the average monthly insurance premium for these first 28 months of her driving career?

_____

d. If Susan Smith had a been a careful driver and kept her original amount of premium unchanged, how much would she have saved in these first 28 months?

_____

Part Seven
Applications in Accounting

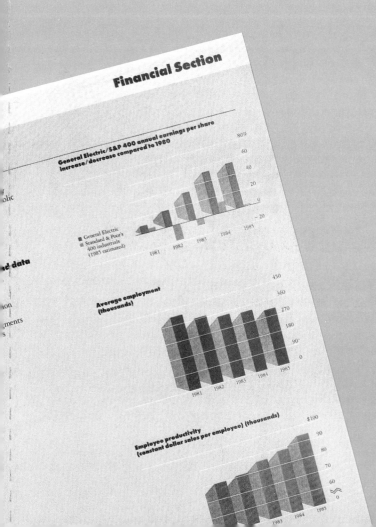

Financial Section

General Electric/S&P 400 annual earnings per share
increase/decrease compared to 1980

■ General Electric
■ Standard & Poor's
400 industrials
(1985 estimated)

1981 1982 1983 1984 1985

Average employment
(thousands)

1981 1982 1983 1984 1985

Employee productivity
(constant dollar sales per employee) (thousands)

1983 1984 1985

Chapter 24
Inventories and Turnover

OBJECTIVES
After completing this chapter, you should be able to:

- **Determine inventory value at cost under each of these three methods: average cost, LIFO, and FIFO**
- **Determine inventory value under lower of cost or market**
- **Estimate ending inventory and cost of goods sold**
- **Calculate average inventory, cost of goods sold, and inventory turnover at both cost and retail**

A company's inventory is the amount of goods it has on hand àt a given point in time. The makeup of the inventory depends upon the type of company. A manufacturing company has three inventory categories: *raw materials* (unused items waiting to become a part of the goods being made); *work-in-process* (partially manufactured goods); and *finished goods* (those items that have completed the manufacturing process).

Wholesale and retail companies usually have only one kind of inventory: *merchandise* (those goods, manufactured by some other firm, that the company offers for sale). This chapter concentrates on mathematics as it is used in accounting for merchandise inventory.

ACCOUNTING FOR INVENTORIES

Inventories are "tracked" mostly through a record keeping system. In the past this system was done on paper. Now almost all businesses keep track of inventory on computer. In addition, an actual counting of the inventory (called a *physical inventory*) must be done at least once a year to detect errors in recording and losses due to damage, theft, and other reasons. When its cost is not too great, a physical inventory may be taken every six months, quarterly, or even monthly.

When inventory is counted, the quantity and description of each item, the unit cost or the retail (selling) price (whichever is used by the company), and the extension (quantity × price) are recorded on an *inventory sheet* as shown in Figure 24-1.

FIGURE 24-1 Inventory Sheet

BIG SKY AUTO PARTS
Inventory Sheet
April 30, 19—

Description	Quantity	Unit Price (Cost)	Extension
Ignition Terminals—#746083	318	$36.14	$11,492.52
Odometer Cables—#007614	73	9.97	727.81
Wiper Blades: Compact—#417654	38	4.71	178.98
Spark Plugs: 0.14—#772034	354	2.34	828.36
Hood/Trunk Latches—#476508	58	13.42	778.36
Total			$14,006.03

After the physical inventory has been taken and the inventory sheet information has been gathered, a calculation of the value of the inventory must be made and compared with the accounting records. Any adjustment to the records is made at that time.

Perpetual and Periodic Inventory Tracking

Many firms keep a running count of all inventory items based on a physical tracking of every item as it comes into and goes out of inventory. This is called a *perpetual inventory*. There are two different kinds of perpetual inventory systems. For businesses that handle a small number of high-cost items such as cars or large appliances the perpetual (dollars) system that keeps track of the items by serial number and price works well. Each individual item can be readily identified as to its actual cost.

On the other hand, businesses that handle large quantities of items purchased at different times and at varying prices (such as candy bars, shoes, or stationery items) have difficulty specifically identifying the actual cost of an item. If a perpetual (units) inventory system is used in those situations, it is keeping a count of the number of units on hand and not individual serial numbers or prices. Recently, this type of perpetual inventory system has become easier for many companies, such as grocery stores, through the use of electronic scanners.

Data for a perpetual (units) inventory system occasionally is kept on special inventory cards but usually is done on a computer. A computer readout of an inventory record sheet is illustrated in Figure 24-2. The last item in the Balance on Hand column tells how many units are on hand at the time of the last recording date. This computer readout of an inventory record shows that there were 354 units of Spark Plugs: 0.14—#772034 on hand on April 30.

An alternative to a perpetual inventory system is the *periodic inventory* system, which does not require a continuous physical monitoring of the units into and out of the inventory stock. Rather, the information about the purchases and sales of items is recorded in the accounting system. That information is compared with the results of the physical inventory and an adjustment to the accounting records is made as needed.

Methods for Valuing Inventory at Cost

In all systems except the perpetual (dollars) system, the cost of the inventory on hand (called *ending inventory*) must be calculated. To make the calculation a business usually adopts one of three generally accepted costing methods: average cost method; first-in, first-out method (FIFO); or last-in, first-out (LIFO). Once selected, the method must be followed consistently.

The *average cost method* assumes that the costs of all items on hand are averaged and shared evenly among all units.

FIGURE 24-2   Inventory Record Sheet

BIG SKY AUTO PARTS HOUSE
Inventory Record Sheet

ITEM: QUICKSTART SPARK PLUG: 0.14   ORDER FORM:
                                            Northwest Distributors
PART NUMBER: #772034   2337 Colfax Avenue
                                            Milbrae, CA 93233
LOCATION: Aisle 72, Bin 4, Box C   Phone—(415) 345-7654

MINIMUM STOCK: 200   MAXIMUM STOCK: 800   ORDER: 100–800

| Purchase Orders (PO) | | | Inventory Control | | | | | |
Date	PO No.	Quantity	Date	Source Code	Units In	Unit Cost	Units Out	Balance On Hand
2/03	F0129	400	1/01	—		$2.10		350
3/15	M1678	300	1/31	SJ01			120	230
3/22	M2076	200	2/28	SJ02			58	172
4/26	A3210	400	3/02	F0129	400	2.36		572
			3/31	SJ03			315	257
			4/03	M1678	300	2.40		557
			4/20	M2076	200	2.64		757
			4/30	SJ04			403	354

a. The average cost of the units on the inventory record sheet for stock part #772034 (Quickstart Spark Plugs: 0.14) illustrated in Figure 24-2 is calculated as follows:

Date	Units	Cost	Extension
1/01	350	$2.10	$ 735.00
3/02	400	2.36	944.00
4/03	300	2.40	720.00
4/20	200	2.64	528.00
	1,250		$2,927.00

Average cost per unit: $2,927 ÷ 1,250 = $2.34
Ending inventory at average cost: 354 units × $2.34 = $828.36

The *first-in, first-out (FIFO) method* assumes that costs for units used are charged according to the order in which the units were purchased. Thus, the inventory remaining is assumed to be composed of the units received most recently.

b. Under the FIFO method the inventory of 354 units shown in Figure 24-2 would consist of the 200 units last purchased plus 154 units from the preceding purchase.

200 units × $2.64 = $528.00
154 units × 2.40 = 369.60
354                $897.60 Ending inventory at FIFO cost

The *last-in, first-out (LIFO) method* assumes the inventory remaining is composed of the units received first.

c. Under the LIFO method the 354 units shown on the inventory record in Figure 24-2 would consist of the 350 units on hand on 1/01 plus 4 units from the first purchase on 3/02.

350 units × $2.10 = $735.00
  4 units × 2.36 = 9.44
354   = $744.44 Ending inventory at LIFO cost

Lower of Cost or Market (LCM) Valuation

In financial statements the ending inventory is presented at either: (a) its cost value (that is, using either average, FIFO, or LIFO costing method) or (b) its *lower of cost or market value (LCM)* (where the cost is the same as in (a) and the *market value* is the dollar amount required to replace the inventory as of the inventory date).

Steps to Determine the Lower of Cost or Market (LCM) Inventory Value

1. Calculate the unit or total cost for each type of inventory item using either average, FIFO, or LIFO costing method.
2. Determine the unit or total market value for each type of inventory item.
3. For each type of inventory item compare the cost value from Step 1 with the market value from Step 2 and choose the lower of the two.
4. If necessary calculate the extension amount for each type of inventory item.
5. Sum each of the amounts selected in Step 3 (and extended in Step 4 if needed) to determine the total inventory value under LCM.

d. Under LCM using the average cost method the total inventory shown in Figure 24-1 would be valued at $13,802.13.

	(A)	Step 1 Unit Price (Average Cost)	Step 2 Unit Price at Market	Step 3 (B) Unit Price at Lower of Cost or Market	Step 4 Extension (A × B)
Description	Quantity				
Ignition Terminals—#746083	318	$36.14	$35.50	$35.50	$11,289.00 market
Odometer Cables—#007614	73	9.97	11.00	9.97	727.81 cost
Wiper Blades: Compact—#417654	38	4.71	4.70	4.70	178.60 market
Spark Plugs: 0.14—#772034	354	2.34	2.64	2.34	828.36 cost
Hood/Trunk Latches—#476508	58	13.42	14.10	13.42	778.36 cost
Total					$13,802.13 Step 5

e. Under LCM using the FIFO cost method the total inventory shown in Figure 24-1 would be valued at $13,905.46.

	(A)	Step 1 FIFO Cost	Step 2 (B) Unit Price	Step 3 Total (A × B)	Step 4 Lower of Cost or Market
Description	Quantity		Market Value		
Ignition Terminals—#746083	318	$11,321.67	$35.50	$11,289.00	$11,289.00 market
Odometer Cables—#007614	73	803.00	11.00	803.00	727.81 cost
Wiper Blades: Compact—#417654	38	192.15	4.70	178.60	178.60 market
Spark Plugs: 0.14—#772034	354	897.60	2.64	934.56	897.60 cost
Hood/Trunk Latches—#476508	58	812.45	14.10	817.80	812.45 cost
Total					$13,905.46 Step 5

ESTIMATION OF INVENTORY VALUE

For monthly financial statements, inventory frequently is "estimated" without a physical count or a perpetual inventory system. The methods for estimating a month-end inventory are varied and identified by such terms as "gross profit method," "markup method," or "retail inventory method." All methods provide for estimating the cost of goods sold (CGS) and subtracting this amount from the sum of the opening inventory and purchases made during the month. Note that *beginning inventory* was the ending inventory the month before and *purchases* are those goods for sale that have been acquired during the current month. These methods are based on the following formula:

> Beginning Inventory (BI)
> + Purchases (P)
> = Cost of Goods Available for Sale
> − Cost of Goods Sold (CGS) (Estimated)
> = Ending Inventory (EI) (Estimate)
> or BI + P − CGS = EI

Without a physical inventory CGS is not known. In this case CGS is estimated by applying a markup rate (percent) to *net sales* (total sales for the time − sales returned and adjustments during that same time). Then the net sales (100%) less this markup rate leaves the cost of goods sold. For instance, if the markup rate were 30%, the cost of goods sold would be 70% (100% − 30%); if the rate of markup were 40%, the cost of goods sold would be 60% (100% − 40%).

f. Assume Big Sky Auto Parts had a beginning inventory of $80,000. During the month the company purchased and received $50,000 in goods and had net sales of $90,000. Throughout the month Big Sky maintained a 40% markup on all sales. Its cost of goods sold would be calculated as follows:

Net sales for the month	$90,000	
Less markup estimated at 40% of net sales	−36,000	($90,000 × 40%)
Cost of goods sold (estimated)	$54,000	($90,000 × (100% − 40%))

Big Sky Auto Parts would then determine its ending inventory (estimated) as follows:

Inventory, beginning of year . . .	$ 80,000
Purchases for month	+ 50,000
Goods available for sale	$130,000
Cost of goods sold (estimated) . .	− 54,000
Ending inventory (estimated) . .	$ 76,000

Sometimes the markup rate (percent) is based on cost rather than sales. In those cases cost of goods sold is estimated by using the following formula:

Net sales ÷ (100% + markup rate based on cost) = estimated CGS

INVENTORY TURNOVER

Inventory turnover is the number of times the average inventory is converted into sales during the year. Inventory turnover is very high for a grocery store or ice cream parlor; it is usually very low for a specialty jewelry store or an antique shop.

Before turnover can be determined, the calculation of average inventory must be done. *Average inventory* is the average of the number of physical inventories taken over a given period of time, usually once a year, every half year, or once every three months. Inventory at retail price is equal to the sum of all units in inventory priced at their selling price at the time the inventory was taken.

Inventory is taken:	*Average inventory (at retail or cost)*
Annually (once a year)	$(BI + EI) \div 2$
Semi-annually (every six months)	$(BI + End\ of\ 6\ months + EI) \div 3$
Quarterly (every three months)	$(BI + End\ of\ 3\ months + End\ of\ 6\ months + End\ of\ 9\ months + EI) \div 5$

Inventory turnover can be calculated based on either retail (selling) price or cost following the steps below.

Steps for Calculating Inventory Turnover at Retail

1. If necessary, determine net sales. Total sales for the year − sales returned and adjustments for the year = net sales.
2. Calculate the average inventory using the retail (selling) price.
3. Calculate inventory *turnover at retail*:
   net sales (Step 1) ÷ average inventory at retail (Step 2).

g. Assume the inventories for the year, based on selling price, are: beginning = $90,000; end of month three = $80,000; end of month six = $100,000; end of month nine = $70,000; and end of month twelve (ending) = $60,000. Net sales for the years equal $520,000. Calculate the inventory turnover at retail.

Step 2   Average inventory = ($90,000 + $80,000 + $100,000 + $70,000 + $60,000) ÷ 5

= $400,000 ÷ 5 = $80,000

Step 3   Inventory turnover at retail
= $520,000 Net sales ÷ $80,000 Average inventory = 6.5 times

Some retail businesses prefer to express their rate of inventory turnover in terms of cost. Inventory *turnover at cost* is obtained by dividing the cost of goods sold during a period by the average inventory for the same period calculated at cost prices. (Note that CGS is simply net sales at cost.)

Steps for Calculating Inventory Turnover at Cost

1. Calculate the cost of goods sold using the formula: BI + P − EI = CGS
2. Calculate the average inventory at cost.
3. Calculate inventory turnover at cost: CGS (Step 1) ÷ average inventory at cost (Step 2).

h. Assuming beginning inventory, purchases, and ending inventory are $60,000, $300,000, and $80,000, respectively, calculate the inventory turnover at cost.

Step 1   Cost of goods sold: Inventory at beginning of year .. $ 60,000
Purchases during year .... + 300,000
Goods available for sale $360,000
Inventory at end of year .... − 80,000
Cost of goods sold $280,000

Step 2   Average inventory = ($60,000 BI + $80,000 EI) ÷ 2
= $140,000 ÷ 2 = $70,000

Step 3   Inventory turnover at cost
= $280,000 CGS ÷ $70,000 Average inventory = 4.0 times

NOTE: The value of the goods sold and the value of the inventory must both be figured at cost, or both at selling price.

COMPLETE ASSIGNMENT 24-2

Chapter terms for review

average cost method
average inventory
beginning inventory (BI)
ending inventory (EI)
finished goods inventory
first-in, first-out (FIFO) costing
   method
inventory sheet
inventory turnover
last-in, first-out (LIFO) costing
   method
lower of cost or market value (LCM)

market value
merchandise inventory
net sales
periodic inventory
perpetual inventory
physical inventory
purchases (P)
raw materials inventory
turnover at cost
turnover at retail
work-in-process inventory

Assignment 24-1: Inventory Cost

A (40 points) — Calculate the extensions and totals (1 point for each correct answer).

1. The inventory of Jim Sutton's Radio-Television shop shows the following items to be figured at the lower of cost or market price. Calculate the total value.

Description	Quantity	Unit Cost Price	Unit Market Price	Extension
Quartz clock and pen set	22	$36.00	$34.80	_____
Travel alarm clock	30	15.60	29.70	_____
Ultrasonic travel clock	16	23.00	23.70	_____
Digital alarm clock	40	19.80	18.60	_____
AM/FM clock radio	112	21.00	17.80	_____
Digital clock radio	9	54.00	57.50	_____
Total				_____

2. A retail furniture dealer counted the following goods in inventory on December 31. An accountant recommends that the inventory items be valued at the lower of cost or market price. Calculate the total value of the inventory based on the lower of cost or market price.

Article	Quantity	Unit Cost Price	Extension at Cost	Unit Market Price	Extension at Market	Inventory Value: Lower of Cost or Market
Armchairs, wood	24	$ 40.00	_____	$ 68.50	_____	_____
Armchairs, tapestry	6	75.00	_____	105.00	_____	_____
Armchairs, Windsor	12	115.00	_____	85.00	_____	_____
Beds, Hollywood	8	52.50	_____	35.00	_____	_____
Bedroom suites	3	297.50	_____	410.00	_____	_____
Chairs, period	30	63.00	_____	84.50	_____	_____
Chairs, kitchen	24	23.00	_____	32.00	_____	_____
Dining tables	8	117.40	_____	87.00	_____	_____
Dining suites	5	288.80	_____	395.00	_____	_____
Sofa sets	9	479.60	_____	325.00	_____	_____
Total			_____		_____	_____

Score for A (40)

B **(60 points) — Calculate the value of ending inventory (10 points for each correct answer).**

3. Garcia Manufacturing Company made purchases of a material as shown in the following listing. The inventory at the end of the year was 3,750 units. Compute the value of the inventory by each of the following methods: (a) average cost; (b) first-in, first-out; and (c) last-in, first-out.

Date	Units	Units Cost	Total Cost
Jan. 5	3,600	$6.20	$ 22,320
Mar. 11	3,000	5.80	17,400
May 14	5,300	6.00	31,800
July 8	1,600	6.30	10,080
Sept. 7	4,000	6.20	24,800
Nov. 10	2,500	6.40	16,000
Total	20,000	—	122,400

a. Average cost: _____

b. First-in, first-out: _____

c. Last-in, last-out: _____

4. The Willand Company had 320 units of item number 345 on hand at the beginning of the year with a cost of $4.20. The number and per unit cost of the units purchased and the number of the units sold are listed below. What would be the value of the ending inventory of 380 units based upon (a) average cost; (b) first-in, first-out; and (c) last-in, first-out.

Date	Units Purchased	Unit Cost	Units Sold	Units on Hand
Jan. 1				320
Feb. 2			190	130
Mar. 28	200	$4.32		330
Apr. 6	300	4.40		630
May 14			280	350
June 9	250	4.48		600
June 30			220	380

a. Average cost: _____

b. First-in, first-out: _____

c. Last-in, last-out: _____

Assignment 24-2: Inventory Estimation and Turnover

A **(50 points)** — **Solve the following problems (2 points for each correct answer as marked).**

1. Fill in the blanks in each of the following with the correct amount. (Beginning inventory + Purchases = Goods available for sale; then Goods available for sale − Cost of goods sold = Ending inventory)

	A.	B.	C.	D.	E.
Beginning inventory	80,000		37,000		42,000
Purchases		97,000		21,000	
Goods available for sale	200,000	215,000	109,000	117,000	89,000
Less cost of goods sold	125,000	72,000		27,000	74,000
Ending inventory			23,000		

2. Each of the five stores in Problem 1 had net sales as shown. What was the average percent of markup, based on cost, for each of the five stores? What was the average percent of markup, based on selling price, for each of the five stores?

	A.	B.	C.	D.	E.
Net sales	200,000	100,000	172,000	40,000	100,000
Markup—based on cost					
Markup—selling price					

3. The Myrick Record Shop takes inventory every six months at retail sales price. Its inventory at the beginning of last year was $39,482, at midyear it was $46,693, and at the end of the year, $40,410. Net sales for the year were $84,390.

a. What was the average inventory? _____

b. What was the turnover? _____

4. Brewer & Adams, a tire shop, began the year with an inventory of $159,700. Purchases during the year totaled $278,182. Their inventory at the end of the year was $109,400.

a. What was the cost of goods sold? _____

b. What was the average inventory? _____

c. What was the turnover? _____

B (50 points) — Solve the following problems (points for each correct answers as marked).

5. The records of Robinson Auto Parts showed the figures below (10 points, 5 points for each correct answer).

	Cost Price	Retail Price
Beginning inventory	$19,794	$32,990
Purchases for the year	47,200	78,667
Net sales for the year	—	61,450
Markup based on sales	40%	—

Calculate the inventory:

a. At cost price: _____

b. At retail price: _____

6. The JM Clothing store kept all merchandise records in terms of selling price. On July 1, the JM books showed the following information:

Beginning inventory, January 1	$23,500
6-month purchases	99,000
6-month net sales	87,800

What was the estimated ending inventory on July 1 (5 points)? _____

7. The JM Clothing store kept all purchase and inventory records on the basis of the cost price. The owner marked up all goods on the basis of 37.5% of the cost price. On July 1, the JM books showed the following information:

Beginning inventory, January 1	104,500
6-month purchases	215,500
Net sales for 6 months	220,000

What was the estimated inventory, at cost, on July 1 (5 points)? _____

8. From the information given below, determine the estimated cost of goods sold and the estimated ending inventory. Round to the nearest dollar (30 points, 1.5 point for each correct answer).

	Beginning Inventory at Cost	Purchases at Cost	Cost of Goods Available For Sale	Net Sales	Markup Based on Cost	Markup Based on Sales	Estimated Cost of Goods Sold	Estimated Ending Inventory
a.	87,000	117,000	204,000	260,000	30%			
b.	87,000	317,000	404,000	260,000		30%		
c.	36,000	408,000	444,000	350,000		27%		
d.	36,000	408,000	444,000	350,000	27%			
e.	19,000	39,000	58,000	50,000	20%			
f.	8,000	360,000	368,000	400,000		60%		
g.	40,000	380,000	420,000	600,000		40%		
h.	80,000	360,000	440,000	360,000	15%			
i.	75,000	40,000	115,000	180,000	60%			
j.	13,000	117,000	130,000	200,000	100%			

Chapter 25
Depreciation

OBJECTIVES

After completing this chapter you should be able to:

- Understand the straight-line, declining balance, and sum-of-the-years-digits methods of depreciation
- Understand the Modified Accelerated Cost Recovery System (MACRS) method of depreciation for income tax purposes
- Calculate full-year and partial-year depreciation expense under the four different depreciation methods covered in this chapter

Depreciation is the decrease in the value of assets owned by a business, such as automobiles, buildings, furniture, computers, or similar articles. It is caused by wear and tear or by *obsolescence* (becoming out-of-date). A typewriter gradually will wear out after a number of years of use. A business computer frequently becomes obsolete in less than 10 years. In automobile plants, many dies and tools last only one or two years because of changes in models of cars. Buildings lose value as wood finishes, electrical wiring, and fixtures deteriorate and as owners' needs change.

In business, depreciation, which is figured on all property owned and in use, is deducted from gross profits as an expense. Many businesses set aside part of their profits in preparation for the future replacement of important depreciating property. Four common methods of calculating depreciation are explained in this chapter.

STRAIGHT-LINE METHOD

The *straight-line method* of determining depreciation is the easiest and most frequently used method. The straight-line method distributes depreciation of an item in equal amounts to designated units or periods (usually months or years) covering the useful life of the item. It assumes the wear and tear is occurring evenly over the life of the property. Three factors are needed to compute depreciation with this method.

1. The *estimated physical life* or *estimated service life* of the asset refers to the amount of usefulness the owner expects to get from the item. The life may be stated as years of usefulness, as the number of hours of use (as in the case of a machine or a high-powered light bulb), or as the number of units that normally may be produced during the life of a piece of machinery.
2. A *resale, scrap,* or *salvage value (SV)* refers to the amount of value the owner of the item expects to receive from disposing of it at the end of its estimated life.
3. The *original cost* of the item includes not only the actual price paid for the item but also any freight charges and cost of installation when the item originally was put into use.

The basic formula for calculating the amount of depreciation under the straight-line method is:

(Original cost − Scrap value) ÷ Estimated total life in units or periods of time = Depreciation amount for 1 unit or period

a. An office computer costing $12,500 has an estimated life of five years and an estimated scrap value (SV) of $900. What is the annual depreciation amount?

$12,500 cost − $900 SV = $11,600 estimated total depreciation
$11,600 ÷ 5 estimated total years = $2,320 annual depreciation

NOTE: The annual percentage rate of depreciation can be calculated by dividing the annual depreciation amount by the cost. For example a. this rate would be 18.56% ($2,320 ÷ $12,500).

b. A machine costing $10,000 has 60,000 estimated hours of operation and an estimated scrap value (SV) of $400. It operated for 2,800 hours in the first year. How much depreciation expense will be shown for the first year?

$10,000 cost − $400 SV = $9,600 estimated total depreciation
$9,600 ÷ 60,000 estimated total hours = $0.16 hourly depreciation
2,800 hours operated × $0.16 = $448 first year depreciation

If the life of the machine is stated as the number of units that it will produce during its lifetime, that number should be divided into the estimated total depreciation amount to get the depreciation per unit.

c. A press that costs $38,000 produces an estimated 3,500,000 units in its life and has an estimated scrap value (SV) of $3,000. It produced 626,000 units this year. How much depreciation will be shown for the year?

$38,000 cost − $3,000 SV = $35,000 estimated total depreciation
$35,000 ÷ 3,500,000 estimated total units = $0.01 depreciation per unit
626,000 units produced × $0.01 = $6,260 first year depreciation

Book Value

The *book value* of an asset is the original cost minus the *accumulated depreciation,* the total of all of the depreciation up to that time.

d. At the end of the first year, the book value of the press in example c. would be calculated:

$38,000 cost − $6,260 accumulated depreciation = $31,740 book value

The book value can be determined at any time in the life of an asset.

e. At the end of the third year the book value of the computer in example a. would be calculated:

$2,320 annual depreciation × 3 years = $6,960 accumulated depreciation
$12,500 cost − $6,960 accumulated depreciation = $5,540 book value after 3 years of use

DECLINING-BALANCE METHOD

The *declining-balance method (DB)* is based on the theory that depreciation is greatest in the first year and is less in each succeeding year.

Steps for Calculating Depreciation (Using the DB Method)

1. Divide 100% by the estimated total years of useful life to determine the basic depreciation rate.
2. Multiply the basic depreciation rate (Step 1) by 2 for the *double-declining-balance method* or by 1.5 for the *150%-declining-balance method* to determine the declining-balance depreciation rate.
3. Multiply the declining-balance depreciation rate (Step 2) by the **book value** of the asset at the **beginning** of the year to determine the depreciation amount for that year. (For the first year the book value at the beginning of the year equals the asset cost.)

NOTE: Step 3 must be repeated each year using the new (declined) book value (last year's beginning book value minus last year's depreciation amount). The same rate is used each year. The declining-balance rate continues to apply until the scrap value is reached. The item may not be depreciated below its scrap value.

f. Using the double-declining-balance method the office equipment from example a. would be depreciated as follows:

Step 1 100% ÷ 5 years = 20%
Step 2 20% × 2 = 40% annual double-declining-balance rate
Step 3

Year	Beginning Book Value			Rate	Depreciation
1	$12,500		×	40% =	$5,000
2	7,500	($12,500 − $5,000) ×		40 =	3,000
3	4,500	(7,500 − 3,000) ×		40 =	1,800
4	2,700	(4,500 − 1,800) ×		40 =	1,080
5	1,620	(2,700 − 1,080) ×		40 =	648
6*	972	(1,620 − 648) ×		40 =	~~388.80~~ $72

*Since book value ($972) is larger than estimated scrap value ($900), there is some depreciation in the sixth year. However, the calculated depreciation ($388.80) is greater than book value minus scrap value ($972 − $900 = $72). Thus, depreciation is limited to the smaller amount ($72).

SUM-OF-THE-YEARS-DIGITS METHOD

The *sum-of-the-years-digits method (SYD)* also calculates a greater depreciation amount in the earlier years of an asset's life. The decrease in the book value is less rapid than under the declining-balance method. The name comes from the calculation done in Step 1.

Steps for Calculating Depreciation (Using the SYD Method)

1. Calculate the sum of all of the years digits in the estimated life of the asset. Use this shortcut formula:

   $\frac{(n + 1) \times n}{2}$ where n = number of years in the estimated life

2. Determine the current year's depreciation fraction by using this formula:

   estimated total years of life remaining at the beginning of the current year ÷ the sum of all digits (Step 1)

3. Multiply the total depreciation amount (cost − SV) of the asset by the depreciation fraction (Step 2) to determine depreciation for the current year.

   NOTE: Each year a new depreciation fraction (Step 2) is determined and Step 3 is repeated. The sum of all digits (Step 1) and the total depreciation amount used in Step 3 are the same every year.

---

g. Using the sum-of-the-years-digits method the office equipment from example a. would be depreciated as follows:

Step 1 $\frac{(5 + 1) \times 5}{2} = 15$ (or 1 + 2 + 3 + 4 + 5 = 15)

Year	Step 2 Fraction	Step 3 Depreciation Total Amount		Depreciation
1	$\frac{5}{15}$	× $11,600	=	$ 3,866.67
2	$\frac{4}{15}$	× 11,600	=	3,093.33
3	$\frac{3}{15}$	× 11,600	=	2,320.00
4	$\frac{2}{15}$	× 11,600	=	1,546.67
5	$\frac{1}{15}$	× 11,600	=	773.33
	Total depreciation			$11,600.00

COMPLETE ASSIGNMENT 25-1

MODIFIED ACCELERATED COST RECOVERY SYSTEM (MACRS)

The depreciation methods described above are used by businesses for financial reporting. However, federal tax laws regulate how depreciation must be taken for income tax purposes. The Internal Revenue Service (IRS) requires that the *Modified Accelerated Cost Recovery System (MACRS)* be used for depreciated property purchased and put into service after 1986.

In the MACRS method the entire cost of depreciable property is recovered over the allowable period. No salvage value is considered.

Under MACRS, assets are classified as follows:

Recovery Period	Includes
3-Year Property	Property with a class life of 4 years or less
5-Year Property	Property with a class life of more than 4 years and less than 10 years—cars, trucks, computers, and office machinery (typewriters, calculators, etc.)
7-Year Property	Property with a class life of 10 years or more but less than 16 years—includes office furniture and fixtures
10-Year Property	Property with a class life of 16 years or more but less than 20 years—includes barges and single-purpose agricultural structures
15-Year Property	Property with a class life of 20 years or more but less than 25 years
20-Year Property	Property with a class life of 25 years or more, other than real property with a class life of 27.5 years or more.
27.5-Year Residential Real Property	Residential real property in which 80% or more of the gross rental income is from dwelling units.
31.5-Year Nonresidential Real Property	Nonresidential real property with a class life of 27.5 years or more

The IRS publishes MACRS depreciation tables. These tables are used to compute depreciation for income tax purposes.

One of the MACRS tables, Table 25-1, gives the annual depreciation percentages for recovery periods: 3, 5, 7, 10, 15, and 20 years when the property is put into use and depreciation starts during the first quarter of the tax year.

If the Recovery Year is:	3-year	5-year	and the Recovery Period is: 7-year	10-year	15-year	20-year
			the Depreciation Rate is:			
1	58.33	35.00	25.00	17.50	8.75	6.563
2	27.78	26.00	21.43	16.50	9.13	7.000
3	12.35	15.60	15.31	13.20	8.21	6.482
4	1.54	11.01	10.93	10.56	7.39	5.996
5		11.01	8.75	8.45	6.65	5.546
6		1.38	8.74	6.76	5.99	5.130
7			8.75	6.55	5.90	4.746
8			1.09	6.55	5.91	4.459
9				6.56	5.90	4.459
10				6.55	5.91	4.459
11				0.82	5.90	4.459
12					5.91	4.460
13					5.90	4.459
14					5.91	4.460
15					5.09	4.459
16					0.74	4.460
17						4.459
18						4.460
19						4.459
20						4.460
21						0.557

TABLE 25-1
MACRS Depreciation Rate

h. Using the table on page 301, the depreciation for the office computer in example a. is computed for tax purposes as follows:

Year	Rate	Unadjusted Cost Basis		Depreciation	Beginning Book Value		Current Depr.		Ending Book Value
1	35.00 ×	$12,500	=	$4,375	$12,500	−	$4,375	=	$8,125
2	26.00 ×	12,500	=	3,250	8,125	−	3,250	=	4,875
3	15.60 ×	12,500	=	1,950	4,875	−	1,950	=	2,925
4	11.01 ×	12,500	=	1,376*	2,925	−	1,376	=	1,549
5	11.01 ×	12,500	=	1,376*	1,549	−	1,376	=	173
6	1.38 ×	12,500	=	173*	173	−	173	=	0

* Rounded

PARTIAL-YEAR DEPRECIATION

For the straight-line method the depreciation amount for a partial year is found by dividing the annual depreciation amount by 12 and then multiplying by the number of months used.

For the declining-balance method the current year's annual depreciation is found, then divided by 12, and multiplied by the number of months used. (This is very similar to the straight-line method.)

For the sum-of-the-years digits method overlapping years must be considered. For the first partial year that year's annual depreciation is found by dividing by 12 and multiplying by the number of months of use. From then on every year will include the remaining fraction of the prior year's depreciation and the partial-year depreciation for the remainder of the current year.

MACRS tables are set up to automatically consider partial year depreciation. As stated earlier, Table 25-1 assumes that depreciation starts sometime during the first quarter (first three months) of the tax year.

i. The office furniture, costing $6,000 and put into use on March 1, is expected to have a useful life of 10 years. Its estimated resale value is $400. Calculate, under each of the four methods, the depreciation expense for March 1 through December 31 of the first tax year and all 12 months of the second year.

Method	Year	Calculation
SL	1st year	$(\$6,000 - \$400) \div 10 \times \frac{10}{12} = \$467^*$
	2nd year	$(\$6,000 - \$400) \div 10 = \$560$
DB (150%)	1st year	$(\frac{100\%}{10} \times 1.5 = 15\%) \times \$6,000 \times \frac{10}{12} = \$750$
	2nd year	$(\$6,000 - \$750) \times 15\% = \$788^*$
SYD	1st year	$\frac{(10 + 1) \times 10}{2} = 55$
		$(\$6,000 - \$400) \times \frac{10}{55} \times \frac{10}{12} = \$848^*$
	2nd year	$(\$6,000 - \$400) \times \frac{10}{55} \times \frac{2}{12} = \$170^*$
		$(\$6,000 - \$400) \times \frac{9}{55} \times \frac{10}{12} = \underline{\$764^*}$
		$\$934$
MACRS	1st year	$\$6,000 \times 25\% = \$1,500$
	2nd year	$\$6,000 \times 21.43\% = \$1,286^*$

*Rounded

COMPLETE ASSIGNMENT 25-2

Part Seven   Applications in Accounting

Chapter terms for review

accumulated depreciation
book value
declining-balance method (DB)
depreciation
double-declining-balance method
estimated physical life
estimated service life
Modified Accelerated Cost Recovery
System (MACRS)

obsolescence
original cost
resale, scrap, or salvage value (SV)
straight-line method
sum-of-the-years-digits method
(SYD)
150%-declining-balance method

Assignment 25-1: Depreciation 1

A (36 points) — Solve the following depreciation problems (points for correct answers as marked).

1. An ice cream company has fast-freeze yogurt machines on which it estimates depreciation by the straight-line method. The following table shows cost, estimated life, years used, and scrap value of each machine. Find the annual depreciation, total depreciation, and book value after the indicated number of years of use (12 points, 1 point for each correct answer).

	Original Cost	Estimated Life	Years Used	Scrap Value	Annual Depreciation	Total Depreciation to Date	Book Value
a.	$ 6,000	10 yrs.	6	$ 350	_____	_____	_____
b.	6,400	7 yrs.	4	800	_____	_____	_____
c.	8,400	12 yrs.	3	none	_____	_____	_____
d.	34,600	15 yrs.	8	1,000	_____	_____	_____

2. The Super Speedy Delivery Service bought two new trucks. The table shows the cost, estimated life (in miles), estimated scrap value, and mileage for the first year. Using the straight-line method based on mileage driven, calculate the first-year's depreciation and the company's book value for each truck at the end of the first year (6 points, 2 points for each correct depreciation amount and 1 point for each correct book value).

	Original Cost	Scrap Value	Estimated Life (in miles)	Mileage for First Year	Depreciation for First Year	Book Value after 1 Year
a.	$19,800	$800	75,000	15,000	_____	_____
b.	27,800	$600	80,000	9,500	_____	_____

3. The Indiana Chemical Company's equipment cost $214,000 in 1991. Its useful life is estimated to be 15 years, and its scrap value is $4,000. The company uses straight-line depreciation (4 points, 2 points for each correct answer).

   a. What is the annual depreciation?

   _____

   b. What is the book value of the equipment at the end of 10 years?

   _____

4. The Jarvis Manufacturing Company purchased a machine for $6,115 on January 1. The freight was $243.80, and the cost of installation was $162. It was estimated that the machine could be operated for 22,800 hours, after which its resale value would be $570. Determine the straight-line depreciation and the book value at the end of each year (14 points, 1 point for each correct answer).

Year	Hours of Operation	Depreciation	Book Value
1	2,300	_____	_____
2	2,750	_____	_____
3	2,500	_____	_____
4	2,480	_____	_____
5	2,800	_____	_____
6	3,100	_____	_____
7	2,950	_____	_____

B (46 points) — Solve the following depreciation problems. Round dollar amounts to two decimal places (points for correct answers as marked).

5. The Holmes Wholesale Videotape Manufacturing Company owns a group of machines, the detail of which are shown in the following table. Holmes uses the double-declining-balance method of calculating depreciation. Calculate the depreciation of each machine for the specific years indicated (24 points, 2 points for each correct answer).

	Original Cost	Estimated Life	Salvage Estimate	Year	Depreciation	Year	Depreciation
a.	$ 4,000	10 yrs.	$ 400	2	_____	4	_____
b.	8,000	4 yrs.	300	1	_____	3	_____
c.	5,940	5 yrs.	100	3	_____	5	_____
d.	7,750	10 yrs.	none	2	_____	3	_____
e.	18,800	8 yrs.	1,225	4	_____	5	_____
f.	3,180	20 yrs.	none	4	_____	6	_____

6. Machinery purchase by the Kansolta Corporation cost $69,800. Depreciation was determined by the double-declining-balance method for an estimated life of 16 years. Calculate the following:

a. Book value after four years (8 points)?

_____

b. Total depreciation after six years (4 points)?

_____

7. The Harris Manufacturing Company bought an engine for $31,500. The engine had an estimated life of 20 years and a scrap value of $5,250. After seven years, the company went out of business and sold the engine for $15,000. If the machine was depreciated by the double-declining-balance method, how much did the company lose on the sale (10 points)?

_____

C (18 points) — Solve the following depreciation problems (2 points for each correct answer).

8. The Western Salvage Service bought three trucks. The table below shows the cost, estimated life, and resale estimate for each truck. Use the sum-of-the-years-digits method to find each truck's depreciation for the first and second years of use. Round answers to the nearest dollar.

	Original Cost	Estimated Life	Resale Estimate	Depreciation for First Year	Second Year
a.	$29,000	6 yrs.	$2,600	_____	_____
b.	25,200	5 yrs.	1,800	_____	_____
c.	22,200	7 yrs.	1,600	_____	_____

9. Using the information in Problem 8, calculate the amount of depreciation for Truck b for the years 3 through 5.

3rd year _____

4th year _____

5th year _____

Assignment 25-2: Depreciation 2

A (43 points) — Solve the following depreciation problems. Round dollar amounts to two decimal places (points for correct answers as marked).

1. Early in 1988, a building contractor bought a cement mixer for $9,000. Its estimated life was six years, and its scrap value was $600. At the end of four years, the machine was worn out and was sold for scrap for $225 (8 points, 4 points for each correct answer).

a. By the straight-line method, how much difference was there between the book value and the cash value of the machine on the date of the sale?

_____

b. In January, 1992 replacement was made with a mixer costing $18,000. What is the book value of the new mixer on December 31, 1993? Use MACRS.

_____

2. E, F, and G were partners in a small textile company. In 1989, they purchased equipment for $54,000 that they agreed would last 8 years and have a resale value of 5% of cost. The three partners could not agree on the depreciation method to use. E was in favor of using the double-declining-balance system, F insisted on the 150%-declining-balance method, and G was sure the sum-of-the-years-digits method would be better. Show the three sets of annual depreciation in the tables below. At the end of four years, what would be the book value under each of the three methods (30 points, 2 points for each correct depreciation amount, 1 point for each correct total, and 1 point for the correct book value)?

Year	E Double-DB	F 150%-DB	G SYD
1	_____	_____	_____
2	_____	_____	_____
3	_____	_____	_____
4	_____	_____	_____
Total	_____	_____	_____
Book Value	_____	_____	_____

3. The Wilcox Company owned a building that cost $1,600,000. Depreciation was figured at a straight-line rate of 3% per year. After 16 years, the company sold the building for $2,350,000. How much greater was the selling price of the building than its book value at the time of the sale (5 points)?

_____

B (21 points) — Solve the following depreciation problems (points for correct answers as marked).

4. On March 1, Botts Realty purchased a new company car for $16,000 with an estimated life of 4 years and an estimated scrap value of $4,000. Botts Realty elected to use the straight-line method for depreciation. On the same date, Wayne Realty bought an identical car at the same price and also estimated the car's life and scrap value to be 4 years and $4,000. Wayne Realty, however, chose the sum-of-the-years-digits method for depreciation.

a. At the end of the first year (10 months of use) and second year how much depreciation did each company calculate (3 points for each correct answer)?

Botts: Year 1   _____

        Year 2   _____

Wayne: Year 1   _____

        Year 2   _____

b. At the end of the second year which company had more accumulated depreciation recorded and what was the difference in the amount (5 points)?

_____

c. Is the following statement true? At the end of the fourth year Wayne Realty will have recorded more accumulated depreciation than Botts Realty (4 points). (Explain why it is or is not true.)

_____

Score for B (21)

C (36 points) — Solve the following depreciation problems. The dates in these problems are important in finding the solutions (points for correct answers as marked).

5. In January, 1990, Brown & Black bought a light duty truck for $20,800. One year later, they bought an additional truck for $21,800. In January, 1992, a third truck was purchased for $23,500. Using MACRS, what was their total allowable cost recovery for 1992 (12 points)?

_____

6. Travis Marcus purchased new office furniture in February of 1991 for $28,100. Using the MACRS method with a 7 year recovery period, show the book value at the end of each year for 1991 through 1998 (24 points, 1 point for each correct rate, depreciation and ending book value amount).

Year	Rate		Unadjusted Cost Basis		Depreciation	Beginning Book Value		Current Depr.		Ending Book Value
1991	____	×	$28,100	=	_____	_____	−	_____	=	_____
1992	____	×	$28,100	=	_____	_____	−	_____	=	_____
1993	____	×	$28,100	=	_____	_____	−	_____	=	_____
1994	____	×	$28,100	=	_____	_____	−	_____	=	_____
1995	____	×	$28,100	=	_____	_____	−	_____	=	_____
1996	____	×	$28,100	=	_____	_____	−	_____	=	_____
1997	____	×	$28,100	=	_____	_____	−	_____	=	_____
1998	____	×	$28,100	=	_____	_____	−	_____	=	_____

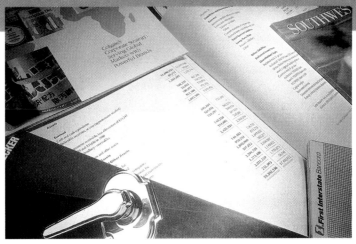

Chapter 26
Financial Statement Analysis

OBJECTIVES
After completing this chapter, you should be able to:

- **Compare and analyze income statements and balance sheets**
- **Use selected ratios in the analysis of financial statements**

Business managers and owners become aware of operating results from information in their *financial statements*. Two important financial statements are the income statement and the balance sheet. Income statements show how much income, expenses, and profit or loss a business has. Balance sheets show how much a business is worth at a given time, including how much it owns, (its assets), how much it owes (its liabilities), and the difference between the two (its net worth).

INCOME STATEMENT ANALYSIS

Businesses keep detailed records of revenues and expenses in order to know their net income. Periodically, the revenues and expenses are summarized on an *income statement*. This statement shows the revenues, the expenses, and the net income for a certain period of time, such as one month, three months (one quarter) or one year.

Income statements are analyzed by comparing other amounts with the net sales figure. Net sales (sales revenue less any returns and allowances given on sales) are considered to be 100%. All other items on the income statement are reported as a percent of net sales. The resulting percents may be compared with similar businesses, percents from past periods for the same company, or percents of budgeted amounts.

The statement in Figure 26-1 is for one year and shows conversion of all dollar amounts to percent based on net sales. Percents are rounded to one decimal place, and dollar amounts are rounded to the nearest whole dollar. Cents are seldom used in reporting annual figures.

FIGURE 26-1   Income Statement

Dolphin Watersports Stores
Income Statement
For the Period from January 1 to December 31, 19X1

	Amount		Percent
Revenue from sales:			
Sales	$988,900		101.4
Less sales returns and allowances	13,900		1.4
Net sales		$975,000	100.0
Cost of merchandise sold:			
Merchandise inventory, January 1	$211,000		21.6
Purchases	423,000		43.4
Merchandise available for sale	$634,000		65.0
Less merchandise inventory, December 31	226,000		23.2
Cost of merchandise sold		$408,000	41.8
Gross profit on sales		$567,000	58.2
Operating expenses:			
Salary and benefits	$294,000		30.2
Rent and utilities	82,000		8.4
Advertising	32,400		3.3
Equipment and supplies	15,800		1.6
General administrative	12,500		1.3
Total operating expenses		$436,700	44.8
Income before income tax		$130,300	13.4
Income tax		30,300	3.1
Net income		$100,000	10.3

Any difference of 0.1% from individual items is due to rounding.

In addition to comparing the items on a single statement, often it is desirable to compare the operations of the current year with those of the preceding year. The statement illustrated in Figure 26-2 is similar to Figure 26-1 except that the information for the preceding year is shown as well.

The statement in Figure 26-2 does not show how much amounts increased or decreased from one year to the next. Very frequently comparative statements will include these differences. Major items were taken from the statement in Figure 26-2 and are shown in this type of comparative statement in Figure 26-3. The percent of change is based on the previous year's figures.

FIGURE 26-2 Comparative income statement

Dolphin Watersports Stores
Comparative Income Statement
For the Period from January 1 to December 31, 19X2 and 19X1

	19X2		19X1	
	Amount	Percent	Amount	Percent
Revenue from sales:				
Sales	$988,900	101.4	$850,000	104.8
Less sales returns and allowances	13,900	1.4	39,000	4.8
Net sales	$975,000	100.0	$811,000	100.0
Cost of merchandise sold:				
Merchandise inventory, January 1	$211,000	21.6	$193,000	23.8
Purchases	423,000	43.4	401,000	49.4
Merchandise available for sale	$634,000	65.0	$594,000	73.2
Less merchandise inventory, December 31	226,000	23.2	211,000	26.0
Cost of merchandise sold	$408,000	41.8	$383,000	47.2
Gross profit on sales	$567,000	58.2	$428,000	52.8
Operating expenses:				
Salary and benefits	$294,000	30.2	$242,000	29.8
Rent and utilities	82,000	8.4	61,400	7.6
Advertising	32,400	3.3	25,700	3.2
Equipment and supplies	15,800	1.6	10,300	1.3
General administrative	12,500	1.3	14,200	1.8
Total operating expenses	$436,700	44.8	$353,600	43.6
Income before income tax	$130,300	13.4	$ 74,400	9.2
Income tax	30,300	3.1	24,400	3.0
Net income	$100,000	10.3	$ 50,000	6.2

Any difference of 0.1% from individual items is due to rounding.

FIGURE 26-3 Comparative income statement

Dolphin Watersports Stores
Comparative Income Statement
For the Period from January 1 to December 31, 19X2 and 19X1

	19X2	19X1	Net Change	%
Change				
Sales	$988,900	$850,000	$138,900	16.3
Sales returns and allowances	13,900	39,000	25,100	64.4*
Net sales	$975,000	$811,000	$164,000	20.2
Cost of merchandise sold	408,000	383,000	.25,000	6.5
Gross profit on sales	$567,000	$428,000	$139,000	32.5
Operating expenses	436,700	353,600	83,100	23.5
Income before income tax	$130,300	$ 74,400	55,900	75.1
Income tax	30,300	24,400	5,900	24.2
Net income	$100,000	$ 50,000	$ 50,000	100.0

Any difference of 0.1% from individual items is due to rounding.
* Decrease

Another analysis used by many businesses is a comparison between actual and budgeted figures. Most businesses use monthly and annual budgets to guide and monitor their operations. The owners and managers note differences between budgeted and actual amounts and make adjustments where necessary. Budgets generally are made for each of the twelve monthly and year-to-date figures. A monthly and year-to-date budget comparison example at the end of June, the sixth month of the year, is illustrated in Figure 26-4.

FIGURE 26-4   Income Statement

Dolphin Watersports Stores
Income Statement
For the Month Ending June 30, 19X2

	June 19X2			Year-to-Date		
	Budget	Actual	% Change	Budget	Actual	% Change
Sales	$85,000	$86,500	1.8	$510,000	$480,000	5.9*
Sales returns & allowances	5,000	3,500	30.0*	10,000	6,000	40.0*
Net sales	$80,000	$83,000	3.8	$500,000	$474,000	5.2*
Cost of merchandise sold	35,000	38,000	8.6	225,000	230,000	2.2
Gross profit on sales	$45,000	$45,000	0.0	$275,000	$244,000	11.3*
Operating expenses	31,000	39,000	25.8	185,000	196,000	5.9
Income before tax	$14,000	$ 6,000	57.1*	$ 90,000	$ 48,000	46.7*
Income tax.............	6,000	1,000	83.3*	40,000	16,000	60.0*
Net income	$ 8,000	$ 5,000	37.5*	$ 50,000	$ 32,000	36.0*

Any difference of 0.1% from individual items is due to rounding.
* Decrease

BALANCE SHEET ANALYSIS

A *balance sheet* is a statement of what is owned (assets), what is owed (liabilities) and the difference between those two (net worth) on a given date. It is a picture of the financial condition of a business at a particular time. With the exception of a budget comparison, the same types of analyses are made with the balance sheet as were made with the income statements.

As in income statement analysis, the amount of each item on the balance sheet is compared with the corresponding item on an earlier statement. Then, the increase or decrease in the amount and percent of increase or decrease are listed. When comparison is made between two statements, the prior (earlier) year is used as the base. These changes measure the growth or decline of the business. Many businesses now use the form of balance sheet illustrated in Figure 26-5.

In Figure 26-5, a single comprehensive sheet is illustrated. It shows a) the percent each asset is to the total assets; b) the percent each liability and net worth item is to the total of the liabilities and net worth; and c) the amount and percent of change for each item for the two years.

Part Seven   Applications in Accounting

FIGURE 26-5   Balance sheet

Dolphin Watersports Stores
Balance Sheet
As of December 31, 19X2 and 19X1

	19X2		19X1		Increase/Decrease	
	Amount	Percent	Amount	Percent	Amount	Percent
Assets						
Current assets:						
Cash....................	$ 207,600	20.0	$152,000	16.5	$ 55,600	36.6
Accounts receivable....................	155,000	15.0	117,500	12.7	37,500	32.0
Merchandise inventory	226,000	21.8	211,000	22.8	15,000	7.1
Total current assets..................	$ 588,600	56.8	$480,500	52.0	$108,100	22.5
Fixed assets:						
Building and improvements	$ 388,900	37.5	$390,800	42.3	$ 1,900	0.5*
Equipment............................	59,200	5.7	52,700	5.7	6,500	0.3
Total fixed assets....................	$ 448,100	43.2	$443,500	48.0	$ 4,600	1.0
Total assets.........................	$1,036,700	100.0	$924,000	100.0	$112,700	12.2
Liabilities						
Current liabilities:						
Notes payable	$ 10,000	1.0	$ 12,000	1.3	$ 2,000	16.7*
Accounts payable	112,100	10.8	93,200	10.1	18,900	20.3
Payroll taxes payable	4,100	0.4	3,800	0.4	300	7.9
Total current liabilities	$ 126,200	12.2	$109,000	11.8	$17,200	15.8
Long-term liabilities:						
Mortgage payable	$ 217,000	20.9	$219,000	23.7	$ 2,000	0.9*
Notes payable over 1 year	24,000	2.3	26,500	2.9	2,500	9.4*
Total long-term liabilities	$ 241,000	23.2	$245,500	26.6	$ 4,500	1.8*
Total liabilities	$ 367,200	35.4	$354,500	38.4	$12,700	3.6
Stockholders' Equity						
Common stock.........................	$ 400,000	38.6	$400,000	43.3	$ 0	0.0
Retained earnings......................	269,500	26.0	169,500	18.3	100,000	59.0
Total stockholders' equity	$ 669,500	64.6	$569,500	61.6	$100,000	17.6
Total liabilities and stockholders' equity	$1,036,700	100.0	$924,000	100.0	$112,700	12.2

Any difference of 0.1% from individual items is due to rounding.

* Decrease

COMPLETE ASSIGNMENTS 26-1 AND 26-2

FINANCIAL ANALYSIS RATIOS

In addition to comparing percent on financial statements, business people
want to study significant relationships between various items on their income
statements and balance sheets. These relationships generally are expressed by
ratios. A *ratio* is the relation of one amount to another. For example, the ratio
of $1 to $0.25 is a ratio of 4 to 1, or 4:1.

In analyzing financial statements six important financial analysis ratios are: the working capital ratio, the acid test ratio, the inventory turnover, the ratio of accounts receivable to sales, the relation of income to sales, and the rate of return on equity.

Working Capital Ratio

The *working capital ratio* comes from the balance sheet. It tells the amount of current assets that would remain if all of the company's current liabilities were paid immediately. This ratio helps the reader of the balance sheet understand how well the company is able to pay its current debts.

Working capital ratio = Total current assets ÷ Total current liabilities

a. The working capital ratio for Dolphin Watersports Stores for 19X2 from Figure 26-5 is:

$588,600 ÷ $126,200 = 4.7 = 4.7:1 in 19X2

This is expressed as a ratio of 4.7 to 1 or 4.7:1 which means that the business has $4.70 in current assets to pay for each $1 in current liabilities.

Acid Test Ratio

The *acid test ratio* is used to determine the amount of assets that can be quickly turned into cash to pay current liabilities. Usually, these current assets are cash and receivables (current assets that easily can be turned into cash).

Acid test ratio = Total of cash plus receivables ÷ Total current liabilities

b. The acid test ratio for Dolphin Watersports Stores for 19X2 from Figure 26-5 is:

Cash	$207,600
Accounts receivable	155,000
Total cash and receivables	$362,600

$362,600 ÷ $126,200 = 2.9 = 2.9:1

Inventory Turnover Rate

In retail stores the cost of inventory often is very high. One way to control inventory costs and increase profit is to maintain a high level of inventory turnover. *Inventory turnover rate* lets management and others know the average number of times inventory is sold during the year. The higher the turnover number the better the movement of inventory. *Average inventory*, found either by averaging monthly, quarterly, or yearly inventory amounts, must be calculated first.

Average inventory = (Beginning inventory + Ending inventory) ÷ 2
(annual)

Inventory turnover rate = Cost of goods sold ÷ Average inventory

c. Based on the information in Figures 26-2 and 26-5 the 19X2 inventory turnover for Dolphin Watersports Stores is:

January 1   December 31
($211,000 + $226,000) ÷ 2 = $437,000 ÷ 2 = $218,500 average inventory

$408,000 cost of merchandise sold ÷ $218,500 = 1.9 times inventory turnover rate

Ratio of Accounts Receivable to Net Sales

When businesses sell on credit they need to be alert to the amount and quality of their accounts receivable. They need to compare the amount of their current receivables to prior years and to analyze the extent of their receivables to those of similar companies. By calculating the *ratio of accounts receivable to net sales* every year management and investors can keep an eye in the percentage of sales that have not yet been paid for by customers. An increasing ratio over the years can indicate problems with collecting payment and should be investigated.

Ratio of accounts receivable to net sales
= Accounts receivable ÷ Net sales

d. The Dolphins Watersports Stores ratio for 19X2 is:

Figure 26-5   Figure 26-2
$155,000 ÷ $975,000 = 0.16 = 0.16:1

Relationship of Net Income to Net Sales

An increase in total sales volume does not necessarily mean that a business is improving, since expenses may be increasing at an equal or greater rate than the revenues. It is important to look at the *relationship of net income to net sales*.

Relationship of net income to net sales = Net income ÷ Net sales

e. Based on information from Figure 26-2 the Dolphin Watersports Stores 19X2 relationship is $100,000 ÷ $975,000 = 10.3% which, compared with the relationship for 19X1 of 6.2% ($50,000 ÷ $811,000), indicates an improvement.

Rate of Return on Investment

Owners want a reasonable return on their investment (equity). A ratio that measures the *rate of return on investment* is the ratio of net income to owners' equity calculated as follows:

Rate of return on investment = Net income ÷ Owners' equity

f. Based on Figures 26-2 and 26-5, the rate of return on the owners' investment for Dolphin Watersports Stores for 19X2 is:

$100,000 ÷ $669,500 = 0.1494 = 14.9% rate of return in 19X2

Chapter terms for review

acid test ratio
average inventory
balance sheet
financial statements
income statement
inventory turnover rate
rate of return on investment

ratio
ratio of accounts receivable to net
    sales
relationship of net income to net
    sales
working capital ratio

Assignment 26-1: Income Statement Analysis

A **(44 points) — Solve the following problem (1 point for each correct answer).**

1. In the following comparative income statement, find for each year the percent of each item in terms of net sales at 100%. Make the percent accurate to one decimal place.

Midwest Products Company
Income Statement
For the period from January 1 to December 31, 19X2 and 19X1

	19X2		19X1	
	Amount	Percent	Amount	Percent
Revenue from sales:				
Sales	$743,900	_____	$517,400	_____
Less sales returns and allowances	39,500	_____	26,400	_____
Net sales	$704,400	_____	$491,000	_____
Cost of merchandise sold:				
Merchandise inventory, January 1	$454,200	_____	$306,200	_____
Purchases	518,600	_____	493,000	_____
Merchandise available for sale	$972,800	_____	$799,200	_____
Less merchandise inventory, December 31	433,500	_____	454,200	_____
Cost of merchandise sold	$539,300	_____	$345,000	_____
Gross profit on sales	$165,100	_____	$146,000	_____
Operating expenses:				
Salary	$ 50,400	_____	$ 41,000	_____
Rent	9,900	_____	7,300	_____
Advertising	3,200	_____	9,000	_____
Delivery	2,100	_____	3,600	_____
Utilities	2,400	_____	1,700	_____
Depreciation	3,200	_____	1,400	_____
Equipment rental	3,300	_____	2,900	_____
Interest	2,700	_____	1,000	_____
Miscellaneous	3,600	_____	16,300	_____
Total operating expenses	$ 80,800	_____	$ 84,200	_____
Income before income tax	$ 84,300	_____	$ 61,800	_____
Income tax	19,300	_____	16,800	_____
Net income	$ 65,000	_____	$ 45,000	_____

Any differences of 0.1 for individual items is due to rounding.

Score for A (44)

B **(44 points) — Solve the following problem (1 point for each correct answer).**

2. In the comparative income statement on page 322, find the amount and percent of net change in each item between 19X2 and 19X1. Make the percents accurate to one decimal place.

Midwest Products Company
Comparative Income Statement
For the period from January 1 to December 31, 19X2 and 19X1

	19X2	19X1	Increase/Decrease* Amount	Percent
Revenue from sales:				
Sales	$743,900	$517,400		
Less sales returns and allowances...........	39,500	26,400		
Net sales	$704,400	$491,000		
Cost of merchandise sold:				
Merchandise inventory, January 1	$454,200	$306,200		
Purchases...............................	518,600	493,000		
Merchandise available for sale	$972,800	$799,200		
Less merchandise inventory, December 31	433,500	454,200		
Cost of merchandise sold	$539,300	$345,000		
Gross profit on sales	$165,100	$146,000		
Operating expenses:				
Salary	$ 50,400	$ 41,000		
Rent	9,900	7,300		
Advertising	3,200	9,000		
Delivery	2,100	3,600		
Utilities	2,400	1,700		
Depreciation	3,200	1,400		
Equipment rental	3,300	2,900		
Interest	2,700	1,000		
Miscellaneous.............................	3,600	$ 16,300		
Total operating expenses	$ 80,800	$ 84,200		
Income before income tax...................	$ 84,300	$ 61,800		
Income tax	19,300	16,800		
Net income	$ 65,000	$ 45,000		

Score for B (44)

C (12 points) — Solve the following problem (1 point for each correct answer).

3. The Midwest Products Company set a monthly budget for operating income and expenses for 19X2. Key budget amounts are shown below. Use data from Problem 2 to determine the year-to-date information. Calculate the percent of change between budget and actual for December and year-to-date.

	December Budget	Actual	% Diff.	Year-To-Date Budget	Actual	% Diff.
Net sales	$50,000	$53,000		$750,000		
Cost of merchandise sold	38,000	34,000		562,500		
Gross profit on sales	12,000	19,000		187,500		
Operating expenses	7,000	11,500		111,500		
Income before income tax	5,000	7,500		76,000		
Net income	4,000	4,000		60,000		

*Decrease

Score for C (12)

Part Seven   Applications in Accounting

Assignment 26-2: Balance Sheet Analysis

A (80 points) — Solve the following problem (1 point for each correct answer).

1. In the following comparative balance sheet, find the percent of each of the assets in terms of the total assets as 100% and of each liability and stockholders' equity in terms of the total liabilities and stockholders' equity as 100%. Then find the net change and the percent changes. Make the percents accurate to one decimal place.

Midwest Products Company
Balance Sheet
As of December 31, 19X2 and 19X1

	19X2		19X1		Increase/Decrease*	
	Amount	Percent	Amount	Percent	Amount	Percent
Assets						
Current assets:						
Cash	$ 205,500	_____	$ 133,400	_____	_____	_____
Accounts receivable	276,000	_____	133,000	_____	_____	_____
Merchandise inventory	433,500	_____	454,200	_____	_____	_____
Total current assets ..	$ 915,000	_____	$ 720,600	_____	_____	_____
Fixed assets:						
Building	$ 698,000	_____	$ 709,400	_____	_____	_____
Equipment	187,000	_____	196,000	_____	_____	_____
Total fixed assets	$ 885,000	_____	$ 905,400	_____	_____	_____
Total assets	$1,800,000	_____	$1,626,000	_____	_____	_____
Liabilities						
Current liabilities:						
Notes payable	$ 262,900	_____	$ 279,900	_____	_____	_____
Accounts payable	363,800	_____	208,300	_____	_____	_____
Payroll taxes payable ..	11,300	_____	8,300	_____	_____	_____
Total current liabilities	$ 638,000	_____	$ 496,500	_____	_____	_____
Long-term liabilities:						
Mortgages payable	$ 480,000	_____	$ 495,500	_____	_____	_____
Notes payable over 1 year	171,000	_____	188,000	_____	_____	_____
Total long-term liabilities	$ 651,000	_____	$ 683,500	_____	_____	_____
Total liabilities	$1,289,000	_____	$1,180,000	_____	_____	_____
Stockholders' Equity						
Common stock	$ 280,000	_____	$ 280,000	_____	_____	_____
Retained earnings	231,000	_____	166,000	_____	_____	_____
Total stockholders' equity	$ 511,000	_____	$ 446,000	_____	_____	_____
Total liabilities and stockholders' equity	$1,800,000	_____	$1,626,000	_____	_____	_____

Any difference of 0.1% from individual items is due to rounding.

Score for A (80)

B **(20 points) — Solve the following problems (points for correct answers as stated).**

2. Using the summary below, supply the information required to complete the table. Round the percents to one decimal place (10 points, 1 point for each correct answer).

	19X4 Amount	19X3 Amount	Net Change	% Change
Sales	$200,000	$115,000	_____	_____
Cost of goods sold	140,000	78,000	_____	_____
Expenses	34,000	24,000	_____	_____
Net profit	_____	_____	_____	_____

3. Use Assignment 26-1, Part A, Problem 1 (Income Statement) to answer the following questions (2 points for each correct answer).

a. If the ending inventory on December 31, 19X2 had been $333,500 instead of $433,500, what would be the cost of merchandise sold?

_____

b. Assuming an ending inventory of $333,500 what would be the gross profit?

_____

c. Assuming an ending inventory of $333,500 and that expenses had remained the same, how much would the business have for its income (or loss) before taxes? Would it have been income or loss?

_____

4. Use Assignment 26-2, Part A, Problem 1 (Balance Sheet) to answer the following questions (2 points for each correct answer).

a. If the ending inventory on December 31, 19X2 had been $333,500, what would be the percent of increase or decrease from the prior year?

_____

b. Assuming an ending inventory of $333,500 what would be the 19X2 retained earnings figure (ignore taxes)?

_____

Assignment 26-3: Financial Ratios 1

A (52 points) — Solve the following problem (1 point for each correct answer).

1. Cindy Davis was considering an investment in a business. The following statements were used in analyzing the Angel Stationery Store. Determine the net changes in the comparative statements. Round the percents to one decimal place.

Angel Stationery Store
Comparative Balance Sheet
December 31, 19X2 and 19X1

	19X2	19X1	Increase/Decrease* Amount	Percent
Assets				
Current assets:				
Cash	$113,800	$104,200	_____	_____
Accounts receivable	138,200	112,800	_____	_____
Merchandise inventory	172,000	133,000	_____	_____
Total current assets	$424,000	$350,000	_____	_____
Fixed assets:				
Building improvements	$ 40,000	$ 48,000	_____	_____
Equipment	136,000	115,000	_____	_____
Total fixed assets	$176,000	$163,000	_____	_____
Total assets	$600,000	$513,000	_____	_____
Liabilities				
Current liabilities:				
Salaries payable	$ 34,600	$ 28,800	_____	_____
Accounts payable	121,400	113,200	_____	_____
Total current liabilities	$156,000	$142,000	_____	_____
Long-term liabilities:				
Notes payable	$159,000	$190,000	_____	_____
Total liabilities	$315,000	$332,000	_____	_____
Owners' Equity				
G.A. Star, capital..........................	$285,000	$181,000	_____	_____
Total liabilities and owners' equity	$600,000	$513,000	_____	_____

Angel Stationery Store
Comparative Income Statement
For the Years Ended December 31, 19X2 and 19X1

	19X2	19X1	Increase/Decrease* Amount	Percent
Net sales	$747,200	$835,000		
Cost of merchandise sold:				
Merchandise inventory, January 1	$133,000	$130,000		
Purchases	574,000	689,000		
Merchandise available for sale	$707,000	$819,000		
Less merchandise inventory, December 31	172,000	133,000		
Cost of merchandise sold	$535,000	$686,000		
Gross profit on sales	$212,200	$149,000		
Expenses:				
Selling	$ 81,000	$ 57,300		
Other	27,200	8,100		
Total expenses	$108,200	$ 65,400		
Net income	$104,000	$ 83,600		

Score for A (52)

B **(48 points) — Solve the following problems (4 points for each correct answer).**

2. Provide the following information for Cindy Davis' consideration.

	19X2	19X1
a. Working capital ratio		
b. Acid-test ratio		
c. Ratio of accounts receivable to net sales		
d. Relationship of net income to net sales		
e. Rate of return on investment		
f. Inventory turnover rate		

Score for B (48)

Assignment 26-4:   Financial Ratios 2

A   (52 points) — Solve the following problems (1 point for each correct answer).

1. Cindy Davis was offered a second business. She received the following statements for years 19X2 and 19X1. Study the statements. Complete calculations for a comparative balance sheet and a comparative income statement of Banner Office Supplies, showing the amount and the percent of change.

Banner Office Supplies
Comparative Balance Sheet
December 31, 19X2 and 19X1

	19X2		19X1		Increase/Decrease*	
	Amount	*%*	*Amount*	*%*	*Amount*	*%*
Assets						
Current assets:						
Cash	$ 41,000	26.8	$ 16,000	14.7	_____	_____
Accounts receivable	12,000	7.9	8,000	7.4	_____	_____
Merchandise inventory	46,000	30.1	31,000	28.4	_____	_____
Total current assets	$ 99,000	64.7	$ 55,000	50.5	_____	_____
Fixed assets:						
Building	$ 39,000	25.5	$ 43,000	39.5	_____	_____
Equipment	15,000	9.8	11,000	10.1	_____	_____
Total fixed assets	$ 54,000	35.3	$ 54,000	49.5	_____	_____
Total assets	$153,000	100.0	$109,000	100.0	_____	_____
Liabilities						
Current liabilities:						
Notes payable	$ 4,500	2.9	$ 5,500	5.1	_____	_____
Accounts payable	9,500	6.2	6,000	5.5	_____	_____
Total current liabilities	$ 14,000	9.2	$ 11,500	10.6	_____	_____
Long-term liabilities:						
Mortgage payable	$ 33,000	21.6	$ 38,000	34.9	_____	_____
Total liabilities	$ 47,000	30.7	$ 49,500	45.4	_____	_____
Owner's Equity						
R.A. Banner, capital	$106,000	69.3	$ 59,500	54.6	_____	_____
Total liabilities and owner's equity	$153,000	100.0	$109,000	100.0	_____	_____

Any differences of 0.1% from individual items are due to rounding.

Banner Office Supplies
Comparative Income Statement
December 31, 19X2 and 19X1

	19X2 Amount	%	19X1 Amount	%	Increase/Decrease* Amount	%
Net sales	$205,000	100.0	$101,000	100.0		
Cost of merchandise sold:						
Merchandise inventory, January 1	$ 31,000	15.1	$ 27,500	27.2		
Purchases...................	154,000	75.1	64,500	63.9		
Merchandise available for sale ..	$185,000	90.2	$ 92,000	91.1		
Less merchandise inventory, December 31	46,000	22.4	31,000	30.7		
Cost of merchandise sold	$139,000	67.8	$ 61,000	60.4		
Gross profit on sales	$ 66,000	32.2	$ 40,000	39.6		
Expenses:						
Selling	$ 31,000	15.1	$ 21,500	21.3		
Other	13,000	6.3	7,250	7.2		
Total expenses	$ 44,000	21.5	$ 28,750	28.5		
Net income	$ 22,000	10.7	$ 11,250	11.1		

Any differences of 0.1% from individual items are due to rounding.

Score for A (52)

B **(48 points) — Solve the following problems (points for correct answers as marked).**

2. Using the figures from Part A, compute the following ratios and comparisons for Banner Office Supplies (4 points for each correct answer).

		19X2	19X1
a.	Working capital ratio..................................		
b.	Acid-test ratio..		
c.	Ratio of accounts receivable to net sales..................		
d.	Relationship of net income to net sales		
e.	Rate of return on investment		
f.	Inventory turnover rate		

3. **a.** As of December 31, 19X2 which of the businesses in Assignment 26-3 and 26-4 has the better return on the owner's equity (2 points)?

b. As of December 31, 19X2, which of the two businesses has the stronger ability to provide working capital for new investment (2 points)?

Score for B (48)

Part Eight
Applications in Finance

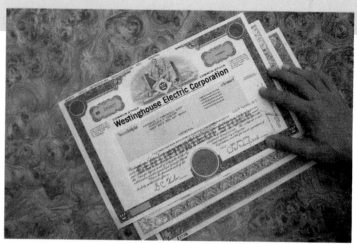

Chapter 27
Corporate Stocks

OBJECTIVES
After completing this chapter, you should be able to:

* Identify the different classes of stock
* Compute the amount of stock dividends
* Compute the costs and proceeds of stock transactions
* Compute the rate of yield
* Determine the gain/loss on sale of stock

Many companies are set up as corporations. Ease in broadening the ownership base and limited liability are two of the reasons why the corporate form is popular. A corporation can receive money by selling shares of ownership. That way the company increases its assets without increasing its debt.

CHARACTERISTICS OF STOCKS

The general term applied to the shares of ownership in a corporation is *capital stock*. Each share of stock is a share of the ownership of the company's assets, over and above its liabilities. The number of shares that a corporation is authorized to *issue*, or offer for sale, is set forth in its *charter*, or basic rules under which the corporation operates. Evidence of ownership of a stock is a *stock certificate*, a special paper containing its own serial number.

The shares of capital stock frequently are assigned an arbitrary monetary figure, known as *par*. The par amount is stated on the stock certificate. For example, a company incorporated with a capital stock of $10,000,000, divided by 1,000,000 shares has a par value of $10 each. The par value is not the same as the market price. Stock may be sold for any amount agreed upon by the buyer and seller. Stock also may be issued without par, in which case it is known as *no-par stock*.

Dividends on Stock

The *board of directors* is a group of people elected by the stockholders to watch over the running of the corporation. The board has the sole authority to distribute earnings to the stockholder. When such action is taken, the directors are said to *declare a dividend*. The rate of dividend is either a certain percent of the par value of the stock or a flat amount of money per share. Thus, a dividend of 8% on a stock with par value of $100 would be $8.00 per share. Most large corporations pay dividends quarterly.

Kinds of Stock

Common stock is the usual type of stock issued by a corporation. Most common stock gives its owners one vote for each share owned. The owners may use their votes at stockholders' meetings to decide who will be on the board of directors.

In order to appeal to a broader investment market, a corporation may provide for one or more classes, or types, of stock with various preferential rights. One kind, *preferred stock*, has a right to share in earnings before common stock does. For example, a company that has a 7% preferred stock must first pay a dividend of 7% of the par value to the holders of preferred stock before anything is paid to the holders of common stock.

a. The ABC Company earned $48,000 last year. The capital stock of the company consists of $400,000 of 7% preferred stock and $200,000 of common stock. If the board of directors declare a dividend of the entire earnings, $28,000 must first be paid to the holders of preferred stock ($400,000 × 7%). The remaining $20,000 ($48,000 − $28,000) then is available for the common stock dividend.

The preferred stockholders' priority right to dividends ordinarily is limited to a specified percentage. Such stock is said to be *nonparticipating preferred stock*. Preferred stock which provides for possible dividends greater than a stated percentage is said to be *participating preferred stock*.

Sometimes preferred stock is cumulative. If a company does not earn enough in any one year to pay a full dividend on preferred stock, or chooses not to declare dividends at all, the unpaid dividends are *in arrears*. Whenever dividends are declared the holders of *cumulative preferred stock* must be paid all dividends in arrears before any current period dividends can be paid.

b. Assume that in example a. the preferred stock is cumulative and that for the preceding year the company had earned only enough to pay a 4% dividend on preferred stock. The earnings of $48,000 would be divided as follows:

Unpaid dividend from preceding year, 3% (7% − 4%)	$12,000
7% dividend for current year	+ 28,000
Total dividend on preferred stock	$40,000

The amount available for dividends on common stock would be $8,000 ($48,000 − $40,000).

Another feature that sometimes makes preferred stock an attractive investment is the possibility of converting the preferred stock into common stock. *Convertible preferred stock* gives the owner the option of converting those preferred shares into a stated number of common shares (for example, conversion of 1 to 3; thus, 1 share of preferred stock could be exchanged into 3 shares of common stock). The conversion feature combines the safety of preferred stock with the possibility of growth through conversion to common stock.

c. John Doe owned 100 shares of ABC convertible preferred stock, $10 par value. He converted each share of preferred into three shares of common. How many shares of common stock did John receive when he converted?

$100 \times 3 = 300$ shares of common stock

If common stock was selling at $17 per share on the date of conversion, how much was John's common stock worth?

17×300 shares $= \$5,100$ common stock value

If John paid $38 per share for his preferred stock, how much had his investment increased?

38×100 preferred stock $= \$3,800$ preferred stock value
$\$5,100 - \$3,800 = \$1,300$ increase in value

If the convertible preferred stock pays 9% annually and the common stock usually pays $0.50 per share, how much more dividend might John expect to receive annually?

$10 par value $\times$ 100 shares $= \$1,000$
$\$1,000 \times 9\% = \$90$ preferred stock dividend
300 shares $\times \$0.50 = \$150$ common stock dividend
$\$150 - \$90 = \$60$ more annual dividends

COMPLETE ASSIGNMENT 27-1

BUYING AND SELLING STOCKS

After stock has been sold by the corporation, it may be sold by the owner at any price desired on the open market, regardless of the par value. Usually, stock is bought or sold through a *stockbroker*, who acts as an agent in the purchase and sale of stock for clients.

Stockbrokers And Stock Exchanges

Basically, there are two kinds of stockbrokers. The *full service broker* not only does the buying and selling upon request for clients but also provides investment advice and manages some of the investments. The *discount broker*, on the other hand, just buys and sells according to the clients' instructions. The operating costs of the discount broker can be kept lower since no additional services are offered. Thus the fees charged clients can be lower than those charged by the full service broker.

Stock exchanges are formal marketplaces set up for the trading of stock. There are a number of stock exchanges in America. The trading of shares of stock is published daily in newspapers. The major listings are the NYSE (New York Stock Exchange), the Amex (American Stock Exchange), or the NASDAQ (National Association of Securities Dealers Automated Quotations) which list the over-the-counter securities.

NOTE: *Securities* are stocks, representing ownership, and bonds, representing debt, that usually can be bought and sold, or traded. *Over-the-counter* means the securities traded are not listed on a stock or bond exchange. (See Chapter 28 for information about bonds.)

Prices quoted are the market values of stocks. A sample stock market report is shown in Figure 27-1. Note that stocks are quoted in dollars and fractions of a dollar. The fractional parts are eighths, quarters or halves. This means that changes in price are at least $0.125.

FIGURE 27-1 Daily Stock Report

| 52 Weeks | | | | | | | | | | | |
High [1]	Low [2]	Stock [3]	Sym [4]	Div [5]	Yld % [6]	PE [7]	Vol 100s [8]	Hi [9]	Lo [10]	Close [11]	Net Chg. [12]
$47\frac{1}{4}$	$35\frac{1}{2}$	Gen Motor	GM	2.75	6.8	5	10725	40	$30\frac{1}{2}$	40	$-\frac{1}{8}$
$123\frac{1}{8}$	$93\frac{3}{8}$	IBM	IBM	4.84	4.6	15	10770	$107\frac{3}{4}$	$104\frac{3}{4}$	105	$-2\frac{7}{8}$
$23\frac{1}{2}$	$18\frac{3}{4}$	PacGE	PCG	1.52	7.4	13	3426	$20\frac{7}{8}$	$20\frac{1}{2}$	$20\frac{5}{8}$	$+\frac{1}{4}$
$33\frac{3}{4}$	$24\frac{1}{8}$	SaraLee	SLE	.84	3.3	13	4583	$26\frac{3}{8}$	$25\frac{5}{8}$	$25\frac{3}{4}$	$-\frac{3}{8}$
$146\frac{1}{2}$	$72\frac{3}{8}$	TimeWar	TWX	1.00	1.3	..	1503	$80\frac{1}{4}$	$79\frac{1}{2}$	$79\frac{3}{4}$	$-1\frac{1}{4}$
$67\frac{3}{8}$	$38\frac{1}{2}$	Xerox	XRX	3.00	7.7	7	753	$39\frac{1}{2}$	$38\frac{7}{8}$	$39\frac{1}{8}$	...

[1] The price per share at the highest point in the previous 52 weeks.

[2] The price per share at the lowest point in the previous 52 weeks.

[3] Company names, often abbreviated to fit in stock tables, are listed alphabetically.

[4] The ticker type symbol is a stock's designation on data bases and quote machines.

[5] The dividend shown usually is the annual rate based on the company's latest payout.

[6] The dividend divided by the closing share price gives the stock's yield.

[7] One measure of a stock's value is its price/earnings ratio (PE). It is based on the per share earnings as reported by the company for the four most recent quarters. The PE number is found by dividing the current price by those most recent four-quarter earnings.

[8] Volume is the number of shares traded, shown in hundreds of shares.

[9] This is the high for the day's trading range.

[10] This is the low for the day's trading range.

[11] This is the closing price on that day.

[12] The net change in price lets you calculate something that isn't in the stock table: the previous day's closing price.

Purchase And Sale Of Stock

The total purchase or selling price of a stock includes the market price of the stock and the charges (*commissions*) made by the broker. The *total cost* paid by the purchaser is made up of the purchase price of the stock plus a brokerage fee (commission). The broker pays the seller *proceeds* equal to the selling price minus the fee or commission. Commission charges are based on a small percentage of the value of the stock, on a flat charge per share, or on an amount negotiated with individual clients. Generally, commissions for brokers are under 1% of the value of the stock or range from $0.30 to $0.80 per share bought or sold. A flat charge of $0.55 per share will be used as the rate for computing the cost of commissions in this book.

d. Cheri bought 200 shares of ITT stock at 90. What was the total cost of the purchase?

$90 × 200 shares = $18,000   purchase price
0.55 × 200   = + 110   commission
$18,110   total cost

e. Joseph sold 1,200 shares of Pacific stock at $48\frac{1}{2}$. What were the proceeds of the sale?

$48.50 × 1,200 shares = $58,200   selling price
$0.55 × 1,200   = − 660   commission
$57,540   proceeds

Round and Odd Lots

Stocks are sold in round lots, odd lots, or a combination of the two. A *round lot* usually is 100 shares. An *odd lot* consists of any number of shares less than 100. 1 to 99 shares is an odd lot for a stock with a 100 share round lot. When odd lots are purchased or sold, the price usually is changed by a small extra charge, or *odd lot differential*. The differential is added to the round lot price for a purchaser and deducted for a seller. In this book a differential of $\frac{1}{8}$ ($12\frac{1}{2}$ cents) will be used as the odd lot rate.

f. Grace sold 140 shares of MJI stock at $161\frac{3}{4}$. What were the proceeds of the sale?

$$
\begin{array}{llll}
\$161.75 \times 100 & = & \$16,175 & \text{round lot price} \\
(161.75 - 0.125) \times 40 & = & \underline{+\ 6,465} & \text{odd lot price} \\
 & & \$22,640 & \text{sale price} \\
\$0.55 \times 140 & = & \underline{-\ 77} & \text{commission} \\
 & & \$22,563 & \text{proceeds}
\end{array}
$$

Finding the Rate of Yield

The *rate of yield* from an investment in stock is the ratio between the dividend and the total cost of the stock.

g. Eric Kam bought 100 shares of MTV stock at 89. A dividend of $5.00 per share was paid this year. What was the rate of yield?

$$
\begin{array}{llll}
\$89.00 \times 100 & = \$8,900 & \text{purchase price} \\
\$\ 0.55 \times 100 & = \underline{+\ 55} & \text{commission} \\
 & \$8,955 & \text{total cost} \\
\$5 \times 100 & = \$500 & \text{dividend for first year} \\
\$500 \div \$8,955 & = 5.58\% & \text{rate of yield}
\end{array}
$$

Gain or Loss on Sale of Stock

For income tax and accounting purposes, the amount of gain or loss on a sale of stock is determined by comparing the proceeds with the total cost.

h. If Eric, in example g., sold his stock at $94, what was the amount and the percent of gain or loss?

$$
\begin{array}{llll}
\$94.00 \times 100 & = \$9,400 & \text{selling price} \\
\$0.55 \times 100 & = \underline{-\ 55} & \text{commission} \\
 & \$9,345 & \text{proceeds}
\end{array}
$$

$9,345 - \$8,955$ (total cost, example g.) = \$390 amount of net gain
$390 \div \$8,955$ = 4.36% percent of gain on sale

i. If Eric wanted to know the total change in the value of his stock (held three years), he would add the $1,500 total dividends received to the proceeds.

$$
\begin{array}{ccc}
\text{total} & \text{total} & \\
\text{proceeds} & \text{dividends} & \text{cost} \\
(\$9,345 & + \$1,500) & - \$8,955 = \$1,890 \text{ total gain in value}
\end{array}
$$

$1,890 \div \$8,955$ = 21.11% gain in value

COMPLETE ASSIGNMENT 27-2

Part Eight   Applications in Finance

Chapter terms for review

board of directors
capital stock
charter
commission
common stock
convertible preferred stock
cumulative preferred stock
declare a dividend
discount broker
full service broker
in arrears
issue
no-par stock
nonparticipating preferred stock

odd lot
odd lot differential
over-the-counter
par
participating preferred stock
preferred stock
proceeds (from sale of stock)
rate of yield
round lot
securities
stock certificate
stock exchange
stockbroker
total cost (for purchaser of stock)

Assignment 27-1: Capital Stock

A (36 points) — The information in Problem 1 also applies to Problems 2 and 3 (points for correct answers as marked).

1. The H&H Company was incorporated with 7% preferred capital stock of $600,000 and common stock of $1,400,000. The par value of the preferred stock was $100 and the par value of the common stock was $50. How many shares of each kind of stock were there (6 points, 3 points for each correct answer)?

   Preferred stock _____

   Common stock _____

2. Last year dividends were declared by the H&H Company which had earnings totaling $640,000 (6 points, 3 points for each correct answer).

   a. What was the total amount of the preferred stock dividend?

   _____

   b. What amount could have been paid on each share of common stock if all the earnings had been distributed?

   _____

3. The directors of the H&H Company actually declared four quarterly dividends of $4.00 a share on the common stock, as well as the regular preferred dividend (6 points, 2 points for each correct answer).

   a. What was the total amount paid by H&H to all common shareholders for each quarterly dividend?

   _____

   b. What was the year's total amount of the common stock dividends?

   _____

   c. What was the total amount of all dividends paid by H&H during the year?

   _____

4. The capital stock of the Addison Company consists of 400,000 shares of preferred stock and 5,500,000 shares of common stock. Last year a dividend of $2.20 a share was declared on preferred stock and four quarterly dividends of $0.25 a share on common stock. How much was the total dividend for the year on each class of stock (6 points, 3 points for each correct answer)?

Preferred stock _____

Common stock _____

5. ComputerMart has 150,000 shares of 6.5% preferred stock, $1 par value, and 1,500,000 shares of common stock. ComputerMart declared total dividends of $250,000 for the current year. How much was the dividend for preferred stock and how much per share on the common stock (6 points, 3 points for each correct answer)?

Preferred stock _____

Common stock (per share) _____

6. Sue bought 300 shares of IBB 6% preferred stock, $10 par value, when it was selling at $60 per share including commission (6 points, 3 points for each correct answer).

a. What was Sue's stock worth at the time of purchase?

_____

b. What was the amount of Sue's quarterly dividend?

_____

Score for A (36)

B (64 points) — Do not consider commission in the following problems (points for correct answers as marked).

7. Pacific Company has 100,000 shares of 8% cumulative preferred stock, $3 par value, and 200,000 shares of common stock. Every three years, Pacific Company pays a total dividend of 50% of its net income. If the company had net income of $62,000 for 1990, $78,000 for 1991, and $80,000 for 1992, how much was the dividend per share for common stock in 1992 (14 points)?

_____

8. Michael Richardson owned 200 shares of Eastern 6.5% convertible preferred stock, $50 par value, for which he paid $56 per share. Two years later, after receiving preferred dividends each year, he converted into 600 shares of Eastern common stock, valued at $23.50 a share at the time of conversion (20 points, 4 points for each correct answer).

a. What was the cost to Michael of the preferred stock?

_____

b. How much did Michael receive in dividends from the preferred stock?

_____

c. What was the value of the common stock Michael received?

_____

d. If he sells the 600 common shares immediately, how much gain will Michael realize, including his dividend?

_____

e. What would be Michael's percent of gain?

_____

9. Texas Air Corp. has issued 5,000,000 shares of 7% preferred stock, $100 par value, and 10,000,000 shares of no-par value common stock. Bob owned 100 shares of preferred. Barbara owned 500 shares of common. In 1990, Texas Air paid $25,000,000 in dividends to its common shareholders. How much more than Bob did Barbara receive (10 points)?

_____

10. Alice Bennett owned 600 shares of TRW 8% convertible stock, $50 par value, for which she paid $35 a share. She received a dividend for one year. She then converted the preferred stock into 400 shares of common stock valued at 98.50 a share (20 points, 4 points for each correct answer).

a. What was the cost to Alice for her preferred stock? _____

b. How much did Alice receive as a dividend for her preferred stock?

_____

c. What was the value of her common stock at the time of conversion?

_____

d. If the common stock paid an annual dividend of $7.00 a share, how much more dividend would she receive annually?

_____

e. What was Alice's percent of increase in annual return as a result of conversion to common stock?

_____

Assignment 27-2: Buying and Selling Stock

A (41 points) — **For calculations use $0.55 a share for commissions and $0.125 for the odd lot differential. Round all percents to two places (points for correct answers as marked).**

1. Juanito purchased 2,000 shares of EKC common stock at 26 and 190 shares of preferred stock at 55 (8 points, 4 points for each correct answer).

   a. What was the total cost of the purchase of common stock? _____

   b. What was the total cost of the purchase of preferred stock? _____

2. Three months later, Juanito sold his 2,000 shares of EKC common stock at $28 and his 190 shares of preferred stock at $58.50 (12 points, 4 points for each correct answer).

   a. What were the proceeds on the sale of common stock? _____

   b. What were the proceeds on the sale of preferred stock? _____

   c. How much did Juanito gain or lose on the purchase and sale of all of his EKC stock?

_____

3. Mr. Bautista purchased 200 shares of City Inc. at $88.50. A dividend of $7.00 per share was paid the first year. What was the rate of yield (5 points)?

_____

4. Jennifer purchased stock for a total cost of $14,800, including commission. She sold the stock a month later for $15,555 after commission (12 points, 4 points for each correct answer).

a. What was her net gain on the sale? _____

b. What was her percent of gain on the sale? _____

c. If Jennifer had held her stock another week and sold for $14,250 after commission, what would have been her percent of loss on the sale?

_____

5. If Jennifer had not sold her stock for $14,250, but waited another three months while the stock fell to a price where she sold and realized net proceeds of $11,780, what would have been her percent of loss (4 points)?

_____

Part Eight   Applications in Finance

B **(59 points) — Solve the following problem (points for correct answers as marked).**

6. Peter, Paul, and Mary each invested $10,000 in different areas. At the end of two years, what was the value of each of their $10,000 investments (15 points, 5 points for each correct answer)?

a. Peter put his $10,000 into a savings account that paid 7.5% interest annually. Add interest on the savings account the first year to the principal before figuring interest for the second year.

Peter _____

b. Paul bought 8%, $75 par value, preferred stock at $50 a share, including commission. He received his full dividend at the end of each year. He sold his stock at the end of the second year. Sales proceeds, after commission, were $50 a share.

Paul _____

c. Mary bought common stock at $40 a share, including commission. Her stock paid quarterly dividends of 90 cents per share, and in two years the stock decreased to a value of $38.50 a share.

Mary _____

7. Find the amount of the dividend per share and the rate of yield per share for each of the following preferred stocks. The cost per share includes all commissions (20 points, 2 points for each correct answer).

a. Cost per share $58, dividend declared $4.00.

Amount of dividend _____

Rate of yield _____

b. Cost per share $80, par value $100, dividend declared 6%.

Amount of dividend _____

Rate of yield _____

c. Cost per share $44.50, dividend declared $2.00.

Amount of dividend _____

Rate of yield _____

d. Cost per share $98, par value $100, dividend declared 4.5%.

Amount of dividend _____

Rate of yield _____

e. Cost per share $82, par value $100, dividend declared 3.5%.

Amount of dividend _____

Rate of yield _____

8. Determine the amount and percent of gain or loss of each of the following transactions. Show a loss in parentheses (). The purchase costs and the sale proceeds include commissions. Round percents to two decimal places (24 points, 3 points for each correct answer).

Number of Shares	Per Share Purchase Costs	Per Share Sale Proceeds	Amount of Gain (or Loss)	Percent of Gain (or Loss)
a. 100	$25.50	$29.00	_____	_____
b. 250	12.00	14.50	_____	_____
c. 140	22.30	20.70	_____	_____
d. 980	19.80	12.75	_____	_____

Score for B (59)

Chapter 28
Corporate and Government Bonds

OBJECTIVES
After completing this chapter you should be able to:

- **Recognize common types of bonds and their differences**
- **Read a bond market report**
- **Compute average annual yield**
- **Compute rate of yield to maturity**

When a corporation or government entity needs additional cash for a long period of time, usually ten years or more, it often will issue long-term notes known as *bonds*. Bonds include the name of the corporation or government entity, the face (maturity) value, the interest rate, and the date of maturity. Bonds are bought and sold on the open market, much like stocks.

BONDS

When first issued, bonds are sold either through brokerage houses or directly to investors at or near the price of $1,000, called par value (or face value). *Par value* represents the investors' principal, the amount that will be paid to the holder on redemption, but does not necessarily represent the market value. If the market value is less, the bond is said to sell at a *discount*. If the market value is more, the bond is said to sell at a *premium*. (The discount or premium amount is the difference between the market value and the par value.)

When a bond issue trades regularly and in quantity, it is said to be *liquid*. This simply means that the holder of the bond can expect to convert the investment to cash readily if cash suddenly is needed.

Kinds of Corporate Bonds

There are many kinds of corporate bonds. Bonds issued by corporations may be *secured* (that is, guaranteed by certain assets) or *unsecured* (not guaranteed). Some of the common types are:

1. *Bearer or coupon bonds.* These are bonds with interest coupons attached, each of which calls for payment of the interest for a period of time, usually six months, on a specified date. Every six months during the life of the bond, another coupon matures. *Title*, or right of ownership, to such bonds is not recorded in the name of the owner, but passes from bearer (holder) to bearer with delivery.

2. *Registered bonds.* These bonds are issued to a person whose name is listed or registered with the corporation (or a designated trustee) so that the interest is paid regularly by check to the registered owner.

3. *Convertible bonds.* These bonds have a provision to be converted into a designated number of shares or a designated value of the corporation's stock.

4. *Debenture bonds.* These bonds have the backing of the corporation but do not specify any of the corporation's tangible assets, such as buildings, equipment or land holdings, as security.

5. *Callable bonds.* Callable bonds have a provision for the issuer to repurchase or call the bonds in at specified dates if the board of directors authorizes the retirement (payoff) of the bonds before their maturity date. Such action by the board of directors would be appropriate if interest rates fall significantly below the interest rate of the callable bond.

Kinds of Government Bonds

1. *Treasury bonds.* These are bonds issued by the United States government.

2. *Municipal bonds.* These are bonds issued by states, cities, school districts, and other public entities.

Facts to Consider Before Purchasing a Bond

Corporate bonds generally provide the highest current yields among fixed-income securities. That high income is fully taxable.

Interest earned on municipal bonds generally is exempt from federal and state income taxes.

Treasury bonds are fully guaranteed and are backed by the full faith and credit of the United States government. Thus, the bondholders are protected against any failure to be paid unless the federal government becomes insolvent.

Because of the safety and tax advantage, government bonds generally carry lower interest rates than debt securities of other issuers, enabling these government units to borrow at favorable interest rates.

Corporate and municipal bonds, unlike treasury bonds, pose a risk that the issuer or borrower may fail to make interest payments or be unable to repay the principal on time. By checking the bond's rating, prospective purchasers of corporate bonds can find out how safe an investment in one bond is compared with another bond. Ratings are information based on experience and research; they are not a guarantee. Three major firms rate bonds: Standard & Poor's Corp., Moody's Investors Service, and Fitch's Investors Service.

In Standard & Poor's system, the rating includes AAA, AA, A, BBB, BB, B, CCC, CC, C, and D. Ratings indicate the relative quality of the bonds. A bond with a low rating is a higher risk bond, and sometimes is known as a *junk bond*. The lower a bond's rating, the higher its yield and its risk.

Information about the market value and sales of bonds on the major exchanges is reported daily in many newspapers. Figure 28-1 shows some of the information usually included in a bond report. The net change is the change from the closing price of the day before.

Bonds	Current Yield	Volume	Close	Net Change
AlaP7½s02	9.1	25	86	-2
ABrnd9⅛ s16	10.4	15	88	$+1$
BkNE9s99	18.4	12	48	$+\frac{1}{2}$
CPoM9s18	9.4	10	96	-1
GMA8¼s16	9.9	10	83	$-\frac{1}{4}$
Monog11s04	27.5	4	40	-9

FIGURE 28-1
Corporation Bonds

Prices of bonds are quoted in percents of face value. For example, a $1,000 bond quoted at 104 would sell at a premium price of $1,040 ($1,000 × 104%). If quoted at 78, the bond would sell at a discounted price of $780 ($1,000 × 78%).

Rule: Prices over 100 (100%) include a premium. Those under 100 (100%) include a discount.

Printed bond reports generally give the interest rate, the method of payment if *semiannual* (every 6 months), and the maturity date. 9s18 shows a 9% interest rate, with interest payable semiannually on bonds maturing in the year 2018. The interest is based on the face (maturity) value of the bond.

a. What will be the amount of the semiannual interest check for the bond shown as 9s18?

$1,000 face value × 9% = $90
$90 ÷ 2 = $45 semiannual interest payment

Commission
The brokerage charge for selling or buying bonds varies with the brokerage house. There is no standard commission. Different brokerage houses follow different practices. For illustrations and problems in this textbook, the charge will be $5 per $1,000 bond.

b. Client B purchased three $1,000 bonds at prices of 93, 82, and 87. What was the amount of commission paid by Client B to the brokerage house?

3 bonds × $5 each = $15 commission

Price of the bonds is irrelevant information since we are assuming a commission based on the face value of each bond.

Interest
Bonds carry interest at a face rate that is fixed and stated on each bond. Some bonds specify that interest accumulates and becomes payable at maturity. On other bonds, the interest payment dates, such as January 1 and July 1 or March 1 and September 1, are stated on the bond. When a bond is sold be-

tween these interest payments dates, it is customary to add the *accrued interest* (interest earned from the last payment date) to the purchase price. This interest is calculated using the actual number of days from the last interest payment date (not counting that date) to the day before the date of the sale and dividing this number by 360.

c. Three $1,000 bonds with interest at 9% on January 1 and July 1 were sold by an investor on September 22 at 102 plus accrued interest. What is the number of days for which accrued interest is paid?

Purchase date: September 22
Number of days of accrued interest: 30 (July) + 31 (August) + 21 (September) = 82 days

What is the purchase cost of the bonds?

$1,000 × 3 = $3,000 face value
$3,000 × 102% = $3,060 market value
$3,000 × 0.09 × $\frac{82}{360}$ = $61.50 accrued interest
$5 × 3 bonds = $15 commission
$3,060 + $61.50 + $15 = $3,136.50 total purchase cost of bonds

Although the accrued interest is an additional cost, the buyer will get it back in the $135 ($3,000 × 9% × $\frac{1}{2}$) full interest payment on the next January 1.

d. What were the proceeds of the sale that the seller in example c. will receive?

$3,060 + $61.50 − $15 = $3,106.50 proceeds to seller

The brokerage house charges commission to both the seller and the buyer.

COMPLETE ASSIGNMENT 28-1

BOND RATE OF YIELD

Interest on bonds provides income to bondholders. This income is referred to as *yield*. There are various methods used to calculate the amount of yield (income) bondholders receive from their bond investments.

Average Annual Yield

Newspapers and bond brokers refer to *average annual yield* as *current yield*. Many newspaper bond reports include a column showing current yield. To calculate the average annual yield from an investment in bonds use the formula:

Annual interest ÷ Total cost = Average annual yield

e. Five $1,000 RGB $9\frac{3}{8}$s04 bonds were purchased at $75\frac{1}{2}$. The commission was $25. What was the average annual yield on the bonds?

$1,000 × 5 = $5,000 face value
$5,000 × $75\frac{1}{2}$% = $3,775 market value
$3,775 + $25 commission = $3,800 total cost
$5,000 × 0.09375 = $468.75 annual interest
$468.75 (annual interest) ÷ $3,800 (total cost) = 0.1234 = 12.34% average annual yield

In this example, the bonds sold at a discount of $1,225 ($5,000 -$3,775) because the investor paid that much less for them than the maturity (face) value. Therefore, the average annual yield of 12.3% is more than the stated interest rate of $9\frac{3}{8}$%.

Rate of Yield to Maturity

Careful investors calculate the yield rate differently to obtain the *rate of yield to maturity*.

Steps to Calculate the Rate of Yield to Maturity

1. Calculate the annual interest by multiplying the face value times the face rate.
2. Determine the *annual discount* (or *premium*) *amortization* (the spreading of the discount or premium amount evenly over the life of the bonds). The amount is computed by dividing the discount (or premium) by the number of years from purchase to maturity of the bonds.
3. Determine the *average principal invested* by adding the maturity value to the cost price and then dividing by 2.
4. Use the following formula to determine the rate of yield to maturity:

$$\frac{\text{Annual Interest + Annual Discount (or − Annual Premium) Amortization}}{\text{Average Principal Invested}}$$

NOTE: Since brokerage charges are such a small part of the cost, they usually are omitted from the calculations of yield to maturity.

---

f. Assume that the RGB bonds matured 20 years after the purchase date.

Step 1 $5,000 × 0.09375 = $468.75 annual interest
Step 2 $1,225 ÷ 20 years = $61.25 annual discount amortization
Step 3 ($5,000 + $3,775) ÷ 2 = $4,387.50 average principal invested
Step 4 ($468.75 + $61.25 = $530) ÷ $4,387.50 = 0.1208 = 12.08% yield to maturity

This rate is somewhat less than the 12.3% annual yield, but it is more accurate with respect to actual income.

Rule: When bonds are sold at *discount,* **the yield rate will be** *higher* **than the stated (face) rate.**

g. To calculate the yield to maturity on bonds sold at a premium, assume that five IntTT8⅝s06 bonds had been bought at the premium price of 123½ and that the bonds will mature in 16 years. The market value of the five bonds would be $6,175. The premium will represent reduced income to the investor if the bonds are held to maturity.

Step 1 $5,000 × 0.08625 = $431.25 annual interest
Step 2   ($6,175 − $5,000 = $1,175) ÷ 16 years = $73.44 annual premium amortization
Step 3   ($5,000 + $6,175) ÷ 2 = $5,587.50 average principal invested
Step 4   ($431.25 − $73.44 = $357.81) ÷ $5,587.50 = 0.0640 = 6.4% yield to maturity

This rate is less than the stated rate of 8⅝ on the premium bonds.

Rule: When bonds are sold at a *premium*, the yield rate will be *lower* than the stated (face) rate.

COMPLETE ASSIGNMENT 28-2

Chapter terms for review

accrued interest	junk bond
annual discount amortization	liquid
annual premium amortization	municipal bonds
average annual yield	par value
average principal invested	premium
bearer bonds	rate of yield to maturity
bonds	registered bonds
callable bonds	secured
convertible bonds	semiannual
coupon bonds	title
current yield	treasury bonds
debenture bonds	unsecured
discount	yield

Assignment 28-1: Bonds

A **(60 points) — Solve the following problems (points for correct answers as marked).**

1. What is the dollar amount of interest per year and the maturity date on each of the following bonds (24 points, 3 points for each correct amount of interest and 1 point for each correct maturity date).

Bond	Interest	Maturity date
a. ATT7s01	_____	_____
b. Avnet8x13	_____	_____
c. CPoWV9s15	_____	_____
d. Fldcst12$\frac{1}{2}$s12	_____	_____
e. OwCor12s10	_____	_____
f. PogoP8$\frac{1}{2}$s05	_____	_____

2. Marcia Upton purchased 20 corporate bonds as shown below. For each transaction determine the cost of the bonds, commission paid, and total purchase costs (36 points, 3 points for each correct cost of bonds, 1 point for each correct commission paid, 1 point for each correct total purchase cost, and 2 points for each correct column total).

Bond	Quantity Purchased	Current Price	Cost of Bonds	Commission	Total Purchase Cost
a. ARich$8\frac{5}{8}$s00	2	$93\frac{1}{2}$	_____	_____	_____
b. DukeP$7\frac{3}{8}$s02	3	84	_____	_____	_____
c. Flwr$8\frac{1}{4}$s05	1	112	_____	_____	_____
d. MACOM$9\frac{1}{4}$s06	6	65	_____	_____	_____
e. PGE$10\frac{1}{8}$s12	4	$98\frac{3}{4}$	_____	_____	_____
f. RalsP$9\frac{1}{2}$s16	4	$91\frac{1}{2}$	_____	_____	_____
Totals			_____	_____	_____

B (40 points) — Solve the following problems (points for correct answers as marked).

3. In each of the following problems, determine the number of days for which accrued interest is paid, the purchase cost of the bonds, and the proceeds of the sale the seller will receive (4 points for each correct number of days, 5 points for correct purchase cost, and 1 point for correct proceeds).

a. Client W: Two $1,000 bonds with interest at 8% on January 1 and July 1 were purchased on September 4, at 103 plus accrued interest:

1. Number of days _____

2. Purchase cost _____

3. Proceeds to seller _____

b. Client X: Three $1,000 bonds with interest at $7\frac{1}{2}$% on January 1 and July 1 were purchased on October 10, at 97 plus accrued interest:

1. Number of days _____

2. Purchase cost _____

3. Proceeds to seller _____

c. Client Y: Four $1,000 bonds with interest at 9% on March 1 and September 1 were purchased on December 3, at 102 plus accrued interest:

1. Number of days _____

2. Purchase cost _____

3. Proceeds to seller _____

d. Client Z: Two $1,000 bonds with interest at $8\frac{1}{2}\%$ on March 1 and September 1 were purchased on April 4, at 84 plus accrued interest:

1. Number of days _____

2. Purchase cost _____

3. Proceeds to seller _____

Score for B (40)

Assignment 28-2: Bond Rate of Yield

A **(52 points) — Solve the following problems (points for correct answers as marked).**

1. An investor bought a 9.85% bond at 95; the commission was $5. The bond would mature in 5 years. Round answers to two decimal places (8 points, 4 points for each correct answer).

    a. What was the average annual yield? _____

    b. What was the rate of yield to maturity? _____

2. In 1988 Jim Ayers bought six LTV 5s03 bonds for which he paid 82. Three years later, he sold the bonds at 84 and bought six Southern Electric $9\frac{1}{2}$s11 bonds at 93. Did he increase or decrease the original rate of yield to maturity and by how much? Round yields to one decimal place (14 points).

    _____

3. On July 29, Rose Mehrer purchased four AMAX $9\frac{1}{2}$s03 bonds at 92. Interest was payable March 1 and September 1. Included in Rose's cost was accrued interest for 149 days (8 points, 4 points for each correct answer).

   a. What was the total purchase cost? _____

   b. What was the average annual yield? Do not consider accrued interest when calculating this rate of yield.

   _____

4. In 1992, James Cooper planned to purchase twenty $1,000 bonds and hold them to maturity. He had two choices. The first was EM&E $8\frac{1}{2}$s05 at $106\frac{1}{2}$. The second was Standard of California 6s02 at 72. Cooper purchased the issue that provided the higher rate of yield to maturity.

   a. Which issue did Cooper purchase (12 points)?

   _____

   b. Upon redemption at the maturity date, how much income would Cooper have averaged monthly if Standard of California had been purchased (3 points)?

   _____

   c. If, in 1995, Cooper purchased EM&E $8\frac{1}{2}$s05 bonds at a price of 89, what would be the yield to maturity (6 points)?

   _____

   d. Which company's bonds would be the better buy: EM&E at 89 or Standard of California (1 point)?

   _____

_____
Score for A (52)

B **(48 points) — Complete the table below. Show yield to maturity to one decimal place (48 points, 2 points for each correct answer).**

	Number Purchased	Price Paid	Discount or Premium	Years to Maturity	Interest Rate	Annual Interest	+ Discount – Premium Amortization	Average Principal Invested	Yield to Maturity
5.	3	96	$ 120.00	4	8				
6.	2	$104\frac{1}{2}$	90.00	15	$11\frac{1}{2}$				
7.	20	73	5,400.00	10	$5\frac{1}{2}$				
8.	7	110	700.00	3	11				
9.	5	105	250.00	20	10				
10.	1	$104\frac{1}{2}$	45.00	$7\frac{1}{2}$	$6\frac{1}{2}$				

Chapter 29
International Business

OBJECTIVES

OBJECTIVES
After completing this chapter, you should be able to:

* **Calculate currency exchange rates**
* **Calculate business transactions with foreign countries**
* **Calculate duty rates on imports**

Businesses in the United States buy (*import*) goods produced in foreign countries and sell (*export*) domestic goods to foreign countries. International business transactions among businesses in various nations account for billions of dollars in trade annually, and constitutes an important part of the economy of most nations in the world. The United States is one of the major importers and exporters in the world, and therefore plays a very important role in international business.

TRADING WITH FOREIGN COUNTRIES

International trade between companies in the United States and foreign countries is under the jurisdiction of the International Trade Administration, a branch of the United States Department of Commerce. Such international trade is subject to a set of rules and regulations known as *The Export Administration Regulations*.

Any company in the United States planning to sell goods to a foreign country must have an export license for the transaction. Export licenses are granted for transactions, not for individuals or companies.

CURRENCY EXCHANGE RATES

For international trade, foreign currencies must be exchanged. Such exchanges normally are made through commercial banks. Most major newspapers include in the financial section a list of foreign exchange rates. These exchange rates change from day to day. Table 29-1 is a typical list of currency exchange rates for most major foreign countries. This table does not include the names of the foreign currencies. Table 29-2 states the name of the currency in each foreign country.

Certain foreign countries call their currency the dollar (Canada, New Zealand, and Singapore). These dollars are not U.S. dollars; each is a separate currency. Several currencies share names, such as franc, mark, peso, or pound. Throughout the world each country prints its currency with that country's name.

TABLE 29-1
Foreign Exchange Rates

	Foreign Currency in Dollars		Dollars in Foreign Currency			Foreign Currency in Dollars		Dollars in Foreign Currency	
	Fri.	Thurs.	Fri.	Thurs.		Fri.	Thurs.	Fri.	Thurs.
Argentina	.0001	.0001	6790.3	6790.3	Lebanon	.001053	.001053	950.00	950.00
Australia	.8240	.8270	1.2136	1.2092	Malaysia	.3723	.3724	2.6860	2.6855
Austria	.0914	.0913	10.94	10.95	Mexico	.000346	.000346	2887.00	2887.00
Belgium	.0311	.0313	32.20	32.00	Netherlands	.5706	.5672	1.7525	1.7630
Brazil	.0152	.0151	65.81	66.11	New Zealand	.6255	.6265	1.5987	1.5962
Britain	1.8928	1.9070	.5283	.5244	Norway	.1659	.1659	6.0270	6.0270
Canada	.8607	.8633	1.1618	1.1583	Pakistan	.0463	.0463	21.61	21.61
Chile	.003396	.003396	294.46	294.46	Peru	.000026	.000026	379218	379218
Colombia	.001912	.001912	523.00	523.00	Philippines	.0405	.0405	24.70	24.70
Denmark	.1681	.1678	5.9500	5.9505	Portugal	.007225	.007239	138.40	138.15
Ecuador	.001115	.001115	950.00	950.00	Saudi Arabia	.2667	.2667	3.7500	3.7500
Egypt	.3685	.3685	2.7134	2.7134	Singapore	.5688	.5721	1.7580	1.7480
Finland	.2712	.2719	3.6875	3.6775	So. Korea	.001396	.001396	716.20	716.10
France	.1919	.1917	5.2110	5.2170	So. Africa	.3883	.3906	2.5750	2.5600
Germany	.6376	.6416	1.5685	1.5525	Spain	.010228	.010199	97.77	98.05
Greece	006458	.006483	154.85	154.25	Sweden	.1744	.1744	5.7325	5.7325
India	.0567	.0568	17.637	17.605	Switzerland	.7612	.7714	1.3137	1.2963
Indonesia	.000541	.000541	1850.00	1850.00	Taiwan	.0371	.0371	26.90	26.90
Ireland	1.7110	1.7220	.5816	.5807	Thailand	.03922	.03922	25.50	25.50
Israel	.5128	.5128	1.9500	1.9500	Turkey	.000374	.000374	2671.65	2676.66
Italy	.000860	.000863	1163.25	1159.00	Uruguay	.000769	.000769	1300.00	1300.00
Japan	.007143	.007105	140.00	140.75	Venezuela	.0205	.0205	48.7000	48.8000
Jordan	1.5221	1.5221	.65700	.65700	Yugoslavia	.09141	.09141	10.94	10.94

TABLE 29-2
Foreign Currencies

Country	Currency	Country	Currency
Argentina	Austral	Malaysia	Ringgit
Australia	Dollar	Mexico	Peso
Austria	Schilling	Netherlands	Guilder
Belgium	Franc	New Zealand	Dollar
Britain	Pound	Norway	Kroner
Brazil	Cruzeiro	Pakistan	Rupee
Canada	Dollar	Peru	Intl
Chile	Peso	Philippines	Peso
Colombia	Peso	Portugal	Escudo
Denmark	Krone	Saudi Arabia	Riyal
Ecuador	Sucre	Singapore	Dollar
Egypt	Pound	So. Korea	Won
Finland	Markkaa	So. Africa	Rand
France	Franc	Spain	Peseta
Germany	Mark	Sweden	Krona
Greece	Drachma	Switzerland	Franc
India	Rupee	Taiwan	New Taiwan dollar
Indonesia	Rupiah	Thailand	Baht
Ireland	Pound	Turkey	Lira
Israel	Shekel	USSR	Ruble
Italy	Lira	Uruguay	Peso
Japan	Yen	Venezuela	Bolivar
Jordan	Dinar	Yugoslavia	Dinar
Lebanon	Pound		

a. The President of Worldwide Industries read in the Friday morning paper that one U.S. dollar had risen a little more than one cent against the Swiss franc. Table 29-1 shows this to be true. Table 29-1 shows in the *Foreign Currency in Dollars* column Switzerland .7612 for Friday, and .7714 for Thursday. This means that on Friday it would take .7612 of a U.S. dollar (76¢) to buy one Swiss franc.

$1.00 × .7612 = $0.76 U.S. currency (or U.S.) (rounding to nearest cent)

Thus, it would take $76.12 U.S. to buy 100 Swiss francs.

$1.00 × .7612 × 100 Swiss francs = $76.12 U.S.

On Thursday, it would have taken 77¢ U.S. ($1.00 × .7714 rounded to the nearest cent) to buy one Swiss franc. To buy 100 Swiss francs would have cost $77.14 U.S.:

$1.00 × .7714 × 100 Swiss francs = $77.14 U.S.

Since on Friday it cost less U.S. currency ($76.12) to buy 100 Swiss francs than it did on Thursday ($77.14) the dollar is more valuable on Friday than on the day before. It has risen in value relative to the Swiss franc.

Because the exchange rate from foreign currency to U.S. dollars is a percent of $1.00 you usually can do the calculation by mental mathematics.

b. How much would 100 Swiss francs be worth Friday in U.S. dollars? The *Dollars in Foreign Currency* column on Friday, Table 29-1, for Switzerland shows the exchange rate is 1.3137. This means that on that day it would take 1.3137 Swiss francs to buy one U.S. dollar:

100 Swiss francs ÷ 1.3137 = $76.12 value in U.S. dollars (rounding to the nearest cent)

One of the hazards of foreign trade is the uncertainty of the future exchange rates between currencies. It is possible that the relative value between the dollar and the buyer's currency will change between the time the contract is signed and payment is received. If the exporter is not properly protected, a devaluation in the foreign currency could cause the exporter to lose dollars in the transaction.

c. Worldwide Industries has contracted to sell certain goods to a company in France. The French company has contracted to pay 750,000 French francs for the shipment. At the time the contract was signed, the *Foreign Currency in Dollars* column in the financial section of the morning paper showed that one French franc was valued at $0.20 U.S. currency. Worldwide Industries expected to receive $150,000 U.S. dollars.

750,000 francs × $0.20 U.S. = $150,000 U.S.

Between the date the contract was signed and the date on which payment was received, the French franc fell to a value of $0.19 U.S. How much did Worldwide Industries lose by agreeing to accept payment in French francs instead of U.S. dollars?

750,000 francs × $0.19 U.S. = $142,500 U.S.

$150,000 U.S. expected − $142,500 U.S. received = $7,500 U.S. lost

d. Worldwide Industries has contracted to buy certain goods from another company in France. Worldwide Industries has contracted to pay one million French francs for the shipment. On the day the contract was signed, the *Dollars in Foreign Currency* column in the morning paper showed that 5.2110 French francs would buy one U.S. dollar. Worldwide Industries expected to pay the equivalent of $191,902 U.S. dollars.

1,000,000 francs ÷ 5.2110 = $191,902 U.S. (rounded to the nearest dollar)

On the date payment was made, the *Dollars in Foreign Currency* column showed that 5.3100 French francs were required to buy one U.S. dollar. How many dollars did Worldwide Industries save by agreeing to pay in French francs?

1,000,000 francs ÷ 5.3100 = $188,324 U.S. (rounded to the nearest dollar)

$191,902 U.S. expected to pay − $188,324 U.S. actually paid = $3,578 U.S. saved

Exporters should be aware of potential problems in currency convertibility. In addition to the fluctuation problems that may occur, not all currencies are fully or quickly convertible into U.S. dollars.

COMPLETE ASSIGNMENT 29-1

DUTIES AND CUSTOMS TERRITORY

All items imported into the United States must go through the U.S. Customs Agency. Many imported items have a *duty* (charge or tax) imposed by the Customs Agency to protect United States manufacturers against foreign competition in domestic markets. Duties vary widely from item to item. A duty may be a set amount, such as $0.50 per item, or an *ad valorem* duty which is a percent of the value of the item.

e. Assume a quartz analog wristwatch in a gold plated case with a metal band has four duty rates imposed upon importation: $0.40 per wristwatch + 6% of the value of the case + 14% of the value of the strap + 5.3% of the value of the battery. Robertson Jewelry Company imported a dozen quartz analog wristwatches from Switzerland. The value of the case was $16; the strap was $10; and the battery was $6. How much duty did the Robertson Jewelry Company pay for the dozen wristwatches (round final answer to nearest cent)?

Duty per wristwatch =	$0.40
Ad valorem duty on case @ $16 × 6% =	.96
Ad valorem duty on strap @ $10 × 14% =	1.40
Ad valorem duty on battery @ $6 × 5.3% =	.318
Total duty per wristwatch:	$3.078

$3.078 per wristwatch × 12 = $36.94 (rounded to nearest cent)

The International Trade Administration encourages the flow of U.S. dollars to some developing countries by allowing duty free importation on certain items, particularly on textiles, from those countries. In contrast, the flow of U.S. dollars to other countries is discouraged by significantly increasing the ad valorem duties on certain items from those countries.

Assignment 29-1: Trading with Foreign Countries

A **(44 points) — Solve the following problems (1 point for each correct answer).**

1. Using the *Foreign Currency in Dollars* columns from Table 28-1, find the amount of U.S. currency necessary to buy 100 units of the currency of each foreign country listed below for Friday and for Thursday. Decide whether the U.S. dollar rose (+) or fell (−) against that currency from Thursday to Friday.

Foreign Currency	Price of 100 units Friday	Price of 100 units Thursday	U.S. dollar rose or fell (+ or −)
a. Australian dollar	_____	_____	_____
b. Austrian schilling	_____	_____	_____
c. Belgian franc	_____	_____	_____
d. Brazilian cruzeiro	_____	_____	_____
e. Canadian dollar	_____	_____	_____
f. German mark	_____	_____	_____
g. S. African rand	_____	_____	_____
h. Swiss franc	_____	_____	_____

2. Using the *Dollars in Foreign Currency* column from Table 28-1, determine the value in U.S. currency of one thousand units of each of the foreign currencies listed below on Thursday and on Friday. Round answers to nearest cent.

Foreign Currency	Value of 1,000 units	
	Friday	Thursday
a. Argentinean austral		
b. British pound		
c. Danish krone		
d. Finish markkaa		
e. Greek drachma		
f. Indian rupee		
g. Irish pound		
h. Italian lira		
i. Japanese yen		
j. Spanish peseta		

Score for A (44)

B (56 points) — Solve the following problems (points for correct answers as stated).

3. Parker Enterprises has contracted to sell certain goods to a company in Britain. The price agreed upon for the goods is 78,000 British pounds. On the date the contract was signed, the *Foreign Currency in Dollars* column in the financial section of the local paper showed that the British pound was valued at 1.9200 U.S. currency.

a. How much U.S. currency value does Parker Enterprises expect to receive for the goods (4 points)?

b. If the value of the British pound fell from 1.9200 to 1.8500 on the date of payment, how much would Parker Enterprises lose by contracting in British pounds instead of American dollars (6 points)?

c. If the British pound rose to 1.9300 on the date of payment, how much would Parker Enterprises gain by contracting in British pounds instead of U.S. dollars (6 points)?

4. Miller Furniture Company is importing 150 chairs from a Danish firm. Each chair is valued at 890 Danish krone. What is the value of the 150 chairs in U.S. currency if the Danish krone is currently shown as .1680 in the *Foreign Currency in Dollars* column of the local paper (6 points)?

_____

5. Major Manufacturers, Inc. is contracting to sell its product to a country whose currency is unstable and difficult to convert to U.S. currency. The value of the goods in U.S. currency is $20,000. The currency of the country to which the goods will be shipped is currently valued at .0040 in the *Foreign Currency in Dollars* column of the local paper. Major Manufacturers, Inc. is willing to accept the currency of a third country. The German mark is agreed upon. The German mark is shown as .6416 in the *Foreign Currency in Dollars* column of the local paper on the date the contract is signed.

a. How many German marks does Major Manufacturers, Inc. expect to receive (round answer to the nearest mark) (4 points)?

_____

b. If the mark does not change before the date of payment, but the value of the currency of the receiving country falls from .0040 to .0003, how much did Major Manufacturers, Inc. save by using the German mark (10 points)?

_____

6. If the British pound is shown as 1.9000 and the Egyptian pound shown as .3700 in the *Foreign Currency in Dollars* column of the local paper, how many more Egyptian pounds than British pounds could a U.S. citizen buy for $1,000 U.S. currency (round answers to the nearest pound) (10 points)?

_____

7. A French designer has contracted to sell to a U.S. chain of clothing stores clothing valued at 80,000 francs. The franc is shown in the *Dollars in Foreign Currency* column of the U.S. newspapers as 5.000.

a. What is the value of the shipment in U.S. currency (4 points)?

_____

b. If payment is contracted to be made as 80,000 francs and the *Dollars in Foreign Currency* changes from 5.000 to 5.500 on payment day, how much will the French designer lose by taking payment in francs instead of U.S. dollars (round answer to the nearest dollar) (6 points)?

_____

Assignment 29-2: Duties and Customs Territory

A (70 points) — Solve the following problems (points for correct answers as stated).

1. Myerson's Department Store ordered from a foreign country 120 music boxes on which an ad valorem duty of 3.2% is charged. Payment is to be made in U.S. currency. The price of each music box is $17.

   a. What is the price of the 120 music boxes before duty is added (2 points)?

   _____

   b. What is the amount of duty charged on the shipment (2 points)?

   _____

   c. What is the total cost to the receiver (2 points)? _____

2. Jewelry International Company is purchasing one gross (144) 20-inch gold necklaces at $70 each, and 6 dozen 18-inch silver necklaces at $55 each from a foreign country. The ad valorem duty for gold and silver jewelry is 6.5%. What is the total cost of the shipment to the buyer (10 points)?

   _____

3. Anthony's Department Store is going to buy 3 gross of vases for the next Christmas season. They can buy porcelain vases or lead crystal vases for $45 each. The duty on porcelain vases is 9%. The duty on lead crystal vases is 6%. How much will Anthony's Department Store save in total cost by purchasing lead crystal instead of porcelain (10 points)?

   _____

4. Melody Piano Store can purchase pianos domestically for $1,360 each. They can purchase pianos from a foreign country for $1,300 plus 5.3% ad valorem duty.

a. Melody Piano Store purchases the pianos with the lower total cost. Do they purchase from a domestic or a foreign manufacturer (8 points)?

_____

b. How much do they save on each piano (2 points)? _____

5. Madison Office Equipment Company purchased the following equipment from a foreign country. Prices and ad valorem rates are shown with each item.

72 automatic typewriters @ $150 each + 2.2% duty
24 addressing machines @ $30 each + 4.2% duty
144 pencil sharpeners @ $12 each + 5.3% duty
24 check writing machines @ $60 each, duty free
72 calculators @ $24 each + 3.9% duty

a. What was the cost of the order before duty (10 points)?

_____

b. What was the cost of the order after duty (round each calculation to the nearest cent) (10 points)?

_____

c. If the 144 pencil sharpeners had been purchased at $12 each from a country with which trade was discouraged and the ad valorem rate was 40%:

1) How much would the pencil sharpeners have cost (5 points)?

_____

2) How much more duty would the pencil sharpeners cost at the ad valorem rate of 40% than at the ad valorem rate of 5.3% (3 points)?

_____

6. Adams Industries could purchase $20,000 worth of textiles from Country A with an ad valorem rate of 2.5%, or from Country B duty free.

a. How much would the shipment cost if purchased from Country A (3 points)?

_____

b. How much did Adams Industries save by purchasing from Country B (3 points)?

_____

_____
Score for A (70)

B (30 points) — Solve the following problems (points for correct answers as stated).

7. The Franklin Computer Company imports some computer components, manufactures other components, and assembles computers for sale within the United States or for export to foreign countries. The company is located in a district which has been designated by the International Trade Administration as a foreign trade zone. The company imported $250,000 worth of monitors having an ad valorem rate of 3.7%, $300,000 worth of power supplies having an ad valorem rate of 3.0%, and $500,000 worth of printers having an ad valorem rate of 3.7%. All products were finished and sold one year later.

a. If all products were sold within U.S. Customs territories, how many dollars of duty did the company pay at the end of the year (2 points)?

_____

b. If 25% of the finished products were moved into U.S. Customs territories for sale and 75% were exported for sale in foreign countries, how many dollars of duty did the company pay at the end of the year (10 points)?

_____

c. If all products were exported for sale, how many dollars of duty did the company pay at the end of the year (2 points)?

_____

d. The company imported $260,000 worth of portable computers having an ad valorem rate of 3.9% and kept 20% of them for exhibition and company use on the premises.

1) If the company repackaged and sold the remaining portable computers in U.S. Customs territories, how many dollars of duty did the company pay on the portable computers (5 points)?

_____

2) If the company repackaged and exported 50% of the remaining portable computers for sale in foreign countries and moved the remaining 30% into U.S. Customs territories for sale, how many dollars did the company pay in duty on the portable computers (5 points)?

_____

8. A company imported 3 million dollars worth of laptop computers having an ad valorem rate of 3.9%. The company repackaged and exported all of the computers for resale. How many dollars did the company save by being located in a foreign trade zone (6 points)?

_____

Score for B (30)

Part Nine
Time Value of Money

Chapter 30
Compound Interest and
Present Value

OBJECTIVES
After completing this chapter, you should be able to:

- Understand and compute compound interest
- Distinguish between future value and present value
- Apply concepts of compound interest to business problems

To effectively manage their cash and other assets, businesses must make many investing and borrowing decisions. Before deciding on an investment, business managers must estimate the amounts that various investment choices could earn. Similarly, before borrowing cash, the business must estimate the costs of different alternatives. Today, these calculations are carefully made, always using compound interest.

COMPOUND INTEREST

Simple interest is calculated with one application of the formula $I = P \times R \times T$, as you learned in Chapter 15. The simple interest on $200 invested for 2 years at 12% is $I = P \times R \times T = \$200 \times 0.12 \times 2 = \$48$. Likewise, the simple interest on an investment of exactly $1.00 invested for 2 years at 12% is $I = P \times R \times T = \$1.00 \times 0.12 \times 2 = \$0.24$.

Compound interest means that the simple interest formula is applied several times during the term. The interest earned by one application is added to the principal before the next interest calculation.

a. Calculate the interest on $200 invested for 2 years at 12% compounded annually (once at the end of each year). Also, calculate the interest on $1.00 invested for 2 years at 12% compounded annually. (Do not round off.)

$200.00	Original principal	$1.00
× 0.12	Interest rate	× 0.12
$24.0000	First-year interest	$0.1200
+ 200.00	First-year principal	+ 1.00
$224.00	Second-year principal	$1.12
× 0.12	Interest rate	× 0.12
4 4800		224
22 400		112
$26.88	Second-year interest	$0.1344
+ 224.00	Second-year principal	+ 1.12
$250.88	Final compound amount	$1.2544
− 200.00	Original principal	− 1.00
$ 50.88	Total compound interest	$0.2544

On the $200 investment, the total compound interest is $50.88 compared with $48 simple interest over the same two years. On the $1.00 investment, the total compound interest is $0.2544 compared with $0.24 simple interest. Observe that 0.2544 × $200 = $50.88.

Since the computations illustrated in the examples are time-consuming, compound interest almost always is calculated using compound interest tables or calculators with special keys.

Table **30-1** on page 376 is an abbreviated compound interest table. The columns represent interest rates and the rows represent the number of times interest is compounded. In the previous example, 12% is compounded 2 times; find the number in the 12% column and the 2nd row: 1.25440. This is the *compound amount factor*. The *compound amount* is equal to the original principal multiplied by the compound amount factor. In example a., 1.25440 × $200 = $250.88 and 1.25440 × $1.00 = $1.2544.

Steps for Using Compound Interest Tables

1. Locate the factor in the proper row and column of the table.
2. Multiply the original principal by the factor. The product is the compound amount.
3. Subtract the original principal from the product. The difference is the total compound interest.

---

b. Find the compound amount and the compound interest for an investment of $200 for 2 years at 12% compounded annually.

Step 1   The compound amount factor from Table 30-1 is 1.25440.
Step 2   Compound amount = $200 × 1.25440 = $250.88
Step 3   Total compound interest = $250.88 − $200.00 = $50.88

Interest may be compounded semiannually, quarterly, monthly, or even daily using the same steps listed above. The only difference is that now the column represents the *periodic interest rate* and the row represents the *number of compounding periods*.

TABLE 30-1 Future Value (Amount) of $1.00

Period (n)	1.00%	1.25%	1.50%	2.00%	3.00%	4.00%	5.00%	6.00%	8.00%	9.00%	10.00%	12.00%	15.00%	18.00%
1	1.01000	1.01250	1.01500	1.02000	1.03000	1.04000	1.05000	1.06000	1.08000	1.09000	1.10000	1.12000	1.15000	1.18000
2	1.02010	1.02516	1.03023	1.04040	1.06090	1.08160	1.10250	1.12360	1.16640	1.18810	1.21000	1.25440	1.32250	1.39240
3	1.03030	1.03797	1.04568	1.06121	1.09273	1.12486	1.15763	1.19102	1.25971	1.29503	1.33100	1.40493	1.52088	1.64303
4	1.04060	1.05095	1.06136	1.08243	1.12551	1.16986	1.21551	1.26248	1.36049	1.41158	1.46410	1.57352	1.74901	1.93878
5	1.05101	1.06408	1.07728	1.10408	1.15927	1.21665	1.27628	1.33823	1.46933	1.53862	1.61051	1.76234	2.01136	2.28776
6	1.06152	1.07738	1.09344	1.12616	1.19405	1.26532	1.34010	1.41852	1.58687	1.67710	1.77156	1.97382	2.31306	2.69955
7	1.07214	1.09085	1.10984	1.14869	1.22987	1.31593	1.40710	1.50363	1.71382	1.82804	1.94872	2.21068	2.66002	3.18547
8	1.08286	1.10449	1.12649	1.17166	1.26677	1.36857	1.47746	1.59385	1.85093	1.99256	2.14359	2.47596	3.05902	3.75886
9	1.09369	1.11829	1.14339	1.19509	1.30477	1.42331	1.55133	1.68948	1.99900	2.17189	2.35795	2.77308	3.51788	4.43545
10	1.10462	1.13227	1.16054	1.21899	1.34392	1.48024	1.62889	1.79085	2.15892	2.36736	2.59374	3.10585	4.04556	5.23384
11	1.11567	1.14642	1.17795	1.24337	1.38423	1.53945	1.71034	1.89830	2.33164	2.58043	2.85312	3.47855	4.65239	6.17593
12	1.12683	1.16075	1.19562	1.26824	1.42576	1.60103	1.79586	2.01220	2.51817	2.81266	3.13843	3.89598	5.35025	7.28759
13	1.13809	1.17526	1.21355	1.29361	1.46853	1.66507	1.88565	2.13293	2.71962	3.06580	3.45227	4.36349	6.15279	8.59936
14	1.14947	1.18995	1.23176	1.31948	1.51259	1.73168	1.97993	2.26090	2.93719	3.34173	3.79750	4.88711	7.07571	10.14724
15	1.16097	1.20483	1.25023	1.34587	1.55797	1.80094	2.07893	2.39656	3.17217	3.64248	4.17725	5.47357	8.13706	11.97375
16	1.17258	1.21989	1.26899	1.37279	1.60471	1.87298	2.18287	2.54035	3.42594	3.97031	4.59497	6.13039	9.35762	14.12902
17	1.18430	1.23514	1.28802	1.40024	1.65285	1.94790	2.29202	2.69277	3.70002	4.32763	5.05447	6.86604	10.76126	16.67225
18	1.19615	1.25058	1.30734	1.42825	1.70243	2.02582	2.40662	2.85434	3.99602	4.71712	5.55992	7.68997	12.37545	19.67325
19	1.20811	1.26621	1.32695	1.45681	1.75351	2.10685	2.52695	3.02560	4.31570	5.14166	6.11591	8.61276	14.23177	23.21444
20	1.22019	1.28204	1.34686	1.48595	1.80611	2.19112	2.65330	3.20714	4.66096	5.60441	6.72750	9.64629	16.36654	27.39303
21	1.23239	1.29806	1.36706	1.51567	1.86029	2.27877	2.78596	3.39956	5.03383	6.10881	7.40025	10.80385	18.82152	32.32378
22	1.24472	1.31429	1.38756	1.54598	1.91610	2.36992	2.92526	3.60354	5.43654	6.65860	8.14027	12.10031	21.64475	38.14206
23	1.25716	1.33072	1.40838	1.57690	1.97359	2.46472	3.07152	3.81975	5.87146	7.25787	8.95430	13.55235	24.89146	45.00763
24	1.26973	1.34735	1.42950	1.60844	2.03279	2.56330	3.22510	4.04893	6.34118	7.91108	9.84973	15.17863	28.62518	53.10901
25	1.28243	1.36419	1.45095	1.64061	2.09378	2.66584	3.38635	4.29187	6.84848	8.62308	10.83471	17.00006	32.91895	62.66863
26	1.29526	1.38125	1.47271	1.67342	2.15659	2.77247	3.55567	4.54938	7.39635	9.39916	11.91818	19.04007	37.85680	73.94898
27	1.30821	1.39851	1.49480	1.70689	2.22129	2.88337	3.73346	4.82235	7.98806	10.24508	13.10999	21.32488	43.53531	87.25980
28	1.32129	1.41599	1.51722	1.74102	2.28793	2.99870	3.92013	5.11169	8.62711	11.16714	14.42099	23.88387	50.06561	102.96656
29	1.33450	1.43369	1.53998	1.77584	2.35657	3.11865	4.11614	5.41839	9.31727	12.17218	15.86309	26.74993	57.57545	121.50054
30	1.34785	1.45161	1.56308	1.81136	2.42726	3.24340	4.32194	5.74349	10.06266	13.26768	17.44940	29.95992	66.21177	143.37064

i. Determine how often compounding occurs in one (1) year. (2 times if semiannually; 4 times if quarterly; 12 times if monthly, etc.)

ii. Divide the stated interest by the number determined in Step *i.* The quotient is the periodic interest rate (column).

iii. Multiply the number of years by the number determined in Step *i.* The product is the number of compounding periods (row).

c. Find the periodic interest rate and the number of compounding periods if 12% is compounded semiannually, quarterly, or monthly.

| | Step *i* | Step *ii* | | Step *iii* |
Stated Interest Rate	*Frequency of Compounding*	*Periodic Interest Rate*	*Investment Term*	*Compounding Periods*
12%	Semiannually (2 times)	12% ÷ 2 = 6%	2 years	2 × 2 = 4
12%	Quarterly (4 times)	12% ÷ 4 = 3%	2 years	2 × 4 = 8
12%	Monthly (12 times)	12% ÷ 12 = 1%	2 years	2 × 12 = 24

d. Find the compound amount and the compound interest if $200 is invested for two years at 12% compounded quarterly. (Use Table 30-1.)

Step *i*   There are 4 compounding periods in one year

Step *ii*   Periodic interest rate = 12% ÷ 4 = 3% per period

Step *iii* Number of periods = 2 years × 4 = 8 periods

Step 1   Use Table 30-1: 3% column and 8th row
             Compound amount factor = 1.26677

Step 2   Compound amount = $200.00 × 1.26677 = $253.354 or $253.35

Step 3   Total compound interest = $253.35 − $200.00 = $53.35

Thus, $200 invested at 12% compounded quarterly will be worth $253.35 in 2 years.

COMPLETE ASSIGNMENT 30-1

PRESENT VALUE OF AN AMOUNT

In the previous example, $200 invested **today** at 12% compounded quarterly will be worth a total of $253.35 in 2 years. The compound amount, $253.35, frequently is called the *future value.* Likewise, the principal, $200, may be called the *present value.* To consumers, the more important number may be the future value because consumers invest for the future. To businesses, however, the more important number very often is the present value. Businesses make decisions that involve spending and borrowing. They expect to make profits in the future. Because they make their decisions in the present, they convert future values into present values.

e. With interest at 12% compounded quarterly, $253.35 two years from now has a present value of $200.

f. With interest at 12% compounded quarterly, $1.00 today has a future value (compound amount) of $1.266770. Therefore, $1.26677 two years from now has a present value of $1.00.

Calculating Present Values with Table 30-1

You can calculate present values using Table 30-1 by reversing the procedure for calculating future value.

$$\frac{\text{Future Value (the compound amount)}}{\text{Compound Amount Factor (from Table 30-1)}} = \text{Present Value}$$

g.

Present Value	×	Table 30-1 Compound Amount Factor	=	Future Value		Future Value	÷	Table 30-1 Compound Amount Factor	=	Present Value
$200	×	1.266770	=	$253.354		$253.35	÷	1.266770	=	$199.99684 or $200.00

h. Find the present value of $1,000 three years from now if interest is 10% compounded semiannually. (Use Table 30-1.)

Step   *i*   There are 2 compounding periods in one year
Step *ii*   Periodic interest rate = 10% ÷ 2 = 5% per period
Step *iii*   Number of periods = 3 years × 2 = 6 periods
Step   1   Using Table 30-1, 5% column and 6th row, compound amount
             factor = 1.34010
             *Present value = $1,000.00 ÷ 1.34010 = $746.21297 or $746.21

             *Remember to divide instead of multiply when finding the present value using Table 30-1.

Calculating Present Values with Table 30-2

For many businesses, being able to calculate quickly present values is more important than being able to calculate future values. Therefore, special tables exist for present values. Table 30-2 is an abbreviated version of one such table.

As shown in example h., you can calculate present values by using Table 30-1 and division. However, without a calculator, dividing $1,000 by a compound amount factor such as 1.34010 is a very tedious operation. Without a calculator, multiplication is a much easier computation. With Table 30-2, look up the *present value factor* following Steps *i–iii* and Step 1. Then, use the following modified version of Step 2: Multiply the **future value** (compound amount) by the **present value factor** to determine the **present value** (principal).

i. How much must you deposit today (present value) in order to have $1,000 three years from now (future value) if interest is 10% compounded semiannually? (Use Table 30-2.)

Step   *i*   There are 2 compounding periods in one year
Step *ii*   Periodic interest rate = 10% ÷ 2 = 5% per period
Step *iii*   Number of periods = 3 years × 2 = 6 periods
Step   1   Using Table 30-2, 5% column and 6th row,
               Present value factor = 0.74622
Step   2
(modified)   Present value = $1,000.00 × 0.74622 = $746.22

The result is identical (except for a small rounding error) to the one in the previous example which was solved using Table 30-1 and division. To solve present value problems, you may use either table. If you prefer to use Table

TABLE 30-2 Present Value of $1.00

Period (n)	1.00%	1.25%	1.50%	2.00%	3.00%	4.00%	5.00%	6.00%	8.00%	9.00%	10.00%	12.00%	15.00%	18.00%
1	0.99010	0.98765	0.98522	0.98039	0.97087	0.96154	0.95238	0.94340	0.92593	0.91743	0.90909	0.89286	0.86957	0.84746
2	0.98030	0.97546	0.97066	0.96117	0.94260	0.92456	0.90703	0.89000	0.85734	0.84168	0.82645	0.79719	0.75614	0.71818
3	0.97059	0.96342	0.95632	0.94232	0.91514	0.88900	0.86384	0.83962	0.79383	0.77218	0.75131	0.71178	0.65752	0.60863
4	0.96098	0.95152	0.94218	0.92385	0.88849	0.85480	0.82270	0.79209	0.73503	0.70843	0.68301	0.63552	0.57175	0.51579
5	0.95147	0.93978	0.92826	0.90573	0.86261	0.82193	0.78353	0.74726	0.68058	0.64993	0.62092	0.56743	0.49718	0.43711
6	0.94205	0.92817	0.91454	0.88797	0.83748	0.79031	0.74622	0.70496	0.63017	0.59627	0.56447	0.50663	0.43233	0.37043
7	0.93272	0.91672	0.90103	0.87056	0.81309	0.75992	0.71068	0.66506	0.58349	0.54703	0.51316	0.45235	0.37594	0.31393
8	0.92348	0.90540	0.88771	0.85349	0.78941	0.73069	0.67684	0.62741	0.54027	0.50187	0.46651	0.40388	0.32690	0.26604
9	0.91434	0.89422	0.87459	0.83676	0.76642	0.70259	0.64461	0.59190	0.50025	0.46043	0.42410	0.36061	0.28426	0.22546
10	0.90529	0.88318	0.86167	0.82035	0.74409	0.67556	0.61391	0.55839	0.46319	0.42241	0.38554	0.32197	0.24718	0.19106
11	0.89632	0.87228	0.84893	0.80426	0.72242	0.64958	0.58468	0.52679	0.42888	0.38753	0.35049	0.28748	0.21494	0.16192
12	0.88745	0.86151	0.83639	0.78849	0.70138	0.62460	0.55684	0.49697	0.39711	0.35553	0.31863	0.25668	0.18691	0.13722
13	0.87866	0.85087	0.82403	0.77303	0.68095	0.60057	0.53032	0.46884	0.36770	0.32618	0.28966	0.22917	0.16253	0.11629
14	0.86996	0.84037	0.81185	0.75788	0.66112	0.57748	0.50507	0.44230	0.34046	0.29925	0.26333	0.20462	0.14133	0.09855
15	0.86135	0.82999	0.79985	0.74301	0.64186	0.55526	0.48102	0.41727	0.31524	0.27454	0.23939	0.18270	0.12289	0.08352
16	0.85282	0.81975	0.78803	0.72845	0.62317	0.53391	0.45811	0.39365	0.29189	0.25187	0.21763	0.16312	0.10686	0.07078
17	0.84438	0.80963	0.77639	0.71416	0.60502	0.51337	0.43630	0.37136	0.27027	0.23107	0.19784	0.14564	0.09293	0.05998
18	0.83602	0.79963	0.76491	0.70016	0.58739	0.49363	0.41552	0.35034	0.25025	0.21199	0.17986	0.13004	0.08081	0.05083
19	0.82774	0.78976	0.75361	0.68643	0.57029	0.47464	0.39573	0.33051	0.23171	0.19449	0.16351	0.11611	0.07027	0.04308
20	0.81954	0.78001	0.74247	0.67297	0.55368	0.45639	0.37689	0.31180	0.21455	0.17843	0.14864	0.10367	0.06110	0.03651
21	0.81143	0.77038	0.73150	0.65978	0.53755	0.43883	0.35894	0.29416	0.19866	0.16370	0.13513	0.09256	0.05313	0.03094
22	0.80340	0.76087	0.72069	0.64684	0.52189	0.42196	0.34185	0.27751	0.18394	0.15018	0.12285	0.08264	0.04620	0.02622
23	0.79544	0.75147	0.71004	0.63416	0.50669	0.40573	0.32557	0.26180	0.17032	0.13778	0.11168	0.07379	0.04017	0.02222
24	0.78757	0.74220	0.69954	0.62172	0.49193	0.39012	0.31007	0.24698	0.15770	0.12640	0.10153	0.06588	0.03493	0.01883
25	0.77977	0.73303	0.68921	0.60953	0.47761	0.37512	0.29530	0.23300	0.14602	0.11597	0.09230	0.05882	0.03038	0.01596
26	0.77205	0.72398	0.67902	0.59758	0.46369	0.36069	0.28124	0.21981	0.13520	0.10639	0.08391	0.05252	0.02642	0.01352
27	0.76440	0.71505	0.66899	0.58586	0.45019	0.34682	0.26785	0.20737	0.12519	0.09761	0.07628	0.04689	0.02297	0.01146
28	0.75684	0.70622	0.65910	0.57437	0.43708	0.33348	0.25509	0.19563	0.11591	0.08955	0.06934	0.04187	0.01997	0.00971
29	0.74934	0.69750	0.64936	0.56311	0.42435	0.32065	0.24295	0.18456	0.10733	0.08215	0.06304	0.03738	0.01737	0.00823
30	0.74192	0.68889	0.63976	0.55207	0.41199	0.30832	0.23138	0.17411	0.09938	0.07537	0.05731	0.03338	0.01510	0.00697

30-1 (the future value table) it still is important for you to understand how to use the present value table method.

RELATIONSHIP BETWEEN TABLES 30-1 AND 30-2

As you might have guessed, there is a close mathematical relationship between the entries in Table 30-1 and the corresponding entries in Table 30-2: they are **reciprocals** of each other. That means that if you take an entry from Table 30-1 and divide it into the number 1, the quotient is the corresponding entry in Table 30-2. The reverse also is true.

$$\frac{1}{\text{Table 30-1 Factor}} = \text{Table } \textbf{30-2} \text{ factor}$$

$$\frac{1}{\text{Table 30-1 Factor}} = \text{Table } \textbf{30-1} \text{ factor}$$

j. Find the reciprocal of the compound amount factor in the 3% column and 8th row of Table 30-1. (Do not round off.) Compare the result with the present value factor in the 3% column and 8th row of Table 30-2.

The compound amount factor in the 3% column and the 8th row is 1.26677
Its reciprocal is $1 \div 1.26677 = 0.789409285$
The present value factor in the 3% column and the 8th row is 0.78941
The only difference is in the rounding.

Likewise, if you take an entry from Table 30-2 and divide it into the number 1, the quotient is the corresponding entry in Table 30-1.

k. Find the reciprocal of the present value factor in the 5% column and 6th row of Table 30-2. (Do not round off.) Compare the result with the compound amount factor in the 5% column and 6th row of Table 30-1.

The present value factor in the 5% column and the 6th row is 0.74622
Its reciprocal is $1 \div 0.74622 = 1.340087$
The compound amount factor in the 5% column and the 6th row is 1.34010
The only difference is in the rounding.

COMPLETE ASSIGNMENT 30-2

Chapter terms for review

compound interest
compound amount
compound amount factor
future value
number of compounding periods

periodic interest rate
present value
present value factor
reciprocal

Assignment 30-1: Compound Amount (Future Value)

A (44 points) — Solve for the compound amount (future value) and the compound interest earned in each of the following investments (3 points for each correct compound amount, 1 point for each correct compound interest).

	Principal	Interest Rate	Time	Compound Amount	Compound Interest
1.	$ 1,000	9% compounded annually	20 years	_____	_____
2.	6,600	12% compounded semiannually	12 years	_____	_____
3.	600	12% compounded quarterly	7 years	_____	_____
4.	11,000	15% compounded monthly	2 years	_____	_____
5.	4,200	16% compounded semiannually	8 years	_____	_____
6.	850	12% compounded annually	6 years	_____	_____
7.	25,000	18% compounded monthly	15 months	_____	_____
8.	1,900	8% compounded quarterly	33 months	_____	_____
9.	16,600	12% compounded monthly	$\frac{3}{4}$ year	_____	_____
10.	500	10% compounded semiannually	10 years	_____	_____
11.	2,800	16% compounded quarterly	$4\frac{1}{2}$ years	_____	_____

Score for A (44)

B (20 points) — Solve for the compound amount (future value) in each of the following (5 points for each correct answer).

12. $1,200 is invested for 5 years at 8% compounded annually.

_____

13. $2,500 is deposited for 11 months into an account that pays 12% compounded monthly.

_____

14. $800 is borrowed for 2 years at 8% compounded quarterly.

_____

15. $10,000 is loaned for 18 months at 12% compounded semiannually.

_____

C (36 points) — Solve for the compound amount (future value) or the compound interest, as indicated (6 points for each correct answer).

16. Ray Wilson put $1,450 cash into his credit union which pays interest of 12% compounded monthly for deposits of two years or more. What will be the compound amount in $2\frac{1}{2}$ years?

_____

17. Mark Curto intends to take his family on a vacation cruise in three years. To have enough money, he invests $4,000 today at a rate that will return 9% annually. How much will his investment be worth at the end of three years?

_____

18. The Piedmont Bank will loan money to small businesses at 8% compounded quarterly. Mary Weifang's stationery store borrows $2,600 for 30 months. How much will Mary have to pay in interest?

_____

19. Wanda Green inherited $3,800. She decided to invest it all to help pay for her daughter's education. What would be the future value of her investment in eight years if she invested it all in a fund that paid 10% compounded semiannually?

_____

20. Davis Plumbing received $32,000 from their insurance company for some fire damage to a warehouse. Rather than use the money now, they were able to invest it at 15% compounded monthly. What will be the value of the investment 17 months from now?

_____

21. Takashi Savings pays 12% compounded quarterly on investments of more than $5,000 for more than five years. How much interest will Takashi have to pay if Ann Tullis deposits $6,600 for 7 years?

_____

Assignment 30-2: Present Value

A **(44 points)** — Solve for the present value (principal) and the compound interest earned in each of the following investments (3 points for each correct present value and 1 point for each correct compound interest).

	Compound Amount	Interest Rate	Time	Present Value	Compound Interest
1.	$12,600	10% compounded semiannually	8 years	_____	_____
2.	1,700	8% compounded quarterly	5 years	_____	_____
3.	3,300	9% compounded annually	15 years	_____	_____
4.	850	15% compounded monthly	2 years	_____	_____
5.	26,500	16% compounded quarterly	3 years	_____	_____
6.	8,100	12% compounded monthly	$1\frac{3}{4}$ years	_____	_____
7.	2,500	6% compounded semiannually	14 years	_____	_____
8.	900	15% compounded annually	10 years	_____	_____
9.	31,600	18% compounded monthly	$1\frac{1}{4}$ years	_____	_____
10.	2,500	12% compounded quarterly	7 years	_____	_____
11.	7,200	8% compounded semiannually	13 years	_____	_____

Score for A (44)

B **(20 points)** — Solve for the present value in each of the following problems (5 points for each correct answer).

12. How much must you invest today at 12% compounded quarterly to have $2,000 in 3 years?

_____

13. How much must you deposit today into an account that pays 10% compounded annually to have $6,400 in 10 years?

_____

14. How much must you invest today at 10% compounded semiannually to have $1,500 in 2 years?

_____

15. How much must you lend today at 15% compounded monthly to be repaid a total (principal and interest) of $800 in 6 months?

_____

C **(36 points) — Solve for the present value, compound amount or compound interest, as indicated (6 points for each correct answer).**

16. Sandee Millet will need $250 in one year. She can earn interest of 12% compounded quarterly. How much should she deposit today?

_____

17. Jim Spurgeon just deposited $14,000 in the Coquille Valley Bank at 12% compounded annually. How much interest will Jim earn if he leaves the entire amount deposited for five years?

_____

18. Karen Ong wants to buy a new copier in two years. She estimates that the cost will be $2,600. How much should she deposit today into an investment that promises to pay 15% compounded monthly?

_____

19. Carol Brandon deposited a large sum of money at 12% compounded quarterly. Then she moved to South America for four years for her job. When she returned, the account contained a total of $12,000. How much money did Carol deposit four years ago?

_____

20. Jeff Atkins will lend money for five years at 10% compounded semiannnually. Lorna Roe borrows $4,600 from Jeff. In five years she repays the amount she borrowed plus all of the interest. How much in total did she repay?

_____

21. John Koramatsu is planning to replace one of his delivery trucks two years from now. He plans that the price of a new truck will then be $20,000. How much does John need to deposit today in a 2-year account that promises to pay 12% compounded monthly?

_____

Chapter 31
Annuities

OBJECTIVES
After completing this chapter, you should be able to:

- Understand the concept of an annuity
- Compute future and present values of ordinary annuities
- Compute the periodic payment of an annuity
- Develop loan amortization tables

The word *annuity* means a series of **equal** payments that are made at **regular, equal** time intervals. Interest is compounded at the end of each time period, coinciding with each payment. There are several commercial applications for annuities: installment payments, some insurance policies, savings and loan payments, and bonds are a few examples.

ANNUITY

Diagram an annuity by drawing a straight line, called a *time line*. Mark off and label the time periods on the time line. Then draw in the regular payments. If there are four payments in the annuity, then there must be four time periods shown on the time line. Likewise, if there are four time periods in the annuity, then there must be four payments.

a. Assume today is December 31, 1992. At the end of each year for four years, $1,000 will be deposited into a bank account. The first deposit will be made on December 31, 1993 and the last will made be on December 31, 1996.

Notice that each $1,000 payment comes at the **end** of a period. This is true in an *ordinary annuity*. There is another type of annuity, called an *annuity due*, where each payment comes at the **beginning** of each period. In this text, we will consider only ordinary annuities.

Notice in Figure 31-1 that there are four payments and four periods. The annuity starts at the beginning of the first period; it is completed at the end of the last period. In this example, the annuity starts on December 31, 1992, even though the first payment is not until December 31, 1993.

FIGURE 31-1
Diagram of an
Ordinary Annuity

Date	12/31/92	12/31/93	12/31/94	12/31/95	12/31/96
Period		1	2	3	4	
Payment	$0	$1,000	$1,000	$1,000	$1,000

FUTURE VALUE OF AN ANNUITY

When people save money at the end of each month, they want to know how much principal and interest they are accumulating. The *amount of an annuity* is the accumulated cash value at the end of the annuity term (at the end of the last period). The amount includes the sum of all payments plus the accumulated compound interest on all payments. Since the amount is the value that will occur in the **future**, the amount often is called the *future value of an annuity*. In this book we generally use the term future value instead of amount. The term amount is correct, but it also has many other meanings.

As shown in example b. the future value of an annuity may be calculated by considering each payment separately and then adding the answers.

b. Assume: today is December 31, 1992; the bank account is empty; at each year-end for four years, $1,000 is deposited into the account; 10% interest is compounded at each year-end; the first deposit will be made December 31, 1993; the last deposit will be made December 31, 1996.

What is the future value of the annuity? That is, what is the value of the annuity on December 31, 1996?

To find the future value of the annuity on December 31, 1996, first use Table 30-1 on page 376 to determine what would be the future value of each of the four payments on December 31, 1996. Then calculate the total.

Amount of Payment	Date	Years of Interest	Future Value on 12/31/96
$1,000	12/31/93	3	$1,000 × 1.33100 = $1,331
$1,000	12/31/94	2	$1,000 × 1.21000 = $1,210
$1,000	12/31/95	1	$1,000 × 1.10000 = $1,100
$1,000	12/31/96	0	$1,000 × 1.00000 = $1,000

Future value of the annuity on 12/31/96 = $4,641

Figure 31-2 illustrates how each of the four payments is moving forward in time to December 31, 1996.

FIGURE 31-2
Future Value of an
Ordinary Annuity

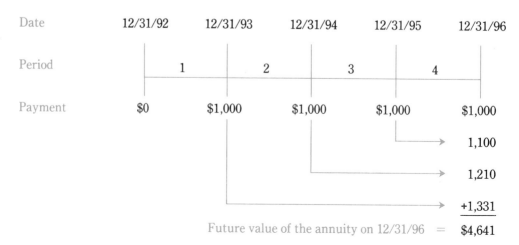

Date	12/31/92	12/31/93	12/31/94	12/31/95	12/31/96
Period		1	2	3	4	
Payment	$0	$1,000	$1,000	$1,000	$1,000
					1,100
					1,210
					+1,331

Future value of the annuity on 12/31/96 = $4,641

ANNUITY TABLES

The annuity calculations above are time-consuming even for just four payments. With 20 or 30 payments, the calculations would be tiresome. Table 31-1 on page 388, which eliminates these tedious computations by providing an *annuity factor*, is used the same as Table 30-1. As in Chapter 30, the column indicates the periodic interest rate and the row indicates the number of periods.

Steps for Using Future Value Annuity Tables

1. Locate the annuity factor in the correct row and column.
2. Multiply the size, in dollars, of each payment by the annuity factor.
3. Multiply the payment amount by the number of payments to determine the total of the payments.
4. Subtract the total of the payments (from Step 3) from the product in Step 2 to determine the total interest.

c. Find the future value of an annuity of four $1,000 annual payments. Each payment is made at the end of the year and 10% interest is compounded each year. Also find the total interest earned over the four years.

Step 1   The annuity factor from Table 31-1 is 4.64100
Step 2   Future value of the annuity = $1,000 × 4.64100 = $4,641
Step 3   Total of the payments = 4 × $1,000 = $4,000
Step 4   Total interest = $4,641 − $4,000 = $641

Finding Annuity Amounts for Periods Other Than One Year

Payments may occur more often than once a year. The only additional requirement for an ordinary annuity is that the interest be compounded at the same time the payments are made. It may occur semiannually, quarterly, monthly, etc. The method is the same as was described in Chapter 30 and Steps *i–iii* are used in this chapter also. However, in this chapter the number calculated in Step *iii* means not only the number of compounding periods but also the number of payments.

d. Find the future value of an annuity where $200 is deposited at the end of each quarter for three years. Interest is 8%, compounded quarterly.

Step   *i*   There are 4 compounding periods in one year
Step   *ii*   Periodic interest rate = 8% ÷ 4 = 2% per period
Step   *iii*   Number of payments = 3 years × 4 = 12 payments
Step   1   Using Table 31-1, 2% column and 12th row annuity factor = 13.41209
Step   2   Future value = $200.00 × 13.41209 = $2,682.418 or $2,682.42

COMPLETE ASSIGNMENT 31-1

PRESENT VALUE OF AN ANNUITY

The annuities above had the equal payments **deposited into** an account each period. However, the equal payments can just as easily be **taken out of** the account each period. The *present value of an annuity* is the dollar amount needed at the **beginning** in order to be able to take out, or pay out, annuity payments of a certain dollar amount at certain regular intervals in the future.

TABLE 31-1   Future Value (Amount) of an Ordinary Annuity of $1.00

Period (n)	1.00%	1.25%	1.50%	2.00%	3.00%	4.00%	5.00%	6.00%	8.00%	9.00%	10.00%	12.00%	15.00%	18.00%
1	1.00000	1.00000	1.00000	1.00000	1.00000	1.00000	1.00000	1.00000	1.00000	1.00000	1.00000	1.00000	1.00000	1.00000
2	2.01000	2.01250	2.01500	2.02000	2.03000	2.04000	2.05000	2.06000	2.08000	2.09000	2.10000	2.12000	2.15000	2.18000
3	3.03010	3.03766	3.04522	3.06040	3.09090	3.12160	3.15250	3.18360	3.24640	3.27810	3.31000	3.37440	3.47250	3.57240
4	4.06040	4.07563	4.09090	4.12161	4.18363	4.24646	4.31013	4.37462	4.50611	4.57313	4.64100	4.77933	4.99338	5.21543
5	5.10101	5.12657	5.15227	5.20404	5.30914	5.41632	5.52563	5.63709	5.86660	5.98471	6.10510	6.35285	6.74238	7.15421
6	6.15202	6.19065	6.22955	6.30812	6.46841	6.63298	6.80191	6.97532	7.33593	7.52333	7.71561	8.11519	8.75374	9.44197
7	7.21354	7.26804	7.32299	7.43428	7.66246	7.89829	8.14201	8.39384	8.92280	9.20043	9.48717	10.08901	11.06680	12.14152
8	8.28567	8.35889	8.43284	8.58297	8.89234	9.21423	9.54911	9.89747	10.63663	11.02847	11.43589	12.29969	13.72682	15.32700
9	9.36853	9.46337	9.55933	9.75463	10.15911	10.58280	11.02656	11.49132	12.48756	13.02104	13.57948	14.77566	16.78584	19.08585
10	10.46221	10.58167	10.70272	10.94972	11.46388	12.00611	12.57789	13.18079	14.48656	15.19293	15.93742	17.54874	20.30372	23.52131
11	11.56683	11.71394	11.86326	12.16872	12.80780	13.48635	14.20679	14.97164	16.64549	17.56029	18.53117	20.65458	24.34928	28.75514
12	12.68250	12.86036	13.04121	13.41209	14.19203	15.02581	15.91713	16.86994	18.97713	20.14072	21.38428	24.13313	29.00167	34.93107
13	13.80933	14.02112	14.23683	14.68033	15.61779	16.62684	17.71298	18.88214	21.49530	22.95338	24.52271	28.02911	34.35192	42.21866
14	14.94742	15.19638	15.45038	15.97394	17.08632	18.29191	19.59863	21.01507	24.21492	26.01919	27.97498	32.39260	40.50471	50.81802
15	16.09690	16.38633	16.68214	17.29342	18.59891	20.02359	21.57856	23.27597	27.15211	29.36092	31.77248	37.27971	47.58041	60.96527
16	17.25786	17.59116	17.93237	18.63929	20.15688	21.82453	23.65749	25.67253	30.32428	33.00340	35.94973	42.75328	55.71747	72.93901
17	18.43044	18.81105	19.20136	20.01207	21.76159	23.69751	25.84037	28.21288	33.75023	36.97370	40.54470	48.88367	65.07509	87.06804
18	19.61475	20.04619	20.48938	21.41231	23.41444	25.64541	28.13238	30.90565	37.45024	41.30134	45.59917	55.74971	75.83636	103.74028
19	20.81090	21.29677	21.79672	22.84056	25.11687	27.67123	30.53900	33.75999	41.44626	46.01846	51.15909	63.43968	88.21181	123.41353
20	22.01900	22.56298	23.12367	24.29737	26.87037	29.77808	33.06595	36.78559	45.76196	51.16012	57.27500	72.05244	102.44358	146.62797
21	23.23919	23.84502	24.47052	25.78332	28.67649	31.96920	35.71925	39.99273	50.42292	56.76453	64.00250	81.69874	118.81012	174.02100
22	24.47159	25.14308	25.83758	27.29898	30.53678	34.24797	38.50521	43.39229	55.45676	62.87334	71.40275	92.50258	137.63164	206.34479
23	25.71630	26.45737	27.22514	28.84496	32.45288	36.61789	41.43048	46.99583	60.89330	69.53194	79.54302	104.60289	159.27638	244.48685
24	26.97346	27.78808	28.63352	30.42186	34.42647	39.08260	44.50200	50.81558	66.76476	76.78981	88.49733	118.15524	184.16784	289.49448
25	28.24320	29.13544	30.06302	32.03030	36.45926	41.64591	47.72710	54.86451	73.10594	84.70090	98.34706	133.33387	212.79302	342.60349
26	29.52563	30.49963	31.51397	33.67091	38.55304	44.31174	51.11345	59.15638	79.95442	93.32398	109.18177	150.33393	245.71197	405.27211
27	30.82089	31.88087	32.98668	35.34432	40.70963	47.08421	54.66913	63.70577	87.35077	102.72313	121.09994	169.37401	283.56877	479.22109
28	32.12910	33.27938	34.48148	37.05121	42.93092	49.96758	58.40258	68.52811	95.33883	112.96822	134.20994	190.69889	327.10408	566.48089
29	33.45039	34.69538	35.99870	38.79223	45.21885	52.96629	62.32271	73.63980	103.96594	124.13536	148.63093	214.58275	377.16969	669.44745
30	34.78489	36.12907	37.53868	40.56808	47.57542	56.08494	66.43885	79.05819	113.28321	136.30754	164.49402	241.33268	434.74515	790.94799

e. On December 31, 1992, a businessman buys a forklift. In addition to the purchase price, he deposits money into an account to provide for four withdrawals of $1000 to be taken out on December 31 each year to pay for maintenance on the forklift. Interest of 10% will be compounded each year. After the fourth withdrawal, the account will be empty. How much needs to be deposited into the account on December 31, 1992?

To find the present value of the annuity on December 31, 1992, first use Table 30-2 on page 379 to find the present value of each of the four payments on December 31, 1992. Then calculate the total.

Amount of Withdrawal	Date	Years of Interest	Present Value on 12/31/92
$1,000	12/31/93	1	$1,000 × 0.90909 = $ 909.09
$1,000	12/31/94	2	$1,000 × 0.82645 = 826.45
$1,000	12/31/95	3	$1,000 × 0.75131 = 751.31
$1,000	12/31/96	4	$1,000 × 0.68301 = 683.01

Present value of the annuity on 12/31/92 = $3,169.86

Example e. is illustrated by the diagram in Figure 31-3 on page 390. The equal withdrawals are shown along the time line and each payment is moved from the "future" back to the "present" (to December 31, 1992). In Figure 31-2, each payment was projected into the future.

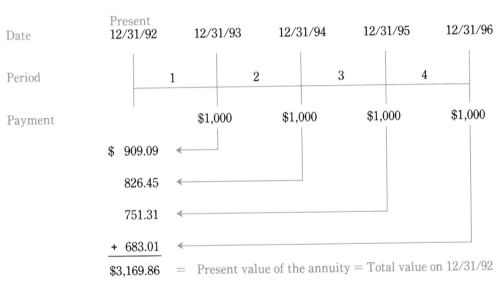

FIGURE 31-3
Present Value of an Ordinary Annuity

The method shown above is useful for instruction but is too time consuming to be practical. To give the same solution quickly, Table 31-2 has been developed.

Steps for Using Present Value Annuity Tables

1. Locate the annuity factor in the correct column and row.
2. Multiply the size of a payment by the annuity factor. The product is the present value of the annuity.

Thus, for example e. using Table 31-2, the factor in the 10% column and 4th row is 3.16987 (Step 1) and $1,000 × 3.16987 = $3,169.87 (Step 2).

The following application may not sound time consuming, but even it would be difficult to do without Table 31-2.

f. You buy an insurance policy that will provide payments of $500 each quarter for five years, from age 65 to 70. Interest of 12% will be paid on the remaining balance in account each quarter. After the last payment at age 70, the account will be empty. This is an annuity. The amount of money that you need in the account at the beginning is called the present value of the annuity.

Step   *i*   There are 4 compounding periods in one year.
Step *ii*   Periodic interest rate = 12% ÷ 4 = 3% per period.
Step *iii* Number of payments = 5 years × 4 = 20.
Step 1   Using Table **31-2**, 3% column and 20th row annuity factor = 14.87747
Step 2   Present value = $500.00 × 14.87747 = $7,438.735 or $7,438.74

FINDING THE SIZE OF THE PAYMENTS

In previous examples, the size of the annuity payment was given. The unknown amounts were either the future value or the present value of the annuity. The problems were solved by using **multiplication** after finding an annuity factor from either Table 31-1 or 31-2. Thus, if the future value or present value of the annuity is given, you can solve for the size of the annuity payment by using **division** and the annuity factor from Table **31-1** or **31-2**.

g. You want to have $5,000 at the end of 2 years. Your bank account pays 12% compounded monthly. How much do you need to deposit each month in order to have exactly $5,000 at the end of two years?

Step   *i*   There are 12 compounding periods in one year
Step *ii*   Periodic Interest Rate = 12% ÷ 12 = 1% per period
Step *iii* Number of Deposits = 2 years × 12 = 24 deposits
Step 1   Using Table **31-1**, 1% column and 24th row annuity factor = 26.97346
Step 2* The future value of the annuity = $5,000. Thus, the size of each deposit = $5,000 ÷ 26.97346 = $185.36739 or $185.37

     * Note: When you solve for the payment, division is used in Step 2 in place of multiplication.

h. You deposit $10,000 in the bank today. You want to withdraw the same amount at the end of each month for 2 years. At the end of the 2 years, after the last withdrawal, the account will be empty. The account pays 12% compounded monthly. What must be the size of each withdrawal?

Step   *i*   There are 12 compounding periods in one year
Step *ii*   Periodic interest rate = 12% ÷ 12 = 1% per period
Step *iii* Number of withdrawals = 2 years × 12 = 24 withdrawals
Step 1   Use Table **31-2**. In the 1% column and 24th row, the annuity factor = 21.24339
Step 2   Size of each withdrawal = $10,000 ÷ 21.24339 = $470.73466 or $470.73 (See *note in example g.)

AMORTIZATION

In Chapter 19 repaying a loan by amortization was introduced. When a loan is amortized, the borrower makes equal payments at the end of every month (or quarter, year, etc.). The payments include both principal and interest on the unpaid balance. This is an annuity because (1) the payments are equal, (2) they come at the end of regular periods, and (3) there is interest

TABLE 31-2 Present Value of an Ordinary Annuity of $1.00

Period (n)	1.00%	1.25%	1.50%	2.00%	3.00%	4.00%	5.00%	6.00%	8.00%	9.00%	10.00%	12.00%	15.00%	18.00%
1	0.99010	0.98765	0.98522	0.98039	0.97087	0.96154	0.95238	0.94340	0.92593	0.91743	0.90909	0.89286	0.86957	0.84746
2	1.97040	1.96312	1.95588	1.94156	1.91347	1.88609	1.85941	1.83339	1.78326	1.75911	1.73554	1.69005	1.62571	1.56564
3	2.94099	2.92653	2.91220	2.88388	2.82861	2.77509	2.72325	2.67301	2.57710	2.53129	2.48685	2.40183	2.28323	2.17427
4	3.90197	3.87806	3.85438	3.80773	3.71710	3.62990	3.54595	3.46511	3.31213	3.23972	3.16987	3.03735	2.85498	2.69006
5	4.85343	4.81784	4.78264	4.71346	4.57971	4.45182	4.32948	4.21236	3.99271	3.88965	3.79079	3.60478	3.35216	3.12717
6	5.79548	5.74601	5.69719	5.60143	5.41719	5.24214	5.07569	4.91732	4.62288	4.48592	4.35526	4.11141	3.78448	3.49760
7	6.72819	6.66273	6.59821	6.47199	6.23028	6.00205	5.78637	5.58238	5.20637	5.03295	4.86842	4.56376	4.16042	3.81153
8	7.65168	7.56812	7.48593	7.32548	7.01969	6.73274	6.46321	6.20979	5.74664	5.53482	5.33493	4.96764	4.48732	4.07757
9	8.56602	8.46234	8.36052	8.16224	7.78611	7.43533	7.10782	6.80169	6.24689	5.99525	5.75902	5.32825	4.77158	4.30302
10	9.47130	9.34553	9.22218	8.98259	8.53020	8.11090	7.72173	7.36009	6.71008	6.41766	6.14457	5.65022	5.01877	4.49409
11	10.36763	10.21780	10.07112	9.78685	9.25262	8.76048	8.30641	7.88687	7.13896	6.80519	6.49506	5.93770	5.23371	4.65601
12	11.25508	11.07931	10.90751	10.57534	9.95400	9.38507	8.86325	8.38384	7.53608	7.16073	6.81369	6.19437	5.42062	4.79322
13	12.13374	11.93018	11.73153	11.34837	10.63496	9.98565	9.39357	8.85268	7.90378	7.48690	7.10336	6.42355	5.58315	4.90951
14	13.00370	12.77055	12.54338	12.10625	11.29607	10.56312	9.89864	9.29498	8.24424	7.78615	7.36669	6.62817	5.72448	5.00806
15	13.86505	13.60055	13.34323	12.84926	11.93794	11.11839	10.37966	9.71225	8.55948	8.06069	7.60608	6.81086	5.84737	5.09158
16	14.71787	14.42029	14.13126	13.57771	12.56110	11.65230	10.83777	10.10590	8.85137	8.31256	7.82371	6.97399	5.95423	5.16235
17	15.56225	15.22992	14.90765	14.29187	13.16612	12.16567	11.27407	10.47726	9.12164	8.54363	8.02155	7.11963	6.04716	5.22233
18	16.39827	16.02955	15.67256	14.99203	13.75351	12.65930	11.68959	10.82760	9.37189	8.75563	8.20141	7.24967	6.12797	5.27316
19	17.22601	16.81931	16.42617	15.67846	14.32380	13.13394	12.08532	11.15812	9.60360	8.95011	8.36492	7.36578	6.19823	5.31624
20	18.04555	17.59932	17.16864	16.35143	14.87747	13.59033	12.46221	11.46992	9.81815	9.12855	8.51356	7.46944	6.25933	5.35275
21	18.85698	18.36969	17.90014	17.01121	15.41502	14.02916	12.82115	11.76408	10.01680	9.29224	8.64869	7.56200	6.31246	5.38368
22	19.66038	19.13056	18.62082	17.65805	15.93692	14.45112	13.16300	12.04158	10.20074	9.44243	8.77154	7.64465	6.35866	5.40990
23	20.45582	19.88204	19.33086	18.29220	16.44361	14.85684	13.48857	12.30338	10.37106	9.58021	8.88322	7.71843	6.39884	5.43212
24	21.24339	20.62423	20.03041	18.91393	16.93554	15.24696	13.79864	12.55036	10.52876	9.70661	8.98474	7.78432	6.43377	5.45095
25	22.02316	21.35727	20.71961	19.52346	17.41315	15.62208	14.09394	12.78336	10.67478	9.82258	9.07704	7.84314	6.46415	5.46691
26	22.79520	22.08125	21.39863	20.12104	17.87684	15.98277	14.37519	13.00317	10.80998	9.92897	9.16095	7.89566	6.49056	5.48043
27	23.55961	22.79630	22.06762	20.70690	18.32703	16.32959	14.64303	13.21053	10.93516	10.02658	9.23722	7.94255	6.51353	5.49189
28	24.31644	23.50252	22.72672	21.28127	18.76411	16.66306	14.89813	13.40616	11.05108	10.11613	9.30657	7.98442	6.53351	5.50160
29	25.06579	24.20002	23.37608	21.84438	19.18845	16.98371	15.14107	13.59072	11.15841	10.19828	9.36961	8.02181	6.55088	5.50983
30	25.80771	24.88891	24.01584	22.39646	19.60044	17.29203	15.37245	13.76483	11.25778	10.27365	9.42691	8.05518	6.56598	5.51681

calculated on the balance at the end of each period. The amount borrowed occurs at the beginning of the annuity arrangement, so it is the present value of the annuity.

1. Locate the annuity factor in the proper table.
2. Divide the amount borrowed (present value) by the annuity factor. The quotient is the size of the monthly (quarterly or annual) payments.

i. Julie Johnson borrows $2,400. Find the size of the payment needed to amortize the loan over four months at 12%.

Step *i* There are 12 compounding periods in one year
Step *ii* Periodic interest rate = 12% ÷ 12 = 1% per period
Step *iii* Number of monthly payments = 4
Step 1 Since the $2,400 borrowed occurs at the **beginning** of the annuity, it is a present value problem and $2,400 = present value of the annuity; use Table **31-2**. In the 1% column and 4th row, the annuity factor = 3.90197
Step 2 Size of each withdrawal = $2,400 ÷ 3.90197 = $615.07392 or $615.07

1. Calculate the interest due for each period by multiplying the period's beginning unpaid balance by the interest rate for the period.
2. Subtract the interest from the annuity payment amount to determine the principal payment.
3. Calculate the new balance by subtracting the principal payment from the period's beginning unpaid balance. For the final payment, calculate the interest as usual; then add the interest to the unpaid balance. The sum is the final payment amount. Note: The final payment frequently is different from the other payments due to rounding.

Table 31-3 presents the amortization schedule for example *i*. Note: Each month's beginning unpaid balance is multiplied by the monthly interest rate (1%).

TABLE 31-3
Amortization
Schedule

Month	Beginning Unpaid Balance	Step 1 (1%) Interest Payment	Annuity Payment	Step 2 Principal Payment	Step 3 New Balance
1	$2,400.00	$24.00	$615.07	$591.07	$1,808.93
2	1,808.93	18.09	615.07	596.98	1,211.95
3	1,211.95	12.12	615.07	602.95	609.00
4	609.00	6.09	615.09	609.00	0

Chapter terms for review

amount of an annuity
annuity
annuity due
annuity factor

future value of an annuity
ordinary annuity
present value of an annuity
time line

Assignment 31-1: Annuities — Future Value

A (44 points) — For each of the following annuities, solve for the missing number (4 points for each correct answer).

	Payment Amount	Payment Periods	Interest Rate	Length of Annuity	Future Value
1.	$10,000.00	annually	10% compounded annually	10 years	
2.		monthly	18% compounded monthly	1 year	2,000.00
3.	750.00	semiannually	8% compounded semiannually	5 years	
4.		quarterly	8% compounded quarterly	4 years	24,250.00
5.	200.00	monthly	12% compounded monthly	2 years	
6.		semiannually	16% compounded semiannually	13 years	64,000.00
7.	2,500.00	annually	6% compounded annually	25 years	
8.		quarterly	12% compounded quarterly	30 months	10,000.00
9.	15,000.00	annually	8% compounded annually	8 years	
10.		semiannually	12% compounded semiannually	6 years	25,000.00
11.	1,200.00	quarterly	16% compounded quarterly	4.5 years	

Score for A (44)

B (20 points) — Solve for the future value or the periodic payment, as indicated (5 points for each correct answer).

12. What is the future value if $600 is invested each quarter for 3 years and interest is 8% compounded quarterly?

_____

13. How much needs to be deposited each year into an account that pays 12% compounded annually in order to have $5,000 at the end of 10 years?

_____

14. What monthly investment is needed to accumulate $7,500 after 18 months if the investment returns 12% compounded monthly?

_____

15. How much will be accumulated at the end of 8 years if $2,500 is invested each six months into an investment that returns 10% compounded semiannually?

_____

C **(36 points) Solve each of the following annuity problems (6 points for each correct answer).**

16. Carol Endo deposited $125 each month into her credit union account which pays interest of 15% compounded monthly. How much will be in her account at the end of $1\frac{1}{2}$ years?

_____

17. Felipe Sanchez is an attorney who invests $4,500 each six months in a fund which returns 10% compounded semiannually. What is the total amount in the fund after 10 years?

_____

18. Rebecca Garland is saving for her retirement. For 7 years she puts $1,500 each quarter into a savings bank account that gives interest of 8% compounded quarterly. How much is in the account after 7 years?

_____

19. Davis Co. will need $500,000 in 10 years to repay a loan. To have the money available Davis plans to deposit a fixed amount each year in an account that will pay 9% compounded annually. What is the annual deposit?

_____

20. Mihalyi Kennels will need a new building in 2 years. The estimated cost is $150,000. How much should they deposit each month into a bank that pays 12% compounded monthly in order to have the $150,000 in 2 years?

_____

21. Olga Rocza is a sculptress who wants to build her own studio. If she can save $12,500 each quarter and get a return of 12% compounded quarterly, how much will she have accumulated by the end of $5\frac{1}{2}$ years?

_____

Assignment 31-2:   Annuities—Present Value

A **(44 points) — For each of the following annuities, solve for the missing number (4 points for each correct answer).**

	Payment Amount	Payment Periods	Interest Rate	Length of Annuity	Present Value
1.	$ 1,100.00	quarterly	16% compounded quarterly	4 years	
2.	_____	semiannually	10% compounded semiannually	11 years	86,200.00
3.	250.00	monthly	15% compounded monthly	2 years	
4.	_____	annually	9% compounded annually	8 years	19,600.00
5.	925.00	quarterly	8% compounded quarterly	3 years	
6.	_____	annually	12% compounded annually	18 years	480,000.00
7.	4,800.00	semiannually	12% compounded semiannually	7 years	
8.	_____	monthly	18% compounded monthly	15 months	1,800.00
9.	12,000.00	semiannually	6% compounded semiannually	9 years	
10.	_____	quarterly	12% compounded quarterly	5 years	14,000.00
11.	8,500.00	annually	8% compounded annually	17 years	

B **(24 points) Solve each of the following annuity problems (6 points for each correct answer).**

12. William Green will receive $300 each month for two years from a man who owes him money. Using an interest rate of 12% compounded monthly, what is the present value of the money William will get?

_____

13. Pete Susick deposited $25,000 in his credit union. He plans to withdraw an equal amount every three months for six years. The credit union pays interest of 12% compounded quarterly. How much is his quarterly withdrawal?

_____

14. Donna Crist wants to put enough money in the bank today so that she can send her son Jeff $2,000 each six months for four years. What amount must she deposit today if her bank will pay her 10% semiannually?

_____

15. A lifetime membership in an alumni club is $500. Assume that interest is 8% compounded annually. Compare the single payment of $500 with the present value of 20 annual payments of $35 per year.

_____

C (32 points) In problems 16-19, find the size of the payment required to amortize the loan (4 points for each correct answer). In problem 20, complete the first two months of the amortization table (16 points).

16. Amount of loan: $9,000
Length of loan: 2 years
Interest rate: 15% cmpd monthly
Period of payment: monthly

Monthly payment: _____

17. Amount of loan: $4,500
Length of loan: 1.5 years
Interest rate: 12% cmpd quarterly
Period of payment: quarterly

Quarterly payment: _____

18. Amount of loan: $12,000
Length of loan: 6 years
Interest rate: 10% cmpd semiannually
Period of payment: semiannual

Semiannual payment: _____

19. Amount of loan: $186,000
Length of loan: 25 years
Interest rate: 8% cmpd annually
Period of payment: annual

Annual payment: _____

20. Carolee Hamilton bought a new car by financing it through the car dealership. The total amount that she financed was $18,000. She will repay her loan over four years by making equal monthly payments of $500.95 with interest paid on the unpaid balance of 1.25% per month (15% annually). Complete the first two months (2 points for each correct answer).

Amortization Schedule

Month	Beginning Unpaid Balance	Interest Payment	Total Payment	Principal Payment	New Balance
1	_____	_____	$500.95	_____	_____
2	_____	_____	$500.95	_____	_____

Part Ten

Advanced Business Applications

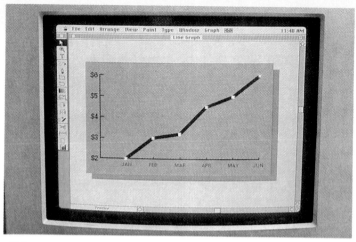

Chapter 32
Business Statistics

OBJECTIVES

When you have completed this chapter, you should be able to:

* Determine the mean, median, and mode of ungrouped and grouped data
* Present statistical data on tables and graphs

Business statistics can be defined as the collection, tabulation, and/or presentation of number information about a business situation. Basic business statistics requires only arithmetic and logical reasoning. The vocabulary of business statistics is important to anyone who reads or uses business data.

STATISTICS

Statistical data often include numbers called averages. Commonly used averages are the mean, the median, and the mode. The purpose of each of the averages is to present a representative or typical value from a group of numbers.

The *mean* of a group of values is found by dividing the sum of the group of values by the number of values in the group.

a. Find the mean salary of five employees whose actual salaries are $22,500, $25,400, $28,000, $33,600 and $35,500.

Sum = $22,500 + $25,400 + $28,000 + $33,600 + $35,500 = $145,000
Mean = $145,000 ÷ 5 = $29,000

The *median* of a group of numbers is found by arranging the numbers in numerical order and finding the middle number. In example a., the median is $28,000 because it is the middle number of the five numbers arranged in order. The median is useful when a value in the group is much larger or much smaller than the rest of the numbers.

b. Find the median salary of five employees whose salaries are $22,500, $25,400, $28,000, $33,600 and $125,500.

The salaries are already in number order; the median is $28,000.

In example b., the mean is $235,000 ÷ 5 = $47,000. But $47,000 is not the representative salary of the five employees. The mean is large because one employee (perhaps the owner) has a very large salary compared to the group. The median salary, $28,000, is more typical of the group.

If there is an even number of employees, the median will be halfway between the two middle numbers. (It is the mean of the middle two numbers.)

c. Find the median salary of six employees whose salaries are $22,500, $25,400, $28,000, $33,600, $35,500 and $125,500.

The median is halfway between the middle two numbers, $28,000 and $33,600. It is ($28,000 + $33,600) ÷ 2, or $61,600 ÷ 2 = $30,800.

The *mode* of a group of numbers is the number that occurs most often. It is useful when the average implies most typical or happening most often. Retail businesses keep track of the items that sell most frequently so that they avoid shortages of those items.

d. Find the mode shoe size of twelve pair of boots, sizes 6, 6, $7\frac{1}{2}$, $7\frac{1}{2}$, 8, $9\frac{1}{2}$, 10, 10, 10, 10, 10 and $10\frac{1}{2}$.

The mode is size 10 because 10 occurred most frequently.

Notice that for example d. neither the mean nor the median make any sense. The mean is 105 ÷ 12 = 8.75 or $8\frac{3}{4}$. The median is halfway between size $9\frac{1}{2}$ and 10, which would be 9.75 or $9\frac{3}{4}$. The store owner could not buy any boots of either size $8\frac{3}{4}$ or $9\frac{3}{4}$. However, the store owner does want to stock enough boots of size 10.

Ungrouped and Grouped Data

The numbers in the previous examples are called *ungrouped data* because they are listed individually. Business applications often involve groups of data that contain thousands of values. To get a feel for the data, it is useful to organize the individual values into groups called *classes of data*. The number of values in each class is called the *frequency*. The resulting table is called a *frequency table* (Table 32-1 on page 400), and now the data are called *grouped data*.

Steps for Developing a Frequency Table

1. Determine the classes of data and list each class in a column.
2. Tally the data by making one mark for each data item across from each item's appropriate class.
3. Count the tally marks for each class and list the amount across from the class.

e. Listed below are salaries of 25 employees. Make a frequency table with five classes: $20,000 up to but not including $25,000; $25,000 up to $30,000; etc.

22500	21300	23500	42400	27500
25400	34600	21000	24400	39100
28000	32000	37500	29500	24000
33600	26200	33500	31800	36400
35500	26000	25200	26000	40800

TABLE 32-1
Frequency Table

Class	Tally	Frequency (F)
$20,000 up to $25,000	ⅢⅡ Ⅰ	6
$25,000 up to $30,000	ⅢⅡ ⅢⅠ	8
$30,000 up to $35,000	ⅢⅡ	5
$35,000 up to $40,000	ⅢⅠ	4
$40,000 up to $45,000	ⅠⅠ	2
Total		25

If the original ungrouped data ever is lost or destroyed, it would be impossible to calculate the mean. You can make a reasonable estimate of the mean by using the frequency table.

Steps for Estimating the Mean Using a Frequency Table

1. Find the midpoint of each class.
2. Multiply each midpoint by the frequency of its class.
3. Add the products (from Step 2) together.
4. Total the frequencies.
5. Divide the Step 3 sum by the total of the frequencies (from Step 4).

f. Calculate the mean of the grouped data in Table 32-1 above.

Class of Grouped Data	F	Step 1 Midpoint	Step 2 F × Midpoint
$20,000 up to $25,000	6	$22,500	$135,000
$25,000 up to $30,000	8	$27,500	220,000
$30,000 up to $35,000	5	$32,500	162,500
$35,000 up to $40,000	4	$37,500	150,000
$40,000 up to $45,000	2	$42,500	85,000
Totals	25		$752,500 (Step 3)

Step 4

Step 5 The mean of the grouped data is $752,500 ÷ 25 = $30,100. (The mean of the ungrouped data was $747,700 ÷ 25 = $29,908.)

TABLES AND GRAPHS

In modern business, statistical information often is summarized clearly and exactly in tables and displayed in graphs. Popular graphs include the histogram, bar graph, line graph, and circle graph. The histogram, bar graph and line graph all have a rectanglar shape. Labels are placed at the left (the vertical axis) and bottom (the horizontal axis).

Histogram

A *histogram* is a diagram that presents the grouped data from a frequency table. The classes are positioned adjacent to each other along the horizontal axis and the frequencies are written along the vertical axis. Figure 32-1 shows the histogram for the frequency table in Table 32-1. The numbers on the horizontal axis increase from left to right. The numbers in the vertical axis increase from bottom to top.

FIGURE 32-1
Histogram of Employee Salaries (thousands of dollars)

Bar Graph

The *bar graph* is similar to the histogram except that there may not be a number scale along the horizontal axis. The bars normally do not touch each other. Table 32-2 shows the sales revenue, cost of goods sold, operating profit, and net profit for each of the first six months of the current year. Also shown are the net profit amounts for the first six months of last year. Figure 32-2 on page 402 is a bar graph which displays only the revenue for the current six months.

TABLE 32-2 Sales Revenues, Expenses, and Net Profit for the Current Year and Net Profit for Last Year (January through June)

Month	Sales Revenue	Cost of Goods Sold	Operating Expenses	Net Profit	Net Profit Last Year
Jan.	$63,000	$31,000	$25,000	$7,000	$6,000
Feb.	60,000	29,000	29,000	2,000	7,000
March	72,000	36,000	27,000	9,000	6,000
April	70,000	37,000	27,000	6,000	8,000
May	75,000	40,000	26,000	9,000	7,000
June	80,000	42,000	33,000	5,000	4,000

FIGURE 32-2
Bar Graph of Sales
Revenues for First
Six Months

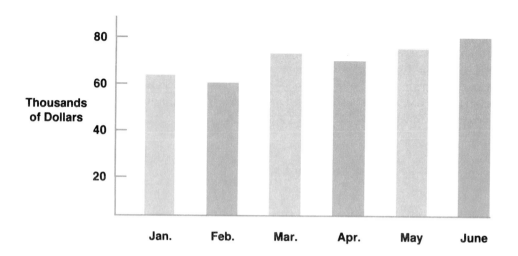

Comparative Bar Graph

Two bar graphs can be drawn together on one grid to make a comparison of statistical data on a *comparative bar graph*. In Figure 32-3, bars for last year and this year's monthly net profit for the first six months are drawn next to each other. There is one pair of bars for each month. Each bar in a pair is colored differently to help the person reading the graph easily tell the bars apart.

FIGURE 32-3
Comparative Bar
Graph of Net
Profits

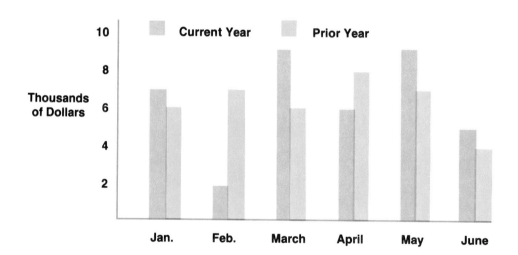

Component Bar Graph

A bar graph that is constructed to show how certain data is composed of various parts is a *component bar graph*. Figure 32-4 shows how the current sales revenue is composed of cost of goods sold, operating expenses, and net profit. Similar to the comparative bar graph, the component parts are colored or shaded to permit easier reading.

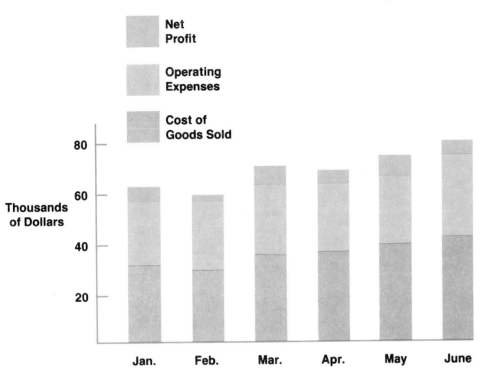

FIGURE 32-4
Component Bar
Graph of the
Current Sales
Revenues

Line Graph

A *line graph* often is used to show data over a period of time. As with bar graphs, the time element usually is plotted on the horizontal axis and the other variable is plotted on the vertical axis. Often, the first time interval is graphed directly on the vertical axis. In Figure 32-5, January is shown on the vertical axis. More than one line can be drawn on a line graph. The same information that was presented in Figure 32-3 is graphed in Figure 32-5. Examine both figures to compare how they differ.

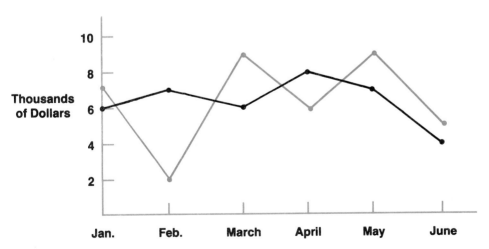

FIGURE 32-5
Line Graph of Net
Profits

Circle Graph

The *circle graph* sometimes is called a *pie chart*. It is similar to a component bar graph because it shows how one quantity is composed of different parts. In a circle graph, however, the parts normally are written as percents. The circle graph in Figure 32-6 shows how sales revenue for March is composed of cost of goods sold, operating expenses, and net profit.

Before the graph is drawn, the data are changed into percents as shown in Table 32-3. The size of each part of the circle can be reasonably estimated by using the fractional equivalents of the percents. In Figure 32-6, cost of goods sold is 50% or $\frac{1}{2}$ of the circle. Operating expenses make up 37.5% or $\frac{3}{8}$ of the circle. The remaining $\frac{1}{8}$ represents net profit.

TABLE 32-3   March Sales Revenue

Item	Amount	Percent
Cost of Goods Sold	$36,000	50.0%
Operating Expenses	27,000	37.5%
Net Profit	9,000	12.5%
Sales Revenue	$72,000	100.0%

$36,000 ÷ $72,000 = 50.0%
$27,000 ÷ $72,000 = 37.5%
$ 9,000 ÷ $72,000 = 12.5%

FIGURE 32-6   Circle Graph of March Sales Revenue

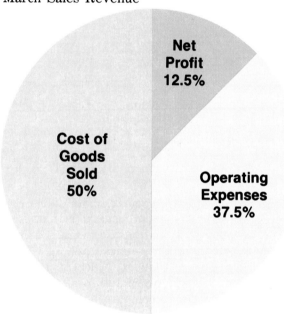

COMPLETE ASSIGNMENTS 32-1 AND 32-2

Chapter terms for review

bar graph
business statistics
circle graph
classes of data
comparative bar graph
component bar graph
frequency
frequency table
grouped data

histogram
line graph
mean
median
mode
pie chart
statistical data
ungrouped data

Assignment 32-1: Statistical Averages

A **(42 points) — Solve the following problems (points for correct answers as marked).**

1. Listed below are the scores on a keyboard speed test (in correct words per minute) given in three different towns to job applicants at the Gas & Electric Company. Find the mean, median and mode for each town. Round to the nearest tenth (27 points, 3 points for each correct answer).

Roseburg	46	57	89	55	46	74	64	89	46	55	60
Tustin	65	44	53	77	58	77	82	66	52		
Woodbury	59	62	47	68	88	78	59	45	59	87	

Gas & Electric Company
Keyboard Speed Test
Statistical Summary

	Mean	*Median*	*Mode*
Roseburg	_____	_____	_____
Tustin	_____	_____	_____
Woodbury	_____	_____	_____

2. John Straley owns a very popular flower shop. He is thinking about opening a flower stand inside a large office building. He decides to compare recent receipts for cut flowers only for 15 days in March and 15 days in July (15 points; 3 points for each correct answer).

March			*July*		
340	260	280	310	240	340
250	190	310	320	370	420
240	350	240	430	320	200
370	360	320	250	220	180
450	470	430	280	230	360

a. Find the mean for March. _____

b. Find the median for March. _____

c. Find the mean for July. _____

d. Find the median for July. _____

e. Find the mean for the thirty days combined.
(Hint: Add the two sums and divide by 30.)

_____

B **(58 points)—Solve the following problems (points for correct answers as marked).**

3. The Gas & Electric Company wants to show all 30 scores of the keyboard speed test in one combined frequency distribution. (See Problem 1.) Create five classes of equal size starting with "40 up to 50," etc. Make all tally marks and determine the frequencies (25 points; 5 points for each correct row).

Gas & Electric Company
Keyboard Speed Test Results

Class	Tally	Frequency

4. PJS Group Sales Corp. was considering the purchase of cellular phones for all sales personnel. They asked 30 local salespersons to estimate the number of telephone calls per week that currently are delayed and that they could make while in their automobiles.

11	46	32	28	24	18
28	39	41	37	16	25
16	44	15	27	35	22
49	27	33	12	34	21
42	26	18	24	14	39

a. Group the data into four classes of equal size beginning with "10 up to 20." Construct a frequency distribution, showing all tally marks (25 points; 5 points for each correct row, including the totals row).

b. Calculate the mean of the grouped data. For midpoints, use 15, 25, 35, and 45. (4 points).

_____

c. Calculate the mean of the ungrouped data (4 points).

_____

PJS Group Sales Corp.
Telephone Call Survey Summary

Class	Tally	Frequency	Midpoint	Freq. × Midpt

_____
Score for B (58)

Assignment 32-2: Tables and Graphs

A (18 points) — Complete the following problem as directed (points for correct answers as marked).

1. PJS Group Sales Corp. was considering the purchase of cellular phones for all sales personnel. They asked 48 salespersons within the state to estimate the number of telephone calls per week that currently are delayed and that they could make while in their cars. The data are given below. (This is similar to problem 3 in Assignment 32-1.)

a. Complete the frequency table (10 points).

b. In the space provided, construct a histogram that shows the four classes on the horizontal axis and the frequency of each class on the vertical axis. (8 points)

28	39	51	37	16	25	23	35	38	37	18	24
16	44	15	27	35	22	11	40	12	27	31	21
49	27	33	12	34	21	44	23	29	12	54	19
42	26	18	24	14	39	38	22	22	24	59	41

Class	Tally	Frequency
10 up to 20	_____	_____
20 up to 30	_____	_____
30 up to 40	_____	_____
40 up to 50	_____	_____
50 up to 60	_____	_____

Score for A (18)

B (54 points) — Complete the following problems as directed (points for correct answers as marked).

2. Sloan Insurance Agency monitors the premiums of insurance policies that it collects each month. It categorizes the policies as life insurance, home (fire) insurance and automobile insurance. The results for the first six months of the year are shown in the table below. In the space provided, create a component bar graph that shows the premiums of each type of insurance during each month. Shade the three components differently (18 points).

Department	Jan.	Feb.	March	April	May	June
Auto	$ 90,000	$ 70,000	$ 70,000	$120,000	$100,000	$ 90,000
Home	45,000	50,000	40,000	40,000	35,000	60,000
Life	45,000	40,000	70,000	40,000	35,000	40,000
Total	$180,000	$160,000	$180,000	$200,000	$170,000	$190,000

3. Martha Jefferson operates printing/copying businesses. One of them, called Jefferson Printing, is located in the financial district and does printing and copying for corporations. The other, Martha's Engraving, is located in a more residential area where the work is primarily social invitations and programs, such as for weddings and banquets. The following table shows the monthly sales revenue for each shop for the last six months.

Store	Jan.	Feb.	March	April	May	June
Jefferson	$120,000	$140,000	$110,000	$115,000	$135,000	$125,000
Martha's	65,000	55,000	50,000	80,000	85,000	75,000

a. Make a line graph showing the monthly sales revenue for each shop. Use a solid line for Jefferson Printing and a dashed line for Martha's Engraving (18 points).

b. Make a comparative bar graph showing the monthly sales revenue for each shop. Shade the bars differently for the two shops (18 points).

Score for B (54)

C (28 points)—Solve the following problems (points for correct answers as marked).

4. Disc-O-Rama, a discount music store, sells compact discs and audio cassette tapes. They categorize the vocal music discs and tapes according to whether they are Rock, Country & Western, Folk, or Classical. Last month they sold the following amounts:

Music Type	Sales	Percent	Fraction
Rock	$48,000	_____	_____
Country & Western	24,000	_____	_____
Folk	12,000	_____	_____
Classical	12,000	_____	_____
Total	$96,000	_____	_____

a. Compute the percent of the total sales for each category of music (8 points).
b. Compute the fraction of the total for each category of music (4 points).
c. Draw a circle graph below which shows the approximate percent for each music type. Label each section of the graph with music type and percent (8 points).
d. Draw another circle graph below to represent sales for a different month which had the percents shown in the table below. Label each section of the graph with music type and percent (8 points).

Rock	50%
Country & Western	25%
Folk	10%
Classical	15%
Total	100%

c.

d.

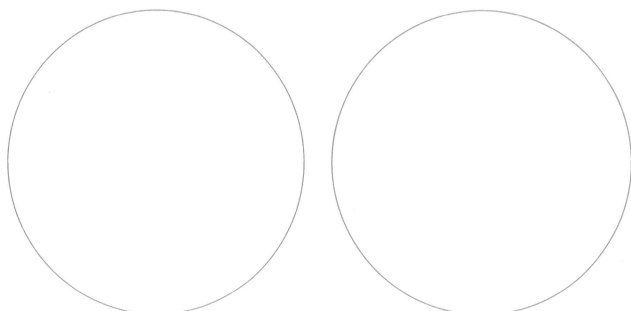

Score for C (28) _____

Chapter 33
Introduction to Algebra

OBJECTIVES
After completing this chapter, you should be able to:

- Apply arithmetic concepts to problems that contain letters or numbers
- Solve simple equations using algebra
- Check a solution by using the original equation

The previous chapters of this text-workbook have been devoted to various topics of business mathematics that involve the basic principles of arithmetic. Chapters 33-34 are devoted to another topic of business mathematics—*algebra*.

ALGEBRA

Everyone who uses mathematics uses the principles of algebra. You have used algebra earlier in this book, but the word "algebra" was not mentioned. In Chapter 15 on simple interest, the fundamental formula Interest equals Principal times Rate times Time, or $I = P \times R \times T$, or $I = PRT$ was introduced. This formula is an algebraic expression because letters are used to represent numbers. It is used to calculate the amount of interest in dollars when the principal, interest rate, and time of the loan or investment are known. Then, in Chapter 16, three more algebraic formulas were given:

$$P = \frac{I}{R \times T}, \ R = \frac{I}{P \times T}, \ \text{and} \ T = \frac{I}{P \times R}.$$

These formulas, which solved for the principal, rate, or time, respectively, are *derived* (developed) from the original formula by using algebra. In Chapters 15 and 16 you probably memorized four different formulas. However, with algebra, you only need to learn the first formula, $I = P \times R \times T$. To find the principal, rate, or time, use the simple interest formula and algebra to calculate the answer.

ARITHMETIC WITH LETTERS

The rules of algebra are the same as the rules of arithmetic, except that letters as well as numbers can be used. Listed below are several arithmetic concepts already used in this book.

1. *Multiply or divide by 1.* When multiplied by or divided by 1, a number does not change.

   a. $8 \times 1 = 8 \qquad 13 = 1 \times 13 \qquad 9 \div 1 = 9 \qquad 22 = 22 \div 1$
   $A \times 1 = A \qquad B = 1 \times B \qquad C \div 1 = C \qquad D = D \div 1$

2. *Cancellation with factors in a fraction.* Study example b. Notice how cancellation is used to simplify the fractions.

   b. $\dfrac{\overset{1}{\cancel{2}} \times 3}{\underset{1}{\cancel{2}}} = \dfrac{1 \times 3}{1} = 3 \qquad\qquad \dfrac{\overset{1}{\cancel{2}} \times P}{\underset{1}{\cancel{2}}} = \dfrac{1 \times P}{1} = P$

3. *Add or subtract 0.* When 0 is added to or subtracted from any number, the number does not change.

   c. $3 + 0 = 3 \qquad\qquad 7 = 0 + 7 \qquad\qquad 24 - 0 = 24$
   $W + 0 = W \qquad\quad X = 0 + X \qquad\quad Y - 0 = Y$

4. *Cancellation in addition.* When the same number is added to and then subtracted from the first number, the first number does not change.

   d. $14 + 5 - 5 = 14 \qquad$ because $5 - 5 = 0$ and $14 + 0 = 14$
   $L - 12 + 12 = L \qquad$ because $12 - 12 = 0$ and $L - 0 = L$

5. *The order of arithmetic operations.* The multiplication and division operations are performed **before** the addition and subtraction operations.

   e. $3 + 2 \times 4 = 3 + 8 = 11$ (not 20) $\qquad$ multiplication before addition
   $22 - 2 \times 3 = 22 - 6 = 16$ (not 60) $\qquad$ multiplication before subtraction
   $10 + 6 \div 2 = 10 + 3 = 13$ (not 8) $\qquad$ division before addition
   $40 - 16 \div 4 = 40 - 4 = 36$ (not 6) $\qquad$ division before subtraction

6. *Parentheses change the order of operations.* Operations inside parentheses are performed first. Parentheses are used to make addition and subtraction happen **before** multiplication and division.

   f. A customer bought 6 items that cost $7 each, minus a discount of $2 per item. Calculate the total cost.

   $6 \times (\$7 - \$2) = 6 \times \$5 = \$30$

   Without parentheses the calculation would have been: $6 \times \$7 - \$2 = \$42 - \$2 = \$40$ since $6 \times \$7$ must be multiplied before subtracting $2.

   Rule: First perform the operations that are within the parentheses. Then perform the multiplication and division operations from left to right. Finally perform the addition and subtraction operations from left to right.

7. *Removing parentheses.* When the operation in front of the parentheses is subtraction, the signs within the parentheses change.

   g. $8 - (5 + 1) = 8 - 5 - 1 = 8 - 6 = 2 \quad$ or $\quad 8 - (5 + 1) = 8 - 5 - 1 = 3 - 1 = 2$
   $9 - (6 - 1) = 9 - 6 + 1 = 9 - 5 = 4 \quad$ or $\quad 9 - (6 - 1) = 9 - 6 + 1 = 3 + 1 = 4$

EQUATIONS

The central concept in algebra is the *equation*. An equation is a sentence that is made up of numbers and/or letters that represent numbers. In the middle of the sentence is an equal sign that separates the equation into two parts—the left-hand side and the right-hand side. Some equations are true while others are false. The following equations involve only numbers. Each is labeled true or false.

h. 2 + 5 = 7   True
    8 − 3 = 4   False, because 8 − 3 is 5
    10 ÷ 5 = 3   False, because 10 ÷ 5 is 2
    2 × 4 + 3 = 11   True

The equations below contain letters as well as numbers. The letter is called a *variable* or an *unknown*. The value or number that makes the equation true is called the *solution* to the equation.

i. 4 × A = 20   The solution is A = 5 because 4 × 5 is 20.
    $9 = \dfrac{B}{4}$ The solution is B = 36 because 36 ÷ 4 is 9.
    13 = C + 11   The solution is C = 2 because 2 + 11 is 13.
    2 × D + 1 = 7   The solution is D = 3 because 2 × 3 + 1 is 7.

NOTE: In algebra, when a letter is the multiplier of a number it is common to show the number and the letter together without the times sign. For example, 4 × A is written as 4A and 2 × D is written as 2D. We will follow this pattern throughtout the rest of the presentation on algebra.

Solving Equations

The procedure of finding the solution to an equation is called *solving the equation*. Equations often can be solved by guessing or by trial and error. Learning algebra, however, means learning how to methodically solve equations. The objective is to isolate the unknown on one side of the equation. To do this, do Step 1 if needed and then select one or more of the components of Step 2 given below.

Steps for Isolating the Variable

---

1.   Simplify each side of the equation, if possible.
2a. Multiply both sides of the equation by the same number.
  b. Divide both sides of the equation by the same number.
  c. Add the same number to both sides of the equation.
  d. Subtract the same number from both sides of the equation.

j. Solve the equation 30 = Y + 6

             30 = Y + 6   Original equation
Step 2d 30 − 6 = Y + 6 − 6   Subtract 6 from both sides
   Thus,   24 = Y   to isolate Y.

Since 10 = 2 × 5 is the same as 2 × 5 = 10 and 3 = J is the same as J = 3, it is acceptable to rewrite an equation so that each side is switched with the other side. Examples k. and m. show such a switch.

k. Solve the equation $24 = Z - 9$

$$24 = Z - 9 \qquad \text{Original equation}$$
$$Z - 9 = 24 \qquad \text{Rewrite with Z on the left.}$$
$$\text{Step 2c} \quad Z - 9 + 9 = 24 + 9 \qquad \text{Add 9 to both sides to isolate Z.}$$
$$\text{Thus,} \qquad Z = 33$$

l. Solve the equation $\frac{P}{5} = 14$

$$\frac{P}{5} = 14 \qquad \text{Original equation}$$

$$\text{Step 2a} \quad \frac{\cancel{5}^{\,1} \times P}{\cancel{5}_{\,1}} = 5 \times 14 \qquad \begin{array}{l}\text{Multiply both sides by 5; the 5s will}\\ \text{cancel on the left and isolate P.}\end{array}$$

$$\text{Thus,} \qquad P = 70$$

m. Solve the equation $48 = 200 \times 0.08 \times T$ for T

$$48 = 200 \times 0.08 \times T \qquad \text{Original equation}$$
$$200 \times 0.08 \times T = 200 \qquad \text{Rewrite the equation to put T on the left.}$$
$$\text{Step 1} \quad 16T = 48 \qquad \text{Simplify the left side.}$$

$$\text{Step 2b} \quad \frac{\cancel{16}^{\,1}T}{\cancel{16}_{\,1}} = \frac{\cancel{48}^{\,3}}{\cancel{16}_{\,1}} \qquad \begin{array}{l}\text{Divide both sides by 16; the 16s will}\\ \text{cancel on the left and isolate T.}\end{array}$$

$$\text{Thus,} \quad T = 3$$

n. Solve the equation $6W + 18 = 114$

$$6W + 18 = 114 \qquad \text{Original equation}$$
$$\text{Step 2d} \quad 6W + 18 - 18 = 114 - 18 \qquad \text{Subtract 18 from each side to isolate 6W.}$$
$$\text{Step 1} \qquad 6W = 96 \qquad \text{Simplify both sides.}$$

$$\text{Step 2b} \qquad \frac{\cancel{6}^{\,1}W}{\cancel{6}_{\,1}} = \frac{\cancel{96}^{\,16}}{\cancel{6}_{\,1}} \qquad \begin{array}{l}\text{Divide both sides by 6 to isolate W;}\\ \text{6s cancel on the left.}\end{array}$$

$$\text{Thus,} \qquad W = 16$$

Checking the Solution in the Original Equation

With algebra you can always check to see whether or not you did the work correctly. To check your answer, substitute the numeric solution in place of the variable in the original equation. (This process is called "plugging in the solution.")

Check of example n.:

$6W + 18 = 114$	Original equation
Does $6 \times 16 + 18 = 114$?	Substitute 16 for W on the left side.
Does $96 + 18 = 114$?	$6 \times 16 = 96$
Yes, $114 = 114$	$96 + 18 = 114$
	Thus, $W = 16$ is the solution

COMPLETE ASSIGNMENTS 33-1 AND 33-2

Chapter terms for review

algebra
derived
equation
solution

solving the equation
unknown
variable

Assignment 33-1:   Algebra 1

A **(24 points)—Remove parentheses and simplify (3 points for each correct answer).**

1. $9 - (2 \times 3) - 2$

2. $48 - 12 \div 6 - 2$

3. $(9 - 2) \times 3 - 2$

4. $(48 - 12) \div 6 - 2$

5. $9 - 2 \times (3 - 2)$

6. $48 - 12 \div (6 - 2)$

7. $(9 - 2) \times (3 - 2)$

8. $(48 - 12) \div (6 - 2)$

Score for A (24)

B **(24 points)—Solve the following equations by removing the parentheses and simplifying (3 points for each correct answer).**

9. $W = 3 \times 9 - 2 \times 4$

10. $R = 36 - 12 \div 4 + 2$

11. $3 \times (9 - 2) \times 4 = X$

12. $36 - 12 \div (4 + 2) = S$

13. $Y = 3 \times (9 - 2 \times 4)$

14. $T = 36 - (12 \div 4 + 2)$

15. $(3 \times 9 - 2) \times 4 = Z$

16. $(36 - 12) \div (4 + 2) = U$

Score for B (24)

C (24 points)—Solve the following multiplication problems by simplifying and by dividing both sides by the proper number (4 points for each correct answer).

17. $5X = 35$

18. $21 + 15 = 4Y$

19. $25 - 3 \times 3 = 4U$

20. $3V = 7 + 16 \div 2$

21. $6Z = 3 \times 11 + 9$

22. $(25 - 3) \times 3 = 11R$

23. $7Q = 30 - (4 + 10 \div 2)$

———————————
Score for C (28)

D (24 points)—Solve the following division problems by simplifying and by multiplying both sides by the proper number (4 points for each correct answer).

24. $\dfrac{P}{3} = 7$

25. $16 - 11 = \dfrac{R}{4}$

26. $3 \times (\dfrac{8}{2} - 1) = \dfrac{T}{6}$

27. $\dfrac{X}{5} = 20 \div (8 - 2 \times 3)$

28. $\dfrac{S}{7} = 9 - 2 \times 3$

29. $16 - 4 \times 2 + 3 = \dfrac{Y}{2}$

———————————
Score for D (24)

Assignment 33-2: Algebra 2

A **(24 points)—Solve the following addition problems by simplifying and by subtracting the proper number from each side (4 points for each correct answer).**

1. $X + 7 = 32$

2. $3 \times 4 + W = 5 \times (7 - 4) + 1$

3. $52 - 18 = Y + (5 + 8)$

4. $4 \times 7 - (4 + 1) = 17 - 8 + V$

5. $2 + 8 + Z = 14 + 3 \times 5$

6. $R + 3 \times 10 = (11 + 4) \times (9 - 4)$

Score for A (24)

B **(24 points)—Solve the following subtraction problems by simplifying and by adding the proper number to each side (4 points for each correct answer).**

7. $X - 9 = 22$

8. $P - 3 \times 7 = 24 \div (3 + 9) + 1$

9. $48 - 39 = Y - (7 + 5)$

10. $(24 \div 3) + 9 - 1 = Q - (6 + 2)$

11. $Z - 2 \times 3 = 29 - 8 \times 3$

12. $R - (1 + 3 \times 3) = 29 - 3 \times 5$

Score for B (24)

C (52 points)—Solve the following equations by simplifying and using multiplication, division, addition or subtraction as required (5 points for each correct answer in #13–#20; 6 points for each correct answer in #21 and #22).

13. $4X - 3 = 29$

14. $\dfrac{P}{4} - 6 = 18 \div (2 + 4)$

15. $33 = 18 + 5Y$

16. $18 \div 2 - 4 = \dfrac{R}{5} - 1$

17. $\dfrac{Z}{4} + 9 = 17$

18. $2 \times 5 + 7S = 25 + 12 \div 2$

19. $7 = \dfrac{W}{3} - 5$

20. $24 - 44 \div 11 = 15 \div 3 + 5T$

21. $5W + 7 = 28 - 3 \times 2$

22. $4 + 4 \times 5 = 3V + 6$

Score for C (52)

Chapter 34
Applications of Algebra

OBJECTIVES
After completing this chapter, you should be able to:

- Use algebra in calculating simple interest, inventory, and cost
- Apply the substitution concept

Using algebra enables business problems to be solved more efficiently than otherwise would be possible. Also, software for personal computers, such as electronic spreadsheets, requires an understanding of the fundamentals of algebra.

SIMPLE INTEREST

In Chapter 33 the equation for simple interest: $I = PRT$ and its three related equations (for finding the principal, rate, and time) were reviewed. The advantage of algebra is that the original equation alone ($I = PRT$) can be used to find values for the principal, the rate, and the time. In examples a., b., and c., the original equation will be used to solve for those three values.

Substitution of One Element for Another

The *substitution* concept refers to the replacement of one value for a different but equal value. This concept is used widely in algebra. As with the other algebra concepts, we have used the substitution concept earlier in this book. It was used in Chapters 15 and 16, which involved simple interest. For example, using the formula $I = PRT$ to find the principal, assume $I = \$10$, $R = 12\%$, and $T = 60$ days. Notice that the previous sentence contains four equations. The last three, though very simple equations, contain both a right-hand side and a left-hand side separated by an equal sign. To solve the problem, information from the last three equations is substituted into the first equation.

a. Substitute $10 for I, 12% (= 0.12 per year) for R and 60 days (= $\frac{60}{360}$) for T. Using algebra, we can solve for P in the equation:

$$I = PRT \qquad \text{Original simple-interest equation}$$

$$\$10 = P \times 0.12 \times \frac{60}{360} \qquad \text{Substitute values for the letters.}$$

$$\$10 = P \times 0.\cancel{12}^{0.02} \times \frac{\cancel{60}^{1}}{\cancel{360}_{1}} \qquad \text{Reduce.}$$

$$\frac{\cancel{\$10}^{\$500}}{\cancel{0.02}_{1}} = \frac{P \times \cancel{0.02}^{1}}{\cancel{0.02}_{1}} \qquad \text{Divide both sides by 0.02 and reduce.}$$

$$\$500 = P$$

Check: $$I = \$500 \times 0.12 \times \frac{60}{360} \qquad \text{Substitute \$500 for P.}$$

$$I = \$500 \times \cancel{0.12}^{0.02} \times \frac{\cancel{60}^{1}}{\cancel{360}_{1}} \qquad \text{Simplify and reduce.}$$

$$I = \$500 \times 0.02 \qquad \text{Multiply.}$$
$$I = \$10$$

Rule: A quantity may be substituted for its equal without affecting the result.

b. Use the equation $I = PRT$ to find the annual interest rate, when $I = \$27$, $P = \$900$, and $T = 120$ days.

$$I = PRT \qquad \text{Original simple-interest equation}$$

$$\$27 = \$900 \times R \times \frac{120}{360} \qquad \text{Substitute values for the letters.}$$

$$\$27 = \cancel{\$900}^{\$300} \times R \times \frac{\cancel{120}^{1}}{\cancel{360}_{1}} \qquad \text{Reduce the right side to lowest terms.}$$

$$\frac{\cancel{\$27}^{9}}{\cancel{\$300}_{100}} = \frac{\cancel{\$300}^{1} \times R}{\cancel{\$300}_{1}} \qquad \begin{array}{l}\text{Divide both sides by \$300 and reduce; } 9 \div \\ 100 = 0.09 = 9\% \text{ on the left side.}\end{array}$$

$$0.09 = R$$

c. Use the equation $I = PRT$ to find the time, when $I = \$45$, $P = \$1,200$, and $R = 15\%$ or 0.15 per year. Give the answer in days.

$$I = PRT \qquad \text{Original simple-interest equation}$$
$$\$45 = \$1,200 \times 0.15 \times T \qquad \text{Substitute values for the letters.}$$
$$\$45 = \$180 \times T \qquad \text{Simplify on the right side.}$$

$$\frac{\cancel{\$45}^{1}}{\cancel{\$180}_{4}} = \frac{\cancel{180}^{1} \times T}{\cancel{180}_{1}} \qquad \begin{array}{l}\text{Divide both sides by \$180 and reduce; } 1 \div \\ 4 = 0.25 = 25\% \text{ on the left side.}\end{array}$$

$$0.25 = T \qquad\qquad 0.25 \text{ year} = \frac{1}{4} \text{ year} = 90 \text{ days}$$

INVENTORY

In Chapter 24 (Inventories and Turnover), you learned this equation:

| Beginning Inventory + Purchases = | Ending Inventory + | Cost of Goods Sold |

If three values are known, the fourth can be calculated with algebra. Assume:

B = Beginning Inventory   E = Ending Inventory
P = Purchases   C = Cost of Goods Sold

Now the equation can be written as B + P = E + C.

d. Use the equation B + P = E + C to find the beginning inventory, when E = $27.3, P = $95, and C = $107. (All numbers are in thousands of dollars.)

B + P = E + C	Inventory equation
B + $95 = $27.3 + $107	Substitute values for the letters.
B + $95 = $134.3	Simplify on the right side.
B + $95 − $95 = $134.3 − $95	Subtract $95 from both sides.
B + 0 = $39.3	Simplify on both sides.
B = $39.3	The beginning inventory is $39.3 ($39,300).

e. Use the equation B + P = E + C to find the ending inventory, when B = $60, P = $125, and C = $136. (All numbers are in thousands of dollars.)

B + P = E + C	Basic inventory equation
$60 + $125 = E + $136	Substitute values for the letters.
$185 = E + $136	Simplify on the left side.
$185 − $136 = E + $136 − $136	Subtract $136 from both sides.
$49 = E + 0	Simplify on the left side.
$49 = E	The ending inventory is $49 ($49,000).

f. Use the equation B + P = E + C to find the amount for purchases, when B = $43.3, E = $47.21, and C = $92.62. (All numbers are in thousands of dollars.)

B + P = E + C	Basic inventory equation
$43.3 + P = $47.21 + $92.62	Substitute values for the letters.
$43.3 + P = $139.83	Simplify on the right side.
$43.3 + P − $43.3 = $139.83 − $43.3	Subtract $43.3 from both sides.
0 + P = $96.53	Simplify on the right side.
P = $96.53	The amount of purchases is $96.53 ($96,530).

g. Use the equation B + P = E + C to find cost of goods sold, given B = $90.5, E = $78.8, and P = $104. (All numbers are in thousands of dollars.)

B + P = E + C	Basic inventory equation
$90.5 + $104 = $78.8 + C	Substitute values for the letters.
$194.5 = $78.8 + C	Simplify on the left side.
$194.5 − $78.8 = $78.8 + C − $78.8	Subtract $78.8 from both sides.
$115.7 = 0 + C	Simplify on the left side.
$115.7 = C	The cost of goods sold is $115.7 ($115,700).

COMPLETE ASSIGNMENT 34-1

COST

To manufacture any product, a company must spend money for labor and materials. These costs are called *variable costs* because the amount varies with the number of products manufactured. There may be other costs such as rent, utilities, office expenses, etc. These costs do not depend on the number of products so they are not variable costs. They are called *fixed costs* because they basically remain fixed no matter how many of the items are manufactured. *Total cost* is the sum of the variable costs and the fixed costs.

$C = V \times Q + F$ where C is the total cost, V is the variable cost per item, Q is the quantity of items produced, and F is the fixed cost

h. The Quin Bicycle Manufacturing Company has calculated that the fixed costs are $2,400 and the variable costs are $20 per bicycle. Therefore, the cost equation is $C = \$20Q + \$2,400$. To find the total cost for producing 60 and 100 bicycles, the values 60 and 100 are substituted in the cost equation.

$$\begin{aligned} C &= \$20Q + \$2,400 \\ &= \$20 \times 60 + \$2,400 \\ &= \$1,200 + \$2,400 \\ &= \$3,600 \end{aligned} \qquad \begin{aligned} C &= \$20Q + \$2,400 \\ &= \$20 \times 100 + \$2,400 \\ &= \$2,000 + \$2,400 \\ &= \$4,400 \end{aligned}$$

i. If the Quin Bicycle Manufacturing Company had total costs of $5,200 last month, how many bicycles were manufactured that month? Substitute $C = \$5,200$ in the equation $C = \$20Q + \$2,400$, and solve for Q.

$C = \$20Q + \$2,400$	Total cost equation
$\$5,200 = \$20Q + \$2,400$	Substitute $5,200 for C.
$\$5,200 - \$2,400 = \$20Q + \$2,400 - \$2,400$	Subtract the fixed cost ($2,400) from both sides.
$\$2,800 = \$20Q$	Simplify both sides.
$\dfrac{\overset{140}{\cancel{\$2,800}}}{\underset{1}{\cancel{\$20}}} = \dfrac{\overset{1}{\cancel{\$20}Q}}{\underset{1}{\cancel{\$20}}}$	Divide both sides by $20 to isolate Q and simplify.
$140 = Q$	140 bicycles were manufactured.

COMPLETE ASSIGNMENT 34-2

Chapter terms for review

fixed costs

substitution

total cost

variable costs

Assignment 34-1: Business Applications—Interest

A **(50 points)** – Solve each problem using the equation **I = P × R × T.** Substitute the given numbers in the equation and then use algebra to find the unknown value. Assume a 360-day year and an annual simple-interest rate (10 points for each correct answer).

1. Find the time (T) when P = $200, R = 12%, and I = $6.80.

_____

2. Find the rate (R) when P = $350, T = 60 days, and I = $8.75.

_____

3. Find the principal (P) when R = 6%, T = 2 years 9 months, and I = $126.

_____

4. Find the rate (R) when P = $1,500, T = 270 days, and I = $101.25.

_____

5. Find the time (T) when P = $675, R = 10%, and I = $157.50.

_____

Score for A (50)

B   (50 points) – Solve each problem using the equation I = P × R × T. Substitute the given numbers in the equation and then use algebra to find the unknown value. Assume a 360-day year and an annual simple-interest rate (10 points for each correct answer).

6. After three months, Harvey Black paid $216 interest to his credit union. How much had he borrowed if the credit union charged him 16% simple interest for the three months?

_____

7. The Cedar Hills Company loaned Roberta Sandos $2,400. After $1\frac{1}{2}$ years, Cedar Hills collected $2,400 plus $324 interest. What was the annual simple-interest rate that Cedar Hills charged?

_____

8. Jurgen Voris borrowed money from his credit union at a 12% annual simple-interest rate. After 210 days, he repaid the principal and $50.40 interest. How much money did Jurgen borrow?

_____

9. John Davison borrowed $850 at an annual simple-interest rate of 8%. At the end of the loan period, John repaid the principal and paid $238 in interest. How long was the loan period?

_____

10. Silvana Forrest loaned $1,000 to her sister Carla. She charged Carla an annual simple-interest rate of 5%. Carla repaid the $1,000 plus $250 in interest. What was the term of the loan?

_____

Score for B (50)

Assignment 34-2: Business Applications—Inventory and Cost

A (50 points) — Solve each problem by using the equation B + P = E + C. Substitute the given numbers in the equation and then use algebra to find the unknown value. Check your solution in the original equation (10 points for each correct answer).

1. Find Purchases (P), when B = \$250,000, E = \$300,000, and C = \$25,000.

   _____

2. Find the Ending Inventory (E), when B = \$745,000, P = \$300,000, and C = \$275,000.

   _____

3. Find the Cost of Goods Sold (C), when B = \$435,750, P = \$135,000, and E = \$427,420.

   _____

4. Find the Beginning Inventory (B), when P = \$64,000, E = \$73,840, and C = \$66,660.

   _____

5. Find Purchases (P), when B = \$184,500, E = \$175,350, and C = \$107,150.

   _____

6. Find the Cost of Goods Sold (C), when B = \$348,500, P = \$245,000, and E = \$291,200.

   _____

_____
Score for A (60)

B (40 points) Use the formula C = V × Q + F to solve each of the following problems for the total cost or for the quantity, as indicated (10 points for each correct answer).

7. Walter Juarez makes children's kites. He estimates that his fixed costs are $3,000 and variable costs are $2.25 per kite. What will be the total cost if he makes 5,200 kites?

_____

8. Sharon Taylor decided to go into the fancy cookie business. She estimated that the necessary fixed costs would be $4,500. The variable costs for materials would be about $0.12 per cookie for a large chocolate chip cookie. What would be the total cost for 100,000 large chocolate chip cookies?

_____

9. North Point Productions, Inc., makes and sells a looseleaf binder for school use. Their fixed costs are $12,000, and their variable costs are $0.80 per binder. How many binders can they make for a total of $75,000?

_____

0. Tanaro River Lighting makes a reading lamp. They anticipate that their fixed costs are $52,000 and that variable costs are $6.40 per lamp. How many reading lamps can they make for a total cost of $480,000?

_____

Appendix: Math in Employment Tests

OBJECTIVES
After completing this appendix, you should be able to:

- **Prepare to take an employment test**
- **Solve rate, time, and distance problems**
- **Solve proportion and relationship problems**
- **Solve time and work problems**
- **Solve measurement problems**
- **Solve percentage problems**

Business math is important in applying for both business and government jobs.   Problems presented in this section frequently appear in employment tests.

RATE, TIME, AND DISTANCE PROBLEMS

In all these problems, the formula is very simple:

Rate (Speed) $\times$ Time = Distance

Given any two factors, it is easy to find the third:

Rate $\times$ Time = Distance
Distance $\div$ Time = Rate
Distance $\div$ Rate = Time

a. X travels at 35 miles per hour for five hours.   How far does X travel?

35 mph $\times$ 5 hours = 175 miles
(Rate $\times$ Time = Distance)

b. X travels 175 miles in five hours.   How fast was X traveling?

175 miles $\div$ 5 hours = 35 mph
(Distance $\div$ Time = Rate)

c. At 35 miles per hour, how long would it take X to travel a total of 175 miles?

175 miles $\div$ 35 mph = 5 hours
(Distance $\div$ Rate = Time)

d. X and Y start traveling toward each other from 300 miles apart.   X is traveling at 35 miles per hour, Y at 40 miles per hour.   How much time will elapse before they meet?

Distance = 300 miles
Total rate = 35 mph (X) + 40 mph (Y) = 75 mph

300 miles $\div$ 75 mph = 4 hours
(Distance $\div$ Rate = Time)

e. X and Y start traveling toward each other from 300 miles apart. X is traveling at 35 miles per hour, Y at 40 miles per hour. How much distance will X travel before they meet?

Total rate = 35 mph (X) + 40 mph (Y) = 75 mph
Time = 300 miles ÷ 75 mph = 4 hours
X's distance = 35 mph (X's rate) × 4 hours (time) = 140 miles

f. Doris walks at 6 miles per hour. Judy walks at 8 miles per hour. If Doris walks in a certain direction one hour before Judy, how far ahead of Doris will Judy be when Judy has walked 44 miles?

Determine time for Judy to walk 44 miles:

$$\text{Time} = 44 \text{ miles} \div 8 \text{ mph} = 5\tfrac{1}{2} \text{ hours}$$

Determine distance Doris walks:

$$\text{Distance} = 6 \text{ mph} \times (1 + 5\tfrac{1}{2}) \text{ hrs.} = 39 \text{ miles}$$

Subtract:
44 miles − 39 miles = 5 miles ahead

g. Harry types 40 words per minute. Jean types 60 words per minute. They each typed a page with 300 words. Harry started 3 minutes before Jean. Who finished first?

Harry's time: 300 words ÷ 40 wpm = $7\tfrac{1}{2}$ min. − 3 min. headstart = $4\tfrac{1}{2}$ min.

Jean's time: 300 words ÷ 60 wpm = 5 min.

Harry's finished first: $4\tfrac{1}{2}$ min. v. 5 min.

PROPORTION PROBLEMS

Proportion problems are used in almost all employment tests. The *unit method* is a simple and fast way to solve proportion problems. To use this method, find a single basic unit of 1 in the problem, and then proceed to the answer. These problems may also be solved by proportionate shares (see example j).

h. To sort 360 letters, 3 clerks require 4 hours. How many letters can 7 clerks sort in 2 hours?

3 × 4 = 12 clerk hours to sort 360 letters
360 ÷ 12 = 30 letters per 1 clerk hour (1 unit)
7 clerks × 2 hours = 14 clerk hours
14 × 30 = 420 letters

i. The number of pennies in a cash box was twice the number of nickels. There were five times as many nickels as there were dimes. All the coins totaled $36. How many pennies were there?

Group the coins:
10 pennies + 5 nickels + 1 dime = 45¢
Determine the number of *single units*:
$36 ÷ $0.45 = 80 units
There are 10 pennies in each of the 80 units, therefore, multiply to find the answer: 80 units × 10 pennies = 800 pennies

j. X, Y, and Z invest in a business as follows: X, \$150; Y, \$250; Z, \$400. Later, the three divide \$1,200 profit in proportion to their investments. How much will each receive?

Total investment = \$150 + \$250 + \$400 = \$800

X's share: $\frac{150}{800}$ × \$1,200 = \$225

Y's share: $\frac{250}{800}$ × \$1,200 = \$375

Z's share: $\frac{400}{800}$ × \$1,200 = \$600

TIME AND WORK PROBLEMS

Time and work problems are another form of problems frequently used in employment tests. The first and most important step in solving time and work problems is to find the *fraction* of the job that can be completed in one unit of time (a day, for example). Once this amount is found, divide the *denominator* by the *numerator* to get your answer.

k. X can do a job in 5 days. Y can do the job in 10 days. How long will it take the two of them working together to do the job?

X takes 5 days: 1 day = $\frac{1}{5}$ of job

Y takes 10 days: 1 day = $\frac{1}{10}$ of job

X and Y together do $\frac{1}{5}$ + $\frac{1}{10}$ or $\frac{3}{10}$ of the job in 1 day

Therefore, they can finish the job in $3\frac{1}{3}$ days (10 ÷ 3 = $3\frac{1}{3}$)

l. X and Y together can do a job in 4 days. X alone can do the job in 16 days. How long would it take Y alone to do the job?

X and Y take 4 days: 1 day = $\frac{1}{4}$ of job

X alone takes 16 days: 1 day = $\frac{1}{16}$ of job

Y alone = $\frac{1}{4}$ − $\frac{1}{16}$ = $\frac{3}{16}$ of the job in 1 day

Therefore, Y can complete the job in $5\frac{1}{3}$ days (16 ÷ 3 = $5\frac{1}{3}$)

MEASUREMENT PROBLEMS

Traditional measurements shown in Figure A-1 are commonly used in employment tests. These should be memorized. Test problems generally involve changing from smaller units to larger or vice versa; adding, subtracting, multiplying, or dividing measures; and reasoning to logically apply units of measure.

m. How many hours equal 5,400 seconds?

5,400 ÷ 60 (sec. in 1 min.) = 90 min.

90 ÷ 60 (min. in 1 hr.) = 1 hr. 30 min.

1 hr. 30 min. = $1\frac{30}{60}$ hrs. = $1\frac{1}{2}$ hrs.

Weight

16 ounces (oz.)	= 1 pound (lb.)
2,000 pounds	= 1 ton

Length

12 inches (in.)	= 1 foot (ft.)
3 feet	= 1 yard (yd.)
5,280 feet	= 1 mile (mi.)
1,760 yards	= 1 mile

Time

60 seconds (sec.)	= 1 minute (min.)
60 minutes	= 1 hour (hr.)
24 hours	= 1 day (da.)
7 days	= 1 week (wk.)
$4\frac{1}{3}$ weeks	= 1 month (mo.)
52 weeks	= 1 year
12 months	= 1 year

Capacity

2 cups	= 1 pint (pt.)
2 pints	= 1 quart (qt.)
4 quarts	= 1 gallon (gal.)
16 ounces (1 lb.)	= 1 pint

Area

144 square inches	= 1 square foot (sq. ft.)
9 square feet	= 1 square yard (sq. yd.)
43,560 square feet	= 1 acre (a.)
640 acres	= 1 square mile (sq. mi.)

Volume

1,728 cubic inches	= 1 cubic foot (cu. ft.)
27 cubic feet	= 1 cubic yard (cu. yd.)
1 cubic foot	= $7\frac{1}{2}$ gallons of water

n. How many inches are there in 5 yards?

5 yards × 3 feet = 15 feet
15 feet × 12 inches = 180 inches

o. Add 2 yards, 1 foot, 9 inches and 3 yards, 2 feet, 6 inches.

Yards	Feet	Inches
2	1	9
3	2	6
5̶ 6	3̶ 4	15
	− 3	− 12*
6	1	3

*This step is used to change units to a higher level.

p. Subtract: 15 yards, 2 feet, 7 inches − 3 yards, 10 inches.

Yards	Feet	Inches
15	2̶ 1	7̶ 19*
− 3		− 10
12	1	9

*Because 10 inches cannot be subtracted from 7 inches, 1 foot (12 inches) is taken from the Feet column and added to the 7, making 19 inches, from which 10 inches can be subtracted.

q. How many square yards of linoleum are used for a floor 32 ft. wide × 36 ft. long?

32 ft. × 36 ft. = 1,152 sq. ft.
1,152 sq. ft. ÷ 9 = 128 sq. yds.

r. If a 14 ft. 9 in. long rod were cut into 3 equal pieces, how long would each piece be?

14 ft. ÷ 3 = $4\frac{2}{3}$ or 4 ft. 8 in.
9 in. ÷ 3 = 3 in.
4 ft. 8 in. + 3 in. = 4 ft. 11 in. each

s. Find the gallons in a tank 22 ft. long by 7 ft. wide filled with 4 ft. of water.

Length × Width × Height = Volume
22 ft. × 7 ft. × 4 ft. = 616 cu. ft.
616 cu. ft. × $7\frac{1}{2}$ gal. per cu. ft. = 4,620 gal.

PERCENTAGE PROBLEMS

A *percent* is a fractional expression whose denominator is 100. Percent may be expressed using a percent sign (%) or a decimal point (.). Fifteen percent is 15% or 0.15.

t. To find percentage: Base × Rate = Percentage

A person receives 15% discount on a purchase of $80. How much is the discount?

$80 × $\frac{15}{100}$ = $12

How much will the person pay for the purchase?

$80 − $12 = $68

u. To find base: Percentage ÷ Rate = Base

If a salesperson's 6% commission amounted to $60, what was the total amount of the sale?

$60 ÷ 0.06 = $1,000

v. To find rate: Percentage ÷ Base = Rate

Of 240 employees in an organization, 192 took public transportation to work. What percent of the employees took public transportation to work?

192 ÷ 240 = 80%

What percent of the employees did not take public transportation to work?

100% − 80% = 20%

w. To find amount of decrease: Amount of decrease ÷ Original amount = Rate of decrease

A company had expenses of $37,200 in 1990 and $31,620 in 1991. What was the dollar amount of decrease?

$37,200 − $31,620 = $5,580

What was the percent of decrease?
$5,580 ÷ $37,200 = 15%

x. To find amount of increase: Amount of increase ÷ Original amount = Rate of increase

A company had expenses of $36,000 in 1990 and $39,600 in 1991. What was the dollar amount of increase?

$39,600 − $36,000 = $3,600

What was the percent of increase?
$3,600 ÷ $36,000 = 10%

RELATIONSHIP PROBLEMS

Relationships in a series of numbers may be found by comparing the first three or four terms in the series.

y. Complete the series: 3, 6, 9, 12, ___, ___

Add 3 to each preceding number. The last two terms are 15 and 18.

A series might combine two or more steps.
Complete the series: 4, 8, 6, 10, ___, ___

Alternately add 4 then subtract 2. The last two terms are 8 and 12.

A series might be progressive.
Complete the series: 1, 3, 6, 10, ___, ___

Add numbers increasing by one for each new calculation. The last two terms are 15 and 21.

Number relationships may be visualized from a verbal description.

z. A person walked 2 miles south, then 3 miles east, then 2 miles north, then 4 miles west. How far was he from his starting point?

1 mile

COMPLETE PRACTICE EMPLOYMENT TEST PROBLEMS 1 AND 2 AND THE PRACTICE CIVIL SERVICE EXAMINATION

Practice Employment Test Problems 1

A (50 points) — Solve the following problems (5 points for each correct answer).

1. Bob can wash 5 cars per hour. Al washes 4 cars per hour. Working together, how many cars can they wash in 9 hours?

_____

2. Group X can do a job in $3\frac{1}{3}$ days. Group Y requires $1\frac{2}{3}$ days. How long will it take both groups working together to do the job?

_____

3. X and Y together can do a job in 9 days. X alone can do the job in 15 days. How long would it take Y alone to do the job?

_____

4. A bricklayer can lay 450 bricks per day. Another can lay 540 per day. Working together, how many days would it take them to lay 6,435 bricks?

_____

5. If X can do a job in 5 days, Y in 8 days, and Z in 10 days, how long would the job take if X, Y, and Z worked together?

_____

6. From Problem 5, how long would it take X and Z working together to do the job?

_____

7. A plane leaves Los Angeles for New York and travels at 600 mph. At the same instant, a plane leaves New York for Los Angeles and travels at 480 mph. If the total distance is 3,600 miles, how much time will elapse before the planes meet?

_____

8. If the Los Angeles to New York plane departed at 8:30 a.m., how many miles would it have traveled at 2:30 p.m.?

_____

9. X and Y start toward each other from 240 miles apart. X leaves 1 hour before Y. X travels at 30 mph, Y at 40 mph. How many miles will Y have traveled when they meet?

_____

10. Al walks at 6 mph. Mike walks at 4 mph. If Mike starts to walk in a certain direction 1 hour before Al, how far behind Al will he be when Al has walked 24 miles?

_____

B   (50 points) — Solve the following problems (5 points for each correct answer).

11. Two cars started toward each other from 375 miles apart. The speed of one car was 25 mph. It met the other car after 5 hrs. What was the speed of the other car?

_____

12. Four clerks require 60 minutes to sort 1,200 letters. How many letters can 10 clerks sort in 8 hours?

_____

13. Three bakers produced loaves of bread in the following proportions: X, 250; Y, 300; Z, 350. Together they baked 12,300 loaves. How many of these did Y bake?

_____

14. X, Y, and Z invest respectively $25,000, $50,000 and $75,000 in a business. Later they sell the business for $96,000 and divide the proceeds in proportion to their original investments. How much did Y get?

_____

15. Add: 5 yds. 2 ft. 9 in.; 4 yds. 1 ft. 7 in.; 1 yd. 6 in.

_____

16. Alice types 50 words per minute. Jerry types 60 words per minute. They each typed a report 2,100 words long. Alice started 5 minutes before Jerry. Who finished first?

_____

17. Subtract: 5 hrs. 20 min. 30 sec. from 10 hrs. 23 min.

_____

18. A cash box had an equal number of dimes and quarters. It had twice as many pennies and three times as many nickels. The total cash was $416. How many nickels were there?

_____

19. A room is 24 feet long and 15 feet wide. How much will it cost to cover the floor with carpet costing $18 a square yard if 4 extra square yards are purchased for matching?

_____

20. A swimming pool is 60 feet long and 30 feet wide. It is 3 feet deep at one end and slopes evenly to a depth of 9 feet at the other end. How many gallons of water will be required to fill it to one foot from the top?

_____

_____
Score for B (50)

Practice Employment Test Problems 2

A   (50 points) — Solve the following problems (5 points for each correct answer).

1. Plane X flies 2,000 miles to New York in 5 hours. Plane Y flies 2,000 miles to New York in 4 hours. If Plane X starts 1 hour before Plane Y, how far ahead of Plane Y will it be when Plane Y has flown 1,500 miles?

_____

2. Swenson plants 14 trees per hour. Johnson plants 12 trees per hour. Working as a team, how many trees can they plant in 22 hours?

_____

3. A car leaves Cleveland for Albuquerque and travels at 55 mph. Simultaneously, a second car leaves Albuquerque for Cleveland and travels at 50 mph. If the total distance is 1,575 miles, how much time will go by until the two cars meet?

_____

4. If the Cleveland to Albuquerque car (from Problem 3) left at 9 a.m., how far from Albuquerque would it be at 6 p.m.?

_____

5. Alberta can sew a dress in 3 days. Allison requires only 2 days. If they combine efforts to do one job to sew 30 dresses, how long will they take to do the job?

_____

6. One manufacturer can produce 800 VCRs per day; another can produce 960 per day. Working together, how many days would it take them to manufacture 39,600 VCRs?

_____

7. If W can do a job in 8 days, X in 6 days, Y in 10 days, and Z in 12 days, how long would it take to complete the job if all four worked together?

_____

8. From Problem 7, how long would it take W and Y to do the job?

_____

9. From Problems 7 and 8, how much less time would it take X and Z than W and Y to complete this job?

_____

10. X and Y start toward each other from 150 miles apart. X leaves 1 hour before Y. X travels at 30 mph, Y at 20 mph. How many miles will Y have traveled when they meet?

_____

_____
Score for A (50)

B (50 points) — Solve the following problems (5 points for each correct answer).

11. How many minutes are there in $1\frac{1}{2}$ days? _____

12. How many inches are there in 32 yards? _____

13. How many gallons of water would it take to fill a swimming pool that was 10 feet wide, 30 feet long, and 5 feet deep?

_____

14. In Problem 3, if water costs 0.7¢ per gallon, how much would it cost to fill the pool?

_____

15. Subtract: 3 yards, 2 feet, 2 inches minus 1 yard, 2 feet, 9 inches.

_____

16. A cash box had an equal number of pennies and nickels. It had twice as many dimes. It had four times as many quarters. The total cash was $75.60. How many dimes were there?

_____

17. In Problem 6, how much of the $75.60 was made up of quarters? _____

18. One computer printer prints at 1,060 words per minute. A second brand prints at 510 words per minute. A third unit prints at 1,430 words per minute. If all three could be used to produce a 250-page report containing 270 words per page, what is the shortest amount of time possible to print the report?

_____

19. A room measures 21 ft. long and 15 ft. wide. How much will it cost to carpet the room with a carpet that costs $18.50 per square yard?

_____

20. If a jacuzzi that was 5 feet long, 4 feet wide, and 3 feet deep were filled with water, how much weight was placed into it?

_____

_____
Score for B (50)

Appendix: Practice Civil Service Examination

A   (100 points)—In the answer space at the right, fill in the space between the two parallel lines under the letter that represents the correct answer. Use a separate sheet of paper for your calculations ($2\frac{1}{2}$ points for each correct answer).

ANSWERS

1. Kay typed 50 letters per day for 7 days; Joe typed 50 per day for 5 days. What is the total number of letters typed by both? **a.** 350 **b.** 600 **c.** 100 **d.** 550 . . . .

      a   b   c   d
   1. || || || ||

2. An automobile traveled for 3 hours 20 minutes at an average speed of 45 mph. How many miles did it travel? **a.** 180 **b.** 135 **c.** 157 **d.** 150

      a   b   c   d
   2. || || || ||

3. A sales representative received commissions of $39.50 in March, $49.20 in April, $18.00 in May, and $97.70 in June. What was the average monthly commission? **a.** $49.20 **b.** $51.10 **c.** $204.40 **d.** $40.00

      a   b   c   d
   3. || || || ||

4. If a person receives a 30% discount on a purchase of $96.80, how much will that person pay? **a.** $29.04 **b.** $93.90 **c.** $32.27 **d.** $67.76 . . . .

      a   b   c   d
   4. || || || ||

5. Of 465 students in school, 93 went to a ball game. What percent of the students did NOT go the game? **a.** 20% **b.** 40% **c.** 60% **d.** 80% . . . . .

      a   b   c   d
   5. || || || ||

6. Two cars are traveling in the same direction, one at 50 mph, one at 55 mph. If the slower car started an hour earlier, how many hours will it take the faster car to catch up to it? **a.** 11 **b.** 9 **c.** 10 **d.** 5.5 . . . .

      a   b   c   d
   6. || || || ||

7. A homeowner has enough lawn seed to plant $\frac{2}{3}$ of a backyard that is 90 ft. by 20 ft. How many square feet will go unplanted? **a.** 330 **b.** 180 **c.** 900 **d.** 600 . . . .

      a   b   c   d
   7. || || || ||

8. X saves twice as much as Y. Y saves twice as much as Z. If X saves a total of 1,500, how much does Z save? **a.** $1,500 **b.** $600 **c.** $375 **d.** $500 ....

8.   a b c d

9. If $15,300 is divided among X, Y, and Z in the proportion of 3, 5, and 9, respectively, how much will X receive? **a.** $2,700 **b.** $5,900 **c.** $5,100 **d.** $900 ....

9.   a b c d

10. Two trains were 780 miles apart. They headed directly toward each other. One traveled at 30 mph. The other traveled at 35 mph. How many hours did it take for the trains to meet? **a.** 26 **b.** 13 **c.** 18 **d.** 12

10.   a b c d

11. At $14.25 per sq. yd., how much would it cost to carpet a room 18 ft. by 27 ft? **a.** $2,308.50 **b.** $692.55 **c.** $769.50 **d.** $6,925.50 ....

11.   a b c d

12. Two partners, X and Y, own a restaurant. They sell $\frac{1}{3}$ interest to Z. If the part of the restaurant X and Y still own is worth a total of $15,000, how much was the original value? **a.** $22,500 **b.** $30,000 **c.** $45,000 **d.** $7,500 ....

12.   a b c d

13. A bus left San Diego at 1:30 and traveled at 50 mph. A train left San Diego at 3:30 traveling in the same direction at 70 mph. At what time will the train catch up with the bus? **a.** 6:30 **b.** 9:00 **c.** 11:18 **d.** 8:30

13.   a b c d

14. If Plane X averages 400 mph and Plane Y averages 800 mph, how many hours will Plane Y travel before it overtakes Plane X if Plane Y has a 2 hour and 30 minute head start? **a.** $1\frac{1}{4}$ **b.** $2\frac{1}{2}$ **c.** 5 **d.** $7\frac{1}{2}$ ....

14.   a b c d

15. How long will it take a car to travel 1,100 miles at an average speed of 55 mph? **a.** 20 hr. **b.** $18\frac{2}{11}$ **c.** 55 hr. **d.** $16\frac{2}{3}$ ....

15.   a b c d

16. Two teenagers who were 60 miles apart walked toward each other. They met in 4 hours. One person averaged 7 mph. How fast did the other person travel? **a.** 7 mph **b.** $8\frac{4}{7}$ mph **c.** $6\frac{3}{7}$ mph **d.** 8 mph ......

16. a ‖ b ‖ c ‖ d ‖

17. Two cars started toward each other 400 miles apart. They met in 5 hours. Car X averaged 45 mph. How many mph did car Y average? **a.** 45 **b.** 55 **c.** 35 **d.** 37 ....

17. a ‖ b ‖ c ‖ d ‖

18. A bus averaging 45 mph leaves New York at 9:30 a.m. How many miles will it have traveled at 4:45 p.m.? **a.** 281.25 **b.** 326.25 **c.** 236.25 **d.** 282.5 ....

18. a ‖ b ‖ c ‖ d ‖

19. A submarine travels at a rate of 12 mph under water and 24 mph on top. In a 100 mile trip, it travels 20 miles below and the rest on top. How many hours does the 100 mile trip take? **a.** $4\frac{1}{6}$ **b.** $8\frac{1}{2}$ **c.** 5 **d.** $7\frac{1}{24}$

19. a ‖ b ‖ c ‖ d ‖

20. How long will it take a train averaging 60 mph to cover its entire route of 400 miles if it loses 45 minutes travel time in stops? **a.** 7 hr. 25 min. **b.** 6 hr. 40 min. **c.** 5 hr. 55 min. **d.** 9 hr. ....

20. a ‖ b ‖ c ‖ d ‖

21. If a hiker travels 18 miles in 4 hours, how many miles will be covered in 7.5 days walking 8 hours per day? **a.** 240 **b.** 262.5 **c.** 320 **d.** 270

21. a ‖ b ‖ c ‖ d ‖

22. X can do a job in 3 days. Y can do the same job in 2 days. How many days would it take them to do the job together? **a.** 1.8 **b.** 1.5 **c.** 1 **d.** 1.2 . . . .

22. | a || b || c || d ||

23. Aren, Warner, and Brown invested $1,000, $1,500, and $3,500 respectively in a business partnership. If the annual profit of $1,500 is divided among them in proportion to their investment, how much will Aren receive? **a.** $300 **b.** $250 **c.** $1,000 **d.** $375 . . . .

23. | a || b || c || d ||

24. Three salespeople, X, Y, and Z, sold a combined total of $8,400. X sold $3,360. Y and Z split the remainder. If a $300 bonus was divided among the three in proportion to their sales, how much did C receive? **a.** $90 **b.** $180 **c.** $50.40 **d.** $75.60 . . . .

24. | a || b || c || d ||

25. From Los Angeles to Dallas, a plane takes 3 hours, 25 minutes. A train takes 1 day, 11 hours, 10 minutes. How many hours are saved by taking the plane? **a.** $7\frac{1}{4}$ **b.** $17\frac{1}{4}$ **c.** $31\frac{3}{4}$ **d.** $19\frac{3}{4}$. . . . .

25. | a || b || c || d ||

26. To 7 gallons, 3 quarts, 1 pint of liquid, are added 2 gallons, 4 quarts. How many pint jars would the total quantity fill? **a.** 87 **b.** 55 **c.** 17 **d.** 173 . . . .

26. | a || b || c || d ||

27. Y and Z start traveling toward each other from 600 miles apart. Y is traveling at 35 mph, B at 40 mph. How many hours will elapse before they meet? **a.** 7 **b.** 8 **c.** 9 **d.** 10 . . . .

27. a b c d ‖ ‖ ‖ ‖

28. Y and Z start traveling toward each other from 600 miles apart. Y is traveling 35 mph, Z at 40 mph. How many miles will Y travel before they meet? **a.** 400 **b.** 320 **c.** 350 **d.** 280 . . . .

28. a b c d ‖ ‖ ‖ ‖

29. Depts. X, Y, and Z had sales of $1,100; $1,900; and $2,500 respectively. A $700 advertising charge was allocated proportionately. How much is Dept. X's share of the advertising charge? **a.** $140 **b.** $350 **c.** $110 **d.** $116.67 . . . .

29. a b c d ‖ ‖ ‖ ‖

30. In Problem 29, what would Dept. Z's expense be if the advertising charge were increased to $2,200? **a.** $100 **b.** $900 **c.** $1,000 **d.** 484 . .

30. a b c d ‖ ‖ ‖ ‖

31. If X and Y together do a job in 6 hours, and X alone does the job in 10 hours, how long does it take Y alone to do the job? **a.** 12 **b.** 20 **c.** 15 **d.** 9 . . . .

31. a b c d ‖ ‖ ‖ ‖

32. A company had expenses of $15,500 in 1984 and $18,600 in 1985. What was the percent of increase? **a.** 15% **b.** $16\frac{2}{3}$% **c.** 25% **d.** 20% . . . .

32. a b c d ‖ ‖ ‖ ‖

33. This year XYZ company had last year's expenses of $24,000 increased by 20%. If $\frac{1}{8}$ of this year's expenses were charged to overhead, what would be the amount? **a.** $2,400 **b.** $3,600 **c.** $4,800 **d.** $3,000 . . . . . .

33. a b c d ‖ ‖ ‖ ‖

34. If an agent's 8% commission for selling a product amounted to $1,200, what was the total amount of the sale? **a.** $12,000 **b.** $9,600 **c.** $8,600 **d.** $15,000 . . . .

```
        a    b    c    d
34.    ||   ||   ||   ||
```

35. How many days will be required for 5 persons to build 5 machines if 5 persons can build 20 machines in 8 days? **a.** 5 **b.** 4 **c.** 2 **d.** 1.6 . . . . . .

```
        a    b    c    d
35.    ||   ||   ||   ||
```

36. Mae Miles drove 231 miles in one day. If this is 40% more than she drove the day before, how many miles were driven the day before? **a.** 165 **b.** 162.7 **c.** 323.4 **d.** 57.75 . . . .

```
        a    b    c    d
36.    ||   ||   ||   ||
```

37. What is the number of square feet on one wall of a 24-ft. by 24-ft. room with a 12-ft. high ceiling? **a.** 48 **b.** 6,912 **c.** 288 **d.** 64 . . . .

```
        a    b    c    d
37.    ||   ||   ||   ||
```

38. Add: 2.001 + 3.14 + 280.3 + 0.7 = **a.** 512.5 **b.** 286.141 **c.** 287.007 **d.** 285.611 . . . .

```
        a    b    c    d
38.    ||   ||   ||   ||
```

39. A secretary earns $700 per month, spends 90% of what is left after deductions of 22%, and saves the rest. How many months will it take the secretary to save $764.40? **a.** 11 **b.** 12 **c.** 13 **d.** 14 . . . .

```
        a    b    c    d
39.    ||   ||   ||   ||
```

40. A $300 lamp is sold with a discount of 40%. 15% of the sales price goes for advertising. What is the advertising cost? **a.** $180 **b.** $60 **c.** $27 **d.** $18 . . . .

```
        a    b    c    d
40.    ||   ||   ||   ||
```

Score for A (100)

Appendix: Aliquot Parts, Computation of Compound Amount and Present Value Factors, and Metric Conversion Tables

ALIQUOT PARTS

	Fraction	Decimal	Percent	Part of 100
Halves	$\frac{1}{2}$	0.5	50%	50
Thirds	$\frac{1}{3}$	0.3333	$33\frac{1}{3}$%	$33\frac{1}{3}$
	$\frac{2}{3}$	0.6667	$66\frac{2}{3}$%	$66\frac{2}{3}$
Fourths	$\frac{1}{4}$	0.25	25%	25
	$\frac{2}{4}$ (see $\frac{1}{2}$)	0.5	50%	50
	$\frac{3}{4}$	0.75	75%	75
Fifths	$\frac{1}{5}$	0.2	20%	20
	$\frac{2}{5}$	0.4	40%	40
	$\frac{3}{5}$	0.6	60%	60
	$\frac{4}{5}$	0.8	80%	80
Sixths	$\frac{1}{6}$	0.1667	$16\frac{2}{3}$%	$16\frac{2}{3}$
	$\frac{2}{6}$ (see $\frac{1}{3}$)	0.3333	$33\frac{1}{3}$%	$33\frac{1}{3}$
	$\frac{3}{6}$ (see $\frac{1}{2}$)	0.5	50%	50
	$\frac{4}{6}$ (see $\frac{2}{3}$)	0.6667	$66\frac{2}{3}$%	$66\frac{2}{3}$
	$\frac{5}{6}$	0.8333	$88\frac{1}{3}$%	$88\frac{1}{3}$
Eighths	$\frac{1}{8}$	0.125	$12\frac{1}{2}$%	$12\frac{1}{2}$
	$\frac{2}{8}$ (see $\frac{1}{4}$)	0.25	25%	25
	$\frac{3}{8}$	0.375	$37\frac{1}{2}$%	$37\frac{1}{2}$
	$\frac{4}{8}$ (see $\frac{1}{2}$)	0.5	50%	50
	$\frac{5}{8}$	0.625	$62\frac{1}{2}$%	$62\frac{1}{2}$
	$\frac{6}{8}$ (see $\frac{3}{4}$)	0.75	75%	75
	$\frac{7}{8}$	0.875	$87\frac{1}{2}$%	$87\frac{1}{2}$

COMPUTATION OF COMPOUND AMOUNT AND PRESENT VALUE FACTORS

If 10% is compounded semiannually for three years, the compound amount (future value) factor in the 5% column and 6th row of Table **30-1** on page 376 is 1.34010. The present value factor for 10% compounded semiannually for three years is found in the 5% column and the 6th row of Table **30-2** on page 379; the factor is 0.74622.

Steps for Calculating Compound Amount and Present Value Factors

1. Determine the periodic interest rate, and write it as a decimal, "i."
2. Determine the number of compounding periods, and call it "n."
3. Multiply $(1+i) \times (1+i) \times (1+i) \times \ldots \times (1+i)$, i.e. ($n$ times). The final product is the compound amount (future value) factor.
4. Divide 1 by the compound amount to determine the present value factor.

---

a. Calculate the compound amount factor and the present value factor if 10% is compounded semiannually for three years.

Step 1   The periodic interest rate is 10% ÷ 2 = 5%, or $i = 0.05$.

Step 2   The number of compounding periods is 3 × 2 = 6.

Step 3   Multiply (1 + 0.05) by itself 6 times: Compound amount factor = 1.05 × 1.05 × 1.05 × 1.05 × 1.05 × 1.05 = 1.34010 (rounded to 5 decimals).

Step 4   Present value factor = reciprocal of compound amount factor: 1 ÷ 1.34010 = 0.74622.

Calculator Keys

In example a., the 6 (3 years × 2 compoundings per year) is called an *exponent*. Some calculators have a key labeled Y^x or X^y which is used to instantly perform all of the multiplications. On most calculators, use the following: 1.05 Y^x 6 = 1.340096 (to six decimals).

Likewise, many calculators have a key labeled 1/x which is for reciprocals: 1.340096 1/x = 0.746215.

Length Conversion Tables (Approximate)

Metric to Traditional			*Traditional to Metric*
1 kilometer (km)	=	0.621 mile	1 inch = 2.540 centimeters (cm)
"	=	3,280.840 feet	1 foot = 0.305 meter (m)
1 hectometer (hm)	=	328.084 feet	1 yard = 0.914 meter (m)
1 dekameter (dam)	=	32.808 feet	1 mile = 1.609 kilometers (km)
1 meter (m)	=	39.370 inches	
"	=	3.281 feet	
"	=	1.094 yards	

Weight Conversion Tables (Approximate)

Metric to Traditional			*Traditional to Metric*
1 metric ton (t)	=	1.102 short tons	1 grain = 0.065 gram (g)
"	=	2,204,623 pounds	1 ounce = 28.349 grams (g)
1 kilogram (kg)	=	2.205 pounds	1 pound = 453.592 grams (g)
"	=	35.274 ounces	" = 0.453 kilogram (kg)
1 hectogram (hg)	=	3.527 ounces	1 short ton = 0.907 metric ton (t)
1 dekagram (dag)	=	0.353 ounce	
1 gram (g)	=	0.035 ounce	
1 decigram (dg)	=	1.543 grains	
1 centigram (cg)	=	0.154 grain	
1 milligram (mg)	=	0.015 grain	

Capacity Conversion Tables (Approximate)

Metric to Traditional			*Traditional to Metric*
1 kiloliter (kL)	=	264.178 gallons	1 pint = 0.473 liter (L)
1 hectoliter (hL)	=	26.418 gallons	1 quart = 0.946 liter (L)
1 dekaliter (daL)	=	2.642 gallons	1 gallon = 3.785 liters (L)
1 liter (L)	=	2.113 pints	1 ounce = 29.573 milliliters (mL)
"	=	1.057 quarts	1 cup = 0.237 liters (L)
"	=	0.264 gallon	
1 deciliter (dL)	=	0.211 pint	
1 centiliter (cL)	=	0.338 ounce	
1 milliliter (mL)	=	0.034 ounce	

Summary

CHAPTER 1

Addition

- Memorize number combinations of 2 and 3 numbers that total 10. By mentally grouping numbers totaling 10 together, you can add columns of numbers quickly.
- Also, counting the number of repeated digits and then multiplying the digit by that number helps add columns of numbers quickly.
- To check addition, add columns again in the opposite direction.
- Column totals added horizontally and row totals added vertically should be equal.

Subtraction

- When the subtrahend is less than the minuend, the result is a positive difference. When the subtrahend is greater than the minuend, the result is a negative difference. In business, a negative difference (sometimes called a credit balance) frequently is shown in parentheses.
- Subtraction is checked with addition.
- A number of horizontal subtractions are checked by adding the columns vertically and then subtracting these totals horizontally.

Multiplication

- Multiplication is "repeated addition" (Steps).
- Check multiplication by dividing the product by the multiplier to obtain the multiplicand.
- To multiply a number by 10, add a zero to the end of the number (Steps). When the multiplier contains one or more zeros, one extra place is left for each 0 in the multiplier.
- Rule: Zero times any number is zero, and any number times zero is zero.
- A shortcut for multiplying by 25 is to multiply by 100 (add two zeros), and divide by 4. A shortcut for multiplying by 50 is to multiply by 100 (add two zeros), and divide by 2.

Division

- Division is the opposite of multiplication.
- Division is the process of finding how many times one number is contained in another (Steps).
- When the partial dividend is smaller than the divisor, a zero must be placed in the quotient above that digit.
- This process is continued until the partial dividend is at least as large as the divisor. Then the long division steps are continued.
- Check division by multiplying the quotient by the divisor and adding the remainder to the product.
- To divide by 10, cut off the digit at the extreme right of the dividend, which will be the remainder. To divide by 100, cut off the two right-hand digits of the dividend, and use them as the remainder.
- When a divisor and dividend both end with zeros, an easy shortcut is to delete the ending zeros common to both, and then divide.
- Estimate a long division whole-number answer (Steps).

CHAPTER 2

Electronic calculators

- See the chapter for review of calculator keys and functions.

CHAPTER 3

Number drills & number sentences

- Practice number drills to improve speed, accuracy, and your ability to think quickly.
- Rule: Moving a number to the opposite side of an equation changes its sign. In addition and subtraction problems, the sign will change from plus to minus or from minus to plus (+ to − or − to +). In multiplication and division problems, the sign will change from multiply to divide or from divide to multiply (× to ÷ or ÷ to ×).

Solving word problems

- Business problems using calculations simply require addition, subtraction, multiplication, and division (Steps).

Quick calculations by rounding

- Rounding odd and difficult-to-calculate amounts to even whole numbers that are easier to calculate is a way to get quick and accurate answers without having to write out the calculations.

CHAPTER 4

Weights and measurements

- Rule: When adding and subtracting weights and measurements, convert smaller units into larger units whenever possible, e.g., ounces into pounds, quarts into gallons, feet into yards. When subtracting weights and measurements, "borrow" quantities needed from the next higher unit.
- Rule: To find the total square feet in an area, multiply its length times its width.
- Rule: To find the number of square yards in a total amount of square feet, divide the total square feet by 9 (number of square feet in each square yard).
- Rule: To find a total cubic measurement, multiply length times width times height.

Numerical averages

- An average of several numbers is obtained by adding the numbers and dividing the total by the number of items added. (This kind of average is known as the *mean*.)
- Use averages and estimates to calculate an approximate value.

CHAPTER 5

Fractions

- A fraction expresses one or more equal parts of a whole unit.

  $$\frac{\text{numerator}}{\text{denominator}} \quad \frac{\text{number of equal parts}}{\text{total parts}}$$

- A proper fraction is smaller than one whole unit. In all proper fractions, the numerator is smaller than the denominator.
- An improper fraction is one or more whole units. The numerator of an improper fraction is greater than or equal to the denominator (Steps).
- A mixed number represents more than one whole unit by combining a whole number and a proper fraction (Steps).
- Rule: If a fraction's numerator and denominator have no common divisor greater than 1, the fraction is in lowest terms (Steps).

- A fraction is raised to higher terms by multiplying both numerator and denominator by the same number. The new denominator must be an even multiple of the old denominator (Steps).

Addition and subtraction of fractions

- Before adding or subtracting, all of the fractions must have the same denominator, a common denominator. The product of the denominators is always a common denominator, but there may be a smaller one (Steps).
- Review the steps for adding and subtracting mixed numbers.

CHAPTER 6

Multiplication of fractions

- When multiplying fractions you do not need common denominators (Steps).
- Cancel common factors before multiplying the numerators and denominators. When all possible cancellation is done the final answer will be in lowest terms.
- When fractions are multiplied, the word "of" very often means to "multiply."
- Review the steps for multiplying a whole number by a fraction and multiplying fractions with mixed numbers.

Division of fractions

- Review the steps for dividing fractions and dividing whole or mixed numbers by a fraction or a mixed number.

Aliquot parts

- When a number (whole or mixed) can be divided by another with no remainder, the divisor is known as an *aliquot part* of the first number.
- Review the common aliquot parts (on page A-21).

CHAPTER 7

Decimals

- A decimal with no whole-number part is a pure decimal, and one with a whole-number part is a mixed decimal.
- The system for reading decimals is just like the system for reading whole numbers: each column represents a different value. Reading from right to left, the columns to the right of the decimal place represent tenths, hundredths, thousandths, ten-thousandths, hundred-thousandths, etc. There is no comma used to separate groups of three digits to the right of the decimal point (Steps).
- Review the steps for adding and subtracting decimals.

Rounding

- When rounding decimals representing money the most you can have is two decimal places. Decimals that are not dollars and cents can be rounded to any number of decimal places.
- Rule: When rounding up, you always increase any partial cent to the next whole cent.

CHAPTER 8

Multiplication of decimals

- Multiplication with one or more decimals is the same as multiplication with whole numbers except that the decimal point must be placed in the correct position in the product (Steps).

Division of decimals

- Division is the same as with two whole numbers except for placement of the decimal (Steps).
- To carry out the division process to several places, it may be necessary to add zeros to the right end of the dividend.
- For a larger divisor and small dividend, it might be necessary to insert zeros in the quotient between the decimal point and the other digits.

- When the dividend is also a whole number, the procedure is the same because the decimal point is at the right end of the dividend.
- In decimal division there are no remainders as there are in whole number division. Instead of remainders, the process carries the quotient to one or more places to the right of the decimal.
- When the divisor is a decimal, change the divisor into a whole number before doing the division (Steps).

Multiplication and division by powers of 10

- Rule: To multiply, move the decimal point in the multiplicand to the right the same number of places as the number of zeros in the multiplier.
- Rule: To divide, move the decimal point in the dividend to the left the same number of places as the number of zeros in the divisor.

Decimal and fractional equivalents

- Every decimal number can be changed into its fractional equivalent. The numerator is the decimal number without a decimal point. The denominator is the correct power of ten.
- Every fraction can be changed into its decimal equivalent by dividing the numerator by the denominator.

Approximating the product and quotient

- The objective is to determine whether a calculated answer is approximately correct. The correct placement of the decimal point is particularly important (Steps).

CHAPTER 9

Bank records

- The balance shown in the checkbook (stub or register) is usually different from the balance on the bank statement. Reasons for the difference usually are: outstanding checks, bank charges to the depositor, credits to the depositor's account, and outstanding deposits (Steps).

CHAPTER 10

Percents

- Review the steps for changing a decimal or a fraction into percents, changing a percent into a decimal, and changing a percent containing a fraction into a decimal.

Base, Rate, & Percentage

- Both Base and Percentage are always the same type of measurement unit. The word "of" means "multiply" when it is preceded by the Rate and followed by the Base.
- Rate times Base equals Percentage or $R \times B = P$
- Rule: When any two elements are known, you can solve for the third element.

To find	You must know	Use this formula
P	R and B	$R \times B = P$
R	P and B	$P \div B = R$
B	P and R	$P \div R = B$

Rates of increase and decrease

- Review the steps for determining the new value after an increase or decrease and finding the rate of change from a base value.

Distribution of overhead costs

- Allocate overhead costs based on a measurement that is related to the total cost (Steps).

CHAPTER 11

Payroll

- A payroll register is a summary of wages earned, payroll deductions, and final take-home pay.
- The payroll deduction for FICA is based on total wages and is not affected by the employee's marital status or the number of dependents.
- The amount of the payroll deduction for income tax varies with the amount of earnings, the employee's marital status, and the number of withholding allowances claimed.
- A withholding allowance is an amount exempted from gross earnings and not subject to federal income tax.
- The two primary methods for calculating how much income tax to withhold from employees are the percentage method and the wage-bracket method (Steps).
- Every employer who withholds federal income tax or FICA tax must file a quarterly return (Form 941) with the IRS within one month after the end of the quarter.

CHAPTER 12

Commissions

- In some companies, the salesperson will receive both a salary and a commission (Steps).
- Normally, goods that are returned or orders that are canceled are not eligible for commission (Steps).
- A system of graduated commission rates give more incentive to the employee (Steps).

Sales and purchases for principals

- When the commission merchant sells goods for the principal:

  Consignor ———— (Consignment goods) ———→ Consignee

  Consignor ←———— (Account sales statement and net proceeds) ———— Consignee

- When the commission merchant buys goods for the principal:

  Consignor ———— (Order to purchase) ———→ Consignee

  Consignor ←———— (Account purchase statement and gross cost) ———— Consignee

CHAPTER 13

Trade discounts

- These generally are based on the quantity purchased.
- Calculate the net price using either the discount method or the complement method (Steps).
- For a series of discounts either of these two methods can be used by repeating the calculation for each discount rate (Steps).
- The complement method can be modified for quicker calculation (Steps).
- To compare a single discount rate to a series of discounts calculate the equivalent single discount rate (Steps).

Cash discounts

- These are used to encourage prompt payment by the buyer.
- A common cash discount—"two ten, net thirty" (2/10, n/30; 2-10, n-30; 2/10, net 30)—means 2% is deducted from the invoice portion that is paid within 10 days of the invoice date.

- Calculate the remittance using either the discount method or the complement method (similar to but not the same as the methods for the trade discount) (Steps).
- There can be more than one discount rate and discount period.
- No discount is given on returned goods or on a freight charge (Steps).
- Steps for calculating the unpaid balance are almost the reverse of the complement method, using division instead of multiplication (Steps).

CHAPTER 14

Markup
- Sales − cost of goods sold = gross profit
- Gross profit − operating expenses = net profit
- Operating expenses + net profit = dollar markup

Markup based on cost
- If markup is based on the cost of the goods for sale:
Dollar markup ÷ cost = markup percent
Cost × markup percent = dollar markup
Dollar markup + cost of goods = selling price
100% + markup percent × cost = selling price

Markup based on selling price
- If markup is based on a percent of the selling price:
Dollar markup ÷ selling price = markup percent
Selling price × markup percent = dollar markup
Selling price − dollar markup = cost
100% − markup percent × selling price = cost

Relationship between cost-based & price-based methods
- Rule: Given equal cost and dollar markup the markup percent for the cost-based method will always be higher than for the price-based method.
- The price-based cost percent = 100% − the desired markup percent of the selling price.
- Cost of goods ÷ price-based cost percent = selling price

Discounted and special sale items
- When both an "original" sales price and a discount sales price are involved, the "original" sales price can be calculated using either a price-based markup or a cost-based markup. This allows the seller to offer a discounted price and still maintain a certain markup percent.

CHAPTER 15

Credit in business
- In business, "short-term" usually means one-year or less in length.

Simple interest
- Interest = Principal × Rate × Time or I = P × R × T (= PRT)
- Since interest usually is stated as an annual rate, dividing an annual rate by 12 will determine the monthly simple interest rate (or by 52 for a weekly simple interest rate).
- The ordinary interest method assumes a 360-day year; the exact interest method assumes a 365-day year (use 366 days for a leap year).
- Calculator steps are performed in the same order as written in the formula.
- Without a calculator it may be possible to simplify the multiplication by cancellation (particularly under the ordinary interest method).

Approximating interest
- Making an estimate of the interest in advance can help you spot a significant calculator error.
- Round the principal, rate and time to numbers that are easy to compute mentally (including assuming a 360-day year).

CHAPTER 16

Promissory notes
- The dollar amount written on the note is the face value (principal) of the note. A note's maturity value (the total amount that must be paid by the borrower when the note becomes due) is equal to its face value plus the total interest in dollars (or MV = P + I).
- Promissory notes may be either interest-bearing or non-interest-bearing.

Determining due date & number of interest days
- When the due date is specified you must calculate the number of interest days (Steps). When the number of interest days is given you must determine the due date (Steps).
- You need to know the number of days in each month.
- When the length of the interest period is expressed in months, the date is advanced by the number of months given. The same day of the month is the due date.

Computing interest variables
- A simple interest problem has four variables: Interest, Principal, Rate and Time.
- RULE: When any three variables are known, you can solve for the fourth variable.

-

To find	You must know	Use this formula
I	P, R, and T	$I = P \times R \times T$
P	I, R, and T	$P = \dfrac{I}{R \times T}$
R	I, P, and T	$R = \dfrac{I}{P \times T}$
T	I, P, and R	$T = \dfrac{I}{P \times R}$

CHAPTER 17

Loans from financial institutions
- Single-payment interest is the most direct method of computing interest on loans (I = PRT).
- When a borrower repays a loan by making regular payments, part of each payment pays the lender the interest owed for the period and the rest repays part of the principal.
- The unpaid-balance interest method is used to recalculate a new interest amount each payment period (Steps).

Borrowing money to make a cash discount
- Can a business save money by borrowing cash to pay the invoice within the discount period? Determine which costs less: (1) the full cost of the invoice paid at the due date, or (2) the cost of the invoice minus the discount plus the loan interest. Do not conclude that borrowing and paying off the invoice within the discount period will always be the better choice.

Discounting notes
- Discounting the note, selling it before it matures, is calculated using percents.
- When selling the note before maturity, the proceeds the seller receives from the buyer is the difference between the maturity value and the discount amount (Steps).
- Discount = Maturity value × Discount rate × Discount period (or D = MV × R × T)
- If the maturity value of a note equals its face value it is a non-interest-bearing note (Steps).
- When banks collect the interest in advance the face value (= maturity value) − proceeds = discount.

Summary

- When a bank uses the discount method, the discount rate is not the interest rate.

CHAPTER 18

Finance charges
- Divide the annual rate by 12 to find the equivalent monthly rate; multiply the monthly rate by 12 to find the equivalent annual rate.
- To calculate simple interest, the rate and time must be the same, either both annual or both monthly. To change time from months to years, divide the number of months by 12.

Effective interest rate
- The stated interest rate may not be the same as the effective interest rate.
- Monthly loan payment schedule:

Month	Unpaid Balance	Interest Payment	Principal Payment	Total Payment	New Balance

(Note: The interest and principal payments are added to determine the total payment amount each month.)

- Whenever (1) the interest is calculated on the unpaid balance every month and (2) the amount paid on the principal is exactly the same every month, you can use the following formula as a short-cut for calculating the total interest paid (n = number of months):

$$\text{Total interest} = \frac{\text{First month's interest} \times (n + 1)}{2}$$

$$= \frac{P \times R \times T \times (n + 1)}{2}$$

- Whenever the effective interest rate is very difficult to calculate, it is appropriate to approximate the effective interest rate (Steps).

CHAPTER 19

Raising the effective rate
- Calculate the approximate effective interest rate using the following formula:

$$R = \frac{2 \times M \times I}{P \times (n + 1)}, \text{ where}$$

R = approximate effective annual interest rate
M = number of payment periods in one year
I = total finance charge (interest plus any extra borrowing fees)
P = amount of the loan, or amount of the purchase that is on credit
n = number of payments in the credit plan

- The lender may raise the rate by charging a fee.
- Generally, the effective interest rate remains unchanged throughout the loan. Also, the amount of each principal payment remains the same over the life of the loan; however, the interest payment amounts vary.

Amortized loans
- When a loan is amortized, the total amount of each payment (principal plus interest) remains unchanged throughout the loan. However, the interest amount, calculated on the unpaid principal balance, decreases with each payment; thus, the principal payment amount increases with each payment.
- The amount of the amortized loan payment can be calculated using a loan factor table (Steps).

S-8

- Monthly amortization schedule:

Month	Unpaid Balance	Interest Payment	Total Payment	Principal Payment	New Balance

(Note: Each month's principal payment is determined by subtracting the interest payment from the total payment.)

CHAPTER 20

Sales tax

- Sales taxes generally are rounded to the nearest cent (Steps).
- Sales taxes on gasoline and cigarettes usually are stated in cents per unit.

Property tax

- Taxes are based on the property's assessed valuation.
- When different percentages of value are used to assess property an equalization, or adjustment, of the assessments may have to be done.
- The tax rate is found by dividing the amount of taxes to be raised by the total assessed valuation of a particular governmental unit.
- A tax rate may be expressed in mills. A *mill* is one tenth of one cent or $0.001. To convert mills into cents, divide by 10.

CHAPTER 21

Individual federal income tax

- If deductions are itemized:
  Taxable income = adjusted gross income − itemized deductions − exemptions
- If deductions are not itemized:
  Taxable income = adjusted gross income − standard deduction − exemptions

Business filings

- Owners of sole proprietorship and partnership businesses include their share of the business revenues and expenses in their own individual federal tax filings. Corporations must file separately using special tax forms.

CHAPTER 22

Life insurance

- Straight (ordinary) life insurance: a certain premium is paid every year until the death of the insured person. The policy then becomes payable to the beneficiary.
- Limited-payment life insurance: a certain premium is paid every year for a specified number of years or until the death of the insured. Generally, upon the death of the insured the policy is payable to the beneficiary.
- Term insurance: a certain premium is paid every year during the specified time period. The policy is payable only in case of death of the insured during the term. The protection stops at the end of the term. Term insurance has no cash surrender value.
- Endowment insurance: provides insurance payable upon the insured's death if it occurs within a specified period, and an endowment of the same amount as the policy, payable if the insured is alive at the end of that period.
- Annuity insurance pays a certain sum of money to the insured every year after the insured reaches a specified age and until the insured's death.
- Additional death benefit (ADB): allows the insured to purchase, at low cost, additional insurance in case of death by accident.

Health insurance

- Employers generally pay most of the premium for employees and participate to a lesser extent in paying premiums for family members of employees.

- Many group plans include a provision for a deductible.
- Another frequent provision in group medical plans is the payment by the insurance company of a percent of costs over the deductible, usually 70% to 90%, with the remaining 10% to 30% paid by the insured.

CHAPTER 23

Property insurance

- Premium rates depend upon the nature of the risk, the location of the property, and the length of time covered by the policy.
- Short rates are rates charged for less than a full term of insurance. If the insurance company cancels the coverage, it must refund the entire unused premium.
- $\dfrac{\text{Amount of insurance carried}}{\text{amount of insurance required}} \times \text{loss} = \text{recovery amount}$ under a policy containing a coinsurance clause (Steps).

Auto insurance

- Auto liability and property damage insurance: protects the insured against personal injuries and property damage claims.
- Auto comprehensive insurance: protects the vehicle of the insured against fire, water, theft, vandalism, falling objects, and other damage that is not caused by collision.
- Auto collision insurance: protects the vehicle against collision damage. It usually includes a deductible amount.
- No-fault insurance covers only the medical costs for injuries to the driver and passengers in insured's own vehicle.

CHAPTER 24

Inventory valuation

- Every company should do a physical inventory at least once a year.
- Inventory is accounted for on either a perpetual or a periodic basis.
- Periodic ending inventories are calculated using one of the methods that assumes a certain flow of inventory costs. Three of these methods are: (1) the average cost method which assumes the costs of all items on hand are averaged and shared evenly among all units; (2) the first-in, first-out (FIFO) method which assumes the costs for units used are charged according to the order in which the units were purchased; and (3) the last-in, first-out (LIFO) method which assumes the inventory remaining is composed of the units received first.
- In financial statements the ending inventory is presented at either: (a) its cost value (that is, using either average, FIFO, or LIFO costing method) or (b) its lower of cost or market value (LCM) (where the cost is the same as in (a) and the market value is the dollar amount required to replace the inventory as of the inventory date) (Steps).

Estimation of inventory value

- $\begin{array}{l} \quad \text{Beginning Inventory (BI)} \\ + \text{ Purchases (P)} \\ \hline = \text{Cost of Goods Available for Sale} \\ - \text{ Cost of Goods Sold (CGS) (Estimated)} \\ \hline = \text{Ending Inventory (EI) (Estimate)} \\ \quad \text{or} \quad BI + P - CGS = EI \end{array}$

- Without a physical inventory CGS must be estimated by applying a markup rate (percent) to net sales:
  Net sales ÷ (100% + markup rate based on cost) = estimated CGS

Inventory turnover	• Inventory turnover, the number of times the average inventory is converted into sales during the year, can be calculated based on either retail (selling) price or cost (Steps).

Depreciation	• Book value = original cost − accumulated depreciation • Four common methods of calculating depreciation are straight-line method (SL), declining-balance method (DB), sum-of-the-years-digits method (SYD), and modified accelerated cost recovery system method (MACRS).
Straight-line	• Distributes the cost in equal amounts to designated units or periods covering the useful life of the item. • Assumes wear and tear is occurring evenly over the life of the property. • The three factors needed to compute straight-line depreciation are (1) the asset's estimated physical or service life; (2) the estimated resale, scrap, or salvage value (SV); and (3) the original cost of the asset. • $\dfrac{\text{Original cost} - \text{scrap value}}{\text{estimated total life in units or periods of time}} =$ depreciation amount for 1 unit or period • Annual percentage rate of depreciation = annual depreciation amount ÷ cost • The depreciation amount for a partial year is found by dividing the annual depreciation amount by 12 and then multiplying by the number of months used.
Declining-balance	• Assumes depreciation is greatest in the first year and is less in each succeeding year (Steps). • Book value should not go below SV. • The depreciation amount for a partial year is found by calculating the current year's annual depreciation, dividing it by 12, and multiplied by the number of months used.
Sum-of-the-years-digits	• Assumes a greater depreciation amount in the earlier years of an asset's life. The decrease in the book value is less rapid than under the declining-balance method (Steps). • Shortcut formula for calculating the sum of all of the years digits: $\dfrac{(n + 1) \times n}{2}$; where n = number of years in the estimated life. • The depreciation amount for a partial year is found by calculating the annual depreciation for the first (partial) year, dividing it by 12, and multiplying by the number of months of use. From then on every year will include the remaining fraction of the prior year's depreciation and the partial-year depreciation for the remainder of the current year.
Modified accelerated cost recovery system	• Must be used for federal income tax depreciation calculation. • The entire cost of depreciable property is recovered over the allowable period (assumes SV = 0). • Use the IRS depreciation tables to compute depreciation. • For determining the depreciation for a partial year, consult the appropriate MACRS table (from the IRS).

Income statement analysis	• All other items on the income statement are reported as a percent of net sales (which is considered to be 100%). • Many businesses compare actual and budgeted figures.

- In addition to comparing the items on a single statement, often it is desirable to compare the operations of the current year with those of the preceding year.

Balance sheet analysis

- With the exception of a budget comparison, the same types of analyses are made with the balance sheet as were made with the income statements.

Financial

- Working capital ratio = total current assets ÷ total current liabilities
- Acid test ratio = total of cash plus receivables ÷ total current liabilities
- Average inventory (annual) = (beginning inventory + ending inventory) ÷ 2
- Inventory turnover rate = cost of goods sold ÷ average inventory
- Ratio of accounts receivable to net sales = accounts receivable ÷ net sales
- Relationship of net income to net sales = net income ÷ net sales
- Rate of return on investment = net income ÷ owners' equity

CHAPTER 27

Corporate stock

- The rate of dividend is either a certain percent of the par value of the stock or a flat amount of money per share.
- Preferred stock has a right to share in earnings before common stock does.
- Nonparticipating preferred stock is limited to a specified percentage of dividends.
- Participating preferred stock provides for possible dividends greater than a stated percentage.
- Cumulative preferred stock must be paid all dividends in arrears before any current period dividends can be paid.
- Convertible preferred stock gives the owner the option of converting those preferred shares into a stated number of common shares.
- A round lot usually is 100 shares of stock; an odd lot is any number of shares less than 100.
- Rate of yield from a stock investment = stock dividend ÷ total cost of the stock
- Gain or loss on a sale of stock = sale proceeds − total cost

CHAPTER 28

Corporate bonds

- Bonds are either secured (guaranteed by certain assets) or unsecured (not guaranteed).
- Bearer or coupon bonds: have interest coupons attached, each of which calls for payment of the interest for a period of time on a specified date. Title (right of ownership) is not recorded in the name of the owner, but passes from bearer (holder) to bearer with delivery.
- Registered bonds: issued to a person whose name is listed (registered) with the corporation (or designated trustee). Interest is paid regularly by check to the registered owner.
- Convertible bonds: can be converted into a designated number of shares or a designated value of the corporation's stock.
- Debenture bonds: are secured by undesignated assets of the corporation.
- Callable bonds: have a provision for the issuer to repurchase or call the bonds in at specified dates if the board of directors authorizes the retirement (payoff) of the bonds before their maturity date.

Government bonds

- Treasury bonds: issued by the United States government.
- Municipal bonds: issued by states, cities, school districts, and other public entities.

Bonds in general
- Prices of bonds are quoted in percents of face value.
- Rule: Prices over 100 (100%) include a premium. Those under 100 (100%) include a discount.
- Interest is based on the face (maturity) value of the bond.
- When a bond is sold between these interest payment dates, accrued interest usually is added to the purchase price. Accrued interest = total interest for the entire interest period × [number of days from the last interest payment date to the day before the date of the bond sale ÷ 360]
- Average annual bond yield = annual interest ÷ total cost
- Rate of yield to maturity (Steps) =
$$\frac{\text{Annual Interest} + \text{Annual Discount (or} - \text{Annual Premium) Amortization}}{\text{Average Principal Invested}}$$
- Rule: When bonds are sold at discount, the yield rate will be higher than the stated (face) rate.
- Rule: When bonds are sold at a premium, the yield rate will be lower than the stated (face) rate.

CHAPTER 29

Currency
- Exchange rates change from day to day.
- $1.00 × foreign currency exchange rate factor × the number of foreign currency units being converted = the cost in U.S. dollars
- The number of foreign currency units being converted ÷ the dollars in foreign currency exchange rate factor = the cost in U. S. dollars
- When the U. S. dollar *cost* of foreign currency *drops*, it means the *value* of the U. S. dollar has *risen*.
- When the U. S. dollar *cost* of foreign currency *rises*, it means the *value* of the U. S. dollar has *dropped*.

Duty
- A duty may be a set amount per item or a percent of the value of the item (an ad valorem duty).

CHAPTER 30

Compound interest
- Compound interest means that the simple interest formula is applied several times during the term. The interest earned by one application is added to the principal before the next interest calculation.
- Using the compound interest tables simplifies the calculation (Steps).
- Future value (compound amount) = principal × compound amount factor (Table 30-1)
- On the factor tables, the column (%) represents the periodic interest rate and the row (n) represents the number of compounding periods (Steps).
- Future value = present value × compound amount factor (Table 30-1)
- Future value − present value (principal) = total interest amount
- Present value = future value ÷ compound amount factor (Table 30-1)
- Present value (principal) = future value × present value factor (Table 30-2)

CHAPTER 31

Annuity
- Review the time lines on pages 389 and 392.
- The amount of an annuity is the accumulated cash value at the end of the annuity term (at the end of the last period).

- Future value = annuity payment amount × future value of an annuity factor (Table 31-1)
- Future value − total amount of the annuity payments = total interest amount (Steps)
- Present value = annuity payment amount × present value of an annuity factor (Table 31-2)
- Annuity payment amount = future value ÷ future value of an annuity factor (Table 31-1)
- Annuity payment amount = present value ÷ present value of an annuity factor (Table 31-2) (Steps)

Amortization

- Amortization schedule (Steps)

Month	Beginning Unpaid Balance	(%) Interest Payment	Annuity Payment	Principal Payment	New Balance

CHAPTER 32

Statistics

- Mean = the sum of the group of values ÷ by the number of values in the group
- Median = the "middle" number of a group of numbers arranged in numerical order
- Mode = the number that occurs most often in a group of numbers
- Frequency table (Steps)

Class	Tally	Frequency (F)

Tables and graphs

- Histogram: a diagram that presents the grouped data from a frequency table.
- Bar graph: similar to the histogram except: (1) the horizontal axis does not have to be a number scale and (2) the bars normally do not touch each other.
- Comparative bar graph: two bar graphs drawn together on one grid to make a comparison of statistical data.
- Component bar graph: a bar graph constructed to show the various data that make up each bar.
- Line graph: (often is used to show data over a period of time) each of the data is shown as a point and all points are connected by a line.
- Circle graph: (sometimes called a pie chart) similar to component bar graph by showing how one quantity is made up of different parts; presented in circle form.

CHAPTER 33

Algebra

- Interest equals Principal times Rate times Time or $I = P \times R \times T$, or $I = PRT$
- $P = \dfrac{I}{R \times T}$, $R = \dfrac{I}{P \times T}$, and $T = \dfrac{I}{P \times R}$

Arithmetic with letters

- When multiplied or divided by 1, a number does not change.
- Cancellation is used to simplify the fractions.
- When 0 is added to or subtracted from any number, the number does not change.
- When the same number is added to and then subtracted from the first number, the first number does not change.

- Rule: First perform the operations that are within the parentheses. Then, perform the multiplication and division operations from left to right and finally the addition and subtraction operations from left to right.
- When the operation in front of the parentheses is subtraction, the signs within the parentheses change.

Equations

- An equation is a sentence that is made up of numbers and/or letters that represent numbers. In the middle of the sentence there is an equal sign that separates the equation into two parts—the left-hand side and the right-hand side.
- The objective is to *isolate* the unknown on one side of the equation so that the equation can be solved (Steps).
- To check your answer, substitute the numeric solution in place of the variable in the original equation.

CHAPTER 34

Substitution

- Rule: A quantity may be substituted for its equal without affecting the result.

Inventory

- If three values are known, the fourth can be calculated with algebra.
- Beginning inventory + purchases = ending inventory + cost of goods sold or $B + P = E + C$

Cost

- $C = V \times Q + F$ where C is the total cost, V is the variable cost per item, Q is the quantity of items produced, and F is the fixed cost.

Challenge Problems

Background Information

C&S Office Supplies, Inc., a medium-size Midwestern company, specializes in computers and office equipment. It serves customers in a five-state area. You have been hired by C&S as a financial assistant and management trainee. Your job will require that you complete various tasks when asked and provide some financial recommendations with statistical information to support your advice.

Each of the following challenges represents typical situations that you must handle. Read each one carefully and complete it as directed.

CHALLENGE 1 (Fractions)

Chuck and Sherry, owners of C&S Office Supplies, Inc., have received a year-end financial report that indicates the net profit on their computer-related equipment sales increased by three fourths over last year's net profit. Because a portion of this increase is due to more effective customer service, the owners decided to give their employees a bonus totaling one third of the increase.

Sherry has asked you to calculate the bonuses for all the employees using the following information: Last year the net profit on computer-related equipment sales was $36,000. The bonus money is to be distributed on the basis of the number of years employed at C&S.

The employees who will receive bonuses are: Laura (6 years), Sam (4 years), Emily (2 years), Robert (2 years), and Travis (1 year).

Each employee's share is to be calculated on her or his fractional part of the total years of employment of all the employees.

Assignment:

A. Calculate the total increase in net profits this year over last year.
B. Calculate the total amount of bonus to be given to employees.
C. Calculate the bonus for each employee.

CHALLENGE 2 (Measurement and Decimals)

Sherry has asked you to determine how much storage space is needed to hold a shipment of inventory that has just arrived. With the help of Robert, who works in the warehouse, you have obtained the following measurements of the shipping cartons:

Carton contents	Length	Width	Height	Quantity
Computer	37 in.	22.75 in.	29.5 in.	14
Printers	40.625 in.	32.5 in.	27 in.	30
Computer paper	27.5 in.	15.1875 in.	18.125 in.	100

Assignment (Round to the nearest whole number):

A. Calculate the smallest volume (in cubic inches) of storage space required to hold all of the shipment.
B. Determine the number of cubic feet that is equal to the answer in A.

CHALLENGE 3 (Percents)

While reviewing the income statement for the past year, Chuck realized that some of the increased profits were due to changes in some of their operating expenses. He noted that, although the salary expense had increased by six percent, the advertising expense had decreased by ten percent and the miscellaneous expense had decreased by seven percent. This year the salary expense is $105,000 and advertising expense is $41,000. Last year miscellaneous expense was $3,000.

Assignment:

A. Calculate last year's salary expense.
B. Calculate last year's advertising expense.
C. Calculate this year's miscellaneous expense.
D. Calculate the total dollar increase or decrease of this year's expense over last year's.
E. Calculate the total percent change of this year's expenses over last year's.

CHALLENGE 4 (Bank Records)

Sherry has asked you to complete the bank reconciliation for the month. She has given you the following information:

Ending checkbook balance: $43,700.73
Ending bank statement balance: $56,503.06

Checks returned with
bank statement:

1658	$	437.63
1659		3,207.90
1660		18,642.57
1661		37,190.10
1662		178.41
1663		72,157.60
1664		2,305.10
1666		493.72
1667		143,770.90
1668		5,107.60
1671		7,562.57
1672		87,508.21
1673		26,623.50

Checks outstanding:

1665	$ 5,488.08
1669	2,100.58
1670	18,905.69
1674	4,685.08

Deposit outstanding: $26,050.10

Promissory note collected by bank: $7,500.00
Collection fee charged by bank: $25.00
Check #1664 recorded in checkbook as: $2,503.10

Assignment:

A. Determine the adjusted bank statement balance.
B. Determine the adjusted checkbook balance.

CHALLENGE 5 (Payroll Records and Commissions)

Any salesperson who has worked for C&S Office Supplies for 4 or more years is paid a salary and a commission on sales made. Laura has worked for C&S for six years. She earns a salary of $325 per week and a commission of 2.5% of all sales over $6,000. Her sales for this week totaled $8,750. Laura is married and has four children but claims only three exemptions. She has $25.00 (nontaxable) deducted each week that is deposited in an investment account for her retirement.

Sam has worked for the company for four years. He earns $250 per week in salary and a commission of 2% of all sales over $5,000. His sales for this week were $9,200. Sam is single and claims one exemption.

Emily, Robert, and Travis are all paid hourly. They each earn $4.10 per hour with time-and-a-half for all hours worked over 40 hours per week. This week Emily worked 48 hours; Robert and Travis each worked 44 hours.

Assignment (Use Tables 11-4 & 11-5 and a 7.65% FICA rate to solve this problem):

A. Calculate the net pay for this week for each of the two salespeople.
B. Calculate the total pay for each of the three hourly employee.

On October 16th C&S Office Supplies purchased from CompuInc. 18 computers. Each computer had a manufacturer's list price of $1,785. The freight charge and invoice terms were $115.60 and 1/15, n30. No trade discount was available. After receiving the computers, C&S discovered that two of them did not work properly; they were returned to CompuInc.

On that date C&S purchased 30 desk chairs and 20 desk lamps from Noll Distributors. The chairs listed at $167.50 each and the lamps listed at $32.70 each. Noll offered a series discount of 20%, 10%, & 5% and invoice terms of 3/20, n60. C&S qualified for the first two trade discounts. A freight charge of $65 was added to the invoice.

Assignment (Ignore sales tax; round to the nearest whole cent):

A. Determine the discount date and the total amount of the discount available to C&S Office Supplies if the CompuInc. invoice is paid within the discount period.
B. Determine C&S Office Supplies' total trade discount from Noll Distributors.
C. Determine the discount date and the total amount paid by C&S Office Supplies if the Noll invoice is paid within the discount period.

CHALLENGE 7 (Markup)

C&S operates with a markup on cost of 45% on electronics and a 30% markup on all other inventory. For this problem assume that the costs to C&S were: each computer—$1,500, each chair—$125, and each lamp—$28.

Assignment:

A. Calculate the amount of markup on each computer, each chair, and each lamp.
B. Assume that C&S sells one of the computers to a customer at the reduced price of $2,000. Determine the markup based on selling price for that sale.

CHALLENGE 8 (Cash Discounts and Simple Interest)

On October 31, C&S Office Supplies purchased 100 boxes of computer paper for inventory. The invoice amount was for $1,800 with terms of 2/10, net 45. In November cash was scarce. Therefore, on the discount date C&S borrowed just enough money from the bank and paid the invoice. The bank charged a 14% annual interest rate. On December 15, C&S paid the bank loan.

Assignment (Assume a 360-day year):

Determine how much C&S saved or lost by borrowing money to pay the invoice within the discount period.

CHALLENGE 9 (Discounting Notes) C&S requires a signed, interest-bearing promissory note from any customer unable to pay within 30 days of the invoice date. Because of cash flow problems, C&S often discounts these notes with the local bank. On June 3 C&S discounted three of the promissory notes at a 12% bank discount rate. The terms of the notes were:

Note 1: a $4,400, 120-day, 7.5% note dated March 18th
Note 2: a $7,350, 150-day, 7% note dated April 15th
Note 3: a $5,000, 60-day, non-interest-bearing note dated May 1

Assignment (Assume a 360-day year):

A. Determine the due date of each note.
B. Calculate the maturity value of each note. (Round to the nearest whole cent.)
C. Calculate the total proceeds C&S received from the bank on June 3.

CHALLENGE 10 (Notes, Interest, and Credit)

On February 15, 1993, C&S Office Supplies sold $22,400 of computer equipment to Hughes Inc. Mike Hughes signed a promissory note dated 2-15-93 at 8% exact interest that was payable in installments. The first payment was for $5,968.22, including interest of $368.22. A second payment of $6,000.00 (including principal and interest) was made after a period of time equal to the first installment period. On the day the second payment was made, Mike & Chuck renegotiated the remaining balance of the note. Mike promised to make the final payment of principal and $163.87 of interest on October 13, 1993, and Chuck agreed to lower the interest rate for the final installment.

Assignment (For money round to the nearest whole cent; otherwise, round to four decimal places):

A. Determine the date of the first payment
B. Determine the amount of interest included in the second payment.
C. Determine the number of days in the final installment period.
D. Determine the new interest rate that had been renegotiated. (Round to the nearest whole percent.)

Hint: It may be helpful to draw a time line.

CHALLENGE 11 (Property Tax)

C&S received its property tax bill for the current year. Brown County, where the company is located, assesses real property at 94.0% of fair market value. The tax bill just received shows a tax of $6,785.00; 36.7% of the total tax is on the land and the balance of the tax is on the improvements. The property tax rate is composed of three separate tax rates. The city of Green Bay has a tax rate of $2.40/$100 of assessed value, the metropolitan sewerage district has a tax levy of $8.75/$1,000, and the Technical College District imposes a tax at a rate of 13.5 mills.

Assignment (Round to the nearest whole cent):

Calculate the fair market value of the land and the improvements using the figures provided.

CHALLENGE 12 (Federal Income Tax)

Sherry has asked you to determine her income tax liability for the past year. She has given you the following figures: Sherry's income from the office supplies business was $36,350. She also earned $4,200 from a small golf equipment repair business she operates out of her home. She received $2,275 for interest on some nontaxable municipal bonds she owns. Last year she paid $2,884 in property tax on her home and mortgage interest on the same property for $5,186. Her husband's income was $42,360. They claim four exemptions.

Use the 1990 tax tables from Chapter 21 to solve this problem.

Assignment:

Compute Sherry and her husband's total federal income tax liability if they file a joint return.

CHALLENGE 13 (Health Insurance)

The owners and all employees of C&S Office Supplies have health care coverage under an HMO plan. C&S pays 100% of the individual coverage for each participant or 70% of the family coverage for those participants wanting that coverage and willing to pay the additional 30%. Monthly coverage costs C&S $75 for each individual policy and $175 for each family policy. One of the 5 employees has chosen not to have the company coverage. Of the remaining 4 employees and the 2 owners, one third have individual coverage; the remaining participants have chosen family coverage. To reduce its costs, C&S is considering increasing the participant's share of the family policy premium to $100 per month.

Assignment:

A. Calculate the total monthly cost to C&S for the health insurance premiums.
B. Determine how much money C&S will save each month if a participant who has chosen the family coverage contributes $100 of the premium cost. Assume all participants that now have family coverage continue that coverage.

CHALLENGE 14 (Property Insurance)

C&S acquired its current building in 1989 for $137,200, including $50,000 for the land. When the insurance policy came up for renewal in 1992, the market value of the building, exclusive of the land, had gone up 13.19%. The replacement cost of the building in 1992 was $95,000. C&S has received its insurance invoice for the year, and you have been requested to verify the quotation. The insurance company bills at a rate of $0.42/$100 of replacement cost. The insurance company has also given C&S the option of prepaying a two-year policy at 1.85 times the annual rate.

Assignment:

A. Determine what the annual premium would be.
B. Determine what the two-year premium would be.

CHALLENGE 15 (Inventory)

On June 30, the end of the fiscal year for C&S, the employees completed a physical count of all unsold merchandise in stock. The number of units on hand, along with a necessary description of each of the types of merchandise, was entered on separate inventory sheets. In July, Sherry summarized some of the inventory records. She has given you a partial list of her summary. Since all of the items on the partial list are new, C&S had none of them in beginning inventory.

MERCHANDISE INVENTORY (June 30)

Office Furniture	In-Stock
Chairs (side)	15
Lamps (floor)	8

Computer Equipment	
Markham CX-1000 computers	6
Johnson Dot-Matrix Printers	9

The purchase records for the preceding items are:

	Date	Units	Unit Cost
Chairs (side):	Nov. 15	10	$ 120.60
	Jan. 23	18	130.25
	Mar. 8	12	135.00
Lamps (floor):	Dec. 2	6	53.58
	Feb. 11	12	67.11
	Apr. 9	5	68.20
Computers:	Oct. 16	16	1,774.38
	Jan. 26	10	1,694.24
	May 19	5	1,589.55
Printers:	Sept. 24	7	465.60
	Mar. 21	13	502.85
	June 3	8	452.56

Sherry is unsure which inventory valuation method would be most beneficial to the company. She has asked for your advice.

Assignment (Round to the nearest whole cent):

A. Calculate ending inventory for each category under the average cost method.
B. Calculate ending inventory for each category under the FIFO cost method.
C. Calculate ending inventory for each category under the LIFO cost method.

CHALLENGE 16 (Depreciation)

Chuck has just asked you to calculate the depreciation on the delivery truck that C&S purchased earlier this year. The acquisition cost was $11,500. Chuck estimates the truck will last 6 years or 100,000 miles and will have a salvage value of $1,000. Since he is unsure about the depreciation method to use, he would like you to determine the expense under several different methods. C&S will recognize one-half year depreciation in the first year.

Assignment (Round percents to the nearest hundredth; round money to the nearest cent):

A. Calculate a 3-year depreciation schedule on the truck using the straight-line method.
B. Calculate a 3-year depreciation schedule on the truck using the double-declining-balance method.
C. Calculate a 3-year depreciation schedule on the truck using the sum-of-the-years-digits method.

CHALLENGE 17 (Financial Statement Analysis)

You have obtained the following C&S financial information figures for two recent years:

1991: Accounts payable .... $ 34,200   Net sales $384,670
      Notes payable   15,000   Cost of goods sold..............   153,868
      Wages payable   8,320   Operating expenses..............   171,400
      Mortgage payable..........   80,000   Net income.....................   59,402
      Owners' equity   133,620

1992: Accounts payable .... $ 29,500   Net sales $418,380
      Notes payable   24,000   Cost of goods sold..............   162,331
      Wages payable   6,100   Operating expenses..............   160,850
      Mortgage payable..........   70,000   Net income.....................   95,199
      Owners' equity   148,700

Assignment (Round percents to the nearest hundredth):

A. Prepare a comparative liabilities and equity section of the balance sheet. Show changes in both dollars and percents.
B. Prepare comparative brief income statements of the two years. Show changes in both dollars and percents.
C. Calculate for 1991 and 1992 the relationship of net income to net sales and the rate of return on investment

CHALLENGE 18 (Stocks, Bonds, and International)

On July 1, 1992, C&S had the following investments:

Stocks		Cost per Share
Atlantic Inc.	300 shares	$43\frac{1}{8}$
Southeast Co.	1,500 shares	$24\frac{1}{2}$
LTHS Co.	850 shares	$18\frac{7}{8}$
GIC Co.	125 shares	$9\frac{1}{4}$

Bonds	Par Value	Face Rate	Interest Pmt. Dates	Cost
SiftCo.	$5,000	11%	Jan. 31 & July 31	$5,500
Nonok	10,000	8%	May 1 & Nov. 1	6,667

At the time of purchase the SiftCo. bond had 4 years left in its 10-year life and the Nonok bond had 12 years of its 20-year life remaining.

On April 24, 1993, C&S sold the following investments:

Stocks		Sale Price per Share
Atlantic Inc.	100 shares	$52\frac{3}{4}$
Southeast Co.	250 shares	$25\frac{5}{8}$
GIC Co.	125 shares	$7\frac{1}{8}$

On June 4, 1993, C&S purchased some the following foreign stocks:

		Cost per Share in Foreign Currency	Foreign Currency in U.S. Dollars
DL Ltd.	50 shares	160 Krone (Denmark)	.1762
Mitsuta Co.	75 shares	9,100 Yen (Japan)	.007293
SKL Co.	200 shares	100 Francs (France)	.1875

Assignment (Round percents to the nearest whole percent; round money to the nearest whole cent):

A. Determine the total gain or loss on sales of the investments.
B. Calculate the average annual yield and the rate of yield to maturity for each bond.
C. Calculate the total cost in U. S. dollars of the foreign stock purchase on June 4, 1993.

CHALLENGE 19 (Compound Interest)

Chuck has decided to invest $2,000 for each of his employees. The money and its accumulated interest will be paid as a bonus to each employee upon reaching his/her eight-year anniversary with the company. Laura will complete her eighth year in two and one-half years, Sam in four years, Emily and Robert in five years and three months, and Travis in six years and nine months.

Laura's money was invested at 10% compounded semiannually; Sam's money was invested at 10% compounded annually; Emily's, Robert's, and Travis' money was invested at 12% compounded quarterly.

Assignment:

Calculate how much each will receive on his/her eighth anniversary.

CHALLENGE 20 (Present Value of an Annuity)

Beginning January 1, 1992, C&S signed a five-year lease agreement for a building to be used for warehousing. The lease calls for a payment of $9,600 at the end of each year with the first payment due on December 31, 1992. C&S deposited enough money into a savings account to insure its ability to make each lease payment when due. The bank is paying 6% interest compounded annually.

Assignment (Round to the nearest whole dollar):

Determine the amount of money to be deposited at the beginning of the lease period to provide for the five yearly payments.

Glossary

A

Account purchase. A detailed statement from the commission merchant to the principal.

Account sales. A detailed statement of the amount of the sales and the various deductions sent by the commission merchant to the consignor.

Accrued interest. Interest earned from the last payment date.

Accumulated depreciation. The total of all the depreciation recognized up to a specified time.

Acid test ratio. Used to determine the amount of assets that can be quickly turned into cash to pay current liabilities; acid test ratio = total of cash plus receivables ÷ total current liabilities.

Ad valorem. Duty that is a percent of the value of the item.

Additional death benefit (ADB). Benefits, available with some life insurance policies, that allow the insured to purchase, at a low rate per thousand dollars of coverage, additional insurance up to the full face value of the policy. In case of death of the insured by accident, both the full value of the policy and the ADB would be paid to the beneficiaries of the insured. If death occurs other than by accident, the full value of the policy is paid but no ADB is paid. Sometimes referred to as accidental death benefit.

Adjusted bank statement balance. The dollar amount obtained by adding to or subtracting from the bank statement balance checkbook activities not yet known to the bank. This should equal the adjusted checkbook balance.

Adjusted checkbook balance. The dollar amount obtained by adding to or subtracting from the checkbook balance those activities appearing on the bank statement that do not yet appear in the checkbook. This should equal the adjusted bank statement balance.

Adjusted gross income. Gross income minus certain income adjustments.

Algebra. A form of mathematics in which letters as well as numbers are used to represent values.

Aliquot part. When a number (whole or mixed) can be divided by another with no remainder, the divisor is known as this.

Allocate. Distribute.

Amortization payment factor. A number which, when multiplied by the per $1,000 loan amount, calculates the amount of each loan payment.

Amortization schedule. A schedule of payments; the schedule shows the amount of interest and the amount of principal in each payment.

Amortizing. The process by which a loan's monthly payments are always equal in dollar amount while the interest amount, which is calculated on the unpaid balance, always varies.

Amount credited. The total amount paid plus the amount of cash discount.

Amount of an annuity. The accumulated cash value at the end of the annuity term (at the end of the last period). The amount includes the sum of all payments plus the accumulated compound interest on all payments.

Amount of decrease. The rate of decrease times the base amount.

Amount of increase. The rate of increase times the base amount.

Annual discount amortization. The spreading of the discount amount evenly over the life of the bonds; annual interest + total cost = average annual yield.

Annual percentage rate (APR). The annual equivalent interest rate charged.

Annual premium amortization. The spreading of the premium amount evenly over the life of the bonds.

Annuity. A series of equal payments that are made at regular equal time intervals.

Annuity due. An annuity in which payment is made at the *beginning* of each time interval.

Annuity factor. A present value factor or a compound amount factor.

Annuity insurance. Life insurance that pays a certain sum of money to the insured every year after the insured reaches a specified age and until the insured's death.

Assessed valuation. A property value determined by a representative of the local or state government.

Asset. Something of value owned by a business or a person.

Auto collision insurance. Insurance that protects the vehicle of the insured against collision damage.

Auto comprehensive insurance. Insurance that protects the vehicle of the insured against fire, water, theft, vandalism, falling objects, and other damage that is not caused by collision.

Auto liability and property damage insurance. Insurance that protects the insured against claims resulting from personal injuries and property damage.

Average. A single number that represents a group of numbers. The process of determining that single number.

Average annual yield. The average annual income rate from an investment; annual interest ÷ total cost = average annual yield.

Average cost method. A method of valuing inventory that assumes that the costs of all items on hand are averaged and shared evenly among all units.

Average inventory. The inventory average calculated by summing each inventory valuation (determined by physical inventory) and divided by the number of physical inventories over a given period of time; average annual inventory = (beginning inventory value + ending inventory value) ÷ 2.

Average principal invested. The maturity value plus the cost price then divided by 2.

B

Balance sheet. The financial statement of what is owned (assets), what is owed (liabilities), and the difference between those two (net worth) on a given date.

Bank statement. A formal accounting by a bank of the adding and subtracting activities that have occurred in one bank account over a stated period of time (usually a month).

Bar graph. A diagram similar to the histogram except that there may not be a number scale along the horizontal axis and the bars normally do not touch each other.

Base (B). The whole quantity or 100% of an amount.

Base value. The amount in the first year, month, or other period of time. A value to which another value is compared.

Bearer bonds. Bonds with interest coupons attached; title to such bonds is not recorded in the name of a person but passes from bearer (holder) to bearer with delivery of the bonds.

Beginning inventory. The cost of inventory on hand at the beginning of a time period.

Beneficiary. A person, a company, or an organization that benefits from the insurance policy.

Board of directors. A group of people elected by the stockholders to oversee the running of the corporation.

Bonds. Long-term notes issued by a corporation or government entity as a means of borrowing money.

Book value. The original cost of an asset minus the accumulated depreciation.

Broker. A person who performs services of buying and/or selling for a commission.

Business statistics. The collection, tabulation, and/or presentation of number information about a business situation.

C

Callable bonds. Bonds that have a provision for the issuer of the bonds to repurchase or call the bonds in at specified dates if the board of directors authorizes the retirement (payoff) of the bonds before their maturity date.

Cancel. "Divide out" common factors that occur in both the numerator and denominator.

Cancellation. Process of dividing out common factors.

Capital stock. The general term applied to the shares of ownership in a corporation.

Cash discount. A reduction in an invoice amount available to the buyer for paying all or part of the amount within a stated period of time.

Cash surrender value. The amount of cash that the company will pay the insured on the surrender, or "cashing-in," of the insurance policy.

Charges. The commission and any other sales expenses, such as transportation, advertising, storage, insurance, etc.

Charter. The basic rules under which the corporation operates.

Check. A written order directing the bank to pay a certain sum to a designated party.

Checkbooks. Checks and check stubs to record deposits, withdrawals, check numbers, dates of transactions, other additions or subtractions, and the account balance.

Check register. A place for recording important information about each cash transaction.

Circle graph. A graph of data presented in circle form; a "pie chart."

Classes of data. Groups of organized individual values.

Coinsurance clause. An insurance policy clause specifying that, if a property is not insured up to a certain percentage of its value, the owner is the bearer of part of the insurance and will not be covered for the full amount of damages.

Commission. Payment to an employee or to an agent for performing or helping to perform a business transaction or service. A fee charged by the broker for buying or selling stock for a client.

Commission merchant. A person who performs services of buying and/or selling for a commission.

Common denominator. A denominator that is shared by two or more fractions. The product of the denominators of two or more fractions is always a common denominator.

Common divisor. A number by which both the numerator and denominator can be evenly divided in order to arrive at a reduced fraction.

Common multiplier. A number by which both the numerator and the denominator are multiplied to raise the fraction to higher terms.

Common stock. The usual type of stock issued by a corporation. Most common stock gives its owners one vote for each share owned.

Comparative bar graph. Two bar graphs can be drawn together on one grid to make a comparison of statistical data.

Complement method. A method for finding the net price.

Complement rate. A rate equal to 100% minus the discount rate; used with the complement method in determining trade or cash discounts.

Component bar graph. A bar graph that is constructed to show how certain data is composed of various parts.

Compound amount. The original principal multiplied by the compound amount factor.

Compound amount factor. A number factor used to shorten the process of calculating a future value (compound amount).

Compound interest. The accumulation of simple interest applied several times during the term.

Consignee. The party to whom a consignment shipment is sent.

Consignment. Goods from a producer to a commission merchant for sale at the best possible price.

Consignor. The party who sends the consignment.

Constant divisors. Divisor is usually the last number entered in and is usually the first number entered in multiplication problems.

Constant multipliers. A calculator feature that provides that a number, once entered, can be automatically repeated as a multiplier by entering the new multiplicand and depressing the equals key.

Convertible bonds. Bonds that have a provision to be converted into a designated number of shares or a designated value of the corporation's stock at the request of the bondholder.

Convertible preferred stock. Preferred stock that gives the owner the option of converting that preferred share into a stated number of common shares.

Corporations. Businesses whose owners are stockholders.

Cost-based markup. The difference between the price and the seller's cost of an item for sale which is calculated as a percent of that cost.

Cost of goods sold. The seller's cost of items (goods) that have been sold during a certain time.

Coupon bonds. Bonds with interest coupons attached; title to such bonds is not recorded in the name of a person but passes from bearer (holder) to bearer with delivery.

Credit balance. A negative difference.

Cross-checking. Adding columns vertically and then adding these totals horizontally.

Cumulative preferred stock. Preferred stock for which all dividends in arrears must be paid before current period dividends can be paid.

Current yield. The average annual yield (income rate) from an investment.

D

Debenture bonds. Bonds that have the backing of the corporation but do not specify any of the corporation's tangible assets.

Decimal equivalent. The presentation of a non-decimal number in decimal form.

Decimal point. The period between two numerals.

Decimal representation. A number containing a decimal part that represents a coin.

Declare a dividend. The authorized distribution of earnings to stockholders; this is done by the board of directors.

Declining-balance method (DB). A depreciation method that assumes a greater use (and greater productivity) in the earlier years of an asset's life; thus depreciation is greatest in the first year and less in each succeeding year.

Deductible. A cost that must be paid by the employee before any cost is paid by the insurance company.

Deductible clause. An insurance policy clause that stipulates that the insured will pay the first portion of collision damage and the insurance company will pay the remainder up to the value of the insured vehicle.

Denominator. In a fraction, the number below the line.

Depreciated. Reduced in value through use.

Depreciation. The decrease in the value of an asset through use.

Derived. Developed.

Difference. The result of subtracting the subtrahend from the minuend.

Discount. A fee charged when someone buys the note before maturity. The difference between a bond's par value and its market value when the market value is less. Rule: When bonds are sold at a discount, the yield rate will be higher than the stated (face) rate.

Discount broker. A stockbroker who buys and sells stock according to the clients' instructions.

Discount date. The last day on which a cash discount may be taken. The day on which a note is discounted (sold).

Discount method. Useful when you want to know both the net price and the actual amount of the trade discount.

Discount period. A certain number of days after the invoice date, in which a buyer may receive a cash discount. The time between a note's discount date and its maturity date.

Discount rate. The percent used for calculating a trade or cash discount. The interest percent charged by the buyer of a discounted note.

Discounting a note. Selling a note before its maturity date.

Dividend. The number being divided.

Divisor. The number used to divide another number.

Dollar markup. The total of operating expenses and net profit. Markup expressed as an amount rather than as a percent.

Double-declining-balance method. A declining-balance method that determines a depreciation amount for the first year that is approximately twice the straight-line rate.

Due date. The final day by which time an invoice is to be paid. After that day the buyer may be charged interest.

Duty. Charge or tax imposed on imported items by the Customs Agency to protect United States manufacturers against foreign competition in domestic markets.

E

Effective interest rate. The actual annual rate of interest.

Eight-digit capacity. The calculator display that is able to show a number up to eight digits long.

Employee's earnings record. Summary by quarter of the employee's gross earnings, deductions, and net pay.

Ending inventory. The cost of the inventory on hand at the end of a time period.

Endowment insurance. Insurance payable upon the insured's death if it occurs within a specified period, and an endowment of the same amount as the policy, payable if the insured is alive at the end of that period.

Equalization. Adjustment of assessments.

Equation. A sentence that is made up of numbers and/or letters that represent numbers, divided into two sections by an equal sign (=).

Equivalent single discount rate. A single trade discount rate that can be used in place of two or more

trade discount rates to determine the same discount amount.

Estimated physical life. The amount of usefulness an owner expects to get from an item before it is physically worn out.

Estimated service life. The amount of usefulness an owner expects to get from an item before it will need to be replaced due to obsolescence.

Exact interest method. The calculation of interest assuming a year that is 365 (or 366) days long.

Exemption. A reduction of adjusted gross income that is allowed for each taxpayer, qualifying spouse, and qualifying dependent.

Export. Domestic goods (produced in the United States) for sale in foreign countries.

F

Face value. The dollar amount written on the note; it is the same as the amount borrowed, or the principal (P).

Factors. Term used in multiplication to mean "numbers."

FICA. Federal Insurance Contributions Act or Social Security tax.

Finance charge. The fee that the seller charges for the privilege of buying on credit.

Financial statements. Statements presenting financial information about a company; two of these statements are the balance sheet and the income statement.

Finished goods. Those items that have completed the manufacturing process.

First-in, first-out (FIFO) costing method. A method of valuing inventory that assumes that costs for units used or sold are charged according to the order in which the units were manufactured or purchased.

Fixed costs. Costs that remain the same even though the number of units manufactured varies.

Floating decimal point. A calculator feature that automatically places the decimal point in its correct location.

Foreign trade zone. Domestic United States site that is considered to be outside U.S. Customs territory.

Form 1040. One of the basic income tax return forms filed by taxpayers.

Form W-2. The wage and tax statement sent to each employee by the employer at the end of the year.

Fraction. A number expression of one or more equal parts of a whole unit.

Fractional equivalent. The presentation of the value of a non-fraction in fraction form.

Frequency table. A schedule of information presenting a tally of data frequency.

Frequency. The number of values in each class of data.

Full service broker. A stockbroker who not only does the buying and selling upon request for clients but also provides investment advice and manages some of the investments.

Future value. The estimated future amount of money being loaned or invested today or over time.

Future value of an annuity. A value that will accumulate at a certain time in the future from the investment of annuity amounts.

G

Graduated commission rates. A system of rates by which graduated commissions increase as the level of sales increase.

Gross cost. The prime cost and all charges paid by the principal.

Gross income. All income received from any source except for that specifically excluded.

Gross proceeds. Whatever price the commission merchant gets for the consignment; also, the full sales price before any allowances, returns, or other adjustments are considered.

Gross profit. The term used by accountants to describe the difference between the sales price and the cost of the sold goods.

Group insurance. Health insurance coverage extended to a group of people. The cost for each person's coverage is less expensive that it would be under an individual policy.

Grouped data. Individual values organized into groups.

H

Health maintenance organization (HMO). Group health insurance coverage with limited options as a means of keeping health insurance costs lower than that of regular group policies.

Higher terms. A fraction in which both the numerator and denominator have been multiplied by the same number.

High risk driver. A driver with a record of numerous citations or accidents.

Histogram. A diagram that presents the grouped data from a frequency table.

I

Import. A good produced in a foreign country and brought into the United States.

Improper fraction. One or more whole units. The numerator is greater than or equal to the denominator.

In arrears. A term used to describe unpaid dividends on cumulative preferred stock.

Income statement. The financial statement that shows the revenues, the expenses, and the net income for a certain period of time.

Insured. For life insurance, this is the person whose life is being insured; for other types of insurance, it is the person who receives the benefit of the insurance.

Interest. A fee, usually charged for the use of money.

Interest-bearing note. A note that has a maturity value that is greater than its face value.

Interest dollars. The interest stated as an amount of money rather than a percent.

Inventory sheet. A form used for recording information when taking a physical inventory.

Inventory turnover. The number of times the average inventory is converted into sales during the year.

Inventory turnover rate. A rate that lets management and others know the average number of times inventory is sold during the year; inventory turnover rate = cost of goods sold ÷ average inventory.

Invoice. A document from the seller requesting payment from the buyer; the supplier's bill.

Invoice date. The date stated on an invoice; the beginning of the discount period.

Issue. To offer a stock or bond for sale.

Itemized deductions. Potential reductions to income allowed for certain payments made during the tax year.

J

Junk bond. A bond with a low rating, thus a higher risk.

L

Last-in, first-out (LIFO) costing method. A method of valuing inventory that assumes that the inventory on hand at the end of a period of time is composed of the units received first.

LC (Liquid Crystal). One type of calculator display; the numbers usually appear in soft white light.

LED (Light Emitting Diodes). One type of calculator display; the numbers usually appear in red or green light.

Levy. A government charge or fee.

Limited-payment life insurance. A certain premium to be paid every year for a certain number of years specified at the time of insuring, or until the death of the insured, should that occur during the specified period. The policy is payable on the death of the insured, although there may be some options available at the end of the payment period.

Line graph. Presentation of data on a graph in which the data points are connected by a line.

Liquid. A term used to describe an investment that can be readily sold for, or "converted to" cash.

List price. The price amount listed in the catalog.

Loan initiation fee. A fee charged by a bank or other lender to cover the cost of processing the loan application.

Loan payment schedules. Loan schedules showing each period's beginning unpaid principal balance, its total down payment, and the amount of interest and of principal in each payment.

Loan value. The amount that the insured may borrow on the policy from the insurance company.

Long-term credit. Loans that are longer than one year.

Lower of cost or market value (LCM). An inventory valuation method by which the lower amount of either the market value or the cost value is chosen.

Lowest terms. A fraction that cannot be reduced by any common divisor.

Low risk driver. A driver with a long-standing, clear driving record.

M

Market value. The dollar amount required to replace the inventory as of the inventory date.

Markup. The difference between the price and the seller's cost of an item for sale. In dollars it is the amount added to the cost of the goods in order to have a gross profit high enough to cover operating expenses and to make a net profit.

Markup percent. When the dollar cost and the dollar markup are known, it is a percent that is calculated by dividing the dollar markup by the cost.

Maturity date. The final day of a note (or bond) on which the borrower (the maker of the note or bond) pays the face value and any interest due to the holder of the note or bond. The due date.

Maturity value (MV). For an interest-bearing note (or bond), it is the sum of the face value (principal) and the interest dollars; $MV = P + I$. For a non-interest-bearing note, it is the same as the face value.

Mean. An "average" that is found by dividing the sum of the group of values by the number of values in the group.

Median. An "average" that is the middle number.

Memory register. A calculator feature that enables the user to store an amount and then add to it, subtract from it, recall it for review, multiply it, or divide it again and again until the register is cleared.

Merchandise. Those goods, manufactured by some other firm, that the company offers for sale.

Mill. One tenth of one cent or $0.001; a tax rate may be expressed in mills.

Minuend. Number from which subtraction is being made.

Mixed decimals. A number containing a decimal point and both a whole-number part and a decimal part.

Mixed number. A number that represents more than one whole unit by combining a whole number and a proper fraction.

Mode. An "average" that is represented by the number that occurs most often.

Modified Accelerated Cost Recovery System (MACRS). The accelerated depreciation method that is required by the IRS.

Modified complement method. A method for finding the net price when two or more trade discount rates are involved.

Multiplicand. The factor that is multiplied.

Multiplier. The factor that indicates how many times to multiply.

Municipal bonds. Bonds issued by states, cities, school districts, and other public entities.

N

Negotiable note. One that can be sold by the lender.

Negotiable promissory note. A promissory note that may be sold to a third party.

Net price. The price the distributor will charge to his customer after any trade discounts have been subtracted from the list price.

Net proceeds. The amount sent to the consignor as a result of consignment sales; gross proceeds minus charges.

Net profit. The return for the owner after all expenses have been subtracted from sales.

Net purchase. The price of the merchandise actually purchased.

Net sales. Total sales for the time period minus sales returned and adjustments made during the same time.

No-fault insurance. Insurance coverage under which the driver of each vehicle involved in an injury accident submits a claim to his or her own insurance company to cover medical costs for injuries to the driver and passengers in that person's own vehicle. The insurance does not cover damage to either vehicle involved in an accident.

No-par stock. Stock issued without par.

Non-interest-bearing note. A note having a maturity value equal to its face value.

Nonparticipating preferred stock. Preferred stock which has a priority right limited to a specified percentage.

Number of compounding periods. The number of time periods of equal length over which interest is calculated.

Number sentence. Numbers used in sentence form.

Number sentence equations. Number sentences in which both sides of the equal sign contain calculations.

Numerator. In a fraction, the number above the line.

O

Obsolescence. Becoming out-of-date.

Odd lot. Any number of stock shares less than 100.

Odd lot differential. A small extra charge by the broker for buying or selling an odd lot.

Of. "Multiply," particularly when "of" is preceded by the Rate and followed by the Base.

150%-declining-balance method. A declining-balance method that determines a depreciation amount for the first year that is approximately one and one-half the straight-line rate.

Operating expenses. The costs of operating the business.

Ordinary annuity. An annuity in which payment is made at the *end* of each time interval.

Ordinary interest method. The calculation of interest assuming a year that is 360 days long.

Original cost. The cost of building or buying an asset and getting it into use.

Overhead costs. General costs not directly related to sales merchandise.

Over-the-counter. A term that means the securities traded are not listed on a stock or bond exchange.

P

Par. An arbitrary monetary figure frequently assigned to capital stock.

Par value. The amount that will be paid to the holder on redemption; not necessarily the market value. The face value of a bond.

Participating preferred stock. Preferred stock that provides for possible dividends greater than a stated percentage.

Partnership. A business that is not incorporated and has more than one owner.

Payee. Party to whom a check is written.

Payment period. The length of time from one payment to the next.

Payroll register. A summary of wages earned, payroll deductions, and final take-home pay.

Percent. A number equal to a fraction whose denominator is 100.

Percentage (P). A portion of the Base.

Percentage method. One of two primary methods for calculating the amount of income tax to withhold from employee paychecks. After the total withholding allowance is subtracted from an employee's gross earnings, the amount to be withheld is determined by taking a percentage of the balance. The percentage to be used is given by the IRS.

Percent key. A calculator key that eliminates the need to convert a percentage to a decimal before multiplying or dividing.

Percent of cost. Markup that is based on the cost of the goods for sale.

Percent of selling price. Markup that is based on the selling price.

Periodic interest rate. The interest rate used to calculate interest at the end of one compounding period.

Periodic inventory. An inventory system that does not require a continuous physical monitoring of the units and unit costs into and out of the inventory stock. The information about the purchases and sales of items is recorded in the accounting system and compared with the results of the physical inventory; an adjustment to the accounting records is made as needed.

Perpetual inventory. A running count of all inventory units and unit costs based on a physical tracking of every item as it comes into and goes out of inventory.

Physical inventory. An actual counting of the inventory.

Pie chart. A circle graph.

Power source. The power supply to a calculator, such as solar energy or a silver-oxide battery.

Powers of 10. Numbers that are multiples of 10, such as 100 and 1,000. The number 1 followed by one or more zeros.

Preferred stock. A type of stock that has a right to share in earnings before earnings are distributed to common stock.

Premium. Fee for insurance coverage, usually paid every year by the insured person. The difference between a bond's par value and its market value when the market value is more. Rule: When bonds are sold at a premium, the yield rate will be lower than the stated (face) rate.

Present value. The estimated worth today of money to be paid or received in the future.

Present value factor. A number factor used to shorten the process of calculating a present value.

Present value of an annuity. The dollar amount needed at the beginning in order to be able to take out, or pay out, annuity payments of a certain dollar amount at certain regular intervals in the future.

Price-based cost percent. When the dollar cost of the item for sale is divided by this percent the selling price of the item is determined.

Price-based markup. The difference between the price and the seller's cost of an item for sale that is calculated as a percent of the selling price.

Prime cost. The price commission merchants pay for the merchandise when they purchase goods for their principal.

Principal. Amount that is borrowed using credit. The person (client) for whom a service is performed.

Proceeds. The amount the seller receives from the buyer of a note being discounted; the difference between the maturity value and the discount amount.

Proceeds (from sale of stock). The amount received from the sale of stock; is equal to the selling price minus the fee or commission.

Product. The answer to a multiplication problem.

Promissory note. An agreement signed by the borrower that states the conditions of a loan.

Proper fraction. Smaller than one whole unit. The numerator is smaller than the denominator.

Property insurance. Insurance against loss of or damage to property.

Property tax. A tax on real estate or other property owned by the business or an individual.

Prorate. Distribute.

Purchases. Those goods for sale that have been acquired during the current time period.

Pure decimal. A number with no whole-number part.

Q

Quotient. The answer to a division problem.

R

Rate (R). The percent of interest that is stated or calculated.

Rate (percent) of decrease. The negative change in two values stated as a percent.

Rate (percent) of increase. The positive change in two values stated as a percent.

Rate of return on investment. A rate that approximates the interest rate the owners are earning on their investment in the company; rate of return on investment = net income ÷ owners' equity.

Rate of yield. The ratio between the dividend and the total cost of stock; one indication of the return on investment in the stock.

Rate of yield to maturity. A more refined estimate of investment yield (income rate) than the average annual yield; annual interest + annual discount (or - annual premium) amortization ÷ average principal invested.

Ratio. The relation of one amount to another.

Ratio of accounts receivable to net sales. Indicates the percentage of sales that have not yet been paid for by customers; ratio of accounts receivable to net sales = accounts receivable ÷ net sales.

Raw materials. Unused items waiting to become part of the goods manufactured.

Reciprocal. The quotient resulting from dividing 1 by the original number; 1 ÷ original number equals the reciprocal of the original number.

Reconciliation of the bank balance. Comparison of the check stubs or check register with the bank statement to determine the adjusted bank balance.

Recovery amount. The maximum amount the insurance company will pay.

Registered bonds. Bonds issued to a person whose name is listed or registered with the corporation.

Relationship of net income to net sales. This ratio indicates the portion of sales that is income; relationship of net income to net sales = net income ÷ net sales.

Remainder. A part of a dividend that is left after even division is complete. The leftover part of division into which the divisor cannot go a whole number of times.

Remittance. Amount a buyer actually pays after deducting the cash discount.

Repeat addition-subtraction. A calculator feature that provides that a number, once entered, can be automatically repeated in addition and subtraction by depressing the equals key.

Resale, scrap, or salvage value (SV). The amount of value the owner of the item expects to receive from disposing of it at the end of the item's estimated useful life.

Round lot. Usually 100 shares.

Rounding. The process of dropping unwanted digits to the right of a certain digit.

Rounding off. Rounding.

Rounding up. The process of changing a certain digit to the next larger whole value and dropping unwanted digits to the right.

S

Sales. The revenue realized by the seller for providing a good or service to a buyer in exchange for something else of value, usually money or a promise.

Sales tax. A government charge on retail sales of certain goods and services.

Secured. Guaranteed by certain assets. A bond that is guaranteed by certain of the issuer's assets.

Securities. Stocks, representing ownership, and bonds, representing debt, that usually can be bought and sold, or traded.

Semiannual. Every 6 months.

Series of discounts. Two or more trade discount rates available to the buyer for different volume purchases.

Short rates. Insurance premium rates charged for less than a full term of insurance.

Short-term credit. Loans that are one year or less in length.

Single-payment interest method. The most direct method of computing interest on loans; the method uses the formula I = P x R x T.

Sole proprietorship. A business that has only one owner and is not incorporated.

Solution. The value or number that makes the equation true.

Solving the equation. The procedure of finding the solution to an equation.

Standard deductions. Set amounts, provided by the IRS, that may be claimed by those individuals who do not itemize their deductions.

Stated interest rate. The interest rate stated on the note or bond, the par on face rate.

Statement of account. A report that shows an opening balance, all deposits and credits, all checks paid, withdrawals recorded, bank service charges, general information about the account, and the balance at the end of the period. A bank statement.

Statistical data. Number facts or information that is organized, summarized, and interpreted.

Stockbroker. An agent in the purchase and sale of stock for clients; a broker.

Stock certificate. A special paper containing its own serial number that is evidence of ownership of a stock share.

Stock exchanges. Formal marketplaces set up for the trading of stock.

Straight (or ordinary) life insurance. Insurance requiring a certain premium to be paid every year until the death of the insured person. The policy then becomes payable to the beneficiary.

Straight-line method. A depreciation method that distributes the depreciable cost of an item in equal amounts to designated units or periods covering its useful life; (original cost - scrap value) ÷ estimated total life in units or periods of time = depreciation amount for 1 unit or period.

Substitution. The replacement of one value for a different but equal value.

Subtrahend. Number being subtracted.

Sum-of-the-years-digits method (SYD). A depreciation method that assumes a greater use (and greater productivity) in the earlier years of an asset's life; the rate of depreciation is greater than the straight-line method but less than the declining-balance method in the earlier years.

T

Tax rate. The percent used to calculate a tax.

Taxable income. The amount of income upon which the income tax is determined.

Term insurance. Insurance protection that is issued for a limited time. A certain premium is paid every year during the specified time period, or "term." The policy is payable only in case of death of the insured during the term. Otherwise, neither the insured nor the specified beneficiaries receive any payment, and the protection stops at the end of the term.

Terms of payment. A statement on the invoice that informs the buyer of any available discount rate and discount date as well as the due date.

Time (T). Stated in terms of all or part of a year, the length of time used for calculating the interest dollars, the rate, or the principal.

Time line. A line representing time onto which marks are placed to indicate the occurrence of certain activities.

Title. Right of ownership.

Total cost. The sum of the variable costs and the fixed costs.

Total cost (for purchaser of stock). The purchase price of the stock plus a brokerage fee.

Trade discounts. Discounts given to buyers that generally are based on the quantity purchased.

Treasury bonds. Bonds issued by the United States government.

Truth in Lending Act. A federal law to assist consumers in knowing the total cost of credit.

Turnover at cost. Inventory turnover determined using an average inventory based on inventory valued at cost.

Turnover at retail. Inventory turnover determined using an average inventory based on inventory valued at retail.

Twelve-digit capacity. The calculator display that is able to show a number up to twelve digits long.

U

Ungrouped data. Numbers listed individually.

Unknown. The letter part of an equation.

Unpaid balance. The remaining loan principal not yet repaid.

Unpaid-balance interest method. A method of calculating interest on loans in which a new interest amount is determined each payment period; the calculation is based upon the unpaid principal balance at the beginning of each payment period.

Unsecured. Not secured. A bond that is not guaranteed by the issuer's assets.

V

Variable. The letter part of an equation.

Variable costs. Costs that vary with the number of products manufactured.

W

Wage-bracket method. One of two primary methods for calculating the amount of income tax to withhold from employee paychecks. This method starts by granting a deduction for each withholding allowance claimed. The amount for each withholding allowance is provided by the IRS in a table. This method uses a series of wage-bracket tables published by the IRS.

Working capital ratio. This ratio tells the amount of current assets that would remain if all of the company's current liabilities were paid immediately; total current assets ÷ total current liabilities.

Work-in-process. Partially manufactured goods.

Y

Yield. Income from an investment; generally stated as a percent, or rate.

Index

Photo Acknowledgments

Simplex Time Recorder Company, page 129
Crocker National Bank, page 345

Progress Record

Part	Chapter	Assignment	Title	Page	Date Assigned	Date Completed	Score/Grade
5	16	16-1	Dates, Time and Interest	195			
		16-2	Solving for Interest Variables	197			
	17	17-1	Borrowing by Business	205			
		17-2	Bank Discount and Discounting Notes	207			
	18	18-1	Finance Charges	217			
		18-2	Charges for Credit 1	219			
	19	19-1	Charges for Credit 2	225			
6	20	20-1	Sales Taxes	235			
		20-2	Property Taxes	239			
	21	21-1	Federal Income Tax 1	251			
		21-2	Federal Income Tax 2	253			
	22	22-1	Life Insurance	263			
		22-2	Life Insurance Settlement Options	267			
		22-3	Health Insurance	269			
	23	23-1	Property Insurance	277			
		23-2	Auto Insurance	279			
7	24	24-1	Inventory Cost	291			
		24-2	Inventory Estimation and Turnover	293			
	25	25-1	Depreciation 1	305			
		25-2	Depreciation 2	309			
	26	26-1	Income Statement Analysis	321			
		26-2	Balance Sheet Analysis	323			
		26-3	Financial Ratios 1	325			
		26-4	Financial Ratios 2	327			
8	27	27-1	Capital Stock	337			
		27-2	Buying and Selling Stock	341			
	28	28-1	Bonds	351			
		28-2	Bond Rate of Yield	355			
	29	29-1	Trading with Foreign Countries	365			
		29-2	Duties and Customs Territory	369			
9	30	30-1	Compound Amount (Future Value)	381			
		30-2	Present Value	383			
	31	31-1	Annuities—Future Value	393			
		31-2	Annuities—Present Value	395			
10	32	32-1	Statistical Averages	405			
		32-2	Tables and Graphs	407			
	33	33-1	Algebra 1	415			
		33-2	Algebra 2	417			
	34	34-1	Business Applications—Interest	423			
		34-2	Business Applications—Inventory and Cost	425			